Personality and Social Encounter

Personality and Social Encounter

Selected Essays

by Gordon W. Allport

Beacon Press   Boston

Preface

What is human personality?

Some would say that it is an ineffable mystery—a shaft of creation, an incarnation. Since no man can transcend his own humanity, he cannot hold the full design of personality under a lens. The radical secret will ever elude us.

Others would say that personality is a product of nature. It is a nervous-mental organization, which changes and grows, while at the same time remaining relatively steadfast and consistent. The task of science is to explain both the stability and the change.

Those who hold either of these views—or both views—are right. And there are other possible answers to our question, likewise paradoxical.

Some say that personality is a self-enclosed totality, a solitary system, a span pressed between two oblivions. It is not only separated in space from other living systems, but also marked by internal urges, hopes, fears and beliefs. Each person has his own pattern, his own unique conflicts; he runs his own course, and he dies alone. This point of view is correct.

But others say that personality is social in nature, wide open to the surrounding world. It owes its existence to the love of two mortals for each other and is maintained through love and nurture freely given by others. Personality is affiliative, symbiotic, sociable. Culture cooperates with family in molding its course. "No man is an island." This view, too, is right.

The essays in this volume, I trust, give full recognition to the truth that lies in all these divergent positions. If Parts I and II favor the "self-enclosed totality," I hope Parts III, IV and V show that personality is "wide open to the world." As for the metaphysical paradox, I hold that any *valid* naturalistic approach must have open doors and clear windows, so that our chance of glimpsing ultimate philosophical and religious truth may not be blocked.

My own approach is naturalistic, but open-ended. Naturalism, as I see it, is too often a closed system of thought that utters premature and trivial pronouncements on the nature of man. But it can and should be a mode of approach that deliberately leaves unsolved the ultimate metaphysical questions concerning the nature of man, without prejudicing the solution. My essays are all psychological, and therefore naturalistic, but they have one feature in common—a refusal to place premature limits upon our conception of man and his capacities for growth and development.

A word about the selection of essays for this volume: they are neither "technical" nor "popular." They have been written either to amplify the theory of personality contained in my book *Personality: a psychological interpretation* (1937) or to express my concern with topical problems in social psychology. My belief that personality is both a self-contained system and open to the world accounts for the title of this collection, *Personality and social encounter*. Five of the papers were previously included in *The nature of personality: selected papers* (1950); but, since that collection is out of print, it seems convenient to reprint them here. Some of the chapters have been revised for the present publication.

In preparing this volume I have had helpful advice and assistance from Professor P. A. Bertocci; from my wife, Ada L. Allport; from Mr. Alan Levensohn, Mrs. Eleanor Sprague and Mrs. Katherine F. Bruner. I should like to express my gratitude to them all, as well as to Edward Darling, director of Beacon Press, who insists that my thoughts are worthy of a fresh printing.

Gordon W. Allport

CAMBRIDGE, MASSACHUSETTS
FEBRUARY 1960

Acknowledgments

I wish to acknowledge with thanks permission to reprint certain materials from the following sources:

AMERICAN JOURNAL OF ORTHOPSYCHIATRY for "The trend in motivational theory," 1953.

AMERICAN PSYCHOLOGICAL ASSOCIATION for two articles from *Journal of Abnormal and Social Psychology*: "What is a trait of personality?" 1931, and "The open system in personality theory," 1960. For three articles from *Psychological Review*: "The ego in contemporary psychology," 1943; "The psychology of participation," 1945; "Scientific models and human morals," 1947.

CRANE REVIEW for "Religion and prejudice," copyright 1959 by Crane Theological School, Tufts University.

BEACON PRESS for "A psychological approach to the study of love and hate," Chap. 5 in P. A. Sorokin (ed.), *Explorations in Altruistic Love and Behavior*, 1950; "Techniques for reducing group prejudice," Chap. 24 in P. A. Sorokin (ed.), *Forms and Techniques of Altruistic and Spiritual Growth*, 1954.

BRITISH JOURNAL OF EDUCATIONAL PSYCHOLOGY, University of Edinburgh, for "Geneticism *versus* ego-structure in theories of personality," 1946.

HARPER & BROTHERS for "Normative compatibility in the light of social science," in A. H. Maslow (ed.), *New Knowledge in Human Values*, 1959.

HOLT, RINEHART & WINSTON, INC., for "What units shall we employ?" Chap. 9 in G. Lindzey (ed.), *Assessment of Human Motives*, Rinehart, 1958.

THE PERSONALIST, School of Philosophy, University of Southern California, for "The psychological nature of personality," 1953.

PUBLIC OPINION QUARTERLY, Princeton University, for "An analysis of rumor" (with Leo Postman), 1946-1947.

SOCIETY FOR THE PSYCHOLOGICAL STUDY OF SOCIAL ISSUES, University of Michigan, for "Guidelines for research in international cooperation," *Journal of Social Issues*, 1947.

SOCIOLOGICAL REVIEW, University College of North Keele, for "Personality: normal and abnormal," 1958.

UNIVERSITY OF ILLINOIS PRESS for "The role of expectancy," Chap. 2 in H. Cantril (ed.), *Tensions That Cause Wars*, 1950.

SOCIETY OF PUBLIC HEALTH EDUCATORS, INC., Health Education Monograph Committee, for "Perception and public health," *Health Education Monograph*, 1958.

TRUSTEES OF COLUMBIA UNIVERSITY for "The limits of social service," in J. E. Russell (ed.), *National Policies for Education, Health and Social Services*, Bicentennial Conference Series, Doubleday, 1955.

Table of Contents

PART I: *An approach to personality*

CHAPTER I

Personality: a problem for science or for art?

There are two principal approaches to the detailed study of human personality: *literature* and *psychology*.

Neither is "better" than the other; each has its distinctive merits and ardent devotees. Too often, however, partisans of one method heap scorn upon the other. This essay attempts a reconciliation and, in so doing, etches a scientific-humanistic frame for the study of personality.

The present essay, based on a lecture at Smith College, first appeared in the Rumanian journal *Revista de Psihologie* in 1938. Some years later the editor of this journal, Nicholas Margineanu, an able psychologist and outspoken social democrat, fell a martyr to the political ravages that swept his native land.

Readers who have a special interest in this topic will find a more extended and more technical discussion in my monograph *The use of personal documents in psychological science* (1942).

Already in the twentieth century three great revolutions have occurred in man's thinking about his own mind. These are, first, Freudian psychoanalysis, with its discovery of the depth and the emotion in mental life; second, Behaviorism, with its discovery of the accessibility of mind to objective study; and, third, Gestalt psychology, with its discovery of the essential orderliness and self-regulation of mind. It is not at all unlikely that these new modes of thought will revolutionize our ways of life during the present century, much as the natural and biological sciences revolutionized ways of life during the past century. We may well expect them to affect profoundly the morals, manners and mental health of our generation and of generations to come. Psychology, it is often said, is destined to become *the* science of the twentieth century.

Now, one of the most significant happenings in the first part of the twentieth century has been the discovery—to which Freudian, Behavioristic and Gestalt psychologies have all contributed—that human *personality* is an accessible subject for scientific probing. It is this event, above all others, I think, that is likely to have the most practical consequences for education, for ethics and for mental health.

3

But before getting into the problem of personality, I should like to dwell for a moment upon the somewhat stormy state of psychological science today. It sometimes seems to me that all the four winds of the intellectual heavens had collided in one storm center, competing for mastery, with the outcome as yet unsure.

According to a division commonly adopted, there are exactly four winds in the intellectual heavens, springing from the four basic provinces of research and learning—the natural sciences, the biological sciences, the social sciences and the humanities. Have you ever thought before that it is in the territory of psychology, and *only there*, that all these four intellectual winds collide and run a tempestuous course? I suppose it is natural enough that they should do so, for only by the aid of all the inventions and all the resources of the mind can the creative mind itself be adequately explored.

From the *natural sciences* comes the colossal impact of scientific methodology. I suppose that in the entire history of human thought there never was a case where one science has been bullied by another science as psychology is bullied by her elder sister science, physics. And I suppose no younger sister ever had so acute an inferiority complex as psychology has in relation to her well-groomed and socially correct elder sister. The desire to emulate the success of physics has led psychology to import at an increasing rate instruments of precision and mathematics into its treatment of mental life. Heaven help the psychologist nowadays who doesn't know his amplifiers and electrical circuits. It is, of course, particularly in the study of sensation that the physical sciences dominate psychology, though it is also true that their influence is felt throughout the entire structure of psychological science.

From the *biological sciences* also come high standards and exacting methods of research, as well as the evolutionary and organismal points of view without which psychology would still be scholastic in character. But the freshening winds of biology have not blown gently and with moderation; they have blown, rather, with the force of a gale, so forcefully that in many quarters they have threatened to push every vestige of humanism out, leaving psychology with a plague of rats. Today it is probably true that more rats are used in the American laboratories of psychology as subjects than men, women and children combined. Some people feel that what psychology really needs is an efficient Pied Piper.

It is, then, the impact of the natural and biological sciences upon psychology that accounts for its obsession to reach the eminence of scientific respectability. The methodological advances have indeed been considerable; but the findings from these points of approach have not as yet by any manner of means solved the problems of human personality. Their value lies chiefly in their advancement of sensory and reflex psychology—or, as someone has a bit derisively called it, "eye-ear-nose-and-throat" psychology.

In recent years the third wind has risen likewise to the force of a gale. *Social science* is causing a tornado all its own. It refuses to blend amicably with natural and biological science, but claims mind pretty much as its own province for study. Anthropologists and sociologists give no quarter. Mind, they insist, takes its form almost wholly in response to cultural demands. Language precedes the individual; so, too, do the religion, the morals, the economic system into which the individual is born. Mind, then, is a matter not for instrumental or biological study but for cultural study. A large number of psychologists have been converted, at least partially, to this view and recently have staged a rebellion within their own ranks, four hundred of them forming a society to investigate as realistically as possible the fate of mind as it is conditioned and constrained by the gigantic movements of contemporary society.

The last wind that blows in our storm center is gentler and less voracious. Yet its presence is always felt. In spite of all counter currents, it is perhaps still the prevailing wind. It is the wind of humanism. After all is said and done, it is philosophy and literature, and not the natural, biological or social sciences, that have fostered psychology throughout the ages. Only in comparatively recent years has psychology detached itself from philosophy and from art to become the storm center that it is.

Now we come to personality. One of the outstanding events in psychology of the present century has been the discovery of personality. Personality, whatever else it may be, is the substantial, concrete unit of mental life that exists in forms that are definitely single and individual. Throughout the ages, of course, this phenomenon of personal individuality has been depicted and explored by the humanities. The more aesthetic philosophers and the more philosophical artists have always made it their special province of interest.

Tardily, psychologists have arrived on the scene. One might almost say they are beginning two thousand years too late. The psychologist's work, it might seem, has been done for him, and done most brilliantly. With his scant and recent background, the psychologist looks like a conceited intruder. And so he is, in the opinion of many literati. Stephan Zweig, for example, speaking of Proust, Amiel, Flaubert and other great masters of characterization, says: "Writers like these are giants in observation and literature, whereas in psychology the field of personality is worked by lesser men, mere flies, who have the safe anchorage of a frame of science in which to place their petty platitudes and minor heresies."

It *is* true that the giants of literature make psychologists, who undertake to represent and to explain personality, seem ineffectual and sometimes a bit foolish in comparison. Only a pedant could prefer the dry collections of facts that psychology can offer regarding an individual mental life to the glorious and unforgettable portraits that the gifted novelist, dramatist or biographer can give. The literary artist creates his account; the psychologist merely compiles his. In the one case a unity emerges, self-consistent even through its subtleties of change. In the other case a ponderous accumulation of discontinuous data piles up.

One critic has put the matter crisply. Psychology, he remarks, whenever it deals with human personality, is only saying what literature has always said, and is saying it much less artfully.

Whether this unflattering judgment is entirely correct, we shall soon see. For the moment it serves at least to call attention to the significant fact that in a sense literature and psychology are competitors; they are the two methods par excellence for dealing with the personality. The methods of literature are those of art; the methods of psychology are those of science. Our question is: which approach is the more suitable for the study of personality?

Literature has had centuries of headstart, and it has been served by genius of the highest order. Psychology is young and has bred as yet few, if any, geniuses in the depiction and explanation of human personality. Being youthful, it would be becoming for psychology to learn a few basic truths from literature.

To show what it can profitably learn, let us take a concrete example. I have chosen one from ancient times in order to show clearly the maturity and ripeness of literary wisdom. Twenty-three hundred years ago, Theophrastus, Aristotle's pupil and successor at the Lyceum in Athens, wrote a number of brief characterizations of certain of his Athenian acquaintances. Thirty of his sketches have survived.

The sketch that I shall select is called "The Coward." Please note its timelessness. The coward of today is essentially the same kind of mortal as the coward of antiquity. Please note also the remarkable directness and economy of the portrait. No words are wasted. It is like a prose sonnet. No one could add or subtract a single sentence to its betterment.

THE COWARD

Cowardliness is a shrinking of the soul caused by fear. The Coward is this sort of person. At sea he thinks cliffs are pirates and directly the sea gets rough inquires anxiously whether all the passengers are initiated [into the mysteries of the Cabeiri]; as he looks up at the sky he asks the steersman if they are halfway and what he thinks of the weather; he tells the person next him that he has had a disturbing dream; he takes off his tunic and gives it to his slave [so that he can swim]; and finally begs to be put on shore. On active service when the infantry are going into action, he calls to the men of his deme to come and stand by him and to keep a good look-out—pretending that it is hard to distinguish who is the enemy. Then hearing the noise of battle and seeing men fall, he tells his comrades that in the hurry he has forgotten his sword; he runs back to his tent and, after getting rid of his slave by sending him out to reconnoitre, hides the sword under his pillow and wastes time in pretending to look for it. If he sees a wounded friend carried in, he rushes up, tells him to keep cheerful, holds him under the arms to support him; then he attends him, wipes the blood off and sits down by him to keep the flies away—in short, does everything except fight. The trumpets sound the charge and, as he sits in the tent, he murmurs: "Curse you! Won't you let the poor man sleep with your everlasting trumpeting!" Covered with the other man's blood he goes out to meet the returning soldiers and tells them he has saved one of his friends at the risk of his own life; and he brings to the bedside the men of his deme and tribe and explains to each visitor that he carried the wounded man to the tent with his own hands.[1]

There is one feature in this classic sketch that I should like to call particularly to your attention. You will note that Theophrastus selects two situations for recording his observations. In one the coward is traveling; in the other he is unwillingly engaged in a battle. In the first situation, seven typical episodes are depicted: the coward's illusion of seeing the cliffs as pirates, his superstitious fear lest some of the passengers might bring bad luck through having neglected a religious rite, his desire to be at least halfway on the dangerous journey, his consulting expert opinion on the weather, his fear of his own disturbing dreams, his preparations for swimming to safety and, finally, his emotional collapse in begging to be put on shore. Even more subtle are the seven telltale episodes during battle. In all there are fourteen situations described; all of them for the coward are equivalent: whatever stimulation he is exposed to arouses the same deep, dominant disposition. His separate acts are quite distinctive, yet all are equivalent in that each is a manifestation of the same dominant cowardly disposition.

In short, Theophrastus, more than two thousand years ago, used a method just now being glimpsed by psychologists—that of defining, with the aid of equivalent stimulations and equivalent responses, the major dispositions of a character.

To state the point yet more broadly: almost all the literature of character—whether sketch writing, as in the case of Theophrastus, or fiction, drama or biography—proceeds on the psychological assumption that each character has certain *traits* peculiar to himself, which can be defined through the narrating of typical episodes from life. In literature a personality is never regarded, as it sometimes is in psychology, as a sequence of unrelated specific actions. Personality is not like a water-skate, darting hither and yon on the surface of a pond, with its several fugitive excursions having no intrinsic relation to one another. Good literature never makes the mistake of confusing the personality of man with that of a water-skate. Psychology often does.

The first lesson, then, that psychology has to learn from literature is something about the nature of the substantial and enduring dispositions of which personality is composed. This is the problem of traits; and by and large, I maintain, it has been handled more successfully through the assumptions of literature than through the assumptions of psychology. More specifically, it seems to me, the concept of the equivalence of stimulation and the equivalence of response, seen so clearly in the ancient sketches of Theophrastus, may serve as a strikingly productive guide for the scientific study of personality—where equivalences may be determined with greater accuracy and greater verifiability than in literature itself. Using the resources of the laboratory and controlled observation outside, psychology might be able to establish for the single individual, far more exactly than literature can, the precise range wherein various life-situations are for him equivalent and the precise range of responses that for him have equivalent significance.

A second major lesson from literature concerns the self-consistency of its products. No one ever asked their authors to prove that the characters of Hamlet, Don Quixote, Anna Karenina, Hedda Gabler or Babbitt were true and authentic. Great characterizations by virtue of their greatness prove themselves. They are plausible; they are even necessary. Every act seems to be in some subtle way both a reflection of and a rounding out of a single, well-knit character. This adhesiveness of behavior meets the test known as self-confrontation: one bit of behavior supports another, so that the whole can be comprehended as a self-consistent, if intricate, unity. Self-confrontation is the only method of validation applied to the work of artists (except perhaps to the work of biographers, who indeed have certain requirements for external validation to contend with). But the method of self-confrontation, I think it may rightly be said, is barely beginning to be applied to the productions of psychology.

Once, in commenting on a character of Thackeray's, Gilbert K. Chesterton remarked, "She drank, but Thackeray didn't know it." Chesterton's quip springs from the demand that all good characterizations possess "systematic relevance" within themselves. Given one set of facts about a personality, other relevant facts should follow. To be sure, a deep and intimate knowledge of a character is required before these necessary inferences can be made. One must know just what the most intimate motivational traits in each case are. For this most central, and therefore most unifying, core of any personality, Wertheimer has proposed the concept of the *radix*—a root from which all stems may grow. He illustrates his conception with the case of a schoolgirl who was a zealous scholar, but at the same time addicted to vivid cosmetics. On the surface there certainly seems to be no systematic relevance here. The two lines of conduct seem to clash. But the apparent contradiction is resolved in this case by exploring beneath the surface for the basic root. In this case, it turned out that the schoolgirl had deep admiration for (a psychoanalyst might call it a fixation upon) a certain teacher who, in addition to being a scholarly woman, had a natural vivid complexion. The schoolgirl simply wanted to be like her teacher. The same facts in another case might betoken a basic desire for power, or simply a double-barreled attempt to capsize the studious boy across the aisle. Whatever the explanation in this case, the point is that with radical understanding it becomes possible to harmonize the apparent inconsistencies in a personality.

Of course, the problem is not always so simple. Not all personalities have basic unity. Conflict, changeability, even the dissociation of personality are common. Much of the *literature* we read exaggerates the consistency of personality; caricatures rather than characters emerge. Oversimplification is found in drama, fiction and biography. The confrontation seems to come almost too easily. The characters of Dickens are a good example of oversimplification. They never have conflicts within themselves; they are always what they are. They may, and usually do, meet unfriendly forces in the environment, but they themselves are entirely perfect in consistency and devoid of inner conflict.

But, if literature often errs through its selectivity in exaggerating the unity of personality, psychology—through its lack of interest and restricted techniques—generally fails to discover or to explore such consistency as does exist.

The greatest failing of the psychologist at the present time is his inability to prove what he knows to be true. No less than the literary artist, he knows that personality is an intricate, well-proportioned and more or less consistent mental structure—but he can't prove it. He makes no use, as the writer does, of the obvious method of self-confrontation of facts. Instead of emulating the artist in this matter, he usually takes safe refuge in the thickets of statistical correlation.

One investigator, thinking to study the virility of his subjects, for a whole population of people, correlates the width of hips and shoulders with interests in sports; another, to find the bases of intelligence, carefully compares the IQ in childhood with the ossification of the wrist bones; a third compares phosphorous per body weight with good-naturedness or with leadership. Investigations such as these, though they are the fashion in research on personality, run their course entirely on a subpersonal level. Devotion to the microscope and to mathematics has led the investigators to shun complex, patterned forms of behavior and thought, even though it is only in these complex forms that personality can be said to exist at all. Bullied by the instruments of physics, many psychologists neglect the most delicate recording instrument ever devised for the relating and proper clustering of facts—namely, their own minds.

Psychology, then, needs techniques of self-confrontation—techniques whereby the togetherness of a personality can be determined. Only a few rudimentary attempts in this direction have been made.[2]

One study employed the English themes of seventy college students. Nine themes were gathered from each student—three in October, three in January and three in May. The topics for the themes were prescribed and were uniform for all students. After the themes were typed and divested of all identifying signs, two experimenters attempted to sort them carefully so that they might, from style alone, group all the themes written by the same student. For both experimenters the results were strikingly positive, well above chance.

The point of interest here is the method by which successful matchings were made. Occasionally, to be sure, some striking mechanical feature caught the eye and aided in identification. Addiction to semicolons would mark the writing of one student, or some other oddity of punctuation or spelling. But most of the identifications were made not on this basis but through a diagnosis of the *personal traits* of the writers. "The investigators found themselves searching for a form-quality of the individual." They felt in each production a reflection of certain complex qualities in the writer himself. These qualities were different in each case and difficult for the experimenter to reduce to words.

In spite of the difficulty of expressing these hypotheses of "form-quality" in words, the fact remains that they were ordinarily the basis of judgment and likewise that the judgments were to a significant degree successful.

It is of interest to note some of the bases upon which this matching proceeded. The production of one student, for example, would be felt always to reflect "a feeling for atmosphere; a well-balanced sense of humor; a quiet, amused tolerance of social relations and situations." Another showed in all his themes "a positive self-assurance; definite, but neither prejudiced nor opinionated; sense of humor." A third was "constantly bored. Looks at life as a monotonous experience in which one follows the easiest course of action." A fourth had a "simple, optimistic attitude toward life and people; simple, direct, declarative sentences."

There is yet another major lesson for psychologists to learn from literature—namely, how to keep a sustained interest in one individual person for a *long* period of time. It was said of a certain famous English anthropologist that although he wrote about savages, he never actually had seen one. He admitted the charge, and added: "And I hope to Heaven I never shall." A great number of psychologists in their professional capacity have never really *seen* an individual; and many of them, I regret to say, hope they never will.

Following the lead of the older sciences, they assume that the individual must be brushed aside. Science, they insist, deals only with general laws. The individual is a nuisance. What is wanted are uniformities. This tradition has resulted in the creation of a vast, shadowy abstraction in psychology called the generalized-adult-human-mind. The human mind, of course, exists in no such form; it exists only in concrete, intensely personal forms. There is no generalized mind. The abstraction that the psychologist commits in measuring and explaining a non-existent mind-in-general is an abstraction that no literary writer ever commits. The literary writer knows perfectly well that mind exists only in singular and particular forms.

Here, of course, we are facing the basic opposition between science and art. Science, it is said, always deals with the general, art always with the particular. But, if this distinction is true, what are we to do about personality? Personality is never general; it is always particular. Must it then be handed over wholly to the arts? Can psychology do nothing about it? I am sure that very few psychologists would accept this solution. Still, it seems to me that the dilemma is inexorable. Either we must give up the individual or we must learn from literature to dwell longer upon him, modifying as is necessary our conception of the scope of science so as to accommodate the single case more hospitably than heretofore.

You may have remarked to yourself that the psychologists you have known, in spite of their profession, are no better than anyone else in understanding people. They are not exceptionally shrewd, nor are they always able to give advice on problems of personality. This observation, if you have made it, is certainly sound. I should go further and say that, because of their habits of excessive abstraction and generalization, many psychologists are actually inferior to other people in their comprehension of the *single* lives that confront them.

When I say that in the interests of a proper science of personality the psychologist should learn to dwell longer on the single case, it might seem that I am poaching upon the domain of biography, whose precise purpose is to dwell exhaustively upon one life.

In England biography began as hagiography and as a recounting of legendary deeds. Neither interest was conducive to objectivity or truthfulness. The term *biography* was first used by Dryden in 1683 and defined by him as "the history of particular men's lives." Reaching a high point in Boswell's *Life of Johnson*, and again in Lockhart's *Life of Scott*, and for a third time in Edmund Gosse's *Father and son*, English biography has had a career of ups and downs. Some biographies are as flat and lifeless as eulogies upon a gravestone; others are sentimental and false.

Increasingly, however, biography is becoming rigorous, and objective, and even heartless. For this trend, psychology has no doubt been largely responsible. Biographies more and more are coming to resemble scientific *autopsies,* performed for the sake of understanding rather than for inspiration or acclaim. There are now psychological and psychoanalytic biographies, and even medical and endocrinological biographies.

The influence of psychological science is felt in autobiography as well. There have been many experiments in objective self-depiction and self-explanation, with improvement upon the disingenuous confessions of Casanova, Rousseau or Barbellion. Two fascinating examples, illustrating the direct influence of psychology, are the *Experiment in autobiography* by H. G. Wells (1935) and *The locomotive god* by W. E. Leonard (1927). But for all their enhanced warmth and intimacy, autobiographers suffer one disadvantage compared with biographers. The autobiographer as a rule cannot bear to disparage himself, and the reader cannot bear to read his praise of himself. Perhaps in time writers may learn how to control their powerful impulse to justify their deeds in the telling, and readers may learn correspondingly to be less suspicious of virtue when it is self-disclosed.

I have mentioned three lessons that the psychologist may learn from literature for the improvement of his own work. The first is the conception held universally in all of literature concerning the nature of traits. Each literary artist proceeds on the assumption that his characters have broadly organized inner dispositions that can be identified and defined. The method that literature uses in identifying and defining traits—namely, the study of equivalent fields of stimulation and equivalent fields of response—needs urgently to find its way into the psychologist's store of methods. The second lesson concerns the test of self-confrontation, which good literature always meets and psychology nearly always avoids meeting. Owing to their neglect of this basic principle of literary validation, psychologists generally fail to find the style and coherence of the personalities that they study. The third lesson calls for more sustained interest in the single case, through longer periods of time. The psychologist should dwell upon one life more exhaustively than he does, no matter if in so doing he sacrifices his impulse to make broad (and usually premature) generalizations about the abstract, nonexistent, average human mind.

In presenting these three advantages of the literary method, I have said little about the distinctive merits of psychology. In conclusion I ought to add at least a few words in praise of my profession. Otherwise you might infer that I am willing and even eager to sell psychology down the river in return for a copy of *Madame Bovary* and a free pass to the Athenaeum.

Psychology has a number of potential advantages over literature. Its disciplined character offsets the subjective dogmatism inherent in imaginative writing. Sometimes literature passes the test of self-confrontation of facts too easily. For example, in one comparative study of biographies of the same person it was found that each version of the life seemed plausible enough but that only a small percentage of the events and interpretations given in one biography were to be found in the others. No one could know which, if any, was the *true* portrait.

It is not necessary for good writers to agree in their observations and in their explanations to anything like the same extent that all good psychologists must agree. Biographers can give vastly different interpretations of a life without discrediting the literary method, whereas psychology is ridiculed when its experts fail to agree with one another.

A psychologist is properly troubled by the arbitrary metaphors of literature. The implication of many metaphors is often grotesquely false, yet they are seldom challenged. In literature one may find, for example, that the docility of a certain character is explained by the fact that "he had menial blood in his veins," the fieriness of another character by the fact that "his temperament he shared with all other redheads" and the intellectuality of a third by the "height of his massive brow." A psychologist would be torn limb from limb if he made any such fantastic assumptions concerning cause and effect.

The artist, furthermore, is permitted and encouraged to be entertaining and engaging, to communicate his own images, to express his own biases. His success is measured by the responsiveness of his readers, who often demand nothing more than that they may languidly identify themselves with a character and escape from their immediate worries. The psychologist, on the other hand, is never permitted to entertain his reader. His success is measured by sterner criteria than the reader's applause.

In gathering his material, the writer draws from his casual observations of life, elides his data and discards troublesome facts at will. The psychologist is held by requirements of fidelity to fact, to *all* facts; and he is expected to secure his facts from controlled and verifiable sources. He must prove his inferences step by step. His terminology is standardized, and he is deprived almost entirely of the use of seductive metaphor. These restrictions surrounding the psychologist make for reliability, verifiability, lessened bias and relative freedom from self-projection into the products of his work.

Psychologists who study personality are, I agree, essentially striving to say what literature has always said, and they are of necessity saying it much less artfully; but as far as they have gone—and it is not very far—they are striving to speak more exactly and, from the point of view of human progress, more helpfully.

The title of this essay, like the titles of many essays, is idly stated. Personality is not a problem for science or a problem for art exclusively, but for both together. Each approach has its merits, but both are needed for even an approximately complete study of the infinite richness of personality.

If in the interests of good pedagogy I am expected to conclude with one pointed bit of advice, it would be this: If you are a student of psychology, read many, many novels and dramas of character, and read biography. If you are *not* a student of psychology, read these too, but *read psychology as well*.

REFERENCES

1. R. Aldington, *A book of characters*, London: Routledge, no date, p. 47.
2. The following experiment is described on pp. 491 ff. of my book *Personality: a psychological interpretation*, New York: Holt, 1937.

CHAPTER 2

The psychological nature of personality

The psychological analysis of human personality must come to terms not only with art but also with philosophy.

The following essay offers in compendious form a psychological theory of personality, but it does so with special reference to the tenets of so-called personalistic philosophy. Written to honor the memory of Edgar Sheffield Brightman (1884-1953), late Bowne Professor of Philosophy at Boston University, the essay appeared in abbreviated form in *The Personalist* (1953).

If you ask whether I consider myself a personalist, I would probably reply, "Does anyone like to have his thought lightly filed away under a label?" But if I am not allowed to evade the question, I would say, "In so far as I am person-centered, yes, I am a personalist." But, as this essay explains, there are areas of serious disagreement.

Readers who are not especially interested in the philosophical issues will still find in this chapter the framework of a strictly psychological theory of personality.

Personalism, says Brightman, is the theory that only persons are real.[1] Thus defined, personalism is basically a metaphysical doctrine. Since a psychologist has no professional competence to argue an ontological position, he could not, as a psychologist, be a personalist —or any other brand of metaphysician.

Having made this pious disclaimer, let us hasten to admit that, whether he knows it or not, every psychologist gravitates toward an ontological position. Like a satellite he slips into the orbit of positivism, naturalism, idealism, personalism. One of these, or some other explicit philosophy, exerts a pull upon his own silent presuppositions, even though he may remain ignorant of the affinity that exists. It is shortsighted of him to deny the dependence—or to refuse to articulate, as best he can, his own thinking about human nature with that brand of philosophy with which it is most closely allied.

In the old days every major philosopher was also a psychologist. His metaphysics and his science of mind were all of a piece. At the present time specialization has reached a point—owing chiefly to the growing dominance of scientific method in psychology—where completely congruent philosophical-scientific views of human nature are exceedingly difficult to achieve.

Take the theory of the person. Within the present century, psychologists have accumulated vast stores of research and insight. But unless I am mistaken, philosophical personalists have not used these findings to any great extent as a testing ground for their own theories. And, vice versa, nearly all of this psychological cumulation has taken place without benefit of the hard thinking of those philosophers who have centered their attention to an equal degree upon the person. It seems as though two separate disciplines have evolved around the same subject matter, each with a distinctive contribution but scarcely aware of the other's existence. The problem is to bring about a more coherent view of the person while respecting the dual approach.

William Stern saw the issue clearly when he proposed that *personalism* be regarded exclusively as a philosophical doctrine and that the portion or type of psychology relevant to the issues of personalism be called *personalistics*.[2] The distinction is meaningful and, up to a point, helpful. It invites the psychologist who agrees in finding personality the most absorbing and insistent topic in the world to say his say without danger of undue presumption. It invites him to collaborate in a cross-disciplinary search without committing himself to propositions beyond his range of competence.

But the distinction breaks down, verbally at least, when the adjective *personalistic*, or the noun *personalist*, is employed. A psychologist interested in personalistics—that is, in the psychology of the person—will almost certainly be labeled a "personalist," and the line of thought he represents will be called "personalistic." Hence, whether he likes it or not, he will be classified with a philosophical school whose interests he shares in part but with whose total position he may hesitate to agree. A typical ground for hesitation, for example, lies in the fact that philosophical personalism has traditionally endorsed "self-psychology" (Brightman, Calkins). Now, a "personalistic" psychologist might find himself in sympathy with the trend of philosophical personalism and yet object to being ticketed as a "self-psychologist," for self-psychology is too dependent on introspection.

It is this confusion, I believe, that has made psychologists, however person-oriented, reluctant to accept the personalistic label. It seems to overcommit them or to align them with a type of psychology they regard as inadequate. While an increasing number of psychological theorists are becoming person-centered, few of them have as yet explicitly accepted the label *personalistic*. One recent exception is represented in the textbook written by Gardner Murphy. He boldly declares that his view of general psychology is "personalistic." We note, however, that his position is more methodological than metaphysical: "The conception is that every psychological act is the act of a whole person, and that the first task of psychology is to focus upon the nature of the person." [3]

There is no doubt that personalistic psychology, conceived even in this limited way, may be a valuable ally of philosophical personalism. It may even be viewed as a necessary propaedeutic. For if, as Brightman insists, truth is a matter of systematic coherence, then all the valid discoveries of psychology pertaining to the nature of personality must find their place without remainder in the philosophy of personalism. Reciprocally, the personalistic psychologist will find the significance of his own researches deepened by his acquaintance with the larger context of philosophical personalism. *What the two disciplines have in common is their conviction that the person is altogether central in the scheme of things, whether the scheme is explored at the psychological or at the philosophical level.*

I

With the exception of a few specialists, psychologists in the present day nearly all deal with the problems of personality. Virtually every textbook, however nomothetically oriented—however predisposed to universal concepts—contains a final chapter on "personality." But the final chapter is often a mere gesture. What it says is seldom geared in with the remainder of the text. Few psychologists center their concern, as Murphy does, in acts-of-whole-persons, nor do they regard it the central task of psychology to focus upon the nature of the person.

Thus most psychologists who talk about personality hold theories that have no relation whatever to a personalistic outlook. For some, personality is an uncemented mosaic of elements, measured perhaps by scales but never vitally interrelated. For others, it is a congeries of "factors" mathematically determined by correlating mental traits in a large population of people (but not in the individual person himself). For still others, it is a passive product of past experience resulting from a succession of pushes, without any contemporary motivation or "go."

It is not my purpose to review all the failures of psychology to give an adequate account of the properties of personality. Readers are already critical enough of the flatness and triviality of many of the prevailing psychological views of personality. The problem to which I wish to address myself is this: *What attributes must a theory of personality have in order to be considered adequate to the empirical facts before us?* If this question can be satisfactorily answered, we shall have in hand the type of theory to which personalistic philosophy—in the interests of systematic congruence—must accommodate itself.

There are, as I see the matter, at least five essential characteristics that an adequate theory of personality must possess. It must possess *all* of these, not only in order to accommodate the empirical facts as known, but also in order to avoid self-contradiction. Let me be clear. I am speaking here of the criteria of personality that appear to be mandatory to a person-centered psychologist. I also believe that the philosophical personalist is required to accept them in one form or another. I shall not object if he wishes to recast my propositions in more congenial terms, provided only that his final product leaves the substance of these criteria available for the psychologist's use in his continued researches.

An adequate theory of personality will (1) regard the human personality as integumented—that is, as centered in the organism; (2) regard the organism as replete, not empty; (3) regard motivation as normally a fact of present structure and function, not merely as an outgrowth of earlier forces; (4) employ units of analysis capable of living synthesis; and (5) allow adequately for, but not rely exclusively upon, the phenomenon of self-consciousness.

Let us now attempt to clarify these requirements.

II

Human personality has a locus—within the skin. To be sure, its imagination and memory range far and wide, but these acts are well grounded in a psychophysical matrix of some order. On another plane of existence, personality may be freed from its space-time bondage; but on the plane where the psychologist dwells, it must be viewed as an organic unity, accessible to study through its acts, its verbal report and even its reflex and physiological functioning. More than one of the body-mind solutions available to personalists would, I think, adequately meet this need. I shall not here attempt to choose among them.

The reason that I stress the criterion of integumentation is that both psychological and philosophical personalists need to rescue human personality from the clutches of those who confuse it with the impression a man makes on others, with his reputation, with his "social stimulus value." Elsewhere I have argued this "biophysical" position at length in contradiction to the view that I have called "biosocial." [4] (Neither term, I think, is well chosen; but their drift is, I hope, clear.) The "biosocial" view takes *your* personality to be what *other* people think and do about you, not what you yourself think and do. To reject this conception is not, of course, to deny that our reputations, whether true or erroneous, may have heavy impact upon others and upon ourselves. But unless we rid ourselves of all definitions that place our personalities in *other* people's minds, we shall never have a secure enough locus for a theory of personality as a system. The biophysical view, unlike the biosocial, would hold that Robinson Crusoe in solitude has "as much" personality before as after the advent of his man Friday.

Besides this crude confusion of person and reputation, there are a number of other partially biosocial views that are almost equally unacceptable. Most of these views evolved in an honest effort to recognize the indisputable fact that the individual is bound into a social context. While one must have deep sympathy with these conceptual attempts, most of them are, in effect, person-destroying. They chisel and chip away at the biophysical nature of personality until it loses its essential characteristics of locus, uniqueness and inner congruence.

For the most part, current theories of this order have to do with the recently popular subject matter in research and teaching that falls under the rubric "Personality and Culture." Two decades ago, in its effort to promote interdisciplinary investigations, the Social Science Research Council promulgated this double-barreled concept, and it was welcomed by scores of psychologists, sociologists and anthropologists. The resulting cross-fertilization of thought has been remarkably productive, not only in furthering research but also in overcoming disciplinary boundaries within universities and colleges. The resulting ferment and realignment, though undoubtedly wholesome, brought forth a number of hasty and misshapen theories.

One type of hasty formulation reduced personality wholly to a mirror-reflection of culture. "Personality is the subjective side of culture" became a popular dictum. It would be hard to imagine a more total reversal of the personalistic emphasis upon the inner coherence-maintaining and purposive properties of the individual. In fact, some writers went so far as to insist that there is no such thing as integration within personality; the only consistency a person shows is a reflection of the orderly and patterned character of his surrounding situation.

A variant of this view is found in current "role" theory. Partisans of this concept are impressed, not by the uniqueness and integrality of the personality system, but by the diverse prescriptions laid upon this system by social expectations. A man is known, not for what he *is*, but for the *roles* he plays—as father, physician, churchman, consumer. He is a composite bundle of roles. That people *do* sometimes behave differently in various environments and in accordance with varying expectations is, of course, not to be denied. The danger with the role concept is that the personal nexus *containing* the role-habits is likely to be overlooked and, correspondingly, the orientation of the person to separate environments overstressed. One is reminded of the exuberance of William James, who declared (though he certainly didn't mean it) that a man "has as many different social selves as there are distinct groups of persons about whose opinion he cares." [5] Personality may be versatile and variable, but it is not capable of dissipation into *n* roles or *n* social selves. Nor is it a mere "equilibrium of roles." There is too much evidence that personality is highly consistent with itself from situation to situation to permit this type of reduction.[6]

A further dubious trend is seen in the currently fashionable conception of "basic" or "modal" personality. We are told that each culture tends to bring up its children according to an approved formula and that children therefore tend to develop similar traits and outlooks. Each culture has a type of personality that corresponds to its cultural pattern. While for certain gross comparisons of culture this conception may be both valid and useful, its coarseness and imprecision limit its value. For one thing, it overlooks the central fact that no single individual reflects all these traits and outlooks, and that some individuals may reflect virtually none of them. It allows not at all for the creative interweaving of cultural threads with threads that are individual and unique. To be sure, the concept does not pretend to cover the "idiosyncratic" determinants of personality; but peril lies in the tendency of certain writers to believe that, having discussed what is "basic" in this sense, they have dealt adequately with the whole subject of personality.

Much of this theoretical vertigo might have been avoided if the initial sponsors of the phrase "Personality and Culture" had changed the particle *and* to *in*. "Personality *in* Culture" poses all the legitimate problems and has the added merit of implying that their solution will be found, not by destroying the integrity of the personal system, but by studying the relation of this self-contained system to cultural and social contexts, which may in turn be regarded as systems of a different order.

In spite of my defense of integumentation, I concede that a genuine weakness in personalistic writing, both philosophical and psychological, is its tendency to sidestep the countless intersections that occur between the personality system and the social system. Even though personalists, by conviction, must ascribe primacy to the former, they can ill afford to leave unsolved the problems created by the intersection. If they persistently do so, their basic contributions will be by-passed and disregarded by advancing social science. The relation of personality to society must somehow be dealt with adequately. It is not enough to assert that a person's traits, attitudes, subjective values or other inner forces account for his conduct. While this statement is true, it disregards situational variance. In spite of a prevailing consistency, one *does* vary one's behavior— within limits—according to social circumstance. To be sure, no one varies it in ways that are not already *his;* but neither is he closed off from, and independent of, the social system. He maintains his own boundaries, but those boundaries are not impermeable.

We need a theory in social science that will allow for the full integrity and primacy of the personal system while relating it adequately to boundary-maintaining social and cultural systems. Important steps in this direction have recently been taken by Parsons and others.[7]

It is Parsons' contention that the personality system is a self-contained unit exerting marked constraints upon the social system. The latter "cannot be so structured as to be radically incompatible with the conditions of function of its component individual actors as biological organisms and as personalities." [8] At the same time, the social system need not meet the needs of *all* its members, but only of a sufficient proportion to maintain its own form of organization. The social system is one in which the individual finds himself related to others in a way that tends to maintain their relationships in equilibrium.[9] The physician and the patient, for example, take certain subtly marked roles in relation to each other in order to fulfill the needs of both; nor could these needs be fulfilled unless these prescribed role relations were observed.

It would seem that this line of thought offers considerable hope for maintaining full recognition of the integral nature of the personality system, while relating it more adequately to its social con-

text. Parsons affirms the ultimate unity of the personality system
and complains that most brands of psychology do not treat personality *as* a system.[10] In short, while offering a theoretical groundwork for social science at large, this sociologist invites and welcomes
a personalistic treatment of the individual.

The need for a social science that will adequately hold the assumptions of personalistic psychology is exceedingly acute. Most
of the theories and trends mentioned in this section seem to veer away
from personality conceived as an integumented system. They illustrate perhaps what Riesman sets forth as the most telling change in
American character—the shift from "inner-directedness" to "other-
directedness." [11] So great today is the demand for peer approval
(children in some schools are graded not on the three R's but on "adjustment") that it seems natural for contemporary social scientists to
think in terms of *basic* personality rather than *full-bodied* personality and in terms of *roles* rather than *being*. It was easier for personalism to have its say in the earlier days of "inner-directedness,"
when it was taken for granted that each person possessed inner purposes and inner balances. In the present day, personalistic psychology and philosophy must fight hard to breast the tide of other-
directedness—the tide of the *Massenmensch*.

III

The influence of modern positivism upon the psychological
study of personality is in part wholesome. Diagnostic instruments
are improving; more exacting standards of evidence prevail; anecdotes
and rumor are discredited; and the preference for operational definition has, in a limited way, made for more intelligible communication.

But positivism also has stultifying effects. Its devotees exclude
explanations in terms of inner traits, purposes, interests; some even
tell us that the nervous system can no longer be invoked in our
explanatory sequences. Since nothing that occurs between the
stimulus and the response is observable, no "intervening variable" is
admissible. We must confine our explanatory efforts, so they say, to
events that lie outside the organism. Even the *habits* of Watsonian
behaviorism must go. One positivist remarked, "When we understand the properties of the stimulus, we shall not need the concept
personality."

What lies behind this methodological craving for an empty
organism? Is it an ascetic desire for scientific chastity, allowing only
minimal assumptions in order to avoid the traps of subjectivism and

circular reasoning? In a thousand years of chaste research built on these meager assumptions, does one hope to achieve a science of behavior having some measure of adequacy? Or could it be that this formula is from the outset an escapist device, designed to protect the harassed scientist from the pulsation of real life around him? He finds it comforting to say that "science is willingness to accept facts even when they are opposed to wishes"; yet his own wish to emulate natural scientists may lead him to reject all facts that are opposed to his wishes. Brightman has shown how the experimental scientist, however positivistic his procedure, is in fact making various silent assumptions that interpose the *self*, as an intervening variable, between the scientist's own stimuli and his own responses.[12]

While adherents of extreme positivism are relatively rare in psychology, their influence is strong enough to create a tone of apology among certain writers who timidly affirm the utility of "intervening variables," "hypothetical constructs" or "inferred tendencies"—in other words, of *traits, values, intentions, self*.

Now, it is obvious that a full-bodied psychology of personality must take precisely the opposite tack from positivism. It must assume from the outset that there is nothing scientifically shameful about postulating a well-furnished personality that *is* something and *does* something—a personality that has internal structures and substructures which "cause," or partially cause, behavior. One may, of course, gain helpful hints from positivism regarding the need for reliable criteria in establishing inferences concerning traits, habits, attitudes, needs and sentiments. Yet no psychologist concerned with personality can avoid altogether the postulation of inner dispositions within the organism to account for its consistency in conduct and for its motivation. In this connection, William McDougall has argued that "inner tendency" is the most indispensable concept in the entire science of psychology.[13] Still, the pressures emanating from positivism are all in the other direction: it is the fashion to unstock the organism, especially to strip it of dynamic power and purpose.

The same trend, to a lesser degree, is seen in what is called "field theory." While Lewin and his followers have never denied the existence of needs and attitudes within the organism, they tend to regard behavior as a function of *all* field-forces, both inner and outer. In practice, there seems to be a predilection for forces in the outer situation that exert pressure upon the individual. Thus the desires and values of the person are squeezed out of many field formulations.[14]

Gestalt psychology, too, postulates a singularly passive, if not actually empty, organism. Outer configurations impinge upon the nervous system, which, through an isomorphic type of response, yields conscious and behavioral equivalents of the stimulus pattern. This psychophysical process, as envisaged by Köhler and others, brings the organism into harmonious relations with its environment, but the organism itself seems to contribute little to the process. Stern, the personalist, felt it necessary to protest vehemently against this passive model. Mental life, he maintained, not only has the self-distributing and isomorphic properties here postulated but also shows the continuous presence of inner activity: *keine Gestalt ohne Gestalter*.

Person-centered psychologists reject the fetish of the empty organism. They cannot see why the enormous potentialities of the human cortex, energized by its own and by autonomic activity, should not allow for *dispositions* as well as for *traces*. Why should the nine billion cells in the cortex act only like iron filings in a magnetic field of force? Their combinations and their properties suggest that, while passive forms of organization (mere "traces") exist, there are also highly dynamic formations, consisting of purposes and interests, which give personality its active, urgent, directed character. We do not know precisely how mental and physical events are related; but it seems obvious that, taken together, they comprise a unified, energy-filled and boundary-maintaining system. The person, thus conceived, is alive and going places.

To be sure, person-centered psychologists do not all view this animated structure of personality in precisely the same way. Some speak of a hierarchical organization of conditioned reflexes, habits, traits and "selves." Others prefer units such as instincts, interests and sentiments. Freudians are partial to the "institutions" of id, ego and superego. While, as I shall soon show, it makes a great deal of difference just what units are chosen, it is enough for now to repeat our contention: any theory of personality pretending adequacy must be dynamic and, to be dynamic, must assume a well-stocked organism.

IV

Yet not every dynamic theory of personality is adequate. Many, indeed most of them, suffer from two shortcomings in their view of motivation: they pay too little attention to the *uniqueness* and to the *contemporaneity* of personal motives.

In their struggle to emulate nomothetic science, most theories regard the desires and intentions of individuals simply as changes rung upon a few uniform themes. These themes may be labeled *drives, instincts, needs, wishes, desires, vectors* or something else. Whatever they are called, the implication is always the same: if we could correctly classify the basic motives of men, we should be able to account for the behavior of each *individual* man. Thus the sex drive, the aggressive instinct, the need for achievement, the wish for security and the desire for dependency become variables to which all personalities may be ordered. While each motivational theory differs in some respects from all others, they have in common this heavily nomothetic bias. For certain purposes it is a defensible bias: often we *do* gain from comparing personalities according to such common categories. But a theory that is completely content with an account of abstract motives, of abstract personalities, fails to provide a foundation sound enough to bear the weight of any single full-bodied personality.

In this connection it is interesting to recall the strongly personalistic flavor of definitions of psychology offered by the founders of the science: Wundt, James and Titchener. The first wrote that psychology "investigates the total context of experience in its relations to the subject"; the second, that "psychology is the science of finite individual minds"; and the third, that "psychology is the study of experience considered as dependent on some person." None of these authors developed his account of mental life to accord with his definition. Yet some vague sense of propriety seemed to guide them in framing their definitions; they knew that mind (as a psychological datum) exists only in finite and in personal forms. Yet each, like the dynamic psychologists of the present day, spent his time exclusively in seeking the laws of mind-in-general and worried little about the concrete formations that mark minds-in-particular. (An exception to this statement is the use made by William James of case-studies in his *Varieties of religious experience*.)

The second shortcoming of current dynamic psychology has to do with its anachronistic handling of motivation. Past-reference dominates the scene. While men are busy leading their lives in the present, with much future-pointing, psychologists are busy tracing these lives backward. Let us take an example. Ask almost any psychologist (psychoanalyst or not) why the son of some famous politician is himself a politician. The answer you will receive is likely to be in terms of father identification, early slanting, conditioning and reinforcement, or something equally freighted with reference to childhood. Such answers are, of course, acceptable enough from a *historical* point of view, but they are likely to be irrelevant and misleading in accounting for the *present* situation. Virtually all psychologies (Freudian, Adlerian, stimulus-response) stress the initial slanting of personal development in the early years of life. While the first outlines may indeed be laid at this time, it does not follow that an adult person normally maintains this style of life for the reasons that were operative in childhood.

Returning to our example: it is indeed probable that our politician did have a father identification at the age of, say, four (most boys do); it is also likely that he was rewarded and praised for his oratorical imitations of Daddy. It is probable that he was thus slanted toward a vocation in politics. But does this bit of history explain the drive, the go, the interest of the politician fifty years later? The father is dead; times have changed; instead of rewards, he receives mostly brickbats. Tens of thousands of personal experiences have intervened, modified and reshaped the initial motivational pattern. His personality *now*, we may say, is centered in his interest in politics, not in his father.

This confusion between the historical roots of motives and the contemporary functioning of motives has seemed to me the most stultifying of all misconceptions that mar current theories of personality. This is not the occasion to examine the damaging consequences of the fallacy or to debate the issue fully.[15] It is necessary only to insist that the forward thrusts of motivation that are so characteristic of human personality cannot adequately be accounted for by any doctrine of pushes, even a sequence of pushes, out of the past. An adequate theory must allow for the effectiveness of a current self-image and for the dynamic character of intentions, of value-orientations and of uniquely patterned psychogenic interest systems in normally healthy adults. Philosophically considered, this shift in emphasis is required in order to discover in the individual the necessary ingredients of freedom and value-orientation that would make personalism tenable.

It is only fair to say that a proper theory must allow for early fixations in personality—for infantilisms, regression and many kindred manifestations of neuroticism. It is not necessary to overlook the epochal discoveries of Freud; it is necessary only to put them in proper perspective. Even our politician *may* be a neurotic. He may still be wistfully identified with his father, and all that he does may be an effort to fill Daddy's shoes (even, conceivably, to displace his father in his mother's affections: the Oedipus complex outlasting the death of the parents). The essential point, however, is that such a condition would be exceptional and abnormal. The Freudian view of motivation may be an acceptable model for neurotic behavior without being an acceptable model for all behavior. My own position, which goes under the designation *functional autonomy of motives,* holds that motivation may be—and in healthy people usually is—autonomous of its origins. Its function is to animate and steer a life toward goals that are in keeping with *present* structure, *present* aspirations and *present* conditions.

In recent years we observe certain marked improvements in theory, shifts in the direction of functional autonomy. What is known as neo-Freudianism shows two striking advances: a fuller recognition of the contributions of culture, and a postulation of a far more active, purposive, forward-reaching "ego." Originally Freud conceived the ego as a relatively helpless, though intelligent, rationalizer, beset by three "tyrants"—the id, the superego and external reality. More often than not, it could do nothing but repress its bitter conflicts, which would finally erupt in neurotic anxiety. Even the most orthodox psychoanalysts now say that Freud died without completing his ego theory. Nor is it customary today to regard this enlarged and improved ego as an agent only of defense; it contains mature motives approximately of the order demanded by the doctrine of functional autonomy.[16]

An equally striking development in the right direction is the revolution in theory implicit in Rogerian or "client-centered" therapy.[17] While the theoretical model underlying this movement in "non-directive counseling" is not yet fully worked out, it is certain to take a form compatible with personalistic psychology. The position, in brief, holds that the self, under proper conditions, is capable of reorganizing its perceptual field and thus of altering behavior. The therapy consists in giving the individual an opportunity to assess and rearrange his own image of his motives and circumstances, and thus to emerge a more coherent and firmly knit person.

Other contemporary movements could be cited along the same line. Whereas terms like *self* and *self-image, ego* and *ego-involvement,* were rarely employed by psychologists a generation ago, they are currently used with great frequency and represent emerging systematic theories of motivation free from the restraints of uniformity and past-reference, which have limited conceptual thinking heretofore.[18]

Personalists should be warned that at least one of their number does not believe that the doctrine of functional autonomy is required in an adequate theory of personality. Bertocci has argued that an instinct theory (such as McDougall's) avoids the predicament of "emergence" that is implied in the present author's position. The issue has been fully discussed in print and need not here be debated.[19] Suffice it to say that both writers agree on the need for unique and forward-pointed motives in an adequate theory of personality, whatever conceptualization is required to achieve this goal.

V

Without some units of analysis, the scientific study of personality would be impossible. The type of unit chosen is important. Person-centered psychology cannot be satisfied with the kinds of variables that are customarily isolated for study. Their weakness lies in the fact that, when synthesized, they fail to reconstitute to a satisfactory degree the personality of the individual who is the object of study. In the endeavor to make instruments (tests, questionnaires, experimental situations) standard, reliable and objective, investigators have invented variables so far removed from the structure and functioning of the particular personality that the knowledge gained often seems useless.

Take the case of vocational tests. It is sometimes assumed that a battery of tests can tell the seeker what vocation he should enter and can tell an employer which applicants to hire and which to reject. Sometimes the instruments are helpful to a degree, but, dealing as they do with "typical" variables, they tell little about the unique motivation, the patterning of skills or the underlying potentialities of the single case.

Not only in applied psychology are "typical variables" tried and found wanting; they are also deficient for the strict purposes of theoretical science. They do not yet (and they seem, in principle, unlikely to) yield a high degree of predictive power, understanding and control—the three desiderata of science. To say that John Brown scores in the eightieth percentile of the "masculinity-feminity" variable, in the thirtieth percentile on "need for achievement" and at average on "introversion-extroversion" is only moderately enlightening. Even with a more numerous set of dimensions, with an avalanche of psychometric scores, patterned personality seems to elude the psychodiagnostician.

It is for this reason that professional, especially clinical, psychologists have recourse to supplementary idiographic methods: to interviewing, life-histories, intuition. These channels of understanding are not yet scientifically "respectable"; they cause method-centered psychologists acute distress. Yet research in personalistic psychology must turn to these more patterned forms of perception if it is to improve our skills in diagnosis and help us identify the central characteristics of the individual person.

I do not mean to imply that the arsenal of painfully accumulated standard methods is worthless. Quite the contrary: for a first approximation to personality, the typical variables (especially if they are reliably scaled) have considerable value. Their strength, like their weakness, lies in their ability to order all personalities to a uniform set of variables, variously called traits, needs, attitudes, dimensions, factors or types. This comparative approach enables us to locate a subject roughly in a population of his peers. Some of the more subtle nomothetic instruments yield more than a single score and thus approach the threshold of the problem of patterning. But even the subtlest of nomothetic methods carries us only to the point where we see that the score on a certain variable is interdependent with other scores on other variables. The *personal nexus* wherein all variables are joined eludes every nomothetic approach.

Elsewhere I have spoken of this "common trait" approach and have shown that it is inferior to the more complex, but ultimately more revealing, "individual trait" approach. While the former is content with uniform variables, the latter seeks to discover the vital foci of organization within individual lives.[20]

The objection has been made that if we stress the individual trait approach, centering attention on the individuality of pattern, then "the science of human nature would come to a dead stop." [21] These generalists argue as follows: Every stone in the meadow is unique, yet the science of mineralogy wholly covers the subject; the accident of uniqueness falls, if anywhere, in the artist's province. Each manifestation of a disease is unique, but biochemistry and other constituent sciences of medicine provide the essential explanations needed. Following these models, psychology as science should seek only uniformities and leave individuality to the practitioner, the biographer or the lover. To clinch the argument, the generalists assert that, if personality is unique, so too is every moment of time during which personality runs its course—and that science cannot hope to deal with such ephemerae.

The weakness of this position, I think, lies in the fact that human personality entails an enduring psychophysical organization, whose intrinsic nature we happen to *want* to study—if we are person-centered. Since it cannot be studied adequately with uniform variables, we have no recourse but to seek the peculiar central and

subsidiary trait-systems that comprise this unique datum. The
effective units in personality happen to be peculiar to the individual.
To acknowledge this central fact does not bring the science of human
nature to a dead stop. On the contrary, it can be demonstrated that a
knowledge of intra-individual patterns of consistency and congruence in behavior gives us enhanced scientific power, for such
knowledge increases our comprehension, predictive ability and control over individual persons beyond the range achieved by unaided
common sense or by nomothetic science. (Whether the individual
should be scientifically "controlled" is an axiological issue that we
need not here discuss. Our present debate is concerned merely with
establishing the scientific respectability of research in the phenomena of uniqueness.)

To date, relatively little progress has been made in theory or
research pertaining to the level of individual traits, largely because
this personalistic requirement has not been admitted in traditional
psychology. Yet some gains have been made. Let me mention, by
way of illustration, a few directions in contemporary investigation
that seem relevant and promising. Studies in expressive behavior are
hopeful, for they tend to disclose the relation of overt movement to
inner patterns of interest, anxiety, temperament. A few mathematical
procedures are promising, especially those that attempt to deal with
patterns of events within the single personality. All work that improves the preparation and use of personal documents (case records,
life-histories and the like) is relevant. The process by which the
human mind forms and checks its judgments of people deserves
sustained study: it seems certain that inference from previous experience is not all that is involved in patterned perception. Important too are studies that fix attention upon the congruence or
disconnection that exists in the motivational systems underlying a
given person's acts: are his conscious and unconscious impulses of a
single piece, or are they discordant? All these problems—and many
more like them—require improved methods for handling pattern and
individuality.[22]

While we are working out new methods for the study of individual traits and personal patterns, there is no reason, of course, to
fall behind in efforts to improve nomothetic variables. Recently my
colleague and critic, Henry A. Murray, on the basis of many years'
labor, proposed a scheme of variables that marks a distinct advance.[23]
The units are in terms of values, vectors and value-vectors. *Values*
include interest in body, progeny, knowledge, freedom, affiliation
and the like; *vectors* are dispositions leading to renunciation, accept-

ance, acquisition, aggression and the like; *value-vectors* ("needs") are the more concrete dispositions to renounce, accept, acquire, construct, maintain and restore a given valued entity. This third type of unit, I believe, since it is concrete, approaches more nearly to adequacy, dealing as it does with the integral intentions (orientations) a person has with reference to his environment, both real and imaginal. The scheme stops somewhat short of recognizing the ultimate manifoldness and uniqueness of each personality, for it still presumes to order all individual patterns to a common, "typical variable" scheme. It may, however, prove to be the most serviceable nomothetic device yet proposed. With its aid we may find that the personality thus analyzed can, with a higher approximation than heretofore, be re-synthesized into its own unique structure and functioning. In so far as it succeeds, we shall have a valuable contribution to the theory and method of personality-research. In so far as it fails, we shall have to carry our search further, pressing ever toward the discovery of more viable units and toward improved means for representing patterned individuality.

VI

With much that I have here written, any personalistic philosopher would, I suppose, agree. He would be bound to approve my insistence that psychology deal adequately with personality as a *system.* He may be saying: Go tell your story to the person-destroying psychologists, not to us. But we come now to a thornier criterion —one that may call for broad concessions on the part of the philosophical personalist; if not, one that at the very least indicates the need for a fresher basis of mutual understanding. The criterion may be stated as follows: *An adequate psychology of personality will allow amply for the concept of self but, unlike some philosophers, will not employ it as a factotum.*

Let us begin by identifying the points where the philosopher and the psychologist are in agreement concerning the properties of the self. In the first place, they must agree that consciousness by no means always involves self-awareness. It seems highly probable that an animal is conscious, but also that its consciousness has no self-reference. As Romanes put the matter, the animal knows but does not know that it knows. Similarly, the dawn of self-awareness in the child is now fairly securely established as a product of maturation and learning gradually developing during the second and third years of life. Among adults, in states of drowsiness and low vitality, there is certainly no awareness of self. And if our criterion of self-awareness is at all exacting (that is, if we require that mental states be clearly recognized as part of a self-system), we might hazard the guess that a person can go through the entire day without being self-aware at all.

A second point of agreement lies in the fact that, despite the ephemerality of self-awareness, it remains the most certain attest we have of personal existence. It is the solid empirical core of human personality. We do not always recognize our consciousness as "owned," but the fact that we occasionally do so is basic to our sense of personal identity and of continuity.

A good deal of modern psychology is concerned with the phenomenological view of the self as datum. One popular, if fairly trivial, line of research has to do with the phenomenal localization of the self in various regions of the body.[24] A more significant interest is in the conditions under which experience is recognized as owned. Recently the topic of the self-image ("ego ideal") has come into prominence, especially in therapeutic literature. Many psychologists see that the *idea* of the self, as well as the *awareness* of the self, constitute a central pivot in the development and change of personality. In this line of work, however, the definition of self is somewhat restricted. Self is regarded only as *the individual as known to the individual*. There is as yet no explicit admission of the self as an *agent*.

But agreement does, I think, proceed further. The person-centered psychologist recognizes that the sense of self, however ephemeral, becomes a vital and active reference point for all conduct. The operation of memory—especially of recognition—brings constantly to mind the indisputable fact of personal identity. The self as anchorage point in consciousness becomes securely established after the first year or two of life, so that the child comes to locate up and down, before and behind, past and future, striving and rejection, in relation to the self he knows.

Thus conation becomes bound into the system. Especially in the second and third year of life, the child grows acutely self-aware and begins to assert himself as a "fighter for ends." (Anyone with a negativistic offspring of this age will need no further proof.) A clamorous self-centeredness sets in, which only with the passing of years becomes socialized and modified into the pursuit of values less egocentric.

Such evidence leads us to assume that, however transient the consciousness of self may be, all sensing, acting and willing are, at bottom, *owned* and that selfhood is the central presupposition we must hold in examining the psychological states of human beings. With this broad inference we agree, though one point remains troublesome. What about the baby? To say that the infant unknowingly "owns" its blurred experience establishes a self prior to the development of the capacity for self-consciousness. Personalists may insist that this is a necessary assumption, but for my part I should like to leave open the possibility that the *emergence* of selfhood in the course of early life may be a defensible proposition.

Up to this point, I assume, personalists and person-centered psychologists are in agreement. Where, then, is there crucial disagreement between them? The chief issue, to my mind, comes from the tendency of the former to overstress the function of consciousness. The tendency takes many forms, whether in connection with discussions of *self*, of *person* or of *personality*. Brightman, for example, writes: "Philosophically, then, personality is restricted to actual consciousness; psychologists will continue to interpret personality as the empirical situation in interaction with a body. This does no harm, unless one becomes confused between the given empirical situation and hypothetical entities, like bodies, which are related to it." [25] And Bertocci, another personalist, writes: "The *I*, the *self*, the *person*, the *conscious being* (all used as synonyms here) *is* the complex unity of activity which consists in sensing, thinking, wanting, imagining, willing, oughting." [26]

Confronted with such overloading of the person with consciousness, the psychologist becomes alarmed lest he be drawn into the camp of simon-pure mentalism and lest he lose the organic unity of personality functioning as he knows it. To Bertocci he would reply that many of the activities of sensing, remembering, imagining, thinking, feeling, willing and the like proceed in a unified way without full—and sometimes without any—participation of consciousness. The person, therefore, is *more* than a conscious unity. To Brightman he would say that, if, philosophically considered, personality is restricted to actual consciousness, the psychologist is talking about a different and wider entity that brooks no such arbitrary psychophysical surgery. It is reassuring to know that the problem troubles personalists themselves and that the door to understanding is not closed.

One way out of the difficulty is offered by William Stern, whose psychophysical neutrality has proved unpalatable to American personalists. Stern, in effect, offers us a *tertium quid,* neither mental nor physical, that maintains the unity and coherence—and represents the metaphysical ultimateness—that the personalist seeks. To him, "The person is living whole, individual, unique, striving toward goals, self-contained and yet open to the world around him; he is capable of having experience." [27]

We note that Stern regards all the listed attributes of the person as compulsory, excepting only "experience." While the person is endowed with the capacity for experience, the guarantee of unity lies at a deeper level. Stern's view is thus opposed to that of both Brightman and Calkins, who hold the self to be mental and to have a body. For Stern, consciousness is merely an important occasional ingredient. Experiences may be salient (*abgehoben*) or deeply imbedded, with a high, low or no degree of self-involvement. Those that are marked by greater personal relevance are of particular interest to the psychologist, but the binding principle is not self (considered either as conscious agent or as datum) but the *person*.

It is true that Stern's position seems to solve the problem by multiplying entities, offering us "neutrality" to juggle along with mind and body. I mention the view here, not with endorsement, but in order to call attention to the fact that one personalist, who was both a philosopher and a psychologist, was deeply concerned with the problem and that he could find no other solution to retain the patent unity of mind and body which here and now marks the organization and functioning of human personality. I doubt that any psychologist whose interest is truly centered in the person could work comfortably within a frame that regards unconscious processes, reflex processes and physiological processes as unintegrated, uncoordinated or less important for the unity of the person than the conscious operations of the self. All these levels of functioning are vital.

VII

In these pages I have attempted to sketch a psychological approach to human personality that seems to me to accord with the scientific evidence available. If I have intruded an unfamiliar vocabulary, and at times a controversial note, I venture to hope and believe that the direction of my argument is compatible with the broad tenets of philosophical personalism. It seems inconceivable to me that two well-intentioned disciplines, working on a common subject matter, can indefinitely remain apart.

REFERENCES

1. E. S. Brightman, *An introduction to philosophy*, rev. ed., New York: Holt, 1951, p. 334.

2. W. Stern, *Studien zur Personwissenschaft. I: Personalistik als Wissenschaft*, Leipzig: Barth, 1930.

3. G. Murphy, *Introduction to psychology*, New York: Harper, 1951, p. xvi.

4. G. W. Allport, *Personality: a psychological interpretation*, New York: Holt, 1937, especially Chap. 2.

5. W. James, *Principles of psychology*, New York: Holt, 1890, I, 294.

6. It may be well to mention some of the kinds of empirical evidence I have in mind. Nearly all "personality tests" tap behavior in *many* situations. A satisfactory "internal reliability" of such tests is *ipso facto* evidence for the inter-situational consistency of personal traits. Intensive studies of refugees whose home culture completely collapsed about their heads show that, in setting up new lives for themselves in new lands, these fugitives did so under the dominance of essentially the same traits, values and modes of adjustment. (G. W. Allport, J. S. Bruner, E. M. Jandorf, "Personality under social catastrophe: ninety life-histories of the Nazi revolution," *Char. & Pers.*, 1941, 10:1-22.) Experiments show that when the central regions of personality are aroused—in other words, when "ego-involvement" is high—the consistency of personality is especially marked. See Chapter 5 of the present volume.

7. T. Parsons and E. A. Shils, *et al.*, *Toward a general theory of action*, Cambridge: Harvard University Press, 1951. T. Parsons, *The social system*, Glencoe, Ill.: The Free Press, 1951. F. H. Allport, *Theories of perception and the concept of structure*, New York: Wiley, 1955, Chap. 21.

8. T. Parsons, *op. cit.*, p. 27.

9. *Ibid.*, p. 542.

10. *Ibid.*, p. 545.

11. D. Riesman, *The lonely crowd: a study of the changing American character*, New Haven: Yale University Press, 1951. It is well to recall in this connection that John Dewey, in *The public and its problems* (New York: Holt, 1927), raised the issue of the dismemberment of the person into mere appendages of many publics—into a taxpayer, an auto owner, a church member, a husband, a bowler, a Civic Leaguer, a dentist, ad infinitum.

12. E. S. Brightman, "The presuppositions of experiment," *Personalist*, 1938, 19:136-43.

13. W. McDougall, "Tendencies, as indispensable postulates of all psychology," *XI Congrès International de Psychologie*, Paris: Felix Alean, 1938, pp. 157-70.

14. This tendency is found in much of Lewin's writing; but in fairness to his breadth of view, it must be said that in certain portions of his work he offers an acceptable analysis of the psychological structure of personality considered as a "differentiated region." Both threads are clearly seen in his posthumous volume, *Field theory in social science* (D. Cartwright, ed.), New York: Harper, 1951. A field-theoretical work that explicitly denies inner dispositions and substitutes the concept of tendency-in-situation is W. Coutu, *Emergent human nature*, New York: Knopf, 1949.

15. See Chapters 3, 4, 6 and 9 of the present volume.

16. Representative of the neo-Freudian books here discussed are: E. Fromm, *Man for himself*, New York: Rinehart, 1947; K. Horney, *New ways in psychoanalysis*, New York: Norton, 1939; F. Fromm-Reichmann, *Principles of intensive psychotherapy*, Chicago: University of Chicago Press, 1951.

17. Cf. C. R. Rogers, *Counseling and psychotherapy*, Boston: Houghton Mifflin, 1942; *Client-centered therapy*, Boston: Houghton Mifflin, 1951; "Some observations on the organization of personality," *Amer. Psychologist*, 1947, 2:358-68.

18. Illustrative of this type of literature are: E. R. Hilgard, "Human motives and the concept of the self" (A Presidential address before the American Psychological Association), *Amer. Psychologist*, 1949, 4:374-82; D. Snygg and A. W. Combs, *Individual behavior*, New York: Harper, 1949; P. Lecky, *Self-consistency: a theory of personality*, New York: The Island Press, 1945; P. M. Symonds, *The ego and the self*, New York: Appleton-Century, 1951.

19. P. A. Bertocci, "A critique of G. W. Allport's theory of motivation," *Psychol. Rev.*, 1940, 47:501-32; G. W. Allport, "Motivation in personality: reply to Mr. Bertocci, *Psychol. Rev.*, 1940, 47:533-54. A more recent statement of Bertocci's well-considered position is found in his *Introduction to the philosophy of religion*, New York: Prentice-Hall, 1951, Chap. 8.

20. *Personality: a psychological interpretation, op. cit.* Chap. 11.

21. H. A. Murray, "Toward a classification of interactions," in T. Parsons and E. A. Shils, *op. cit.*, Part IV, Chap. 3.

22. Chapters 3-9 of the present volume deal with some of the issues here too briefly mentioned.

23. *Op. cit.*, especially pp. 463 ff.

24. Cf. E. L. Horowitz, "Spatial localization of the self," *J. Soc. Psychol.* 1935, 6:379-87.

25. E. S. Brightman, "What is personality?" *Personalist*, 1939, 20:138.

26. P. A. Bertocci, *Introduction to the philosophy of religion, op. cit.*, p. 203.

27. W. Stern, *General psychology from the personalistic standpoint* (trans. by H. D. Spoerl), New York: Macmillan, 1938, p. 70. In German: *Die Person ist eine individuelle, eigenartige Ganzheit, welche zielstrebig wirkt, selbstbezogen und weltoffen ist; fähig ist zu erleben.*

CHAPTER 3

The open system in personality theory

If personality theory must come to terms with literature and with philosophy, it must also come to terms with natural and biological science. The concept of "system" is employed by many present-day psychologists in the hope that it will unify their work with that of their fellow scientists. In part their hope seems justified—provided only that the personality system is allowed to remain as open as its nature requires.

This essay was written by invitation of Division 8 (the Division of Personality and Social Psychology) of the Amercan Psychological Association. It was delivered at the fourteenth annual meeting of the Division in Cincinnati in September 1959, and appeared in the *Journal of Abnormal and Social Psychology* (1960).

Our profession progresses in fits and starts, largely under the spur of fashion. The average duration of our fashions I estimate to be about ten years. McDougall's instinct theory held sway from 1908 to approximately 1920. Watsonian behaviorism dominated the scene for the next decade. Then habit hierarchies took command, then field theory—and now phenomenology. We never seem to solve our problems or exhaust our concepts; we only grow tired of them.

Presently it is fashionable to investigate such phenomena as response-set, coding, sensory deprivation and person perception, and to talk in terms of system-theory—a topic to which we shall soon return. Ten years ago, fashion called for group dynamics, Guttman scales and research on the unsavory qualities of the authoritarian personality. Twenty years ago it was frustration-aggression, Thurstone scales and national morale. Nowadays we watch with some consternation the partial eclipse of psychoanalysis by existentialism. And so it goes. Fortunately, most surges of fashion leave a rich residue of gain.

Fashions have their amusing and their serious sides. We can smile at the way bearded problems receive tonsorial transformation. Having tired of "suggestibility," we adopt the new hairdo known as "persuasibility." Modern ethology excites us, and we are not troubled by the recollection that a century ago John Stuart Mill staked down the term to designate the new science of human character. We like the neurological concept of "gating," conveniently forgetting that

American functionalism always stood firm for the dominance of general mental sets over specific. Reinforcement appeals to us but not the age-long debate over hedonism. The problem of freedom we brush aside in favor of "choice points." We avoid the body-mind problem but are in fashion when we talk about "brain models." Old wine, we find, tastes better from new bottles.

The serious side of the matter enters when we and our students forget that the wine is indeed old. Picking up a recent number of the *Journal of Abnormal and Social Psychology,* I discover that the twenty-one articles written by American psychologists confine ninety per cent of their references to publications of the past ten years, although most of the problems they investigate have gray beards. In the same issue of the *Journal,* three European authors locate fifty per cent of their references prior to 1949. What this proves I do not know, except that European authors were not born yesterday. Is it any wonder that our graduate students reading our journals conclude that literature more than a decade old has no merit and can be safely disregarded? At a recent doctoral examination the candidate was asked what his thesis on physiological and psychological conditions of stress had to do with the body-mind problem. He confessed he had never heard of the problem. An undergraduate said that all he knew about Thomas Hobbes was that he sank with the *Leviathan* when it hit an iceberg in 1912.

A Psycholinguistic Trifle

Our windows are pretty much shuttered toward the past, but we rightly rejoice in our growth since World War II. Among the many happy developments is rejuvenation in the field of psycholinguistics. (Even here, however, I cannot refrain from pointing out that the much-discussed Whorfian hypothesis was old stuff in the days of Wundt, Jespersen and Sapir.) Be that as it may, I shall introduce my discussion of open systems in personality theory by a crude Whorfian analysis of our own vocabulary. My research (aided by the kind assistance of Stanley Plog) is too cursory to warrant attempting a detailed report.

What we did, in brief, was to study the frequency of the prefixes *re-* and *pro-* in psychological language. Our hypothesis was that *re-* compounds, connoting as they do again-ness, passivity, being pushed or maneuvered, would be far more common than *pro-* compounds connoting futurity, intention, forward thrust. Our sample consisted of the indexes of the *Psychological abstracts* at five-year in-

tervals over the past thirty years; also, all terms employing these
prefixes in Hinsie and Shatzky's *Psychiatric dictionary* and in English and English's *Psychological dictionary*. In addition, we made a
random sampling of pages in five current psychological journals.
Combining these sources, it turns out that *re-* compounds are nearly
five times as numerous as *pro-* compounds.

But, of course, not every compound is relevant to our purpose.
Terms like *reference, relationship, reticular, report* do not have the
connotation we seek; nor do terms like *probability, process* and
propaganda. Our point is more clearly seen when we note that the
term *reaction* or *reactive* occurs hundreds of times, while the term
proaction or *proactive* occurs only once—and that in English's *Dictionary*, in spite of the fact that Harry Murray has made an effort to
introduce the word into psychological usage.

But even if we attempt a more strict coding of this lexical material, accepting only those terms that clearly imply reaction and response on one side and proaction or the progressive programming of
behavior on the other, we find the ratio still is approximately 5:1.
In other words, our vocabulary is five times richer in terms like
*reaction, response, reinforcement, reflex, respondent, retroaction,
recognition, regression, repression, reminiscence* than in terms like
production, proceeding, proficiency, problem-solving, propriate and
programming. So much for the number of different words available.
The disproportion is more striking when we note that the four terms
reflex, reaction, response and *retention* together are used one hundred
times more frequently than any single *pro-* compound except *problem-solving* and *projective*—and this latter term, I submit, is
ordinarily used only in the sense of reactivity.

The weakness of the study is evident. Not all terms connoting
spontaneous, future-oriented behavior begin with *pro*. One thinks of
expectancy, intention, purpose. But neither do all terms connoting
passive responding or backward reference in time begin with *re*. One
thinks of *coding, traces, input-output* and the like. But, while our
analysis leaves much to be desired, it prepares the way for our
critique of personality theory in terms of systems. The connecting
link is the question whether we have the verbal, and therefore the
conceptual, tools to build a science of change, growth, futurity and
potential; or whether our available technical lexicon tends to tie us
to a science of response, reaction and regression. Our available
vocabulary points to personality development from the past up to
now, more readily than to its development from here on out into the
future.

The Concept of System

Until a generation or so ago, science, including psychology, was preoccupied with what might be called "disorganized complexity." Natural scientists explored this fragment and that fragment of nature; psychologists explored this fragment and that fragment of experience and behavior. The problem of interrelatedness, though recognized, was not made a topic for direct inquiry.

What is called system-theory today—at least in psychology—is the outgrowth of the relatively new organismic conception reflected in the work of Von Bertalanffy and Goldstein and in certain aspects of Gestalt psychology. It opposes simple reaction theories, where a virtual automaton is seen to respond discretely to stimuli as though they were pennies in the slot. Interest in system-theory is increasing in psychology, though perhaps not so fast as in other sciences.

Now, a system—any system—is defined merely as *a complex of elements in mutual interaction.* Bridgman, as might be expected of an operationist, includes a hint of method in his definition. He writes that a system is "an isolated enclosure in which all measurements that can be made of what goes on in the system are in some way correlated." [1]

Systems may be classified as *closed* or *open.* A closed system is defined as one that admits no matter from outside itself and is therefore subject to entropy according to the second law of thermodynamics. While some outside energies, such as change in temperature and wind, may play upon a closed system, it has no restorative properties and no transactions with its environment, so that like a decaying bridge it sinks into thermodynamic equilibrium.

Some authors, such as Von Bertalanffy,[2] Brunswik[3] and Pumpian-Mindlin,[4] have said or implied that certain theories of psychology and of personality operate with the conception of closed systems. But in my opinion these critics press their point too far. We had better leave closed systems to the realm of physics where they belong (although even here it is a question whether Einstein's formula for the release of matter into energy does not finally demonstrate the futility of positing a closed system even in physics). In any event it is best to admit that all living organisms partake of the character of open systems. I doubt that we shall find any advocate of a truly closed system in the whole range of personality theory. At the same time, current theories do differ widely in the amount of openness they ascribe to the personality system.

If we comb definitions of open systems, we can piece together four criteria: (1) There is intake and output of both matter and energy. (2) There is the achievement and maintenance of steady (homeostatic) states, so that the intrusion of outer energy will not seriously disrupt internal form and order. (3) There is generally an increase of order over time, owing to an increase in complexity and differentiation of parts. (4) Finally, at least at the human level, there is more than mere intake and output of matter and energy; there is extensive transactional commerce with the environment.[5]

While all of our theories view personality as an open system in some sense, they can be fairly well classified according to the varying emphasis they place upon each of these criteria and according to how many of the criteria they admit.

Criterion 1

Consider the first criterion: material and energy exchange. Stimulus-response theory in its purest form concentrates on this criterion to the virtual exclusion of all the others. It says, in effect, that a stimulus enters and a response is emitted. There is, of course, machinery for summation, storage and delay, but the output is broadly commensurate with the intake. We need study only the two poles of stimulus and response with a minimum of concern for intervening processes. Methodological positivism goes one step further, saying, in effect, that we do not need the concept of personality at all. We focus attention on our own measurable manipulations of input and on the measurable manipulations of output. Personality thus evaporates in a mist of method.

Criterion 2

The requirement of steady states for open systems is so widely admitted in personality theory that it needs little discussion. To satisfy needs, to reduce tension and to maintain equilibrium—this comprises, in most theories, the basic formula of personality dynamics. Some authors, such as Stagner[6] and Mowrer, regard this formula as logically fitting in with Cannon's[7] account of homeostasis.[8] Man's intricate adjustive behavior is simply an extension of the principle involved in temperature regulation, balance of blood volume, sugar content and the like in the face of environmental change. It is true that Toch and Hastorf warn against over-extending the concept of homeostasis in personality theory.[9] I myself doubt that Cannon would approve the extension, for to him the value of homeostasis lay in its capacity to free man for what he called "the priceless unessentials" of life.[10] When biological equilibrium is attained, the priceless unessentials take over and constitute the major part of human activity. Be that as it may, most current theories clearly regard personality as a *modus operandi* for restoring a steady state.

Psychoanalytic theories are of this order. According to Freud, the ego strives to establish balance among the three "tyrants"—id, superego and outer environment. Likewise, the so-called mechanisms of ego-defense are essentially maintainers of a steady state. Even a neurosis has the same basic adjustive function.[11]

To sum up: Most current theories of personality take full account of two of the requirements of an open system. They allow interchange of matter and energy, and they recognize the tendency of organisms to maintain an orderly arrangement of elements in a steady state. Thus they emphasize stability rather than growth, permanence rather than change, "uncertainty reduction" (information theory) and "coding" (cognitive theory) rather than creativity. In short, they emphasize *being* rather than *becoming*. Hence, most personality theories are biologistic in the sense that they ascribe to personality only the two features of an open system that are clearly present in all living organisms.

There are, however, two additional criteria, sometimes mentioned but seldom stressed by biologists themselves, and similarly neglected in much current personality theory.

Transatlantic Perspective

Before examining Criterion 3, which calls attention to the tendency of open systems to enhance their degree of order, let us glimpse our present theoretical situation in cross-cultural perspective. In this country our special field of study has come to be called "behavioral science" (a label now firmly stuck to us with the glue of the Ford millions). The very flavor of this term suggests that we are occupied with semi-closed systems. By his very name the behavioral scientist seems committed to study man more in terms of behavior than in terms of experience; more in terms of mathematical space and clock-time than in terms of existential space and time; more in terms of response than of programming; more in terms of tension reduction than of tension enhancement; more in terms of reaction than of proaction.

Now let us leap our cultural stockade for a moment and listen to a bit of ancient Hindu wisdom. Most men, the Hindus say, have four central desires. To some extent, though only roughly, they correspond to the developmental stages of life. The first desire is for *pleasure*—a condition fully and extensively recognized in our Western theories of tension reduction, reinforcement, libido and needs. The second desire is for *success*—likewise fully recognized and studied in our investigations of power, status, leadership, masculinity and need-achievement. The third desire is to do one's duty and discharge one's responsibility. (It was Bismarck, not a Hindu, who said, "We are not in this world for pleasure but to do our damned duty.") Here our Western work begins to fade out: except for some pale investigations of parental punishment in relation to the development of childhood conscience, we have little to offer on the "duty motive." Conscience we tend to regard as a reactive response to internalized punishment, thus confusing the past "must" of learning with the "ought" involved in programming our future.[12] Finally, the Hindus tell us that for many people all these three motives pall, and they then seek intensely for a grade of understanding—for a philosophical or religious meaning—that will liberate them from pleasure, success and duty.[13] (Need I point out that most Western personality theories treat the religious aspiration in reactive terms—as an escape device, no different in kind from suicide, alcoholism and neurosis?)

Now we retrace our steps from India to modern Vienna and encounter the existentialist school of logotherapy. Its founder, Viktor Frankl, emphasizes above all the central place of *duty* and *meaning*, the same two motives that the Hindus place highest in their hierarchy of desire. Frankl reached his position after a long and agonizing incarceration in Nazi concentration camps, where, with other prisoners, he found himself stripped to naked existence.[14] In such extremity, what does a person need and want? Pleasure and success are out of the question. One wants to know the meaning of his suffering and to learn how, as a responsible being, he should acquit himself. Should he commit suicide? If so, why; if not, why not? The search for meaning becomes supreme.

Frankl is aware that his painfully achieved theory of motivation departs widely from most American theory, and he points out the implication of this fact for psychotherapy. He specifically criticizes the principle of homeostasis as implying that personality is a quasi-closed system.[15] To cater to the internal adjustments of a neurotic, or to assume that he will regain health by reshuffling his memories, defenses or conditioned reflexes, is ordinarily self-defeating. In many cases of neurosis, only a total breakthrough to new horizons will turn the trick.

Neither Hindu psychology nor logotherapy underestimates the role of pleasure and success in personality. Nor would Frankl abandon the hard-won gains reflected in psychoanalytic theory and need-theory. He says merely that in studying or treating a person we often find these essentially homeostatic formulations inadequate. A man normally wants to know the whys and wherefores. No other biological system does so; man stands alone in that he possesses a degree of openness surpassing that of any other living system.

Criterion 3

Returning now to our main argument, we encounter a not inconsiderable array of theories that emphasize the tendency of human personality to go beyond steady states and to strive for an enhancement and elaboration of internal order, even at the cost of considerable disequilibrium.

I cannot examine all of these or name all the relevant authors. One could start with McDougall's proactive sentiment of self-regard, which he viewed as organizing all behavior through a kind of "forward memory" (to use Gooddy's apt term).[16] Not too dissimilar is the stress that Combs and Snygg place on the enhancement of the phenomenal field. We may add Goldstein's conception of self-actualization as tending to enhance order in personality, as well as Maslow's theory of *growth motives* that supplement *deficiency motives*. One thinks of Jung's principle of individuation leading toward the achievement of a self—a goal never actually completed. Some theories, those of Bartlett and Cantril among them, put primary stress on the "pursuit of meaning." Certain developments in post-Freudian "ego-psychology" belong here.[17] So, too, does existentialism, with its recognition of the need for meaning and of the values of commitment. (The brain surgeon Harvey Cushing was speaking of open systems when he said, "The only way to endure life is to have a task to complete.") No doubt we should add Woodworth's recent advocacy of the "behavior primacy" theory as opposed to the "need" theory, Robert White's emphasis on "competence" and Erikson's "search for identity."

These theories are by no means identical. The differences between them merit prolonged debate. I lump them here simply because all seem to me to recognize the third criterion of open systems—

namely, the tendency of such systems to enhance their degree of order and become something more than they now are.

We all know the objection to theories of this type. Methodologists with a taste for miniature and fractionated systems complain that they do not lead to "testable propositions." [18] The challenge is valuable in so far as it calls for an expansion of research ingenuity. But the complaint is ill-advised if it demands that we return to quasi-closed systems simply because they are more "researchable" and elegant. Our task is to study what *is,* not merely what is immediately convenient.

Criterion 4

Now for our fourth and last criterion. Virtually all the theories I have mentioned up to now conceive of personality as something integumented, as residing within the skin. There are theorists (Kurt Lewin, Martin Buber, Gardner Murphy and others) who challenge this view, considering it too closed. Murphy says that we overstress the separation of man from the context of his living. Hebb has interpreted experiments on sensory deprivation as demonstrations of the constant dependence of inner stability on the flow of environmental stimulation.[19] Why Western thought makes such a razor-sharp distinction between the person and all else is an interesting problem. Probably the personalistic emphasis in Judeo-Christian religion is an initial factor; and as Murphy has pointed out,[20] the industrial and commercial revolutions further accentuated the role of individuality. Buddhist philosophy, by contrast, regards the individual, society and nature as forming the tripod of human existence. The individual as such does not stick out like a raw digit. He blends with nature, and he blends with society. It is only the merger that can be profitably studied.

Western theorists, for the most part, hold the integumented view of the personality system. I myself do so. Others, rebelling against the setting of self over against the world, have produced theories of personality written in terms of social interaction, role relations, situationism or some variety of field theory. Still other writers, such as Talcott Parsons[21] and F. H. Allport,[22] have admitted the validity of both the integumented personality system and systems of social interaction, and have spent much effort in harmonizing the two types of system thus conceived.

This problem, without doubt, is the knottiest issue in contemporary social science. It is the issue that, up to now, has prevented us from agreeing on the proper way to reconcile psychological and sociocultural science.

In this matter my own position is on the conservative side. It is the duty of psychology, I think, to study the person-system, meaning thereby the attitudes, abilities, traits, trends, motives and pathology of the individual—his cognitive styles, his sentiments, his individual moral nature and their interrelations. The justification is twofold: (1) There is a persistent though changing person-system in time, clearly delimited by birth and death. (2) We are immediately aware of the functioning of this system. Our knowledge of it, though imperfect, is direct, whereas our knowledge of all other outside systems, including social systems, is deflected and often distorted by their necessary incorporation into our own apperceptions.

At the same time, our work is incomplete unless we admit that each person possesses a *range* of abilities, attitudes and motives, which will be evoked by the different environments and situations he encounters. Hence we need to understand cultural, class and family constellations and traditions in order to know the schemata the person has probably interiorized in the course of his learning. But I hasten to warn that the study of cultural, class, family or any other social system does not automatically illumine the person-system, for we have to know whether the individual has accepted, rejected or remained uninfluenced by the social system in question. The fact that one plays the role of, say, teacher, salesman or father is less important for the study of his personality than to know whether he likes or dislikes, and how he defines, the role. But, unless we are students of sociocultural systems, we shall never know what it is the person is accepting, rejecting or redefining.

The provisional solution I would offer is the following: the personality theorist should be so well trained in social science that he can view the behavior of an individual as fitting any system of interaction; that is, he should be able to cast this behavior properly in the culture where it occurs, in its situational context and in terms of role theory and field theory. At the same time he should not lose sight—as some theorists do—of the fact that there is an internal and subjective patterning of all these contextual acts. A traveler who moves from culture to culture, from situation to situation, is none the less a single person; and within him one will find the nexus, the patterning, of the diverse experiences and memberships that constitute his personality.

Thus, I myself would not go so far as to advocate that personality be defined in terms of interaction, culture or roles. Attempts to do so seem to me to smudge the concept of personality and to represent a surrender of the psychologist's special assignment as a scientist. Let him be acquainted with all systems of interaction, but let him return always to the point where such systems converge and intersect and are patterned—in the single individual.

Hence, we accept the fourth (transactional) criterion of the open system, but with the firm warning that it must not be applied with so much enthusiasm that we lose the personality system altogether.

General Systems Theory

There are those who see hope for the unification of science in what James Miller has called *general behavior systems theory*.[23] This approach seeks formal identities between physical systems, the cell, the organ, the personality, small groups, the species and society. Critics—for example Buck[24]—complain that all this is feeble analogizing, that formal identities probably do not exist and that attempts to express analogies in terms of mathematical models result only in the vaguest generalities. As I see it, the danger in attempting to unify science in this manner lies in the inevitable approach from below—that is, in terms of physical and biological science. Closed systems or systems only partly open become our model; and if we are not careful, human personality in all its fullness is taken captive into some autistic paradise of methodology.

Besides neglecting the criteria of enhanced organization and transaction, general systems theory has an added defect. The human person is, after all, the observer and interpreter of systems. This awkward fact has recently been haunting the founder of the operational movement, P. W. Bridgman.[25] Can we as scientists live subjectively within our system and at the same time take a valid objective view thereof?

Some years ago Elkin published the case of "Harry Holzer" and invited thirty-nine specialists to offer their conceptualizations.[26] As might be expected, many different conceptualizations resulted. No theorist was able entirely to divest the case of his own preconceptions. Each read the objective system in terms of the subjective. Our theories of personality—all of them—reflect the temperament of the author fully as much as the personality of *alter*.

This sad specter of observer-contamination should not, I think, discourage us from the search for objectively valid theory. Truth, as

the philosopher Charles Peirce has said, is the opinion that is fated
to be ultimately agreed to by all who investigate. My point is that
the opinion fated to be ultimately agreed to by all who investigate is
not likely to be reached through a premature application of general
systems theory or through devotion to any one partially closed theory.
Theories of open systems hold more promise, though at present they
are not in agreement among themselves. But somewhere, sometime,
I hope and believe, we shall establish a theory of the nature of personality that all wise men who investigate, including psychologists,
will eventually accept.

Some Examples

In the meantime, I suggest that we regard all sharp controversies
in personality theory as probably arising from the two opposed points
of view: the quasi-closed and the fully open.

The principle of reinforcement, to take one example, is commonly regarded as the cement that stamps in a response, as the glue
that fixes personality at the level of past deeds. An open system interpretation is very different. Feigl, for instance, has pointed out that
reinforcement works primarily in a prospective sense.[27] It is only
from a *recognition* of consequences (not from the consequences
themselves) that the human individual binds the past to the future
and resolves to avoid punishment and to seek rewards in similar
circumstances—provided, of course, that it is consonant with his
interests and values to do so. Here we no longer assume that reinforcement stamps in; it is taken as one factor among many to be
considered in the programming of future action.[28] What a wide
difference it makes whether we regard personality as a quasi-closed or
an open system!

The issue has its parallels in neurophysiology. How open is the
nervous system? We know it is of a complexity so formidable that
we have only an inkling as to how complex it may be. Yet one thing
is certain: high level gating often controls and steers lower level
processes. While we cannot tell exactly what we mean by "higher
levels," they surely involve ideational schemata, intentions and generic
personality trends. They are instruments for programming, not merely
for reacting. In the future we may confidently expect that the neurophysiology of programming and the psychology of proaction will
draw together. Until they do so, it is wise to hold lightly our self-
closing metaphors of sow bug, switchboard, giant computor and
hydraulic pump.

Finally, an example from motivation theory. Some years ago I argued that motives may become functionally autonomous of their origins. (And one lives to regret one's brashness.)

Whatever its shortcomings, the concept of functional autonomy succeeds in viewing personality as an open and changing system. As might be expected, criticism has come chiefly from those who prefer to view the personality system as quasi-closed. Some critics say that I am dealing only with occasional cases where the extinction of a habit system has failed to occur. This criticism, of course, begs the question, for the precise point at issue is: why do some habit systems fail to extinguish when no longer reinforced? And why do some habit systems that were once instrumental get refashioned into interests and values having a motivational push?

The common counterargument holds that "secondary reinforcement" somehow miraculously sustains all the central desires of a mature person. The scientific ardor of Pasteur, the religio-political zeal of Gandhi and, for that matter, Aunt Sally's devotion to her needlework are explained by hypothetical cross-conditioning, which somehow substitutes for the primary reinforcement of primary drives. What is significant for our purposes is that these critics prefer the concept of secondary reinforcement, not because it is clearer, but because it holds our thinking within the frame of a quasi-closed (reactive) system.

Now is not the time to reargue the matter, but I can at least hint at my present views. I would say first that the concept of functional autonomy has relevance even at the level of quasi-closed systems. There are now so many indications concerning feed-back mechanisms, cortical self-stimulation, self-organizing systems and the like[29] that I believe we cannot deny the existence of self-sustaining circuit-mechanisms, which we can lump together under the rubric *perseverative functional autonomy*.

But the major significance of the concept lies in a different direction and presupposes the view that personality is a wide open system seeking progressively new levels of order and transaction. While drive motives remain fairly constant throughout life, existential motives do not. It is the very nature of an open system to achieve progressive levels of order through change in cognitive and motivational structure. Since in this case the causation is systematic, we cannot hope to account for functional autonomy in terms of specific reinforcements. This condition I would call *propriate functional autonomy*.

Both perseverative and propriate autonomy are, I think, indispensable conceptions. The one applies to the relatively closed part-systems within personality; the other, to the continuously evolving structure of the whole.

A last example. It is characteristic of the quasi-closed system outlook that it is heavily nomothetic: it seeks similarities among all personality systems—or, as in general behavior systems theory, among *all* system. If, however, we elect the open system view, we find ourselves forced in part toward the idiographic outlook. For now the vital question becomes: what makes the system hang together in any one person? [30] Let me repeat this question, for it is the one that more than any other has haunted me over the years: *what makes the system cohere in any one person?* That this problem is pivotal, urgent and relatively neglected will be recognized by open system theorists, even while it is downgraded and evaded by those who prefer their systems semi-closed.

Final Word

If this essay has seemed polemical, I can only plead that personality theory lives by controversy. In this country we are fortunate that no single party line shackles our speculations. We are free to pursue any and all assumptions concerning the nature of man. The penalty we pay is that, for the present, we cannot expect personality *theory* to be cumulative—although, fortunately, to some extent personality *research* can be.

Theories, we know, are ideally derived from axioms—or, if axioms are lacking (as in our field), from assumptions. But our assumptions regarding the nature of man range from the Adlerian to the Zilborgian, from the Lockean to the Leibnitzian, from the Freudian to the Hullian, from the cybernetic to the existentialist. Some of us model man after the pigeon; others view his potentialities as many-splendored. And there is no agreement in sight.

Nils Bohr's principle of complementarity contains a lesson for us. He showed that if we study the position of a particle, we do not at the same time study its momentum. Applied to our own work, the principle tells us that if we focus on reaction, we do not simultaneously study proaction; if we measure one trait, we do not fix our attention on pattern; if we tackle a subsystem, we lose the whole; if we pursue the whole, we overlook the part-functioning. For the single investigator, there seems to be no escape from this limitation. Our only hope is to overcome it by a complementarity of investigators and of theorists.

While I myself am partisan for the open system, I would shut no doors. (Some of my best friends are quasi-closed systematists.) If I argue for the open system, I plead more strongly for the open mind. Our condemnation is reserved for that peculiar slavery to fashion which says that conventionality alone makes for scientific respectability. We still have much to learn from our creative fumblings with the open system. Among our students, I trust, there will be many adventurers.

REFERENCES

1. P. W. Bridgman, *The way things are,* Cambridge: Harvard University Press, 1959, p. 188.
2. L. Von Bertalanffy, "Theoretical models in biology and psychology," in D. Krech and G. S. Klein (eds.), *Theoretical models and personality theory,* Durham, N.C.: Duke University Press, 1952.
3. E. Brunswik, "The conceptual framework of psychology," *International Encyclopedia of Unified Science,* Chicago: University of Chicago Press, 1955, Vol. I, No. 10.
4. E. Pumpian-Mindlin, "Propositions concerning energetic-economic aspects of libido theory," *Ann. N.Y. Acad. Sci.,* 1959, 76:1038-52.
5. Von Bertalanffy's definition explicitly recognizes the first two of these criteria as present in all living organisms. A living organism, he says, is "an open system which continually gives up matter to the outer world and takes in matter from it, but which maintains itself in this continuous exchange in a steady state, or approaches such steady state in its variations in time" [*Problems of life* (trans. of *Das biologische Weltbild,* 1949), New York: Wiley, 1952, p. 125]. But elsewhere in this author's writing we find recognition of the additional criteria (*Ibid.,* p. 145; "Theoretical models and personality theory," *op. cit.,* p. 34).
6. R. Stagner, "Homeostasis as a unifying concept in personality theory," *Psychol. Rev.,* 1951, 58:5-17.
7. W. B. Cannon, *The wisdom of the body,* New York: Norton, 1932.
8. In a recent review ["A cognitive theory of dynamics" (review of R. S. Woodworth, *Dynamics of behavior*), *Contemp. Psychol.,* 1959, 4:129-33], H. S. Mowrer strongly defends the homeostatic theory. He is distressed that the dean of American psychologists, Robert Woodworth (*Dynamics of behavior,* New York: Holt, 1958), has taken a firm stand against the "need-primacy" theory in favor of what he calls the "behavior-primacy" theory. With the detailed merits of the argument we are not here concerned. What concerns us at the moment is that the issue has been sharply joined. Need-primacy, which Mowrer calls a "homeostatic" theory, does not go beyond our first two criteria for an open system. Woodworth, by insisting that contact with and mastery of the environment constitute a pervasive principle of motivation, recognizes the additional criteria.
9. H. H. Toch and A. H. Hastorf, "Homeostasis in psychology," *Psychiatry,* 1955, 18:81-91.
10. W. B. Cannon, *op cit.,* p. 323.

11. When we speak of the "function" of a neurosis, we are reminded of the many theories of "functionalism" current in psychology and social science. Granted that the label, as Merton has shown (R. K. Merton, *Social theory and social structure*, rev. ed., Glencoe, Ill.: The Free Press, 1957, Chap. 1.), is a wide one, still we may safely say that the emphasis of functionalism is always on the usefulness of an activity in maintaining the steady state of a personality or social or cultural system. In short, "functional" theories stress maintenance of present direction, allowing little room or none at all for departure and change.

12. G. W. Allport, *Becoming: basic considerations for a psychology of personality*, New Haven: Yale University Press, 1955, pp. 68-74.

13. H. Smith, *The religions of man*, New York: Harper, 1958; New York: Mentor, 1959.

14. V. E. Frankl, *From death camp to existentialism*, Boston: Beacon, 1959.

15. V. E. Frankl, "Das homöostatische Prinzip und die dynamische Psychologie," *Z. Psychoth. Med. Psychol.*, 1959, 9:41-47.

16. W. Gooddy, "Two directions of memory," *J. Indiv. Psychol.*, 1959, 15: 83-88.

17. Pumpian-Mindlin (*op cit.*, p. 1051) writes, "The focus of clinical psychoanalysis on ego psychology is a direct result of the change from a closed system to an open one."

18. Cf. T. B. Roby, "An opinion on the construction of behavior theory," *Amer. Psychologist*, 1959, 14:127-34.

19. D. O. Hebb, "The mammal and his environment," *Amer. J. Psychiat.* 1955, 111:826-31. Reprinted in E. E. Maccoby, T. M. Newcomb, E. L. Hartley (eds.), *Readings in social psychology*, New York: Holt, 1958, pp. 335-41.

20. G. Murphy, *Human potentialities*, New York: Basic Books: 1958, p. 297.

21. T. Parsons, *The social system*, Glencoe, Ill.: The Free Press, 1951.

22. F. H. Allport, *Theories of personality and the concept of structure*, New York: Wiley, 1955.

23. J. G. Miller, "Toward a general theory for the behavioral sciences," *Amer. Psychologist*, 1955, 10:513-31.

24. R. C. Buck, "On the logic of general behavior systems theory," in H. Feigl and M. Scriven (eds.), *Minnesota studies in the philosophy of science*, Vol. I, 1956.

25. *Op. cit.*

26. F. Elkin, "Specialists interpret the case of Harry Holzer," *J. Abnorm. Soc. Psychol.*, 1947, 42:99-111.

27. H. Feigl, "Philosophical embarrassments of psychology," *Amer. Psychologist*, 1959, 14:117.

28. G. W. Allport, "Effect: a secondary principle of learning," *Psychol. Rev.*, 1946, 53:335-47.

29. Cf. D. O. Hebb, *The organization of behavior*, New York: Wiley, 1949; J. Olds and P. Milner, "Positive reinforcement produced by electrical stimulation of septal area and other regions of rat brain," *J. Comp. Physio. Psychol.*, 1954, 47:419-27; H. T. Chang, "The repetitive discharge of cortico-thalamic reverberating circuit," *J. Neurophysiol.*, 1950, 13:235-57.

30. Cf. J. G. Taylor, "Experimental design: a cloak for intellectual sterility," *Brit. J. Psychol.*, 1958, 49:106-16.

CHAPTER 4

Scientific models and human morals

The present chapter, like Chapter 3, is based on a talk to the Division of Personality and Social Psychology of the American Psychological Association. It was delivered as the president's address at the first annual meeting, September 1946, and was published in the *Psychological Review* (1947).

The essay expresses dissatisfaction with the root-metaphors employed in depicting human nature. It argues that theoretical systems require concepts that reflect the basic nature of conduct, goal-directed and intentional. Current fashionable models—derived from animal, child and machine—overstress the purely reactive side of personality and, in so doing, handicap the psychologist in his efforts to understand and improve the human lot.

In forming this Division of Personality and Social Psychology, we are stating our readiness to assume a certain responsibility. We are announcing, in effect, that as a group of scientists we believe we have a contribution to make in interpreting and remedying some of the serious dislocations in our society.

The test of our fitness to exist and to prosper, I submit, will be our ability to contribute substantially in the near future to the diagnosis and treatment of the outstanding malady of our time. The malady I refer to is not war, for modern warfare is but a symptom of an underlying morbid condition; it is not the threatening fission of one world into two, ominous as this threat may be; nor is it our apparent inability to control for our safety and profit the transformation of matter into atomic energy, though this crisis too is now upon us. I speak rather of the *underlying* ailment, of the fact that man's moral sense is not able to assimilate his technology.

While technological warfare, technological unemployment and the atomic age—all by-products of physical science—have overtaken us, mental and moral science have made no corresponding gains in allaying the rivalries and anxieties induced by technology, in devising methods of social control or in enhancing human cooperation and solidarity. It is, I venture to point out, precisely our own young science that has failed to keep pace with the needs of the times.

Public officials are urgently seeking the aid of psychologists.

Many of us who have been approached are embarrassed by the scarcity of scientific findings, and even of serviceable concepts and well-formulated problems, that psychology has to offer *of the type that is being sought.* What is asked for is instant help in discovering the sources and conditions of man's moral sense in order that this sense may be enlarged and brought into focus. What is asked for is aid from a science of human relationships, whose assistance Franklin D. Roosevelt likewise invoked in his last speech before his death.[1] Yet we may comb the entire file of the *Psychological Abstracts* and find very little that has any bearing upon the improvement of human relationships on an international scale.

Why have we so relatively little to offer? Is it simply that we are young? Or have we gotten off to a thoroughly bad start through our adoption of root-metaphors that lead away from, rather than toward, the problem at hand? Three generations ago psychology was commonly classified as a "moral science." Though we may not favor the aura of this term, how can we expect anything other than a science *of* moral conduct to discover the conditions that will bring the needed counterpoise to technology run wild?

In taking stock of this situation, I observe how many of us seem so stupefied by admiration of physical science that we believe psychology, in order to succeed, need only imitate the models, postulates, methods and language of physical science. If someone points out the present inutility of mechanical models in predicting any but the most peripheral forms of human behavior, we are inclined to reply: Wait a thousand years if necessary, and you will see that man is a robot and that all his mental functions can be synthesized in kind as successfully as we now synthesize table salt, quinine or a giant calculator. While we righteously scorn what one of us has called "the subjective, anthropomorphic hocus pocus of mentalism," [2] we would consider a colleague emotional and mystical should he dare speak of "the objective, mechanomorphic focus of physicalism."

Let our progress be gradual, we say. By sticking to the peripheral, visible operations, we may someday be able to approach complex problems of motivation, and then come within hailing distance of the distresses of mankind. We hope that these distresses will keep a thousand years until we are ready to cope with them and that in the meantime a free science will be permitted to linger along and take its time. But, even if such improbable conditions were fulfilled, I question whether we should endorse this counsel of patience or the premises upon which it rests.

Besides the mechanical model, there are two other currently

popular paradigms in psychology that are, in my opinion, only slightly less inept in guiding significant research or theory concerning the foundations of social morality. I refer to the phylogenetic model and to the infant mind. Although both these models during the past two generations have brought new insights and correctives into our work, they have not proved adequate to the needs of clinical, personnel and social psychology.

When any one of us undertakes a piece of research, he inevitably adopts, according to his preference, one or another of the fundamental models available to psychologists. My thesis is that now if ever we need to test our preferred model for its capacity to yield discoveries that have some sure relevance to moral nature and to social ills.

Expectancy and Intention

The machine model in psychology had its origin, not in clinical or social experience, but rather in adulation of the technological success of the physical sciences.

If I interpret the matter correctly, American psychology naturally adapted mechanical models because our culture has always been action-oriented and technological. By and large, our psychology is a motorized psychology and is only now widening its concept of action to include the ego-involved participation of the human organism in matters affecting its own destiny.[3] The earlier extreme position, represented by E. B. Holt and J. B. Watson, held personality to be essentially a battery of trigger-release mechanisms. This view paid no attention to the sustained directions of striving that are characteristic of moral behavior—to what in this essay I shall call "intentions."

This trigger-model, still preferred by a few, gave way gradually to a more purposive behaviorism. The concept of "sign-Gestalt expectancy" was introduced by Tolman and mercifully shortened by Hilgard and Marquis to "expectancy."[4] It is an interesting fact that these authors seem to regard the principle of expectancy as the most purposive of all the essentially mechanical theories derived from the multitudinous experiments on the conditioned reflex.[5] In other words, some version of the principle of expectancy is as far as many psychologists have come in their conception of the nature of personal and social conduct.

The principle holds that in the presence of certain signs the organism expects a certain goal to appear if it follows the customary behavior route. If the goal is reached, the expectation is confirmed;

if not, the organism may vary its behavior.[6] The principle, while allowing for the importance of attitude, is essentially stimulus-bound. We behave according to the cues we have learned, according to our expectancies.

In order not to complicate my argument, I shall leave out of consideration the law of effect, which, it would be easy to show, likewise ascribes behavior wholly to past experience, to learned cues and to mechanical reinforcements.[7] Both principles, so far as I can see, accord nothing to the *un*rewarded, *un*realized, yet persistive intentions of man's moral nature.

The trouble with these currently fashionable concepts, drawn from the phylogenetic model, is that while they seem to apply aptly enough to animal behavior, whence they were derived, they have only a limited or else a remote analogical bearing on the activities of human beings. We may know a person's expectancies and even his past rewards; yet we are singularly unable to predict or control his future behavior unless we know also his basic intentions, which are by no means a stenciled copy of his previous expectancies and rewards.[8]

To take an example, the sign-Gestalten today are such that we may reasonably expect future crises in our relations with Russia. Does this fact tell in any degree what we can, should or will do about it? This precise area of conflict is a novel one (as, indeed, all important situations are). The best predictive basis we have lies in our own national and personal *intentions* regarding Russia. It is our purposes, not our expectancies, that are now the issue.

As if aware of the scantiness of the expectancy principle, Tolman advises us to embrace also a "need-cathexis psychology." [9] But the situation here turns out to be parallel. Need-cathexis psychology—of course I oversimplify—holds essentially that a handful of physiological drives get attached to this, that or the other object. A man who, in Tolman's pleasing vernacular, is "raised right" meshes his drive into a socially acceptable gear. A man "raised wrong" does not. But what is so striking about human motivation is that so often a desire or aspiration is meshed into no gear. It simply reaches forward hungrily into the future like the tip of a scarlet runner bean, groping for a goal that it does not know about.

The embarrassment of the need-cathexis type of psychology is reflected in the apologetic language it uses when referring to this expansive aspect of human motivation. Accustomed to work with animals or with infants, need-cathexis psychology labels adult human intentions "secondary drives," "derived drives" or "drive conversions."

With such depreciating concepts, both the mechanical and the phylogenetic psychologists apparently seek to dispose of those morally relevant desires and aspirations that are in fact so different from the
drive-impelled excursions of the cozy robot or cozy rodent.[10]

My objection to the animal paradigm for personality and for
social psychology is not so much that animals lack culture—a fact
that Tolman in his sparkling paper first frankly admits and then
amiably represses—but rather that the motivational structure of man
and of lower animals seems to be in only a slight degree similar.
In this respect, as with his evolutionary brain development (to quote
Julian Huxley), "man stands alone." [11] Animals are demonstrably
creatures of stimulus-expectancy and need-cathexis. Man, in all that
is distinctive of his species, is a creature of intentions. We may well
doubt that the basic equation for intentional morality, or that for
intentional learning, can be written from a study of organisms that
lack propositional symbols. To this point I shall return.

While I am disapproving of current models, I shall state my
final grievance, this time against the rigid ontogenetic stencils that
derive from Freudianism. Odd as it may appear, Freud resembles
the mechanical and phylogenetic psychologists in wanting his doctrine of motivation anchored to neuro-anatomy. I assume that this
is his desire, because he refuses to see anything at all in the cooperative, socialized, affiliative undertakings of mankind except goal-
inhibited sexuality. To the sex drive he adds principally the impulses of aggression, destruction and death. It seems obvious that
Freudianism, even though eagerly adopted by many who have found
the mechanical and animal models inadequate, offers an equally
meager basis for a serviceable study of man's moral conduct.

The trouble lies chiefly in the excessive emphasis upon infantile
experience. We are asked to believe that an individual's character-
structure is, in all essentials, determined by the time his last diaper
is changed. Even Suttie, who postulates as the foundation of morality
an original and embracing instinct of tenderness, affection and social
symbiosis, believes its fate is sealed according to the manner in
which the mother handles this affiliative impulse before and after
weaning.[12] If the chances for peace in the world depend to such
a degree upon infant fixations, ought we not disband this Division
and register as wet nurses to the mewling citizens of tomorrow?

The concept of intention, which I am here opposing to reactivity, expectancy and infantile fixation, is not immediately congenial to American psychology. Yet its adoption in some form or

another is necessary. With some malice aforethought I have selected the term *intention*—spiced, as it is, by an aggravating flavor of mentalism—to signify those aspects of thought and of motivation that play a leading, but now neglected, part in the complex, affiliative, moral conduct of men. I believe it is precisely the "private" worlds of desire, aspiration and conscience that must be studied if we are to succeed in the task of social engineering.

In using the term *intention*, however, I am not arguing surreptitiously for phenomenology, though in order to improve our grasp on the subtleties of man's intentions we would do well to emulate the refinement of its descriptive method.[13] Nor am I arguing for a revival of Brentano, though we have neglected unduly the central proposition of Act Psychology: that, at every moment, man's mind is directed by some intention—loving, hating, comparing, understanding, desiring, rejecting, planning or some similar mental act.

Let us define intention simply as *what the individual is trying to do*. Naïve as this definition may sound, it is in reality the product of decades of sophisticated wrestling with the problems of human motivation. In this concept influences as diversified as Brentano, Darwin, Freud, Cannon and Wertheimer are brought into focus. In essence it no longer draws the sharp distinction, advanced by both Kant and Schopenhauer, between will (or drive) on the one hand and intellect on the other. The machine, rat and infant models we have been following (though I am sure they'd be surprised and grieved to know it) preserve this irreconcilable Kantian dichotomy. They side somewhat more, however, with Schopenhauer in regarding the functions of the intellect as wholly instrumental and secondary. Without forgetting for a moment what we have learned about rationalizing and about the untrustworthiness of introspective reports on motives, we may safely declare that the opposing of motive and thought-process has gone much too far. Usually the individual is trying to do something in which his wants and his plans easily cooperate. Instead of being at opposite poles, his emotion and his reason canalize into a single endeavor. The direction of his endeavor I designate as the intention, and offer this concept as an improvement upon the one-sided irrationalistic doctrines of drive, need, instinct and cathexis.

In deference to the discoveries of psychoanalysis, we readily admit that an individual does not always know precisely what his own intentions are. *Consciously* he may misinterpret the line of his own endeavor; a neurotic frequently does so. In such cases, insight is either lacking or partially lacking. But as a rule, the "posture or lay of consciousness" reflects accurately enough that inextricable fusion of driving and planning that we find in the dynamics of mature human conduct.[14]

It is the mark of an intention that it is directed toward the future. Yet it is typical of the models we have followed that they lead to preoccupation with adjustments in the past. While people are living their lives forward, psychologists are busy tracing them backward. The model we need for our investigations of human relationships will escape from our present excessive dependence on geneticism in all its forms.[15]

A geneticist—for example, one who places great weight on the expectancy-principle—is inclined to define personality as a peculiar set of reaction-tendencies. An intentionist, on the other hand, sees personality as a peculiar set of subjective values. There is a difference. The one learns at best only about moral *accomplishment;* the other gains additional light on moral *potential.*

It may be argued that the models I am presuming to criticize do deal both with "goal reactions" and with "anticipatory goal reactions." Hull, for example, offers "anticipatory goal reaction" as a "physical mechanism," which he says he regards as equivalent to the concept of "guiding ideas," or what I am calling *intention.*[16] The difficulty with "anticipatory goal reaction," as with "expectancy," is that men often have values without having any specific goal in mind. They may have a consistent direction of striving, but their goals are either transient or else undefinable. All of a rat's, but only a small bit of human, behavior can be characterized in terms of concrete goals whose attainment will de-tension specific drives. For the most part the course of man's behavior runs according to certain schemata, or in prolonged channels. Only now and then are these channels marked by lights or buoys that represent specific goals.

A simple example may be borrowed from Lecky's analysis of childhood thumb-sucking. The following statement distinguishes neatly between expectancy and what I am here calling intention; that is, between behavior regulated by habit and behavior ordered to nonspecific schemata: "Certainly the child who sucks his thumb gives the act plenty of exercise and gets enough satisfaction from it to fix it indelibly. Therefore if the habit theory is true, we should be able to predict absolutely that the child will continue to suck his thumb for the rest of his life. But what really happens? Every year millions of children who have industriously sucked their thumbs since birth, and who have successfully resisted every effort to force them to change their behavior, quit the practice spontaneously when they are five or six years old. The reason is that they are beginning at this age to think of themselves as big boys or girls, and they recognize that thumb-sucking is inconsistent with the effort to maintain this new idea." [17]

An intention often takes the form of a self-image, as in the case of Lecky's reformed thumb-sucker. Having adopted a conception of what we want to be, we are constrained to make good in the role we have assumed. The specific goals we set for ourselves are almost always subsidiary to our long-range intentions. A good parent, a good neighbor, a good citizen, is good, not because his specific goals are acceptable, but because his successive goals are ordered to a dependable and socially desirable set of values. We now know that juvenile delinquency and adult criminality were sadly misconceived so long as they were regarded as a matter of bad habit-formations. For years, reformatories have trained habits but have achieved few reformations. Only a radical shift of outlook and intention remakes a criminal, alcoholic or neurotic character.

The models we have been following lack the long-range orientation that is the essence of morality. Infant and rodent have immediate goals and indulge in anticipatory goal-reactions, but have no directive schemata. By contrast, a child in puberty develops a desire to become a successful and respected man of affairs, and he acquires this generalized objective long before he knows what concrete goals he has to work for. Thus, customarily, image and intention seem to antedate and to define goal-reactions. The essence of moral behavior is of this sort. It presupposes long-range purposes, whose directions precede their specifications.

When President Roosevelt enunciated the Four Freedoms, he was speaking of certain common intentions of the human race. An important feature of his historic formulation lies in his assumption that *all* men, in *all* cultures, intend (that is, long for) freedom from want, freedom from fear, freedom of speech and of worship. Note how this assumption contrasts with the prevailing creed of modern social science. Cultural relativity, really a doctrine of stimulus-expectancy, has laid such a heavy hand upon us that we have overlooked the possibility of universal intentions. Yet, unless Roosevelt's bold assumption is found justified, we can scarcely hope to find a psychological basis for effective world organization.

In all probability Roosevelt's formulation is psychologically not the best that can be made; nor dare we underestimate the incompatibility of nationalistic intentions and rivalries. But the psychologists' perspective should be equally bold. It is up to us to find out whether there are in fact common purposes that might provide ground for international solidarity. To do so, social psychologists in all lands might well join in a search, through modern instruments of polling, clinical interviewing, child study and life-histories, for existent moral bases on which international cooperation can be built.

It is conceivable—I think probable—that such research would discover the ruthless pursuit of personal and national power to be a result of the frustration of basically affiliative intentions. In clinical practice we know how often the clamorous manifestations of egotism gain the upper hand when men are denied a proper continuation of the originally friendly and symbiotic relationship with family, friends and neighbors. It seems probable that every child in every nation, the world over, at a time when he is most plastic, wants security, affection and an affiliative, comprehending relation to the surrounding world. It is conceivable that the same basic intentions exist in most adults, although thwarting and perversion of this relationship have engendered a vast amount of hatred, emotional instability and warlike impulse.

Basic research would discover why the taboo on tenderness, on nurturant desires, has grown so excessive that the development of cooperative and affiliative behavior outside one's own family is, at least in our culture, generally disapproved. It would seek to discover under what conditions the impulse to love and to be loved is turned into the impulse to hate and to invite hatred. If it is the child's nature to trust everyone, why is it the nature of national or ethnic groups to distrust nearly everyone? The models we have been following tend to deflect our attention from problems of human affection and the conditions for its development. When a bit of human friendliness is discovered—and it can be discovered only accidentally with models now current—it is likely to be labeled "goal-inhibited sexuality," and, thus tagged, forgotten. Up to now the sexual activity of rat and man has received incomparably more attention from psychologists than has the cooperative activity of men and nations.

Besides the study of affection and hatred, the possibilities for peace require research into many other strictly human capacities— among them the use of humor, the function of creeds and the processes of communication. For moral development depends on many factors other than root-desires and intentions. But every aspect of moral conduct that one can name depends intricately upon the employment of symbols.

Signs and Symbols

Perhaps the clearest symptom of the present conceptual confusion in our field is the extent to which we confound symbols with signs, or—if one prefers Morris' terminology—symbols with signals.

We know that all animals, as well as men, respond to signals. The principle of expectancy says so and, in this respect, is right. A signal is something that exists in the physical world; it is an identifiable stimulus. But even the most behavioristically inclined theorists cannot and do not claim that animals can handle propositional symbols—those self-produced signs *of* signs that are man's prized and troublesome possession. An animal, says Thorndike, can "think things," but it cannot "think about things." [18] And Yerkes asserts that symbolic processes in chimpanzees are rare and difficult to observe. One may, he says, fairly continue to question their existence, though it may be that signal responses can be regarded in some way as "antecedents of human symbolic processes." [19]

Surveying relevant investigations and opinions, Cassirer concludes: "In all literature of the subject there does not seem to be a single conclusive proof of the fact that any animal ever made the decisive step from subjective to objective, from affective to propositional, language." [20]

Cassirer argues, reasonably enough, that the symbolic system creates a wholly new dimension of reality for man. Instead of dealing directly with things themselves or with their visible signals, man deals with their ideational surrogates: [21] "He has so enveloped himself in linguistic forms, in artistic images, in mythical symbols or religious rites, that he cannot see or know anything except by the interposition of this artificial medium." [22]

Even so behavioristic a writer as Morris admits that the theory of sign-response as developed by himself carries over with difficulty to the human sphere: ". . . Non-human beings seldom produce the signs which influence their behavior, while human individuals in their language and post-language symbols characteristically do this and to a surprising degree. Here is a basic difference between men and animals, and until behavioral theory develops a semiotic adequate to this difference it will remain what it is today: a careful study of animals and a pious hope for a science of the human person." [23]

Morris seems to be saying with fine candor that there is a world of difference between signal and symbol, and that even his own careful system of semiotic fails adequately to bridge the gap. Though I have not actually counted the illustrations in his book, I have the impression that a majority of them refer to animal responses to signals and that relatively few deal with human responses to symbols. In any case, it is clear that Morris, like many psychologists, is enamored of the phylogenetic model.

I venture to cite another brilliant and candid passage from his book. He writes of the fact that a sign may be *iconic*—that is to say, it may itself resemble the properties of its denotatum. Thus a motion picture is highly iconic; an onomatopoeic word less so; a wholly arbitrary sign not at all iconic. He then offers this highly significant observation: "One of the dangers of the use of models in science, for instance, arises out of the temptation to ascribe to the subject matter of a theory properties of the model illustrating the theory which are not involved in the theory itself." [24]

From this warning would it not follow that an adequate theory of symbols can hardly be derived from the animal model in which *signals* alone predominate? How can we expect to understand human symbolism in terms of the phylogenetic type when, as Morris himself asserts, we are tempted to overextend the properties of our type-model and force them to serve in place of the independent theory we need to develop?

The Model We Need

To sum up: The designs we have been using in our studies of motivation, of symbol and hence of the foundations of moral behavior are not—to borrow Morris' crisp term—sufficiently iconic with our subject matter. Addiction to machines, rats or infants leads us to overplay those features of human behavior that are peripheral, signal-oriented or genetic. Correspondingly, it causes us to underplay those features that are central, future-oriented and symbolic.

What sort of a model, then, do we need? This question opens systematic vistas that lie beyond the scope of this essay. Yet, lest my numerous criticisms indicate a despair that I do not actually feel, I shall mention a few recent signs and portents that signify a newer—and, to my mind, more wholesome—outlook.

Most noteworthy is the fact that the war led many psychologists to deal directly with the integrated behavior of the GI, the factory worker, the civilian. We then learned that the interests of morale, psychotherapy, personnel placement and psychological warfare could not be pursued successfully by clinging to our threadbare models. Our inadequate root-metaphors went into the ash can for the duration. It is because of this conceptual discard, with its resultant wartime success in the promotion of social engineering, that I have presumed at this time to bring into the open a conflict that many, perhaps most of us, have secretly felt. Must we now resume the tattered stencils that we so recently abandoned with such good effect?

There are various indicators of improvement in theoretical outlook. I have in mind the new and vital conception of the ego that has come into psychotherapy;[25] the discovery and application of psychological principles involved in bringing the worker into a participant relation with his job;[26] the discovery and application of procedures leading to successful administration.[27] We discern an accelerated movement toward the development of such theories as can have their acid test here and now, not a thousand years hence. These theories neither strain the credulity nor stretch an inappropriate model beyond its logical breaking point.

We happily find more emphasis than before on the structuring activities of the person, on the importance of centrally initiated motive patterns, on cognitive dynamisms—including ideology, schemata of meaning and frames of reference. We find the contemporaneity of motives stressed, as well as the important functions of self-esteem and ego-involvement. Though symbols are still confused with signals, we are beginning, through content-analysis and interviewing, to study symbols both in their own right and as the basic ingredients of all complex conduct, including all morally relevant thought and behavior. We have learned, through improved polls and other methods of inquiry, to ascertain the direction of social purpose as it resides in individual minds. From such knowledge it should be possible to fashion a domestic and international social policy that will be sufficiently realistic to succeed.

All these and many more signs indicate the growing dependence of modern theories upon a model that is none the less scientific for being humane. As this design for personality and social psychology gradually becomes better tempered to our subject matter, we shall cease borrowing false notes—whether squeaks, squeals or squalls. We shall read the score of human personality more accurately for the benefit of the world audience that waits to listen.

REFERENCES

1. "Today we are faced with the preëminent fact that, if civilization is to survive, we must cultivate the science of human relationships—the ability

of all peoples, of all kinds, to live together and work together, in the same world, at peace."

2. E. G. Boring, "Mind and mechanism," *Amer. J. Psychol.*, 1946, 54:173-92.

3. See Chapter 12 of the present volume.

4. E. R. Hilgard and D. G. Marquis, *Conditioning and learning*, New York: Appleton-Century, 1940.

5. *Ibid.*, p. 101.

6. *Ibid.*, p. 88.

7. G. W. Allport, "Effect: a secondary principle of learning," *Psychol. Rev.*, 1946, 54:335-47.

8. See Chapter 9 of the present volume.

9. E. C. Tolman, "A stimulus-expectancy need-cathexis psychology," *Science*, 1945, 101:160-66.

10. It is instructive to read the perorations of two presidential addresses by psychologists, one preferring the machine model, the other the rat model. Though good-humored and witty, both authors candidly acknowledge their own escapist motives. To paraphrase Carlson's quip concerning Cannon's theory of emotions: the authors seem to entertain their models because the models entertain them.

"I believe that robotic thinking helps precision of psychological thought, and will continue to help it until psychophysiology is so far advanced that an image is nothing other than a neural event, and object constancy is obviously just something that happens in the brain. That time is still a long way off, and in the interval I choose to sit cozily with my robot, squeezing his hand and feeling a thrill—a scientist's thrill—when he squeezes mine back again." (E. G. Boring, *op. cit.*, p. 192).

"And, as a final peroration, let it be noted that rats live in cages; they do not go on binges the night before one has planned an experiment; they do not kill each other off in war; they do not invent engines of destruction, and if they did, they would not be so dumb about controlling such engines; they do not go in for either class conflicts or race conflicts; they avoid politics, economics and papers on psychology. They are marvelous, pure and delightful. And, as soon as I possibly can, I am going to climb back again out on that good old philogenetic limb and sit there, this time right side up and unashamed, wiggling my whiskers at all the dumb, yet at the same time far too complicated, specimens of *homo sapiens*, whom I shall see strutting and fighting and messing things up, down there on the ground below me" (E. C. Tolman, *op. cit.*, p. 166).

11. J. Huxley, *Man stands alone*, New York and London: Harper, 1941.

12. I. D. Suttie, *The origins of love and hate*, London: Kegan Paul, 1935.

13. An excellent example is Bertocci's analysis of man's sense of moral obligation (P. Bertocci, "A reinterpretation of moral obligation," *Phil. Phenomenol. Res.*, 1945, 6:270-83). He shows that, when we study the *ought-consciousness* phenomenologically, we discover how entirely different it is from the *must-consciousness*. This discovery leads to a justifiable suspicion that, whatever conscience may be, it does not derive merely from fear of punishment or from social coercion. Too hastily and heedlessly have psychologists accepted Freud's identification of the superego with threat of parental punishment.

14. McDougall specifically objected to the concept of intention on the

grounds that conscious intention merely obscures the instinctive motive at work (W. McDougall, *Outline of psychology*, New York: Scribner, 1923, pp. 121 f.). He had in mind the indubitable fact that men's verbal reports of their intentions may be rationalizations. But in my use of the term I do not confine intention to reportable purpose. Sometimes the essential direction of an intention is understood well enough by the subject, sometimes not. If the term, as I propose, is taken to mean *both* the understood and the non-understood direction of an act, I maintain that it can serve as a proper designation for "ultimate motives" and not merely for proximate or rationalized motives.

To my mind, it is unnecessary to have recourse to a doctrine of underlying needs or instincts. McDougall, for example, allowed far too little for the ever changing panorama of man's intentions, which, as they evolve from an original genetic equipment, undergo complete change of form and functional significance (G. W. Allport, "Motivation in personality: reply to Mr. Bertocci," *Psychol. Rev.*, 1940, 47:533-54).

15. See Chapter 9 of the present volume.

16. C. L. Hull, "Goal attraction and directing ideas conceived as habit phenomena," *Psychol. Rev.*, 1931, 38:487-506.

17. P. Lecky, *Self-consistency: a theory of personality*, New York: The Island Press, 1945, p. 122 f.

18. E. L. Thorndike, *Animal intelligence*, New York: Macmillan, 1911, p. 119.

19. R. M. Yerkes, *Chimpanzees: a laboratory colony*, New Haven: Yale University Press, 1943, p. 189.

20. E. Cassirer, *An essay on man*, New Haven: Yale University Press, 1945, p. 30.

21. Even in human beings we occasionally encounter a sharp break between symbols and signs. Some of Goldstein's aphasic patients, for example, seem capable of responding to signs but not to symbols, as in the case of the man who could understand the word-signs "drink it" when a glass full of water was presented to him, but was unable to go through the symbolic motions of drinking it if the glass was empty (K. Goldstein, *Human nature in the light of psychopathology*, Cambridge: Harvard University Press, 1940, p. 44).

Without symbols we could not make believe, dissimulate or lie; we could not form plans for our future or hold in mind those schemata that make possible consistency in moral conduct.

22. E. Cassirer, *op. cit.*, p. 25.

23. C. Morris, *Signs, language and behavior*, New York: Prentice-Hall, 1946, p. 198.

24. *Ibid.*, p. 23.

25. See Chapter 9 of the present volume.

26. See Chapter 12 of the present volume.

27. A. H. Leighton, *The governing of men*, Princeton: Princeton University Press, 1945.

PART II: *Motivation and structure in personality*

CHAPTER 5

The ego in contemporary psychology

This essay argues that the concept of self—that is, of ego—must be given a prominent position in psychological theory. It deplores the fact that, following the publication of William James's *Principles of psychology*, the self for a time suffered a virtual eclipse.

Since the first publication of this essay in the *Psychological Review* (1943), the concept has in fact been reintroduced at a rapid rate. There is much agreement concerning need for it, but less agreement concerning its precise place in personality theory. The analysis offered in the present chapter is developed more fully in my book *Becoming: basic considerations for a psychology of personality* (1955).

The essay was the presidential address at the fourteenth annual meeting of the Eastern Psychological Association at Hunter College in April 1943.

Introduction

One of the oddest events in the history of modern psychology is the manner in which the ego—or self—became sidetracked and lost to view. I say it is odd, because the existence of one's own self is the one fact of which every mortal person—every psychologist included—is perfectly convinced. An onlooker might say, "Psychologists are funny fellows. They have before them, at the heart of their science, a fact of perfect certainty, the one warrant for the being of all other things, and yet they pay no attention to it. Why don't they begin with their own egos, or with our egos—with something we all know about? If they did so, we might understand them better. What is more, they might understand us better."

Back in the 1880s, of course, it was good form for James, Royce, Dewey and their contemporaries to speak freely of the ego, the self or even the soul. The soul, to be sure, was giving way under Wundt's onslaughts, and everyone was finding it exhilarating to shake off the alleged theological domination and to emerge unfettered and positivistic into the era of the New Psychology. They forgot that their predecessors had endorsed the soul, not because of their theological leanings, but because associationism did not recognize or explain to their satisfaction the *coherence, unity* and *purposiveness* that they thought prevailed in mental life. Granted that the "soul" also failed to explain these properties, it at least called attention to their existence.

After the expulsion of the soul, these unifying properties of mental life were occasionally referred to under the designation of *self*. For a time, thanks to James, Calkins, Prince, and the French psychopathologists, self was a reasonably popular concept. But gradually it too fell into disuse.

The total eclipse of soul and the partial eclipse of self were due in part, as I have just said, to the rise of positivism in psychology. Positivism, we all know, is a scientific program for moral rearmament, whose imperatives include absolute monism, absolute objectivity and absolute reductionism—in short, absolute chastity. From this ascetic point of view, subjective certainties are suspect, selves seem a bit indecent and any hint of metaphysics (that is, of nonpositivistic metaphysics) savors of laxness. As Gardner Murphy has pointed out, there was no prestige to be gained from a psychology of the self.[1]

But for all its sumptuary control, positivism had one undisputed merit: it engendered a wholesome dislike for question-begging explanations. Much of the older psychology, it showed, suffered from a tendency to labor over words as if words were the essence of things. Thanks to positivism, faculty psychology, resting as it did on verbal realism, became discredited, and dialectics fell into disrepute. Much of self-psychology, we must now admit, dwelt on the unenlightening plane of dialectics. Its statements were often redundant or circular: in the manner of Gertrude Stein, it sometimes asserted that a self is a self is a self. Not being, by nature, especially lyrical, psychologists failed to see any deeper significance in this exalted formula. Quite understandably, they refused to admit such a stammering self to the gray citadel of their laboratories.

But when a concept becomes taboo, it is probable that the taboo will irradiate to cover a whole range of problems associated with the concept. Something of this sort seems to have happened. It is not only the soul and the self that suffered ostracism. Along with them went a vast array of problems having to do with the coherence and unity of mental life; with pride, ambition and status; with values, ideals and outlook on the future. The eclipse, of course, has not been total, but it has been considerable.

As if to compensate for the neglect of these interests within the field of psychology proper, psychoanalysis rose upon the horizon, emitting a spectacular, if sporadic, light. Small wonder that the world at large turned to psychoanalysis for guidance in dynamic psychology. There was precious little other guidance to be had. I am inclined to believe that history will declare that psychoanalysis marked an interregnum in psychology—between the time when it lost its soul, shortly after the Franco-Prussian War, and the time when it found it again, shortly after World War II.

Until psychoanalysis becomes finally fused into a broader and more adequate psychology, it may take pride in having preserved and advanced the study of certain functions of the self that positivistic psychology had consigned to oblivion. It may take credit, too, for preserving one term, more or less cognate with *self*, from the dark taboo of which I have spoken. *Ego* has featured prominently in psychoanalytic literature from its beginning. This term I am now appropriating to signify the recentering that is taking place in psychological theory.

But it is not from psychoanalysis alone that we draw our threads. The position of the ego in contemporary psychology is determined by certain other historical trends as well.

Main Conceptions of the Ego

Among the different conceptions of the ego found in psychological literature, the following are certainly the most important:

The ego as knower. The nominative form of the word *ego* implies that some subject is busily engaged, as Brentano would say, in "intending" his relations to the universe. The problem of the knower, or "Pure Ego," has been of little interest to psychologists since James gave it his lengthy *coup de grâce* in the *Principles*. It is enough, says James in effect, to admit that knowing goes on. A separate knowing-ego is not a necessary assumption. For phenomenologists[2] and personalists,[3] of course, the problem of the subject-object relationship remains uppermost. But, for the most part, since the time of Brentano and James, psychologists have passed the problem by.[4] For our purposes, we need only record this first usage and note its relative rarity.

The ego as object of knowledge. Some investigators have set themselves the problem of the nature of our experience of the self.[5] This approach, limited as it is to the deliverances of introspection, has not been particularly rewarding. It yields relatively unenlightening localizations for the ego, which is felt to lie "between the eyes" or to consist of "motions in the head" or to be situated "between right and left," "between up and down," "between behind and before." Following this line of investigation, Horowitz came upon such a diversity of results (reports locating the ego in the head, heart, chest, face, brain, genitals) that he concludes: "The localization of the self as it is reported in the literature quoted, in the responses on our questionnaire, in informal discussion, in the investigation of children, is not the basic phenomenon one might hope for to ease an analysis of the structure of the self and personality." [6]

There seem to be only two facts upon which there is general agreement: (1) Infants, all writers concur, do not recognize themselves as individuals; they behave in what Piaget calls an "undifferentiated absolute" composed of self and environment. Only gradually and with difficulty does a segregated ego evolve. (2) The ego of which we are aware is variable in its dimensions. Sometimes it includes less than the body and sometimes more. In a semi-doze we lose all sense of our egos, though we may be conscious enough of impersonal items. Our feet, perhaps, are suddenly perceived as strange objects not belonging to us. In pathological conditions, remarkable experiences of depersonalization take place.[7] Conversely, we sometimes think of a tool we are using as part of our extended ego-system, and at times we regard our children, our lodge or our ancestors as an intimate part of our extended selves. It is agreed that, in this manner, the ego-systems of which we are aware contract and expand in a most variable fashion.[8]

The ego as primitive selfishness. A century ago Max Stirner wrote *Der Einzige und Sein Eigenthum,*[9] a volume in which he developed the thesis that man is by nature unalterably egoistic. In 1918 the French biologist Felix Le Dantec handled the same theme more brilliantly in his *L'egoïsme: seule base de toute société.*[10] Unquenchable egoism is the foundation of the social edifice, says Le Dantec, and hypocrisy is its keystone. Psychologists are partial to such hardheaded realism and have themselves gone far in unveiling the hypocrisy in man's nature. Projections, rationalizations, defense mechanisms have been exposed for what they are—the whitewashing of ego-centric motivation. During this century psychologists have joined with historians, biographers and novelists in the fashionable sport of debunking human motives.

The ego as dominance-drive. Related to this view of primitive egoism, we find many investigations that deal with dominance feelings, with ascendance, with pecking orders, with euphoria. From this point of approach, the ego is that portion of the personality that demands status and recognition. The negative states of anxiety, insecurity, defensiveness, resistance are just as truly indicators that, whenever the ego is debased, there arise impulses for its defense and restoration to status.

Ego as a passive organization of mental processes. Psychoanalysis, we all know, has contributed much to the interpretation of human nature in terms of egoism. Its whole theory of motivation is based upon the assumption of hedonistic self-interest. But in psychoanalysis, egoism, oddly enough, is ascribed not to the ego but to the urges arising from the id. For Freud the ego proper is a passive percipient, devoid of dynamic power, "a coherent organization of mental processes" that is aware of the warring forces of the id, superego and external environment.[11] The ego, having no dynamic power, tries as well as it can to conciliate and to steer the warring forces; but when it fails, as it often does, it breaks out in anxiety. The ego is born of restraint of the instinctual impulses, and it continually needs strengthening. But even when, through the analytic process, it is strengthened, it is still essentially nothing more than a passive victim-spectator of the drama of conflict.

Dissatisfied with Freud's denial of dynamic power to the ego, later psychoanalytic writers, French and Hendrick among them,[12] have ascribed more *momentum* to the ego. It is the agent that plans, that strives to master as well as to conciliate the conflicts. One analyst, Heinz Hartmann, departing considerably from Freud, holds that "adaptation to reality—which includes mastery of it—proceeds to a large extent from the ego and in particular from that part of the ego which is free from conflict; and it is directed by the organized structure of ego-functions (such as intelligence, perception, etc.) which exist in their own right and have an independent effect upon the solution of conflicts."[13] To such writers the ego-ideal is no longer, as it was with Freud, a passive reflection of the superego, which in turn is conceived as a mere legacy of the parent. The ego through its ideals reaches into the future, becomes an executive, a planner, a fighter.

Ego as a "fighter for ends." We are brought, then, by some of the more modern psychoanalysts to a position not unlike that of McDougall, or of James in his more teleological moments. For McDougall self-regard was the master and controlling sentiment, in whose interest all other sentiments function.[14] The phrase "fighter for ends" I borrow from James,[15] who at times was intensely dynamic and personalistic in his conception of the self.

The purposive view of the ego may be linked to Koffka's postulate that there is ever active "a force which propels the ego upwards."[16] The same position is represented in those dynamic psychologies that recognize the subservience of the biological drives to one central drive of ego-satisfaction. One of the most forceful expressions of this point of view is to be found in Goldstein's *Human nature in the light of psychopathology*.[17]

The ego as a behavioral system. In spite of his postulation of "a force which propels the ego upwards," Koffka's position is characteristically somewhat less dynamic than that just described. The ego, he says, is only one segregated system within an homogeneous field. Much behavior occurs with no reference to the ego. Not all perception, not all action, not all emotion and not all consciousness are related to an ego-system. The ego varies widely in its boundaries from time to time and, under certain circumstances, acts as a system that determines the course of events, as does any other dynamic system according to the theory of Gestalt. But, much of the time, behavior is free from the influence of an ego-system.

More influential because of its experimental fruitfulness is Lewin's treatment of the subject.[18] Although he seldom uses the term *ego,* he too allows for a central subsystem within the person. Not all behavior is ego-linked, but many kinds of experimentally obtained results can be accounted for only by reference to the special types of tension that exist whenever the ego is "engaged." The shifting aspiration level is, most obviously, a phenomenon of ego-tensions. Satiation, substitution, encapsulation, resistance, irreality and power-field are among the Lewinian concepts whose characteristics represent various properties of ego-tensions.[19]

It is clear that Lewin, no less than Koffka, wishes to avoid thinking of the ego as a single entity and prefers to regard it as the variable set of forces that are aroused whenever the person enters into some novel and perhaps dangerous relation to his environment.

Ego as the subjective organization of culture. In recent years, as everyone knows, there has been a drawing together of psychology, psychoanalysis and social anthropology. The resulting commensalism has produced a new conception of the ego. The picture of the selfish and unsocialized ego bequeathed us by Stirner and Le Dantec has been broadened. Sherif, for example, points out that, although the ego is a "genetic psychological formation," it is acquired by the child under the ceaseless impact of influence by parents, teachers and associates, with the result that the ego "is chiefly made up of social values." [20] Since the process of segregating the ego in childhood is achieved largely by giving the child a name, a status, a code of behavior, a social sense of guilt and social standards for making his judgments, Sherif concludes that the ego is nothing but the social part of man.[21] This author's position is extreme, for if the ego is nothing but "the social in man," one wonders what to call all the antisocial impulses and the solitary strivings that are normally called *egoistic?*

Cantril's view is similar to, but less extreme than, Sherif's. Cantril admits that "a person's ego and, consequently, the way in which he regards himself, are by no means always entirely bound by the surrounding culture." [22] But what an individual regards as himself is, undeniably, in large part socially determined. When his nation's flag is torn down, *he* is insulted; when disparaging remarks are made of his parents, *he* is involved; when his political candidate loses a contest, *he* has been defeated.

By stressing the cultural content of the ego, these authors in effect eradicate the artificial Freudian distinction between ego and superego. They also rescue the ego from the antisocial solipsism of Stirner and Le Dantec and make of it a socialized agent ready to enter as an integrated unit into the complex relations of social life.

From this historical glance I have omitted many writers who have made their contribution to the literature of the ego. Nevertheless, I believe I have mentioned the chief ways in which, up to now, the ego has been conceived—that is, as knower, as object of knowledge, as primordial selfishness, as dominator, as a passive organizer and rationalizer, as a fighter for ends, as one segregated behavioral system among others and as a subjective patterning of cultural values.

The question immediately arises as to whether these eight uses of the term *ego* have anything in common, or whether, as is often the case, a single term is allowed to obscure entirely different problems. Is the ego as knower the same ego that seeks status? Is the I that is known also a fighter for ends? Has the ego-system proposed by Koffka any kinship with Freud's ego, who atempts through insight to reclaim the id?

These are questions that cannot yet be answered. We cannot say whether these eight conceptions reflect irreconcilable theories, or shade imperceptibly into one another, or are all ultimately to be subordinated under one inclusive theory of the ego.

In favor of the last possibility, I should like to point to recent experimental studies that, if I mistake not, lend support to several of these conceptions simultaneously. *The experiments result in one common finding—namely, that ego-involvement, or its absence, makes a critical difference in human behavior.* When a person reacts in a neutral, impersonal, routine atmosphere, his behavior is one thing. When he is behaving personally, perhaps excitedly, seriously committed to a task, he behaves quite differently. In the first condition his ego is not engaged; in the second condition it is. And it is my belief that, in most of the experiments I shall report, one finds that the ego is acting in several, if not all, of the eight capacities I have listed. In other words, *ego-involvement* is, as the phrase implies, a condition of total participation of the self—as knower, as organizer, as observer, as status seeker and as socialized being. But now for the experimental evidence.

Experimental Evidence

Generality and specificity. A few years ago I found myself involved in a controversy in the field of personality. Certain experimenters claimed that their findings demonstrated a situational specificity in human conduct. For example, a child honest in one situation would not be found honest in another,[23] a person confident of one judgment would not be confident of another.[24] Whole books were written in defense of specificity.[25] Other investigators, by other methods, found a person honest in one situation to be honest in another,[26] a person confident in one judgment to be confident in another;[27] and whole books were written in defense of generality.[28] It was a pleasant battle while it lasted. An arbitrator arose, a peacemaker by temperament—Gardner Murphy was his name—and he proposed a compromise. "Honesty," he suggested, "is either a general characteristic or a set of specific habits, depending on your interest and your emphasis."[29] Murphy was right, but it was not until recently that the deciding interest and critical emphasis became clear, at least to me. For my own belated insight I am indebted to an experiment by Klein and Schoenfeld.[30]

These investigators gave to a group of subjects a series of mental tests under two experimental conditions. In the first, the atmosphere was neutral, dull, *non-ego-involved.* The workers were merely laboratory subjects going through routine motions. After each of the six tests, they were required to rate the degree of confidence they felt in the accuracy of their performances. For each individual, there was little consistency in these certainty ratings.

After an interval of time, a second, equivalent set of tests was administered. This time the atmosphere was markedly changed. The subjects were placed under greater strain; they were told to try hard, since the results of these "intelligence" tests would be entered on their college records. For this set of tests, the confidence ratings were markedly consistent. A student who felt assured in one test felt assured in the other five; a student who lacked confidence in one of

his performances generally lacked confidence in the other performances. The authors conclude that confidence is a personality trait
when the ego is involved, but that it is specific to each situation
when the subject has no deep interest at stake.

This experiment supplies the hypothesis needed to settle a long-
standing controversy: when there is ego-involvement, there are general traits; when there is no ego-involvement, there are no general
traits.

From an entirely different source comes evidence to the same
effect. In connection with its polling investigations, the Office of
Public Opinion Research has found that *intensity* of feeling goes
with *consistency* of opinion.[31] For example, in the pre-Pearl Harbor
era it was found that those who felt most intensely in favor of aid to
Britain were, by and large, those who endorsed all sorts and varieties
of interventionist propositions. On the other hand, those who were
lukewarm in their support of aid to Britain were far more inconsistent
and specific in their answers. Sometimes they gave interventionist,
and sometimes isolationist, replies. The measure obtained between
the intensity scale and the generality of the attitude was a coefficient
of correlation of +.63.

Judgment. Eli Marks worked on judgments of skin color among
Negroes. He found them, in part, a function of the objective scale
but also, in part, a function of an egocentric scale. A Negro of
medium coloration is likely to be judged dark by a Negro of lighter
complexion and to be judged light by a Negro of darker complexion.[32]
For decades psychophysicists have dealt with judgments of hue as a
function of wave length, but Marks makes clear that judgments of
hue may be also a function of one's sense of social status. Wave
length is perceived by the sensitized retina, but it is perceived no
less by the sensitized ego.

In the field of simple predictive judgment, it was found in the
public opinion polls of 1940 that, of the people who were strong
Willkie supporters, 71 per cent predicted that he would win the
election; of those who were weak Willkie supporters, only 47 per
cent made this prediction.[33] Assuming, as we must, that intensity of
an attitude indicates ego-involvement, we find here a clear quantitative demonstration that a 24 per cent difference in the number of
predictions exists when the ego-regions of the personality are engaged. Admittedly, the ego's wish is only one factor in predictive
judgments; but if conditions are right, it can become the crucial
factor.

Polling research has uncovered yet another important fact concerning judgment. If you ask respondents to tell you to your face what they think about the British, or about some minority group in this country, or even about their own educational level, you obtain one set of results; but if you ask them to write their answers to the same questions privately and deposit them in a padlocked ballot box, on the average your results will be significantly different.[34] Now this difference between open and secret expressions of opinion seems to exist only when the answers might jeopardize the respondent's sense of status or affect his prestige in the interviewer's eyes. The discrepancy is great enough to warrant the use of secret balloting whenever questions are of a type that might expose the person to humiliation.

Judgments concerning one's self are remarkably interesting things to study. We know, for example, how inaccurate people are in rating their own economic status. Nearly all prefer to overlook the objective evidence and to identify themselves with the great middle class.[35] We know something about the distortions that result when people report their own traits. Frenkel-Brunswik found the self-protective devices so powerful that her subjects would omit, justify or completely reverse the facts in their accounts of their own deficiencies.[36] Although it is trite to point out what all psychologists know so well, that lack of objectivity is the rule when our egos are involved, it is not trite to remark that very little work has been done on the extent and nature of the distortion, or on the curious and momentous question why some personalities attain objectivity even in the face of extreme ego-involvement. Insight, it would seem, grows more and more difficult to achieve as the inner regions of the personality are approached. And yet some individuals accomplish remarkable feats of self-objectification. Why do they succeed and others fail?

Memory. Thanks to Bartlett we know how cultural schemata alter our memory traces.[37] Here, of course, is an example of the silent influence of an ethnocentric frame. But within any given culture, striking memory-efforts can be traced to egocentric frames as well.

Edwards has demonstrated that, if memory material fails to fit comfortably into an ego-involved frame, it contorts itself until it does so. Selecting three groups of students, each with a different attitude toward the New Deal (favorable, neutral or opposed) he first read them a ten-minute passage concerning the relations of the New Deal to communism. The subjects knew they were to be tested for the accuracy of their retention.

"Immediately after the reading, a multiple choice recognition test consisting of 46 items was given to the subjects. Half or 23 of the items on the test were answered in the passage in a manner favorable to the New Deal, the other 23 were answered in a manner unfavorable. The items on the test offered opportunities for rationalization of one's answer, if the correct answer was opposed to one's attitude. The subjects were re-tested after an interval of 21 days.

"Analysis of variance of the data showed that rationalization was directly associated with the degree of conflict between the correct answer and the attitudinal frames of reference of our subjects. In general the results show—as do many other studies—that it is almost impossible to expect objectivity and accuracy in perception, learning, remembering, thinking, etc., when ego-involved frames of reference are stimulated." [38]

Here one might cite also the memory experiments of Zillig, which show how members of the male sex recall fewer aphorisms favorable to women than to men.[39] Or the Watson and Hartmann study concerning the distortions that occur in memory for theological arguments, depending upon the subject's previous commitment to atheism or to theism.[40] Or Wallen's ingenious demonstration that, after an interval of time, subjects recall ratings of their own personalities in a manner that makes them compatible with their own preconceived opinions of themselves.[41]

Levine and Murphy demonstrated that pro-Communist sympathizers memorize pro-Communist textual material more easily than they do anti-Communist textual material.[42] What is more, they forget the antipathetic text more rapidly and more completely than the sympathetic text. In anti-Communists the effects are exactly reversed. It was a brilliant stroke for these authors to demonstrate in one experiment that both learning and forgetting are functions of the political identifications of the ego.

Frame of reference. Some of the studies I have mentioned have been conducted in relation to what their authors have called a "frame of reference." Now, a frame of reference seems to signify *any spatial-temporal or cultural orientation that relates many of an individual's attitudes, habits and judgments to one another and that influences the formation of new judgments, attitudes and habits.* A general orientation favorable to the New Deal will, according to Edwards, determine our specific remembrance of items from speeches concerning the New Deal.[43] A general orientation regarding various other subjects, Sells has shown, will affect our logical reasoning in all matters pertaining to them.[44]

It is important to note that not all frames are ego-involved. If I locate Ninth Avenue or East Twelfth Street readily, it is because I have a geographic frame in mind for New York City. In my case this spatial orientation is not at all ego-involved. The point I am making is that research on the problem of frames of reference is not necessarily research on the problem of ego-involvement. Many cultural frames having to do with language, etiquette or dress determine our perceptions, our memory, our conduct, but their influence is not felt as personally relevant. Margaret Mead has expressed her anthropological astonishment at the odd custom Americans have of appearing at her lectures with clothes on; but to most of us this quaint folkway causes no ego-concern, at least as long as it is operative.

But an interesting discovery came to light in World War II. Certain cultural frames, which had previously been indifferent, suddenly became acutely personal. Probably no one in Alsace felt concerned about the bilingual frame of reference until the Nazis decreed that only German should be spoken and that only Germanized names and inscriptions should appear on the tombstones. Bilinguality had always been taken for granted; but when this familiar, habitual frame was suppressed and placed under attack, it became of central importance, and people reacted as to a personal insult. Many of us have discovered that hitherto indifferent frames of reference, such as the constitutional guarantees we enjoy, previously taken for granted, have suddenly become ego-involved and, once in jeopardy, are defended as if they were parts of our physical bodies. Suppose we were forbidden to speak the English language. How enraged we would become! What had always been a mere ethnocentric frame would immediately become ego-involved.

Ethnocentric and egocentric frames both affect our conduct, and under certain conditions the ethnocentric frame is experienced also as an egocentric frame. But I think it is a mistake to confuse the concept of the ego with that of the socius (or cultural portion of our personalities) as Sherif has done. Under normal social conditions, only a relatively small portion of our culture is ego-involved.

Learning. The longest and most difficult chapter in psychology, no one will deny, is the chapter on learning. The 1942 Yearbook of the National Society for the Study of Education is devoted entirely to this subject. One searches its 463 pages in vain for any mention of the ego, and almost in vain for any recognition of the importance of *interest.* True, one finds occasional remarks to the effect that "the teacher who neglects the simple but powerful word of praise does so at her pedagogical peril," [45] but the potential significance of such remarks for learning theory seems lost to view.

Clinical, educational and industrial psychologists know that the first rule of all applied psychology is that every child and every adult needs some experience of success and social approval. John E. Anderson advises the teacher to go far out of her way if necessary to find an area in which these feelings can be engendered. He adds: "Success in one area may more than compensate for failure in many areas; some accomplishment furnishes an integrating center about which the personality may be integrated." [46]

Note especially Anderson's statement that "success in one area may more than compensate for failure in many areas." Only in terms of ego-psychology can we account for such fluid compensation. Mental health and happiness, it seems, do not depend upon the satisfaction of any specific drive; they depend, rather, upon the *person* finding *some* area of success *somewhere*. The *ego* must be satisfied—not the hunger drive, nor the sex drive, nor the maternal drive, however temporarily insistent these segmental tensions may be.

Most theories of learning lean heavily upon the assumption of multiple drives. A segmental tension exists; the organism behaves; the tension is relieved; and the response is set. In this sequence it is often assumed that all drives are equally potent for learning. The satisfaction of any drive, through the principle of reward or confirming reaction, is held to bring about an equal degree of learning. If this is so, how can we account for the fact that praise is found almost uniformly to be the leading incentive in school, in factory and in ordinary life? If we are to hold to the theory of multiple drives at all, we must at least admit that the ego-drive (or pride, or desire for approval—call it what we will) takes precedence over all other drives.

Not only does human learning proceed best when the incentive of praise and recognition is used, but the individual's *capacity* for learning actually seems to expand under this condition. Every psychometrist knows that if he is to obtain a valid IQ, the subject must be encouraged. Terman's instructions on this point are well known: "Nothing contributes more to a satisfactory *rapport* than praise of the child's efforts. . . . In general, the poorer the response, the better satisfied one should appear to be with it. . . . Exclamations like fine! splendid! etc., should be used lavishly." [47]

In other words, to maximize the child's intelligence we must maximize his ego. For psychological theory this is really a momentous fact. Intelligence is the ego's tool for solving its own problems. It is manifestly unfair to estimate intelligence on the basis of performance in which the individual himself has no interest. For this reason, through the device of praise, the subject must be encouraged to make the test-items into ego-involved problems, which he can attack with maximally motivated effort. Intelligence is the individual's capacity to solve problems of importance to himself.

One unfavorable condition for learning must be admitted lest we oversimplify the issue. Too intense an ego-involvement may be disruptive. Its normal integrative value may be actually undetermined when eagerness or self-consciousness reach a degree of intensity that leads to embarrassment or over-anxiousness. No one learns or performs well if his autonomic nervous system is in a turmoil. We need a rule that will help us determine the optimum degree of ego-involvement required for enhancing efficiency of learning and performance.[48]

One word about the law of effect. Its principal shortcoming, I think, stems from the assumption that rewarded *responses* tend to recur. Many experiments, in fact, show that rewarded responses do not blindly recur whenever an appropriate stimulus returns. Hoppe points out that people normally do not strive again for a goal successfully achieved.[49] What they do is to raise their aspirations to a point where they clearly risk failure. A student who makes an A record in a course in college shows no tendency to repeat that course. He prefers to take new risks in the same general area. And an experiment by Rosenzweig indicates that it is definitely infantile to choose to repeat successful acts.[50] For example, a puzzle once solved, even if accompanied by a burst of elation, no longer attracts the mature individual. He wants new worlds to conquer. Reward may bring merely satiation and boredom.

The fallacy, I repeat, lies in our speaking of rewarding a *response*. The law of effect would be truer if it held simply that a *person,* being rewarded, employs his past successes in whatever way he thinks is likely to bring him satisfaction in the *future.* Israeli has shown that, except for certain psychopaths, people are much more interested in their futures than in their pasts.[51] Since this is so, an individual's past performances often mean little or nothing to him. Only if the ego would be served thereby does he engage in a repetition of the successful act. More often he chooses to vary and refine his behavior so that he may feel that he himself is growing toward new successes in the future.

The relation between success and repetition, I suspect, is much closer in the case of non-ego-involved behavior than in the case of ego-

involved behavior. Over and over again I use the same motor combinations in typewriting, in driving my car, in dealing with trades-
men. They are reasonably successful acts; why should I change them?
But I do not repeat successful research work; I do not repeat a
gratifying conversation with a friend; nor do I restate the same goal
in an aspiration-level experiment. Ego-involved tasks often demand
changing goals and new responses. Rewarded behavior, it would
seem, becomes stereotyped only in lower animals, or in human
activities of such a routine nature that they fail to engage the ego.

To summarize this brief discussion: It would seem that, in order
to employ the law of effect with human learning, we must view it
as secondary to the principle of ego-involvement. The law of effect,
like cue reduction, conditioning, bond-formation and most other
popular principles of learning, has been worked out for the most part
on animal subjects or on human beings deprived, for the duration of
the experiment, of their egos. The principles may be good ones, but
when the ego is engaged they operate in a contingent fashion. Learning theory of the future, let us hope, will not remain so peripheral
to the ego.

Motivation. You may be thinking, "But, we've always known
that one must be motivated in order to secure a response. Are you
talking about anything more than the importance of motivation?"
Yes. I am saying that there are two forms of motivation, one ego-
involved and one not, and I am attempting by repeated citations
from experiments to show the differences that exist between them.

Take, for example, the work of Huntley and Wolff on judgments based upon records of expressive behavior.[52] These investigators, working independently, instructed their subjects to make
judgments concerning the personalities of many people from their
handwritings, from their recorded voices, from photographs of their
hands and from their style of storytelling. The subjects were motivated in a routine manner, as is any laboratory subject. Suddenly,
in the midst of the series, they were confronted with samples of their
own expressive behavior, which had been recorded without their
knowledge. In the large majority of cases the subjects did not consciously recognize their own records and continued innocently with
their characterizations. But something had happened. The characterizations began to take a different form. Even though a judge
was wholly unaware that a certain expression was his own, he generally gave it a much more favorable rating than he gave similar
expressive records taken from other subjects. Occasionally he gave it
a vehemently unfavorable rating. Practically never did he give it an

indifferent rating. Other people's records might arouse no affect, but not his. Whenever a subject became half-conscious, as it were, that a record might possibly be his, his judgments were still more intensely partisan; but, when he fully recognized his own record, his social sense of modesty prevailed, and his judgments returned to the noncommital level.

In these experiments we have a particularly neat demonstration of the fact that ego-involved systems may operate in a wholly silent manner, affecting judgments in a most extreme way without the subject knowing the reason. The experiments also prove that the limen of ego-involvement is lower than the limen for self-recognition, an interesting finding, which warns us once more that conscious report and introspection will never be a sufficient method for exploring the operations of the ego-system. But the important point for our present purpose is to note that routine motivation to perform a task is one thing and ego-charged motivation is quite another. Routine motives yield one set of results, ego-motives a different set.

When is motivation ego-involved, and when is it not? A partial answer seems to lie in the degree of frustration involved. As we have already noted, many customary frames of reference are not felt to be personally relevant and do not behave like egocentric frames, until their continuance is threatened. Many drives, too, run their course without engaging the ego unless they are interfered with. But serious frustration may instigate the clamor, the jealousy, the possessiveness often characteristic of ego-involvement. Yet frustration by no means always produces this effect, especially if one has compensated for drive-frustration by success in other realms. And, to complicate the situation further, we cannot say that ego-involvement is absent when there is no frustration. Many smooth-running instances of goal-seeking behavior are obviously ego-involved. A mother feels just as closely identified with her child when it is in good health as when her maternal care meets with frustration. A businessman is as much absorbed in his enterprise in times of prosperity as in times of adversity. Let us say, then, that frustration of goal-seeking behavior or any kind of threat to the individual is very likely to engage the ego-system, but that normally this ego-system is made up of the ordinary values that spell out the significance of life to the individual.

The level of aspiration. The history of ten years' research on this Lewinian problem is too intricate to trace here, but, unless I am mistaken, every investigation has directly or indirectly confirmed Hoppe's initial claim that the subject behaves in such a manner as to maintain his self-esteem at the highest possible level.[53] Of course, many investigators have not used the conception of the ego at all. Yet, whatever results are found, all seem to point to the essential inescapability of Hoppe's original hypothesis. Frank, for example, found that subjects in whom "self competition, and consciousness of social pressure" were present had D-scores three to seven times as large as did subjects who had no such sense of personal involvement in the situation. (D-scores, of course, indicate the discrepancy between performance and the goal that the individual wishes or expects to achieve.) Frank also found that subjects who are ego-involved do not change their estimates with every little variation in their performance. They try and try again before trimming their aspirations to fit their capacities. Subjects not ego-involved, on the other hand, quickly yield to the immediate realities of the situation and lower their aspiration level.[54] We know too that competitiveness, surely a symptom of ego-involvement, usually produces a rise and greater consistency in the aspiration level.[55] But we cannot say that competitiveness always has this effect, because subjects who dread competition will lower their level of aspiration consistently in order to avoid the risk of humiliation.[56]

In short, it seems always to be the ego-demand of the individual subject that determines the behavior of the aspiration level. Some subjects are adventurous, some cautious; their egos demand different types of satisfaction, and it is this fact that is repeatedly reflected in the results of the experiments. It is worth pointing out that historically the aspiration level may well be regarded as the door by which the ego re-entered the cloisters of academic psychology.

Industrial psychology. Most of us, I suppose, have been impressed by the demonstrations of Roethlisberger and Dickson,[57] Watson[58] and others that employees in industry are not "economic men" so much as they are "ego men." What they want, above all else, is credit for work done, interesting tasks, appreciation, approval and congenial relations with their employers and fellow workers. These satisfactions they want even more than high wages or job security. The employer's estimate of the worker's wants correlates just about zero with the worker's own report of his wants.[59] The employer thinks that wages and security are the dominant desires, whereas in reality the ego-satisfactions are primary. What a different outlook there would be on our economic life if we took firm hold on the issues of status and self-respect in industry and replanned our industrial society in a manner that would rescue the worker's ego from oblivion.

The Nature of the Ego

In the experiments I have cited, and in many others of analogous nature, it turns out that one group of subjects (those who are personally aroused and committed to a task) behave in ways quite unlike other subjects (who are not so committed). In some instances there are measurable quantitative differences as great as 50 or 60 per cent, sometimes much more. In other instances there are qualitative changes that elude measurement. Thus we are here confronted with some parameter that makes a vast difference in our experimental results.

We have seen that under conditions of ego-involvement the whole personality manifests greater consistency in behavior; it reveals not specificity in conduct but generality and congruence. In the field of judgment, we have seen how ego-involvement results in significant distortions of the ordinary psychophysical scales. In memory, we find that ego-involved retention is characteristically superior (though at times repressions also may be more likely to occur, and rationalizations may creep into memory). In intelligence, we note that ego-involvement is indispensable if we would obtain optimum performance. In learning theory, reforms seem indicated to make room for the demonstrable influence of the ego upon the acquisition of skill and knowledge. In motivation, the craving for recognition, status and personal appreciation turns out to be supreme, so much so that our conceptions of procedure and policy in industrial relations, in education and in psychotherapy are profoundly affected. And these are only a few of the operational criteria by which we may demonstrate the existence of the ego.

Its admittance to good standing in contemporary psychology has been advocated by several psychologists besides myself. Koffka, Lewin and the psychoanalysts have done so, as has Murray, who makes a distinction between "peripheralist" psychology and "centralist" psychology.[60] The thesis set forth in Rogers' book *Counseling and psychotherapy*[61] seems to me especially clear evidence that the ego is coming into its own. Rogers, in effect, asks counselors to sit back and, with little more than an occasionally well-placed *m-hm*, to encourage the patient himself to restructure and re-plan his life. The patient's ego takes command. It's about time it should.

Although we have given an adequate operational demonstration of the ego, we have not yet faced the difficult problem of definition.

Earlier we saw that eight conceptions seem to prevail. But whenever we encounter ego-involvement, the ego in *several* of its historical senses seems to be active. Furthermore, these historical conceptions seem to have much in common.

For one thing, it seems clear that all of the conceptions are less embracing than "personality." All writers seem agreed that the ego is only one portion, one region—or, as the Freudians say, one "institution"—of the personality. Many skills, habits and memories are components of personality, but seldom if ever become ego-involved. Writers seem also agreed that the ego is nonexistent in early childhood, evolving gradually as the child comes to mark himself off from his environment and from other human beings. They seem to agree in viewing the ego as the portion of the personality that is in proximate relation to the external world: it senses the threats, the opportunities and the survival significance of both outer and inner events. It is that portion of the personality, so to speak, that meets the world head-on. It is the contact-region of the personality. For that reason it is also the conflict-region. Yet it is coextensive neither with consciousness nor with unconsciousness; for much that we are conscious of is unimportant to our egos, and many unconscious stimuli silently but effectively engage them.

There is also agreement that the subjective sense of the ego varies greatly from time to time, now contracting to include less than the body, now expanding to include more. Its content keeps changing; at one moment the ego seems preoccupied with one activity and soon thereafter with a wholly different activity. This shifting scene, however, does not mean that there is no stable and recurring structure. On the contrary, if you know a person well enough, you find that you are able to predict with marked success what items will and what items will not be linked to his ego. By many writers the ego is represented as a layered structure. Certainly there are *degrees* of ego-involvement: a person may be moderately partisan or intensely partisan.

There seems to be one other property of the ego that is less often discussed—namely, its customary preoccupation with the future. Israeli, it will be remembered, reports that among his subjects over 90 per cent expressed themselves more interested in their futures than in their pasts.[62] This finding is worth stressing, for, as a rule, psychologists are more interested in a person's past than in his future. In other words, the psychologist and his subject customarily face in different directions, and that is unfortunate.

The admittance of the ego to good standing in psychology does not mean a reimportation of the *deus ex machina* of pre-Wundtian psychology. It does mean, however, a recognition of the fact that our predecessors, who regarded psychology as the science of the soul, were not wrong in setting the problems of unity and personal relevance before us. What they called the soul we may now, with good conscience, call the ego. In so doing, no clocks need to be set backward. Dialectics has already given way to experiment, to the clinic and to still newer methods for studying the common man in his normal social setting.

But, disregarding the problems of method, which are beyond the scope of this essay, we may safely predict that ego-psychology in the twentieth century will flourish increasingly. For only with its aid can psychologists reconcile the human nature that they study and the human nature that they serve.

REFERENCES

1. G. Murphy, "Psychology and the post-war world," *Psychol. Rev.*, 1942, 49:298-318.

2. M. Beth, "Zur Psychologie des Ich," *Arch. f. d. Ges. Psychol.*, 1933, 88:323-76; T. K. Oesterreich, *Phenomenologie des Ich in ihren Grundproblemen*, Leipzig: J. A. Barth, 1910.

3. For example, J. S. Moore, "The problem of the self," *Phil. Rev.*, 1933, 42:487-99.

4. Private correspondence with Koffka concerning his own usage of the term brought out the interesting fact that, in writing his chapters on the ego, he had never thought of ego in the role of the knower (K. Koffka, *Principles of Gestalt psychology*, New York: Harcourt, Brace, 1935). "To be quite frank, I never put this question to myself." He adds, "That my solution will be similar to Brentano's I doubt. At the moment it seems to me that it will be found in the theory of Ego subsystems, more particularly in the relation of the Self-system to other Ego-systems."

5. E. W. Amen, "An experimental study of the self in psychology," *Psychol. Monogr.*, 1926, Vol. 35, No. 165; E. L. Horowitz, "Spatial localization of the self," *J. Soc. Psychol.*, 1935, 6:379-87; H. Lundholm, "Reflections upon the nature of the psychological self," *Psychol. Rev.*, 1940, 47:110-26.

6. E. L. Horowitz, *op. cit.*, p. 386.

7. H. Delgado, "Psicologia y psicopatologia de la conscientia del yo," *An. Inst. Psicol.*, University of Buenos Aires, 1938, 2:135-76; P. Federn, "Narzissmus im Ichfuge," *Int. Z. f. Psychoanal.*, 1927, 13:420-38.

8. H. Lundholm, *op. cit.*

9. M. Stirner, *The ego and his own* (trans. by S. T. Byington), London: A. C. Fifield, 1912.

10. F. Le Dantec, *L'egoïsme, seule base de toute société*, Paris: Flammarion, 1916.

11. S. Freud, *The ego and the id* (trans. by J. Rivière), London: Hogarth Press, 1927.

12. R. M. French, "Some psychoanalytic applications of the psychological field concept," *Psychoanal. Quart.*, 1942, 11:17-32; I. Hendrick, "Instinct and the ego during infancy," *Psychoanal. Quart.*, 1942, 11:33-58.

13. H. Hartmann, "Ich-psychologie und Anpassungsproblem," *Int. J. Psychoanal.*, 1940, 21:214.

14. W. McDougall, *The energies of men*, New York: Scribner, 1933, p. 383.

15. W. James, *Principles of psychology*, New York: Holt, 1890, I, 141.

16. K. Koffka, *op. cit.*, p. 670.

17. "On the basis of our discussion I believe we are in no way forced to assume the existence of special drives. . . . They are special reactions in special situations, and represent the various forms by which the organism as a whole expresses itself. . . . The traditional view assumes various drives which come into the foreground under certain conditions. We assume only one drive, the drive of self-actualization, but are compelled to concede that under certain conditions the tendency to actualize one potentiality is so strong that the organism is governed by it" (K. Goldstein, *Human nature in the light of psychopathology*, Cambridge: Harvard University Press, 1940, pp. 144 f.).

18. K. Lewin, *Principles of topological psychology*, New York: McGraw-Hill, 1936, p. 181.

19. A particularly suggestive contribution of Lewin pertains to the difference between nationalities in terms of the relative ease with which the ego becomes "engaged." Thus the American is less defensive, less touchy, less reticent than the German, because the barriers of the German's ego lie nearer the "surface." He protects himself against familiarity and intrusion, whereas the American leads a much more "public" life and protects only the "core" of his personal life from public gaze (K. Lewin, "Some social-psychological differences between the United States and Germany," *Char. & Pers.*, 1936, 4:265-93).

20. M. Sherif, *The psychology of social norms*, New York: Harper, 1936, p. 179.

21. *Ibid.*, p. 186.

22. H. Cantril, *The psychology of social movements*, New York: Wiley, 1941, p. 44.

23. H. Hartshorne and M. May, *Studies in deceit*, New York: Macmillan, 1928.

24. W. C. Trow, "The psychology of confidence," *Arch. Psychol.*, 1923, No. 67.

25. P. M. Symonds, *The nature of conduct*, New York: Macmillan, 1928.

26. D. W. MacKinnon, "Violation of prohibitions," in H. A. Murray (ed.), *Explorations in personality*, New York: Oxford University Press, 1938, pp. 491-501.

27. D. M. Johnson, "Confidence and speed in two-category judgment," *Arch. Psychol.*, 1939, No. 241.

28. G. W. Allport, *Personality: a psychological interpretation*, New York: Holt, 1937.

29. G. Murphy and G. Jensen, *Approaches to personality*, New York: Coward-McCann, 1932, p. 385.

30. G. S. Klein and N. Schoenfeld, "The influence of ego-involvement on confidence," *J. Abnorm. Soc. Psychol.*, 1941, 36:249-58.

31. H. Cantril, *Gauging public opinion*, Princeton: Princeton University Press, 1943, Chap. 3.

32. E. Marks, "Skin color judgments of Negro college students," *J. Abnorm. Soc. Psychol.*, 1943, 38:370-76.

33. H. Cantril, *Gauging public opinion, op. cit.*

34. *Ibid.*, Chap. 5.

35. *Ibid.*

36. E. Frenkel-Brunswik, "Mechanisms of self-deception," *J. Soc. Psychol.*, 1939, 10:409-20.

37. F. C. Bartlett, *Remembering: a study in experimental and social psychology*, Cambridge, England: Cambridge University Press, 1932.

38. A. L. Edwards, "Rationalization in recognition as a result of a political frame of reference," *J. Abnorm. Soc. Psychol.*, 1941, 36:234.

39. M. Zillig, "Einstellung und Aussage," *Z. f. Psychol.*, 1928, 106:58-106.

40. W. S. Watson and G. W. Hartmann, "Rigidity of a basic attitudinal frame," *J. Abnorm. Soc. Psychol.*, 1939, 34:314-36.

41. R. Wallen, "Ego-involvement as a determinant of selective forgetting," *J. Abnorm. Soc. Psychol.*, 1942, 37:20-39.

42. J. M. Levine and G. Murphy, "The learning and forgetting of controversial material," *J. Abnorm. Soc. Psychol.*, 1943, 38:507-17.

43. A. L. Edwards, "Political frames of reference as a factor influencing recognition," *J. Abnorm. Soc. Psychol.*, 1941, 36:34-50.

44. S. B. Sells, "The atmosphere effect: an experimental study of reasoning," *Arch. Psychol.*, 1936, No. 200.

45. National Society for the Study of Education, *The psychology of learning*, Forty-first Yearbook, Part 2, Bloomington: Publ. School Pub. Co., 1942, p. 118.

46. *Ibid.*, p. 349.

47. L. M. Terman, *The measurement of intelligence*, Boston: Houghton Mifflin, 1916, p. 125.

48. One formulation of the needed rule is suggested by French: "So long as the tension does not exceed the available energy of the integrative mechanisms, so long will the integrative capacity of the goal-directed striving increase with increasing tension. But as soon as the tension of the need begins to exceed the available energy of the integrating mechanism, the effect of increasing tension will be the opposite" (R. M. French, "Goal, mechanisms and integrative field," *Psychosom. Med.*, 1941, 3:245).

49. F. Hoppe, "Erfolg und Misserfolg," *Psychol. Forsch.*, 1930, 14:1-62.

50. S. Rosenzweig, "Preferences in the repetition of successful and unsuccessful activities as a function of age and personality," *J. Genet. Psychol.*, 1933, 42:423-41.

51. N. Israeli, "The social psychology of time," *J. Abnorm. Soc. Psychol.*, 1932, 27:209-13.

52. C. W. Huntley, "Judgments of self based upon records of expressive behavior," *J. Abnorm. Soc. Psychol.*, 1940, 35:398-427; W. Wolff, "Selbstbeurteilung und Fremdbeurteilung im wissentlichen und unwissentlichen Versuch," *Psychol. Forsch.*, 1932, 16:251-329.

53. F. Hoppe, *op. cit.*

54. J. D. Frank, "Some psychological determinants of the level of aspiration," *Amer. J. Psychol.*, 1935, 47:285-93.

55. M. G. Preston and J. A. Bayton, "Differential effect of a social variable upon three levels of aspiration," *J. Exp. Psychol.*, 1941, 29:351-69.

56. J. D. Frank, "Individual differences in certain aspects of the level of aspiration," *op. cit.*

57. F. J. Roethlisberger and W. J. Dickson, *Management and the worker*, Cambridge: Harvard University Press, 1939.

58. G. Watson, "Work satisfaction," in G. W. Hartmann (ed.), *Industrial conflict: a psychological interpretation*, New York: Cordon Press, 1939, Chap. 6.

59. *Ibid.*, p. 119.

60. H. A. Murray, *Explorations in personality*, New York: Oxford University Press, 1938.

61. C. R. Rogers, *Counseling and psychotherapy*, Boston: Houghton Mifflin, 1942.

62. N. Israeli, *op. cit.*

CHAPTER 6

The trend in motivational theory

What methods shall we use to assess a person's motives? The answer, of course, depends on what theory of motivation we hold.

This essay argues—in agreement with modern "ego-psychology"—that conscious values and intentions are important, far more important than Freudian and other irrationalist theories of motivation would allow. It holds that the best way to discover what a person is trying to do is to *ask* him (with, of course, due precautions), though the more sly "projective" methods also have their uses. The essay calls for a systematic use of both indirect and direct methods, all in accordance with a balanced theory of motivation.

Originally the essay appeared in *The American Journal of Orthopsychiatry* (1953).

Motivational theory today seems to be turning a corner in the road of scientific progress. In attempting to characterize this change in direction I wish to pay special attention to the problem of psychodiagnostic methods, for the successes and failures of these methods can teach us much about psychodynamic theory.

Let us start by asking why projective methods are so popular in both diagnostic practice and research. The answer, I think, is to be found in the history of motivational theory during the past century. All of the major influences have pressed in a single direction. Schopenhauer, with his doctrine of the primacy of the blind will, had little respect for the rationalizations invented by the individual's intellect to account for his conduct. Motives, he was sure, could not be taken at their face value. Darwin followed with his similar anti-intellectual emphasis on primordial struggle. McDougall refined the Darwinian stress on instinct, retaining in his horme the flavor of Schopenhauer's will, Darwin's struggle for survival, Bergson's *élan* and Freud's libido. All these writers were irrationalists—confident that underlying genotypes in motivation should be sought, rather than the surface phenotypes. All of them were reacting against the naïve intellectualism of their predecessors and against the rationalizations offered by self-justifying mortals when called on to account for their conduct. Among these irrationalists who have dominated Western psychology for the past century, Freud, of course, has been the leading figure. He, like the others, perceived that the mainsprings of conduct may be hidden from the searchlight of consciousness.

In addition to irrationalism, modern dynamic psychology has developed another earmark: geneticism. The original instincts laid down in our nature are regarded as decisive; or if not, then the experiences of early childhood are held to be crucial. At this point, the leading non-dynamic school of thought—stimulus-response psychology—joins forces with geneticism. Stimulus-response theorists agree with instinct psychologists and psychoanalysts in viewing adult motives as conditioned, reinforced, sublimated or otherwise elaborated editions of instincts or drives, or of an id whose structure, Freud said, "never changes."

Not one of these dominating theories of motivation allows for an essential transformation of motives in the course of life. McDougall explicitly denied the possibility, asserting that our motivational structure is laid down once and for all in our equipment of instincts. New objects may become attached to an instinct through learning, but the motive power is always the same. Freud's position was essentially identical: the concepts of sublimation and of shifting object cathexis chiefly accounted for whatever apparent alterations occur. Stimulus-response psychology is likewise geared to the assumption of remote control operating out of the past. We respond only to objects that have been associated with primary drives in the past, and we do so only in proportion to the degree that our responses have been rewarded or gratified in the past. From the stimulus-response point of view, the individual can hardly be said to be *trying* to do anything at all. He is simply *responding* with a complex array of habits that somehow were rewarded year before last. The prevailing dictum that motivation is always a matter of "tension reduction" or of "seeking equilibrium" is consistent with this point of view but scarcely consistent, I think, with all the known facts.

This prevailing atmosphere of theory has engendered a kind of contempt for the "psychic surface" of life. The individual's conscious report is rejected as untrustworthy, and the contemporary thrust of his motives is disregarded in favor of a backward tracing of his conduct to earlier formative stages. The individual loses his right to be believed. And while he is busy leading his life in the present with a forward thrust into the future, most psychologists have become busy tracing it backward into the past.

It is now easy to understand why the special methods invented by Jung (fifty years ago), Rorschach (forty years ago) and Murray (thirty years ago) were seized upon with enthusiasm by psychodiagnosticians. At no point do these methods ask the subject what his interests are, what he wants to do or what he is trying to do. Nor do the methods ask directly concerning the subject's relation to his parents or to authority figures. They infer this relationship entirely by assumed identifications. So popular is this indirect, undercover approach to motivation that many clinicians and many university centers spend far more time on this type of diagnostic method than on any other.

Occasionally, however, a client may cause the projective tester consternation by intruding his unwanted conscious report. The story is told of a patient who remarked that a Rorschach card made him think of sexual relations. The clinician, thinking to tap a buried complex, asked him why. "Oh, because," said the patient, "I think of sexual relations all the time, anyway." The clinician scarcely needed a Rorschach card to find out this motivational fact.

Still, it is probably true that most psychologists prefer to assess a person's needs and conflicts by going the long way around. The argument, of course, is that everyone, even a neurotic, will accommodate himself fairly well to the demands placed upon him by reality. Only in an unstructured projective situation will he reveal his anxieties and unmasked needs. "Projective tests," writes Stagner, "are more useful than reality situations for diagnostic purposes." [1] To my mind, this uncompromising statement seems to mark the culmination of a century-long era of irrationalism, and therefore of distrust. Has the subject no right to be believed?

Fortunately, the extensive use of projective methods at the present time is yielding results that enable us to place this technique in proper perspective and to correct the one-sided theory of motivation upon which their popularity rests.

Let us consider first the wartime research conducted with thirty-six conscientious objectors who lived for six months on a semistarvation diet.[2] Their diet was so rigorously meager that on the average they lost one quarter of their initial body weight in the course of the six months. The food need was agonizingly great, their incessant hunger most poignant. Unless occupied with laboratory or other tasks, they found themselves thinking of food almost constantly. Typical daydreaming is reported by one subject as follows: "Today we'll have Menu No. 1. Gee, that's the smallest menu, it seems. How shall I fix the potatoes? If I use my spoon to eat them, I'll be able to add more water. . . . If I eat a little faster, the food would stay warm longer—and I like it warm. But then it's gone so quickly."

Now, the curious thing is that, while these men were clearly obsessed by their food drive and all their energy seemed directed toward its fulfillment, on projective tests the need failed to appear. The investigators report that, among the tests used (free word association, first letters test, analysis of dreams, Rorschach and Rosenzweig's P-F Study), only one gave a limited evidence of the preoccupation with food—the free association test.

Here is a finding of grave significance. *The most urgent, the most absorbing motive in life failed completely to reveal itself by indirect methods.* It was, however, entirely accessible to conscious report. Part of the explanation may be that the subjects turned in relief to laboratory tasks to forget for a while their obsessive motive. They responded to the projective tests with heaven knows what available, habitual associational material. The failure of night dreams to reveal a significant amount of wish fulfillment is somewhat more perplexing. It can scarcely be ascribed to a defensive mental set. But both types of result suggest a possible law: unless a motive is repressed, it is unlikely to affect distinctly the perception of, and responses to, a projective test. It is too early to tell whether this is a valid generalization, but it is a hypothesis well worth testing.

Other studies on hunger seem to yield supporting evidence.[3] Their trend suggests that, on projective tests, the number of explicit food associations actually declines in longer periods of fasting, apparently because the motive itself gradually becomes completely conscious and is not repressed. It is true that instrumental associations (references to ways of obtaining food) continue to appear in the subject's word-responses as the state of hunger grows. This finding, however, is quite consistent with the hypothesis, since, while hunger is fully conscious, the subject in the experimental situation is prevented from seeking satisfaction and thus is still repressing his instrumental action-tendencies.

Another revealing line of evidence comes from the research of J. W. Getzels.[4] This investigator utilized two forms of a sentence completion test—one couched in the first person and one in the third. His pairs are of the following type:

When they asked Frank to be in charge he. . . .
When they asked me to be in charge I. . . .

When Joe meets a person for the first time he usually. . . .
When I meet a person for the first time I usually. . . .

In the experiment, of course, the items were randomized. In all there were twenty diagnostic items of each type. The subjects were sixty-five veterans, twenty-five diagnosed as well adjusted; forty were psychoneurotic cases discharged from service with disability involving personality disorder.

It turned out that, to a highly significant degree, the well-adjusted men gave *identical* responses to the first- and to the third-person completions. If we assume that the third-person sentence is a "projective method," then the results obtained by this method for well-adjusted subjects squared almost perfectly with the results obtained from the direct, first-person questioning. The psychoneurotics, on the other hand, to a highly significant degree varied their responses. They said one thing when queried directly (for example, "When they asked me to be in charge I agreed") and another on the projective item ("When they asked John to be in charge he was afraid"). The first-person completion is so direct that in the psychoneurotic it invokes the mask of defense and elicits a merely conventionally correct response.

Thus the direct responses of the psychoneurotic cannot be taken at their face value. The defenses are high; the true motives are hidden and are betrayed only by a projective technique. The normal subjects, on the other hand, tell you by the direct method precisely what they tell you by the projective method. They are all of a piece. You may therefore take their motivational statements at their face value, for, even if you probe, you will not find anything substantially different.

This research adds weight to the tentative judgment we formed in the case of the starving subjects. It is not the well-integrated subject, aware of his motivations, who reveals himself in projective testing. It is, rather, the neurotic personality, whose façade belies the repressed fears and hostilities within. Such a subject is caught off guard by projective devices; but the well-adjusted subject gives no significantly different response.

There is, however, one difference between the two researches. The starving subjects actually *avoided* any betrayal of their dominant motive in the projective tests. The well-adjusted veterans, on the other hand, gave essentially the *same* type of response in both direct and projective testing. It may be that the dissimilar nature of the tests used in the two situations accounts for this difference in results. But this detailed difference need not detain us here. What seems to be important is the implication of these researches that *a psycho-*

diagnostician should never employ projective methods in the study of motivation without at the same time employing direct methods. If he does not use direct methods, he will never be able to distinguish a well-integrated personality from one that is not. Nor will he be able to tell whether there are strong conscious streams of motivation that are entirely evading the projective situation (as in the case of the starving subjects).

The trend of evidence seems to indicate that a normal, well-adjusted individual with strong goal-directedness may, on projective tests, do one of two things—either give material identical with that of conscious report, in which case the projective method is not needed, or give no evidence whatever of his dominant motives. Only when the projective responses reveal emotionally laden material that is contradictory to conscious report, or to other results of direct assessment, do we find special value in projective testing. And we shall never know whether or not a neurotic situation prevails unless we use *both* diagnostic approaches and compare the yield.

Consider for a moment the diagnosis of anxiety. Using various responses on the Rorschach and TAT cards, the clinician might infer a high level of anxiety. Now, this finding taken by itself tells us little. The subject may be the sort of person who is enormously effective in life because he harnesses his anxiety to performance. He may know perfectly well that he is a harried, worried, bedeviled overachiever. Anxiety is an asset in his life, and he has enough insight to know the fact. In this case the yield by projective methods is matched by the yield from direct methods. The projective technique was not really needed, but it does no harm to use it. Again, as in our starvation cases, we might find that projective protocols reveal no anxiety, while in actuality we are dealing with a person who is as harried, worried and bedeviled as our first subject. The explanation may be, quite simply, that he effectively controls his jitters and that his large measure of control enables him to tackle the projective tests with some mental set unrelated to his anxious nature. But we may also find—and here is where projective methods have their uses—that an apparently bland and calm individual, denying all anxiety, reveals profound disturbance and fear in projective performances. It is this type of dissociated nature that projective tests help to diagnose; yet they cannot do so unless direct methods also are employed.

In speaking so frequently of direct methods, I have referred chiefly to conscious report. To ask a man his motives, however, is not the only type of direct method that we may employ. It is, however, a good one—especially to start with.

When we set out to study a person's motives, we are seeking to find out what that person is trying to do in this life—including, of course, what he is trying to avoid and what he is trying to be. I see no reason why we should not start our investigation by asking him to tell us the answers as he sees them. If the questions in this form seem too abstract, they can be recast. Particularly revealing are people's answers to the question, "What do you want to be doing five years from now?" Similar direct questions can be framed to elicit anxieties, loyalties and hostilities. Most people, I suspect, can tell what they are trying to do in this life with a high degree of validity, certainly not less on the average than the prevailing validity of projective instruments. Yet some clinicians disdain to ask direct questions.

But by direct methods I mean also to include standard pencil-and-paper measures, such as the Strong Interest Inventory and the Allport-Vernon-Lindzey Study of Values. It often happens that the yield on such instruments is not what would come from the subject's conscious report. The subject may not have known, for example, that compared with most people his pattern of values is, say, markedly theoretical and aesthetic, or far below average in economic and religious interest. Yet the final score on the Study of Values is itself merely a summation of a series of separate conscious choices that he has made in forty-five hypothetical situations. While his verbal report on the pattern as a whole may be faulty, this pattern not only squares with all his separate choices but is known on the average to have good external validity. People with certain patterns of interests as measured by the test do in fact make characteristic vocational choices and do in their daily behavior act in ways that are demonstrably consistent with the test results.

To sum up: Direct methods include the kind of report that is elicited in careful interviewing, whether it be the simple psychiatric variety, or the sort employed in vocational or personal counseling, or in non-directive interviewing. Autobiographic methods, when employed at their face value, are likewise direct. So too are the results of any kind of testing where the final scores represent a sum or pattern of a series of conscious choices on the part of the subject.[5]

The currently fashionable term *psychodynamics* is often equated explicitly with psychoanalytic theory. Projective techniques are considered psychodynamic because they are thought to tap the deepest layers of structure and functioning. We have already indicated reasons for doubting the sufficiency of this assumption. Many of the most dynamic motives are more accurately tapped by direct methods. At the very least, the discoveries by projective techniques cannot be properly interpreted unless they are compared with discoveries yielded by direct methods.

Devotees of psychodynamics often say that no discoveries are of value unless the unconscious is explored. This dictum we find in the valuable book by Kardiner and Ovesey, *The Mark of oppression*,[6] dealing with the seriously disordered and conflictful motivational systems of Negroes in a Northern city. Unless I am greatly mistaken, however, the authors discover little or nothing about their cases through psychoanalytic probes that is not evident in the manifest situation. The conscious handicaps of a Negro in our society, the economic misery, the deteriorated family situations, the bitterness and despair constitute a painful psychodynamic situation in individual lives that in most instances receives no further illumination when depth analysis is employed.

Most of the psychodynamic evidence given by Kardiner and Ovesey concerning their cases is, in fact, drawn from straightforward autobiographical report. Their use of this method is acceptable and their findings highly instructive. But their theory seems to me out of line with both the method actually used and the findings obtained. Psychodynamics is not necessarily a hidden dynamics.

This point is well made by the psychiatrist J. C. Whitehorn[7] who holds that psychodynamics is a general science of motivation. Into its broad principles one may fit the specific contributions and insights of psychoanalysis, but psychoanalysis itself is by no means the sum and substance of psychodynamics. Whitehorn insists that the proper approach to psychotic patients, especially to those suffering from schizophrenic or depressive disorder, is through such channels of their normal interest systems as remain open. It is not the region of their disorder that requires primary attention, but those psychodynamic systems that still represent sturdy and healthy adaptations to reality. In Whitehorn's words, the therapist should seek "to activate and utilize the resources of the patient and to help him thereby to work out a more satisfying way of life with a less circumscribed emphasis upon these special issues." [8]

Sometimes we hear it said that psychoanalytic theory does not do justice to psychoanalytic practice. What is meant is that, in the course of therapy, an analyst will devote much of his time to a direct discussion with his patient of his manifest interests and values. The analyst will listen respectfully, accept, counsel and advise concerning these important and *not* buried psychodynamic systems. In many instances, as in the cases presented by Kardiner and Ovesey, the motives and conflicts are taken at their face value. Thus the method of psychoanalysis as employed is not fully sustained by the theory that is affirmed.

Nothing that I have said denies the existence of infantile systems, troublesome repressions or neurotic formations. Nor does it deny the possibility of self-deception, rationalization and ego-defense. My point is merely that methods and theories dealing with these aberrant conditions should be set in a broad conception of psychodynamics. The patient should be assumed insightful until he is proved otherwise. If you asked a hundred people who go to the icebox for a snack why they did so, probably all would answer, "Because I was hungry." In ninety-nine of these cases we may—no matter how deeply we explore—discover that this simple, conscious report is the whole truth. In the hundredth case, however, our probing shows that we are dealing with a compulsive overeater, with an obese seeker after infantile security, who, unlike the majority of cases, does not know what he is trying to do. It is peace and comfort he is seeking—perhaps his mother's bosom—and not the left-over roast. In this case, and in a minority of all cases, we cannot take the evidence of his overt behavior, nor his account of it, at their face value.

Freud was a specialist in precisely those motives that cannot be taken at their face value. To him, motivation resided in the id. The conscious, accessible region of personality that carries on direct transactions with the world—that is, the ego—he regarded as devoid of dynamic power.

It is a misfortune that Freud died before he had remedied this one-sidedness in his theory. Even his most faithful followers tell us now that he left his ego-psychology incomplete. In recent years many of them have labored to redress the balance. Without doubt the principal current in psychoanalytic theory today is moving in the direction of a more dynamic ego. This trend in theory is apparent in the work of Anna Freud, Hartmann, French, Horney, Fromm, Kris and many others. In a communication to the American Psychoanalytic Association, Kris points out that the attempt to restrict interpretations of motivation to the id aspect only "represents the older procedure." Modern concern with the ego does not confine itself to an analysis of defense mechanisms alone. Rather, it gives more respect to what he calls the "psychic surface." Present psychoanalytic techniques, he tells us, tend to link "surface" with "depth." [9] In a similar vein Rapaport has argued that a measure of true autonomy must now be ascribed to the ego.[10]

To illustrate the point at issue, we might take any psychogenic interest of maturity—say, the religious sentiment. Freud's handling of the matter is well known. To him religion is essentially a neurosis in the individual, a formula for personal escape. The father image lies at the root of the matter. One cannot therefore take the religious sentiment, when it exists in a personality, at its face value. A more balanced view of the matter would seem to be this: *sometimes* one cannot take this sentiment at its face value, and *sometimes* one can. Only a careful study of the individual will tell. In a person in whom the religious factor serves an obviously egocentric purpose—talismanic, bigoted, self-justificatory—we can infer that it is a neurotic, or at least immature, formation in the personality. Its infantile and escapist character is not recognized by the subject. On the other hand, in a person who has gradually evolved a guiding philosophy of life where the religious sentiment exerts a generally normative force upon behavior and confers intelligibility to life as a whole, we infer that this particular ego-formation is a dominant motive and that it must be accepted at its face value. It is a master motive and an ego-ideal whose shape and substance are essentially what appear in consciousness.[11]

Let us consider a final example. It is well known that most boys around the age of four to seven identify with their fathers. They imitate them in many ways. Among other things, they may express vocational aspirations for daddy's job. Many boys, when grown, do in fact follow their fathers' footsteps.

Take politics. Father and son have been politicians in many families: the Tafts, Lodges, Kennedys, La Follettes and Roosevelts, to mention only a few. When the son is at a mature age, say fifty or sixty, what is his motivation? Is he working through his early father identification, or is he not? Taken at its face value, the interest of the son in politics now seems to be absorbing and self-contained, a prominent factor in his own ego-structure. In short, it seems to be a mature and normal motive. But the strict geneticist would say: "No, he is now a politician because of a father fixation." Does the geneticist mean that an early father identification started him in a political direction of interest? If so, the answer is yes, of course. All motives have their origin somewhere. Or does he mean, "This early fixation now, today, sustains the son's political conduct"? If so, the answer is normally no. The political interest is now a prominent part of the ego-structure, and the ego is the healthy man's source of energy. To be sure, there may be cases where a person mature in years is still trying to curry Father's favor, to step into his shoes, to displace him with the mother. A clinical study of a second-generation politician may conceivably show that his behavior is compulsively father-identical. If so, his daily conduct is in all probability so compulsive, so ungeared to realistic situational needs, so excessive that the diagnosis can be suspected by any skilled clinical observer. But such instances are relatively rare.

To sum up: We need in our motivational theory to make a sharper distinction between infantilisms and motivation that is strictly contemporary and at age.

I am fully aware of my heterodoxy in suggesting that there is, in a restricted sense, a discontinuity between normal and abnormal motivation, and that we need a theory that will recognize this fact. Discontinuities are distinctly unpopular in psychological science. One theory of abnormality tells us that we are merely pleased to regard the extremes on our linear continuum as abnormal. Some culture theorists insist that abnormality is a relative concept, shifting from culture to culture and from one historical period to another. Likewise, there are many borderline cases which even the most experienced clinician could not with confidence classify as normal or as abnormal. Finally —and most important—one can, by scratching deeply enough, find *some* infantilism in the motivation of many normal people.

Granted all these familiar arguments, there is still a world of difference, if not between normal and abnormal people, then between the healthy and unhealthy mechanisms involved in the development of motivation. What we call integrative action of the nervous system is basically a wholesome mechanism that keeps motivation up to date. It tends to bring about both an internal consistency and a reality testing among the elements entering into motivational patterning. Effective suppression is another healthy mechanism, harmless to the individual and making possible the arrangement of motives in an orderly hierarchy.[12] With the aid of effective suppression, the individual ceases to act out infantile dramas. Insight, a clear self-image and the little-understood factor of homeostasis may be mentioned among the balancing mechanisms.

As Getzel's experiment shows, direct and projective performances in healthy people are all of a piece. A further test of normality—unfortunately, one psychologists have not yet developed—may lie in the harmony of expressive behavior (facial expression, gestures, handwriting) with the individual's fundamental motivational structure. There is evidence that discoordination between conscious motives and expressive movement is an ominous sign.[13] This lead for research should be followed through.

In unhealthy motivation, unbalancing mechanisms have the upper hand. There is always some species of dissociation at work. The individual represses ineffectively; repressed motives erupt in autistic gestures, in tantrums, in nightmares, in compulsions, perhaps in paranoid thinking. Above all, self-knowledge is lacking in large regions of the life. But normally the balancing mechanisms have the upper hand. Sometimes, in certain badly disordered lives, the unbalancing mechanisms take over. Occasionally we find them operating in a segmental way in lives that are otherwise healthy. When the clash in mechanisms is marked, diagnosis is aided by the use of projective techniques. But, when there is essential harmony within the personality system, projective methods will teach us little or nothing about the course of motivation.

From what has been said, it is clear that a satisfactory conception of psychodynamics will have the following characteristics: (1) It will never employ projective methods or depth analysis without allowing for a full diagnosis of motives by direct methods as well. (2) It will assume that, in a healthy personality, the great bulk of motivation can be taken at its face value. (3) It will assume that normal motivation of this order has a present and future significance for the individual, which is by no means adequately represented by a study of his past life. In other words, it will allow that the present psychodynamics of a life may in large part be functionally autonomous, even though continuous with early motivational formations.[14] (4) It will, at the same time, retain the epochal insights of Freud and others to the effect that infantile fixations sometimes occur and that we do well to check on conscious report and to supplement direct methods by indirect.

Before such an adequate conceptualization can be achieved, one current dogma in motivational theory must be re-examined. I refer to the oft-encountered statement that all motives aim at "the reduction of tensions." This doctrine—found in instinctivism, psychoanalysis and stimulus-response psychology—operates to keep us on a primitive level of theorizing.

We cannot, of course, deny that basic drives seem to seek "reduction of tension." Oxygen need, hunger, thirst and elimination are clear examples. But these drives are not a trustworthy model for all normal adult motivation. Goldstein remarks that patients who seek only tension reduction are clearly pathological. They are preoccupied with segmental irritations from which they seek relief. There is nothing creative about their interests. They cannot take suffering or delay or frustration as a mere incident in their pursuit of values. Normal people, by contrast, are dominated by their "preferred patterns" of self-actualization. Their psychogenic interests are modes of sustaining and directing tension rather than escaping it.[15]

We should, I think, agree that tension reduction is not an adequate statement of the functioning of mature psychogenic motives. At the time of his inauguration as president of Harvard, James Bryant Conant remarked that he was undertaking his duties "with a heavy heart but gladly." He knew he would reduce no tensions by committing himself to the new job. Tensions would mount and mount and, at many times, become almost unbearable. While he would, in the course of his daily work, dispatch many tasks and feel relief, the over-all commitment—his total investment of energy—would never result in any equilibrium. Psychogenic interests are of this order: they lead us to complicate and strain our lives indefinitely. "Striving for equilibrium," "tension reduction" and "death wish" seem trivial and erroneous representations of normal adult motivation.

The postwar years, as I have said, brought a wholesome turn in theorizing. Few authorities on war neuroses, for example, wrote in terms of tension reduction; they spoke, rather, of "firm ego structure" or "weak ego structure." Grinker and Spiegel say, "As the ego becomes stronger the therapist demands increasing independence and activity from the patient."[16] After successful therapy, these and other writers sometimes remark, "The ego now seems in full control." In such expressions as these—and one encounters them with increasing frequency—we meet post-Freudian ego psychology again. True, the flavor of these theoretical statements varies. Sometimes they still seem close to the conception of the ego as rationalizer, rider and steersman. But often, as in the statements just quoted, they go far beyond. They imply that the ego is not only normally able to avoid malignant repression, chronicity and rigidity, but is also a differentiated dynamism —a fusion of healthy psychogenic motives that can be taken at their face value.

There is no need to take fright at the conception of an "active ego." As I see the matter, the term *ego* does not refer to a homunculus, but is merely a shorthand expression for what Goldstein calls "preferred patterns." The term means that normally healthy personalities have various systems of psychogenic motives. They are not limitless in number; indeed, in a well-integrated adult they may be adequately indicated on the fingers of two hands, perhaps one. What a person is trying to do persistently, recurrently, as a function of his own internal nature, is often surprisingly well focused and well patterned. Whether these leading motives are called desires, interests, values, traits or sentiments does not greatly matter. What is important is that motivational theory—in guiding diagnosis, therapy and research—should take these structures fully into account.

REFERENCES

1. R. Stagner, "Homeostasis as a unifying concept in personality theory," *Psychol. Rev.*, 1951, 58:5-17.

2. J. Brozek, H. Guetzkow, M. V. Baldwin and R. Cranston, "A quantitative study of perception and association in experimental semi-starvation," *J. Pers.*, 1951, 19:245-64.

3. R. Levine, I. Chein and G. Murphy, "The relation of the intensity of a need to the amount of perceptual distortion: a preliminary report," *J. Psychol.*, 1942, 13:283-93; R. N. Sanford, "The effect of abstinence from food upon imaginal processes," *J. Psychol.*, 1936, 2:129-36.

4. J. W. Getzels, "The assessment of personality and prejudice by the methods of paired direct and projective questionnaires," unpublished thesis, Harvard College Library, Cambridge, 1951.

5. For the purposes of the present argument, this simplified discussion of direct and indirect techniques is adequate. Psychodiagnosis requires, however, a much more discriminating classification of the methods currently employed and of the "levels" of organization that each normally taps. An excellent beginning is Rosenzweig's proposal that three classes of methods be distinguished, each adapted in principle to tapping three levels of behavior (S. Rosenzweig, "Levels of behavior in psychodiagnosis with special reference to the picture-frustration study," *Amer. J. Orthopsychiat.*, 1950, 20:63-72). What he calls *subjective* methods require the subject to take himself as a direct object of observation (questionnaires, autobiographies). *Objective* methods require the observer to report on overt conduct. *Projective* methods require both subject and observer to "look the other way" and to base the diagnosis on the subject's reaction to apparently "ego-neutral" material. Broadly speaking, Rosenzweig's subjective and objective procedures correspond to what I here call direct methods, and projective procedures to indirect methods.

Especially noteworthy is Rosenzweig's statement that the significance of projective methods, such as his own P-F Study, cannot be determined unless the subject's projective responses are examined in the light of his subjective and objective responses.

6. A. Kardiner and L. Ovesey, *The mark of oppression*, New York: Norton, 1951.

7. J. C. Whitehorn, "Psychodynamic considerations in the treatment of psychotic patients," *Univ. West. Ontario Med. J.*, 1950, 20:27-41.

8. *Ibid.*, p. 40.

9. E. Kris, "Ego psychology and interpretation in psychoanalytic therapy," *Psa. Quart.*, 1951, 20:15-30.

10. D. Rapaport, "The autonomy of the ego," *Bull. Menninger Clin.*, 1951, 15:113-23.

11. G. W. Allport, *The individual and his religion*, New York: Macmillan, 1950.

12. L. Belmont and H. G. Birch, "Re-individualizing the repression hypothesis," *J. Abnorm. Soc. Psychol.*, 1951, 46:226-35, D. V. McGranahan, "A critical and experimental study of repression," *J. Abnorm. Soc. Psychol.*, 1940, 35:212-25.

13. G. W. Allport and P. E. Vernon, *Studies in expressive movement*, New York: Macmillan, 1933.

14. G. W. Allport, *The nature of personality: selected papers*, Cambridge: Addison-Wesley, 1950, especially pp. 76-113.

15. K. Goldstein, *Human nature in the light of psychopathology*, Cambridge: Harvard University Press, 1940.

16. R. R. Grinker and J. P. Spiegel, *War neuroses*, Philadelphia: Blakiston, 1945, p. 94.

CHAPTER 7

What units shall we employ?

Turning from the problem of motives to the problem of structure, we ask: what are the building blocks that comprise the edifice of a given personality?

The leading historical answers to this question include such proposed units as traits, sentiments, attitudes, schemata, factors and syndromes of temperament. While each of these has certain advantages, the best solution seems to lie in identifying the unique dynamic *trends* peculiar to the structure of each individual life.

This essay was orginally part of a symposium held at Syracuse University and published under the title *Assessment of human motives* (1958).

Man's nature, like all of nature, seems to be composed of relatively stable structures. The success of psychological science, therefore, as of any science, depends in large part upon its ability to identify the major structures, substructures and microstructures (elements) of which its assigned portion of the cosmos is composed.

Early Inadequate Units

From the fourth century B.C. to the seventeenth century A.D., the life sciences—indeed, all the sciences—were badly frozen because they had chosen unproductive units of analysis: the Empedoclean elements of earth, air, fire and water. These units and these alone are the "root of things"—so said Hippocrates and Galen; so said all the sages of the Middle Ages and the Renaissance, including both Christian and Islamic scholars.[1] Personality theory, such as it was, was written entirely in terms of the four temperaments arising, men said, from the humoral distillations of the four cosmic elements: black bile (*melancholic*), yellow bile (*sanguine*), blood (*choleric*) and phlegm (*phlegmatic*). "Quatuor humores in nostro corpore regnant," sang the thirteenth-century medical poem. This rigidity of analysis endured at least until the time of Harvey, whose discovery of the circulation of the blood in 1628 cast doubt upon the whole humoral doctrine.[2]

Freed at last from this incubus, psychology perversely entered a second ice age by adopting the conception of *faculties*—units scarcely

more productive than the humors. The faculties set forth by the
Thomists, by Christian Wolff, by the Scottish school and by the
phrenologists have a certain common-sense appeal, but they do not
satisfy modern theorists.

Under the influence of Darwin, personality theorists traded
faculties for *instincts*. The ensuing era, lasting approximately sixty
years, cannot be called an ice age, for it brought with it McDougall's
elegant and consistent defense of instincts and their derivatives, the
sentiments. More than anyone else, McDougall fixed our attention
upon the possible existence of uniform motivational units. Freud
reinforced the search, though, unlike McDougall, he himself offered
no clear taxonomic scheme. During this era innumerable instincts
were discovered, postulated, invented. In 1924, Bernard reported
that more than 14,000 different instincts had been proposed and that
no agreement was yet in sight.[3]

Sensing disaster in this direction, psychologists started fishing in
fresher waters. The doctrine of *drives* (a limited form of instinct)
continued to hold the behaviorist fort, and to some extent still does,
but most psychologists nowadays seem to agree with Hebb[4] that to
equate motivational structure with simple drives or biological needs is
a wholly inadequate procedure.

Difficulties and Complexities of Contemporary Search

I mention these fragments of history in the hope that they will
give perspective to our contemporary search. It is clear that we have
not yet solved the problem of the units of man's nature, though the
problem was posed twenty-three centuries ago. It is equally clear that
psychology lags far behind chemistry, which has its periodic table of
elements; behind physics, with its verifiable, if elusive, quanta; and
even far behind biology, with its cell. Psychology does not yet know
what its "cell" may be. It is partly for this reason that skeptics question psychology's right to be called a science. Its investigators have
not yet reached agreement on what units of analysis to employ.

Some of the trouble lies in the fact that psychology could make
little use of a "cell," even if it discovered one. (It has given up the
"reflex arc," which for a time seemed to serve the purpose.) Psychology's peculiar problem lies in the existence of many different levels
of organization, whose number and nature are as yet unascertained.
Units of structure may be smaller or larger, depending on our interests. If we happen to be concerned with an elementary behavioral
problem, such as the alternate extension and flexion of the leg, we

may adopt *spinal innervation* as our unit. If we wish to classify forms of motor activity, *walking* seems a more acceptable unit. Should we be interested in interpersonal behavior, we can conceivably establish a measurable habit of *walking away from people* (thus approaching Karen Horney's conception). If our concern is with the generalized dispositions of personality, we may consider some such unit as a *trait of withdrawal*. Fine-grained or coarse-grained—units of both orders have their place. Ultimately, of course, our hope is to be able to reduce molar units to molecular and, conversely, to compound molecular units into molar.

But we are far from this goal. Even at the coarser levels of analysis, we are not in agreement on the kinds of units we seek. Shall they be habits or habit systems; needs or sentiments; vectors, factors, trends or traits? Shall they be drives or dimensions; *Anschauungen* or attitudes; regions, syndromes, personal constructs or ergs? All have been proposed and empirically defended.

The most hopeful note in the confused situation is that for the past thirty years there has been boundless zeal for both measurement and theory. By now the measured aspects of personality cannot fall far short of the 14,000 instinctive units reported by Bernard. When psychologists face up to this orgy of units, let us hope they will not fall into the state of collapse that terminated the earlier search for instincts. There seems to be no immediate danger, for one reads in the *American Psychologist*: "A Ford Foundation grant of $238,400 will enable a research team of the University of Minnesota to conduct a five year study aimed at developing a more adequate system of descriptive, diagnostic, and dynamic categories. . . . The team will work toward developing terms or systems of terms maximally descriptive of personality." [5]

I should like to discuss this bewildering topic, not because I have a secret solution for a two-thousand-year-old problem or because I am so clairvoyant that I can previse the final Minnesota results, but because I believe that our present research lacks perspective on its own efforts, and I should like to achieve a balanced view of the efforts of assessors to date. Toward the end of this essay, I shall venture one somewhat radical proposal for a shift of direction in our research.

Central Propositions for a New Approach

First, a few central propositions on which I hope we can all agree. It seems clear that the units we seek in personality and in motivation are relatively complex structures, not molecular. They lie in the upper reaches of what Hull called the habit hierarchy, and not at the level of specific habits. We do not seek cells or even cell assemblies; we do not seek reflexes, hedons, traces or quanta of endocrine discharge, or the gating processes of the nervous system. Ultimately, of course, we should like to translate complex structures into microelements and discover their neurohumoral counterparts. But at present, and for some time to come, we must be satisfied to search out the generalized units that define relatively broad forms of organization.

The second proposition may admit of equally rapid agreement. Methodologists tell us than we can never observe a motive, or a trait, or any similar unit directly. We agree. They tell us that any unit we discover is only a "hypothetical construct" or an "intervening variable." Here, too, they are right, though for my part I vote for "hypothetical construct," which, in the usage proposed by Mac-Corquodale and Meehl,[6] implies that the units we seek, though invisible, are factually existing. Methodologists tell us, furthermore, that we must have sound and repeatable operations for establishing the units we fix upon; we may not bring them into being by merely naming them, as did the addicts of instinct a generation or two ago. Again we agree. In fact, we do well to accept all the cautions and safeguards of modern methodology, save only that excess of zeal which holds all units to be fictional, existing only in the manipulations of the investigator.

A third proposition will detain us longer, for it has to do with the greatest stumbling block of all in our search for objectively existing structures. I refer to the unquestioned variability of a person's behavior from situation to situation. Motivational units discovered under laboratory conditions often seem to evaporate when the subject moves from the laboratory to his office, to his home, to his golf club. Indeed, his behavior in these familiar settings may often seem contradictory. Situational variability has led many social scientists to the conviction that any search for a consistent personality with specifiable motives and traits is doomed to failure.

Recently I attended a conference of psychologists working on the problem of the "perception of persons."[7] At this conference one heard much about perception but little about persons, the object of perception. The reason, I think, is that the participants were keenly aware of the chameleon-like changes that mark a person as he moves from situation to situation. They much preferred to study the perception-of-a-person-in-a-situation and thus evade the question of what the person is really like. Not only does the individual vary his behavior, but our perception of him is heavily affected by our subjective sets, by our degree of liking for him and by his degree of similarity to ourselves. The perceiver himself may, therefore, be the principal source of variance; the situation in which the object-person acts may be the second source of variance; and the fixed traits and motives of the object-person may be only a minor factor.

The hope for an accurate assessment of motives and traits is thus badly bedeviled by the person's variability and the perceiver's bias. It is also badly bedeviled by the uncertainty of criteria. When are we to know that our assessment is accurate and veridical? Not by comparing our assessment with ratings by others, who may be subject to both common and idiosyncratic errors. Not by the self-report of the subject, who is capable of self-deception. Not by prediction of future behavior, which will depend to a considerable extent on the situation that evokes this behavior. Not by other tests and measurement, for these too are fallible.

Situational Variables

All these objections are sound, and their combined force is today leading many investigators away from the assessment of motives and persons. One tempting escape is found in the concept of *role*. Emanuel Brown, to use one example, is no longer viewed as a single person: he is a colligation of roles. As a teacher he meets certain expectancies; as a father, others; still others as a citizen and as a Rotarian. In one of his enthusiastic moments, William James took the same way out. "A man," he says, "has as many selves as there are distinct groups of persons about whose opinion he cares." [8]

The extreme version of this situational doctrine is found in Coutu's book *Emergent Human Nature,* where the author argues that the search for traits of personality and their assessment is chimerical; that the most we can say of any person is that in a given situation he has a specific tendency to respond in a certain limited way. The only acceptable unit, therefore, according to Coutu, is the "tinsit" or "tendency-in-a-situation." [9]

Unless we can successfully refute the extreme forms of role theory and tinsit theory, and James's statement about the social self, our work should cease here and now. What is the use of assessing motivation or personality if behavior is as dependent on the situation as these theories assert? Let us see what may be said on the other side.

In the first place, some of our assessment methods have built into them a safeguard against situational variability. They explicitly vary the situation. Thus a person's disposition to be ascendant, or his aesthetic value, or his neurotic tendency is tested by a wide range of items depicting a great variety of situations commonly experienced. While some studies show that a trait measured in this way does vary, say, from the academic to the business situation, or from the athletic to the purely social, it is more common to find that the person carries with him, by and large, his typical level of anxiety, a typical amount of aesthetic interest and of ascendance, a typical aspiration level and a fairly constant degree of prejudice.

In the second place, it is obviously not true that a man has as many social selves as there are groups whose opinion he prizes. A man who is deferential, ambitious or compulsive in the office is not likely to shed these characteristics at home or on the golf course. Their intensity may vary, and their mode of expression may alter, but true Jekyll and Hyde cases are exceedingly rare. So far as roles are concerned, is it not a fact that characteristic styles run through a person's conduct even when he is playing diverse roles? Is it not also true that a person *seeks* the roles that are most congenial to his personality, avoiding others that cramp his style or put an undue strain upon his internal motivational structure?

That some persons are forced into roles they do not like we must admit, just as we must admit that a range of variation marks anyone's behavior according to the circumstances in which he finds himself. But though these factors greatly complicate our search for structures, they need not discourage us. There is too much consistency, too much dependability, too much sameness in a person's behavior to warrant the surrender of our task.

There are two steps we can take to meet this problem. We can continue to seek methods of assessment that cross over many situational boundaries. Pencil-and-paper techniques can do so more easily than experimental techniques, since the former can ask the subject about his behavior in many daily contexts. But if a technique is limited to a given experimental situation (as is the Rorschach, for example), we can at least insist that our diagnosis be confirmed by additional evidence drawn from ancillary techniques.

Elsewhere I have deplored our reliance on too limited a battery.[10] Projective tests, for example, need the supplement of direct methods, for otherwise we may obtain a picture of certain latent tendencies without ever knowing whether these are separated from or integrated with conscious interests and self-knowledge. It makes a world of difference whether anxiety, or homosexuality, or aggression is a repressed tendency or whether it is fully accepted and known. Projective devices alone would never answer this question.

Besides using multiple or wider devices to enlarge the coverage of situations, we may often need frankly to admit the limited range covered by our assessment. We can say, for example, that this college student in a series of tests at college displays such and such characteristics. Just what he will do at home or in business we cannot be sure. In another case, we might say that this patient, manifestly disturbed, shows such-and-such propensities, but that owing to his condition no wider generalization is allowable at this time.

Situationism, in short, is a serious obstacle to overcome. Diagnosticians should be more aware of the problem and strive for broader coverage in their instruments; at the same time, they should safeguard their statements about motivation by making clear the conditions covered by the battery.

But let us not join the camp of skeptics who say that an individual's personality is "a mere construct tied together with a name" —that there is nothing outer and objectively structured to be assessed. No scientist, I think, could survive for long if he heeded this siren song of doubt, for it leads to shipwreck. An astronomer spots a star. Like any good realist, he assumes that it has properties, elements and structure—all of which it is his scientific duty to search out and to study. When a botanist dissects a plant, he does not assume that he is dissecting a construct tied together by a name. It is a plant; and its structure and its functioning interest him. Similarly, the psychologist of personality wants to come as close as he can to the veridical structure of the person he studies; and he does so in spite of the extensive and troublesome situational variability, and in spite of his own errors of observation and measurement, which he tries constantly to reduce.

A theoretical task for the future is to relate the intra-individual structure to the recurrent situational patterns, which in themselves may be regarded as complex social or cultural structures. In the terms of F. H. Allport, we have to deal both with *trend structures* in the personality and with *tangential collective structures*. Between them exists some degree of *interstructurance*. Analytical research, such as that carried out by Tannenbaum and Allport,[11] should help us determine the differentials of energy in the individual's pattern of behavior that may be ascribed to internal-trend structures, on the one hand, and to tangential collective structures, on the other.

Units of Motivation and Units of Personality

We move now nearer to the heart of our subject. What is the relation between units of motivation and units of personality? I would suggest that all units of motivation are at the same time units of personality, but that not all units of personality are simultaneously units of motivation. Only a few writers have made this distinction systematically. Murray does so when he distinguishes motivational needs, or *vectors*, from the styles or manners of fulfilling needs represented by actones and verbones.[12] Similarly, McClelland distinguishes motives from traits and from schemata.[13] Traits he limits to recurrent patterns of expressive or stylistic behavior; schemata, to additional orientations, cognitive and symbolic habits, and frames of reference. To him motives alone are the dynamic or casual forces, and these he finds satisfactorily designated by the term *needs*.

We will all agree that some characteristics of personality are of a highly dynamic order, while some are of an instrumental or stylistic order. There is, for example, a distinct difference between a hate-filled complex or a driving ambition, on the one hand, and a style of urbanity or a hesitating manner, on the other. In Lewin's terms, certain regions are capable of greater tension than others. And some regions (the stylistic) are called into play only to guide the individual in the execution of more central motives. Thus a young man who is hungry for friendships goes out in the evening on a quest, but conducts himself according to his own peculiar style of timidity or confidence, reticence or garrulity. His need for affiliation and his style of seeking it are both characteristics of personality, the one being more dynamic (more motivational) than the other.

At the same time, we are not all in agreement about what constitutes a motivational unit. If we were to follow Murray, McClelland or Freud, we would put on the one side only the inferred forces called needs, instinctual energies or id impulses. On the other side we would put the schemata, traits, cathexes and features of ego-structure. The implication here is that there are raw, primary, urge-like forces that alone constitute units of motivation. It is chiefly these, of course, that the projective tests seek to assess.

But, for my part, I cannot believe that motivational units are as abstract as this procedure implies. Let me illustrate my misgiving by reference to a certain man's interests. He is, let us say, profoundly interested in politics. This simple statement tells you a great deal about his motivational structure. Is it helpful, for purposes of assessment, to dissipate this integral structure in some such analysis as follows? He has an aggressive drive, a need for externalization and a modicum of father fixation—all of which are cathected on politics; he has certain cultural schemata that he has learned, and has a habit of reading the political news in the morning paper, together with a history of reinforcement so far as civic participation is concerned. Or, to make the point simpler, shall we say that his need for aggression (which some might hold to be the ultimate motivational unit in his case) is somehow arbitrarily cathected by politics? Or shall we say—I think more accurately—that his aggression and his interest are now all of a piece? His passion for politics is one true structural fact, no matter what his past behavior history may have been. You will recognize that I am here enlisting the principle of functional autonomy.

There is no need to debate this issue now. I want merely to point out that ultimate motivational units are not limited to the unconscious urges, ergs, needs or instinctual energies favored by certain forms of psychodynamic theory; nor are they accessible solely through projective techniques, even though these are certainly legitimate tools to use in a total battery of assessment methods.

Classes of Units in Current Assessment Research

Let us ask now what classes of units we find in current assessment research. No single investigator deals with them all, for each specializes in his own pet dimensions. Our question is what picture emerges if we try to catch a glimpse of all the investigators at work at once.

The preference of many investigators for multivariate scales makes difficulty at the outset for our attempt at orderly classification. A generation ago we were content with one test for ascendance-submission, a wholly separate test for extroversion-introversion, and so on. While such single scales are still with us, our hunger for omnibus instruments has grown. Take the field of neuroticism. At first (in 1917) we had the Woodworth Personal Data Sheet, which measured one and only one alleged unit: a neurotic disposition. The Cornell Index developed by Weider in 1945 still yielded a general score for the selection or rejection of armed services personnel, but at the same time differentiated various types of neurotic maladjustment. More widely used today is the MMPI [Minnesota Multiphasic Personality Inventory], with its 550 items subdivided into 26 unitary tendencies. Most of these relate to pathological trends, but one cannot say that the units sought are conceptually uniform.

Our multiphasic instruments, our many-faceted inventories, our multiple-factor devices and our miscellaneous profiles make it hard to sort out the types of units involved. The current vogue is to assess everything all at once; but in the process, the possibility of theoretical analysis seems to suffer. I wonder whether this desire is not caused in part by the fact that the Rorschach Test at first claimed to measure "the total personality." Such an intoxicating possibility led us to give up our earlier slingshot scales and adopt the shotgun inventory.

In spite of the shotgun's scatter, let us try to classify the units sought in personality assessment. Without claiming any finality for my listing, I call attention to ten classes of units that seem to me to be widely studied today:

INTELLECTUAL CAPACITIES. This area is so large in its own right that we ordinarily segregate it from both motivation and personality assessment. I mention it here only because a complete assessment could not possibly leave it out of account. Someday, I hope, we may be able to relate intellectual functioning more intimately than we now do to motivational and personal functioning.

SYNDROMES OF TEMPERAMENT. In this group we note recent progress; one thinks of the work of Sheldon, Thurstone, Cattell, Guilford and others. Thanks to their efforts, we can now assess such units as general activity, sense of well-being, restraint, emotional stability, lability and somatotonia. One could wish for a stricter limitation of the concept of temperament than some of these investigators employ, but they deal constructively with units representing the prevailing "emotional weather" in which personalities develop.

UNCONSCIOUS MOTIVES. Without doubt the greatest interest of clinical psychologists is in units of this general class. Sometimes they are called needs (though no one insists that all needs are unconscious); often they involve dimensions with a Freudian flavor, such as anxiety, aggression, oral or anal trends and Oedipal fixation. Freudian theory holds that such deep and buried motives are somehow more real and basic than units tapped by other methods. This contention, as I have already indicated, can never be proved unless both direct methods and projective methods are used for the same variables with the same personalities.

SOCIAL ATTITUDES. Here are units of quite a different order. While they have been evolved chiefly in social psychology, they are part and parcel of any complete clinical assessment program. We want to know how our subject views the church or how he regards Russia. We want to know his liberal or conservative tendencies and his score on scales for authoritarianism, ethnocentrism, dogmatism and traditional family ideology. These last-mentioned units illustrate the inevitable arbitrariness of our classification, for, while they deal with social attitudes, they pretend to disclose deeper aspects of character structure and thus overlap with our other categories.

IDEATIONAL SCHEMATA. Growing out of the study of social attitudes, we find today considerable concern with generalized thought-forms. One may cite Klein's efforts to discover general styles, or *Anschauungen*, which cut through both motivational and cognitive functions; or Kelly's proposal to study the constructs a person employs in viewing the world around him. Witkin and others establish the syndromes of "field dependence" and "field independence." [14] Though Witkin's diagnostic method is anchored in perceptual measurement, he finds that the "field dependent" person is characterized also by anxiety, fear of his impulses, poor impulse control and a general lack of awareness of his own inner life.

INTERESTS AND VALUES. In contrast to unconscious motivational units, we find many dimensions that deal with structured motives rather than with their presumed underlying dynamics. Here we would cite measures of interest in art, farming or salesmanship; or the six Spranger units, as measured by the Allport-Vernon-Lindzey *Study of Values*. Perhaps here, too, we would locate the summary measure of masculinity-femininity, based on a potpourri of conscious choices.

EXPRESSIVE TRAITS. A number of units seem to fall halfway between motivational and stylistic dimensions. For want of a better term, we may call them *expressive*. Among these we may include dominance tendencies, extroversion, persistence and empathy, as well as sociability, self-control, criticalness, accessibility and meticulous, or "just so," trends.

STYLISTIC TRAITS. This group receives least attention, probably because psychologists regard stylistic traits as lying on the surface of personality. One might include here politeness, talkativeness, consistency, hesitancy and other measurable manners of behaving. Ultimately we may expect that these stylistic characteristics will be related to deeper structural units, but they are also measurable in their own right.

PATHOLOGICAL TRENDS. Many investigators prefer to analyze motivation and personality in familiar clinical terms. Hysteric, manic, neurotic and schizoid dispositions are the sort of units we find employed in the assessments of both normal and abnormal personalities. We have spoken of the evolution of these measures from the Woodworth PD Sheet to the MMPI. One could mention as equally illus-

trative of this group the Humm-Wadsworth Test and other derivations from the Kraepelin and Kretschmer classifications.

FACTORIAL CLUSTERS. As yet I have not referred to factors. Factorial units in part belong in the classes we have already considered.
Clearly, Thurstone's "primary mental abilities" are properly classified
under intellectual capacities. Most of the factors proposed by Guilford and Zimmerman can be located under temperament syndromes
or under expressive traits. Most of Cattell's factors can be similarly
sorted. At the same time, many of the factors that result from summarizing mathematically the data from many tests used with many
people often defy conceptual analysis in any of the preceding classes.
Thus Guilford and Zimmerman report an "unidentified" factor, called
C_2, which represents some baffling blend of impulsiveness, absent-
mindedness, emotional fluctuation, nervousness, loneliness, ease of
emotional expression and feelings of guilt.[15] When units of this sort
appear—and it happens not infrequently—one wonders what to say
about them. To me they resemble sausage meat that has failed to pass
the pure food and health inspection.

I am not saying that factorial analysis does not have its place in
the search for units. It seems to me that when factor analysts start
with a conceptually defined field, such as extroversion and introversion, they often succeed in improving for us the clarity and accessibility of dimensions. In other words, factors are better when they
follow theory than when they create it.

Factors are simply a summary principle of classification of many
measures used with (usually) many people. This property does not
suddenly endow them with new power. They are not, as some en-
thusiasts hold, "the cause of all human conduct," nor are they "source"
traits as opposed to "surface" traits, nor are they the "influence" underlying all behavior. They are neither more nor less motivational than
other units. Usually they are nothing more than empirically derived
descriptions of the average man.

In this respect, factors do not differ markedly from the other types
of units we have described. All of them presume to offer scalable
dimensions—that is to say, they are common units in respect to which
all personalities can be compared. None of them corresponds to the
cleavages that exist in any single personality, unless the single personal structure happens to be like that of the empirically derived
average man. Still, scalable dimensions are useful dimensions, and I
hope that work will continue until we reach firmer agreement concerning their number and nature.

I cannot claim that the thousands of dimensions proposed to guide our analysis of motivation and personality can all be neatly included in this tenfold scheme; but it may be helpful to our thinking.

As yet investigators have reached little or no agreement; they are not yet able to say, "These are the most useful units to employ." For the guidance of elementary students, Woodworth and Marquis, basing their classification on Cattell,[16] ventured a "List of the most clearly established primary traits": "Easy-going, intelligent, emotionally stable, dominant, placid, sensitive, trained and cultured, conscientious, adventurous, vigorous, hypersensitive, friendly." [17] But professional psychologists are not yet ready to fix upon this or any other "primary" list.

A word should be said about the intercorrelation of traits. Factor analysis in its earlier years hoped to eliminate this troublesome phenomenon by seeking factors orthogonal to one another, but even factor analysts now admit that this goal is impracticable. A certain tendency to coexist must be expected among human qualities. Of course, if correlations are very high (as they would certainly be between scales for "dominance" and "ascendance," for example, or for "depression" and "melancholy"), it would be foolish to retain separate scales for synonymous or nearly synonymous traits.

One of the most insistent intercorrelations that occur indicates a general soundness, or strength, or dependability of character structure, or the opposite syndrome. Vernon shows how this pattern—he calls it "dependability"—emerges in factorial studies.[18] The Grant Study at Harvard, working intensively with normal young men, was forced to adopt a general over-all measure of "soundness." [19] In general, it does not seem that a "halo" effect deriving from the bias of raters can account for this finding.

When such persistent intercorrelations occur between any clusters of traits, what shall we call them: types? syndromes? far-reaching dimensions? My own preference would be for *syndrome*, since the term clearly indicates coexistence among conceptually distinct variables. The term *type*, I fear, would lead us into trouble, since the term has many additional meanings.

Individual Structural Pattern

Now let us turn finally to a somewhat alarming possibility. What shall we do if the cleavages in any single life do not correspond to the empirical cleavages derived from studies of the average man? Can it be that our unending search for common units, now multiplying year by year, is a kind of nomothetic fantasy? Can it be that the structural organization of Joseph Doakes's personality is unique?

If such a possibility seems too traumatic to face, let us ask the question in a milder way. Suppose we leave our common units unmolested and apply them as seems helpful in our assessment work; what shall we do when a given case seems to be completely by-passed by the common dimensions? A. L. Baldwin, for example, discussing four nursery school children, writes that the group analysis gave reasonably accurate interpretations of the behavior of three of the four children, but the fourth was not described adequately in terms of the group factors. "Even in cases where group factors were approximately accurate, some aspects of the individual's personality were not revealed." [20]

Perhaps what we need is fewer units than we now use, but units more relevant to individual structural patterns.

To gain some preliminary insight into this matter I tried a simple pilot exercise with ninety-three students. I asked them to "think of some one individual of your own sex whom you know well," then to "describe him or her by writing in each space provided, a word, phrase, or a sentence that expresses fairly well what seems to you to be some essential characteristic of this person." The page provided eight spaces, and the students were told to "use as many spaces as you need." The term "essential characteristic" was defined as "any trait, quality, tendency, interest, etc. that you regard as of major importance to a description of the person you select."

After the student had finished with the first page, he received a second page that added two additional blank spaces for further characteristics. The question was then asked, "Do you feel the need for more than ten essential characteristics? If so, about how many more do you think you would need?" A further question asked, "Do you feel that some of the characteristics you have named are duplicates (that is, more or less synonymous), so that really fewer would have sufficed? If so, about how many in all would have been sufficient?"

Faulty though this method may be, the results are not without interest. Only 10 per cent of the subjects felt that they needed more than ten essential characteristics, and for the most part these subjects were vague regarding the total number that would be required: two said they needed an additional ten, one needed fifty, others did not know.

Ninety per cent of the students, however, found the exercise meaningful and the total of ten spaces provided fully adequate. On the average, they indicated that 7.2 essential characteristics would cover their needs, the range being from 3 to 10.

One might object that the method employed had the effect of suggesting a rather small number of essential characteristics. Perhaps this is so, though I shall in a moment cite independent supporting evidence for the proposition that a relatively small number of structural units covers the major aspects of personality.

From my point of view, the weakness of the experiment lies chiefly in the somewhat sketchy definition of "essential characteristic." Many students, though not all, were content with common trait names, such as *friendly, loyal, intelligent, dependable.* I should not expect such terms ordinarily to do justice to the peculiar coherent structure of friendliness, loyalty, intelligence or dependability that mark the life in question. Here we are confronted with the universal problem in all idiographic research: adjectives cut slices *across* people rather than *within* people. It requires more deftness with language than most of us possess to put together a phrase or sentence that will pinpoint *individual* structure. It is precisely here that the gifts of the novelist and biographer exceed those of the psychologist.

Turning for a moment to the field of biography, we find confirmation of our point in Ralph Barton Perry's definitive volumes on *The thought and character of William James.*[21] Summing up his exhaustive study of this complex and fascinating figure, Perry concludes that, in order to understand him, one must deal with eight leading "traits" or "ingredients." He first lists four "morbid" or "pathological" traits—tendencies that taken by themselves would have proved to be severe handicaps. These are hypochondria, preoccupation with "exceptional mental states," marked oscillations of mood and repugnance to the processes of exact thought. Blended with, and redeeming, these morbid trends are four "benign" traits: sensibility, vivacity, humanity and sociability. While, like the students in our exercise, Perry uses common trait names, he proceeds immediately to define them in such a way that the peculiar Jamesian flavor of each ingredient is brought to light. Clinical psychologists need some of the biographer's skill in particularizing terms. Standing alone, such terms are only hollow universals.

It seems to me that George Kelly in his *Psychology of personal constructs* is approaching the same goal from a different direction.[22] He holds that the important thing about any person is the major way in which he construes his life-experiences, including his social contacts. Hence, in order to understand a person, we should adopt what Kelly calls the "credulous approach." Through interviewing or by studying self-characterizations, perhaps with the aid of the Role Construct Repertory (REP) Test, we arrive at our diagnosis. The method yields constructs that are unique to the individual, as well as constructs he has in common with others. Further, it leads to the discovery of the unique pattern of relations among the several constructs of a given person. Speaking of widely used scaling and factoring procedures, Kelly observes that, while such methods provide a quick and sure exploitation of common constructs (applicable to all people), they prevent us from discovering new and unique constructs and fall into the additional error of assuming that the greatest commonality defines the greatest truth.

In a personal communication, Professor Kelly tells me that he is not yet prepared to say how many major constructs the average individual uses, but that sometimes an individual's responses to REP "can be condensed into one or two major dimensions with two or three rows left over as specific constructs." It is true that people with an intellectual bent often seem to produce a variety of constructs, but their large vocabulary does not entirely obscure the relative simplicity of their patterns. Kelly speaks likewise of a useful therapeutic rule of thumb: "The patient may change the topic in the middle of an interview but he rarely changes the theme." Themes are persistent and recurring. While each person may have certain specific and concrete constructs that apply to limited and special areas of experience, Kelly concludes that the clinician does not ordinarily identify more than "four of five major construct dimensions." We hope that work with the REP Test and with other quantitative clinical instruments will continue until we find a firm answer to our question.

A similar promising lead lies in the techniques of "personal cluster analysis" set forth by Alfred Baldwin.[23] Analyzing an extensive written correspondence from an elderly woman, he discovers only four or five major ideational and value-laden themes.

Another related proposal was put forward some years ago by F. H. Allport, who suggested measuring the consistency of an individual's acts in relation to his own principal life purposes or "teleonomic trends." [24] The investigator could, from previous acquaintance, hypothesize the principal themes or trends—or "constructs," or "clusters"—he expects to find in a given life. He could then by observation—with due checks for reliability—order the daily acts of the individual to these hypothesized dimensions. If we use this method systematically, we might well find, as do Perry, Kelly and Baldwin, that a handful of major structures covers the life surprisingly well, even though specific and unrelated minor trends may likewise appear.

The proverbial visitor from Mars would, I think, find it incomprehensible that so little sustained work has been done in this promising direction of individuality. He would say to the earth-bound psychologist: "Human nature on your planet is infinitely diverse. No two people are alike. While you give lip service to this proposition, you immediately discard it. What is more, people's internal structural organization—individual by individual—may be far simpler and more accessible than you think. Why not take the cleavages nature offers you and follow them through? Even granted that uniformities run through nature at its lower levels of organization (the chemical elements composing the body are identical), at the higher levels of organization where the psychologist works, the units you seek are not uniform at all. A baby, once started on the road of life, will fashion—out of his unique inheritance and special environment —nodes of accretion, foci of learning and directions of growth that become increasingly individual as the years roll along. And won't you have a good laugh at yourself when you discover this elementary fact? Then, perhaps, you'll look for your units where you ought to look for them—in each developing life."

I venture to hope we shall heed the admonition of the visitor from Mars. That we have not done so is due, of course, to the prevailing conviction that science cannot deal with individual cases at all, except as they exemplify general laws or display uniform structures. The philosophers of the Middle Ages felt the same way, their dogma being *scientia non est individuorum*. But isn't the definition of science at best an arbitrary matter—at worst, an idol of the den?

Summary

In the interest of perspective, let me summarize my principal points. The search for the units that comprise motivation and compose personality is very ancient. Not until the past generation or two has appreciable progress been made. During recent years, however, we have followed a bewildering array of approaches, many of them fresh and imaginative, and resulting in more measured aspects than anyone can conveniently compute. Broadly speaking, these uncounted thousands of nomothetic units fall into ten classes: intellectual capacities, syndromes of temperament, unconscious motives, social attitudes, ideational schemata, interests and values, expressive traits, stylistic traits, pathological trends and factorial clusters not readily classifiable in the other nine categories. Some investigators, of course, propose units that combine two or more of these classes. While I suspect there may be some overenthusiasm for certain categories (the overzealous use of projective tests for tapping unconscious motives, for example, and the over-addiction to factorial units), I would not discourage research in any of these directions.

We must accept the fact that up to now relatively little agreement has been achieved. It seems that each assessor has his own pet units and uses a pet battery of diagnostic devices. But it is too early to despair. Instead of discouragement, I hope that our present disagreement will lead to continuous and wholesome experimentation. Essential to continued progress is a firm belief in the "outer reality" of personal and motivational systems. The fact that the units we seek are invisible should not deter us. Nor should we yield to the destructive skepticism of certain extreme methodologists, who hold that the whole search is chimerical. Finally, while we must admit the variabilities of the structures we seek, which are caused by changing situations without and continual growth and change within, we should take this fact into our design and theory, and not surrender our belief that reasonably stable personal and motivational structures exist.

Such, in brief, is the present state of affairs with nomothetic assessment, as I see it. But I have argued, in addition, that we will do well to turn to the fresher possibilities that lie in improved idiographic analysis. Nor should we be deterred by preconceived ideas about what science can and cannot with propriety do. The conquerors of Mt. Everest did not allow themselves to be blocked by the sacred cows they encountered in the streets of Darjeeling. Nor should we. But perhaps the goal ahead is not so formidable as Mt. Everest. It may turn out to be only as high and as wide and as human as the personality of John Citizen, who is, after all, our old and familiar friend.

REFERENCES

1. See C. Sherrington, *Man on his nature*, 2nd ed., New York: Doubleday Anchor, 1953, Chap. 1.

2. See G. W. Allport, *Personality: a psychological interpretation*, New York: Holt, 1937, Chap. 3.

3. L. L. Bernard, *Instinct: a study in social psychology*, New York: Holt, 1924, p. 220.

4. D. O. Hebb, *The organization of behavior*, New York: Wiley, 1949.

5. *Amer. Psychol.*, 1957, 12:51.

6. K. MacCorquodale and P. E. Meehl, "On a distinction between hypothetical constructs and intervening variables," *Psychol. Rev.*, 1948, 55:95-107.

7. See R. Tagiuri and L. Petrullo (eds.), *Person perception and interpersonal behavior*, Palo Alto: Stanford University Press, 1958.

8. W. James, *Psychology: briefer course*, New York: Holt, 1910, p. 179.

9. W. Coutu, *Emergent human nature*, New York: Knopf, 1949.

10. See Chapter 6 of the present volume.

11. A. S. Tannenbaum and F. H. Allport, "Personality structure and group structure: an interpretative study of their relationship through an event-structure hypothesis," *J. Abnorm. Soc. Psychol.*, 1956, 53:272-80.

12. H. A. Murray, *et al.*, *Explorations in personality*, New York: Oxford University Press, 1938.

13. D. C. McClelland, *Personality*, New York: Dryden, 1951. See also his "Personality: an integrative view," in J. L. McCary (ed.), *Psychology of personality*, New York: Logos, 1956.

14. H. A. Witkin, H. B. Lewis, M. Hertzman, K. Machover, P. Meissner and S. Wapner, *Personality through perception*, New York: Harper, 1954.

15. J. P. Guilford and W. S. Zimmerman, "Fourteen dimensions of temperament," *Psychol. Monogr.*, 1956, No. 417.

16. R. B. Cattell, *Description and measurement of personality*, Yonkers, N.Y.: World Book, 1946.

17. R. S. Woodworth and D. G. Marquis, *Psychology*, New York: Holt, 1947.

18. P. E. Vernon, *Personality tests and assessments*, London: Methuen, 1953.

19. C. W. Heath, *What people are*, Cambridge: Harvard University Press, 1945.

20. A. L. Baldwin, "The study of individual personality by means of the intraindividual correlation," *J. Pers.*, 1946, 14:168.

21. R. B. Perry, *The thought and character of William James*, Boston: Little, Brown, 1936, Vol. II, Chaps. 90-91.

22. G. A. Kelly, *The psychology of personal constructs*, New York: Norton, 1955, I, 34.

23. A. L. Baldwin, "Personal structure analysis: a statistical method for investigating the single personality," *J. Abnorm. Soc. Psychol.*, 1942, 37:163-83.

24. F. H. Allport, "Teleonomic description in the study of personality," *Char. & Pers.*, 1937, 6:202-14.

CHAPTER 8

What is a trait of personality?

This is an early essay. It is included because it represents probably the first attempt to formulate what has come to be called "trait theory." The issues it raises are still basic to the psychology of personality.

Traits, though they may be called by various names, seem to be the "hypothetical constructs"—that is, the inescapable assumptions—in every theory that seeks to depict high-level integration of personality.

The essay was read at the Ninth International Congress of Psychology, held in New Haven in 1929, and published in the *Journal of Abnormal and Social Psychology* (1931). Later developments of trait theory will be found in *Personality: a psychological interpretation* (1937), as well as in various chapters of the present volume.

At the heart of all investigation of personality lies the puzzling problem of the nature of the unit or element that is the carrier of the distinctive behavior of a man. *Reflexes* and *habits* are too specific in reference and connote constancy rather than consistency in behavior. *Attitudes* are ill-defined and, as employed by various writers, refer to determining tendencies that range in inclusiveness from the *Aufgabe* to the *Weltanschauung*. *Dispositions* and *tendencies* are even less definitive. But *traits*, although appropriated by all manner of writers for all manner of purposes, may still be salvaged, I think, and may be limited in their reference to a certain definite conception of a generalized response-unit in which resides the distinctive quality of behavior that reflects personality. Foes as well as friends of the doctrine of traits will gain from a more consistent use of the term.

The doctrine itself has never been explicitly stated. It is my purpose, with the aid of eight criteria, to define *trait* and to state the logic and some of the evidence for the admission of this concept to good standing in psychology.

1. *A trait has more than nominal existence.* A trait may be said to have the same kind of existence that a habit of a complex order has. Habits of a complex, or higher, order have long been accepted as household facts in psychology. There is no reason to believe that the mechanism that produces such a habit (integration, *Gestaltung*

or whatever it may be) stops short of producing the more generalized habits which are here called traits of personality.

2. *A trait is more generalized than a habit.* Within a personality there are, of course, many independent habits; but there is also so much integration, organization and coherence among habits that we have no choice but to recognize great systems of interdependent habits. If the habit of brushing one's teeth can be shown, statistically or genetically, to be unrelated to the habit of dominating a tradesman, there can be no question of a common trait involving both these habits; but, if the habit of dominating a tradesman can be shown, statistically or genetically, to be related to the habit of bluffing one's way past guards, there is the presumption that a common trait of personality exists that includes these two habits. Traits may conceivably embrace anywhere from two habits to a legion of habits. In this way, there may be said to be both major, widely extensified traits and minor, less generalized traits in the same personality.

3. *A trait is dynamic, or at least determinative.* The stimulus is not the crucial determinant in behavior that expresses personality; the trait itself is decisive. Once formed, a trait seems to have the capacity of directing responses to stimuli into characteristic channels. This emphasis upon the dynamic nature of traits, ascribing to them a capacity for guiding the specific response, is variously recognized by many writers. The principle is nothing more than that which has been subscribed to in various connections by Woodworth, Prince, Sherrington, Coghill, Kurt Lewin, Troland, Lloyd Morgan, Thurstone, Bentley, Stern and others.

From this general point of view, traits might be called "derived drives" or "derived motives." Whatever they are called, they may be regarded as playing a motivating role in each act, thus endowing the separate adjustments of the individual to specific stimuli with that *adverbial* quality that is the very essence of personality.

Some psychologists may balk at the doctrine of the absorption of driving power into the integrated mechanism of traits. If so, it is equally possible, without violence to the other criteria of this essay, to accept the view that a trait is a generalized neural set, which is activated ecphorically or redintegratively. But it seems to me that this second doctrine is only slightly less dynamic than the first. The difference is simply one between trait considered as a drive aroused through the operation of a specific stimulus, and trait conceived as powerfully directive when an effective stimulus arouses the organism to action.

4. The existence of a trait may be established empirically or statistically. In order to know that a person has a habit, it is necessary to have evidence of repeated reactions of a constant type. Similarly, in order to know that an individual has a trait, it is necessary to have evidence of repeated reactions that, though not necessarily constant in type, seem none the less to be consistently a function of the same underlying determinant. If this evidence is gathered casually by mere observation of the subject or through the reading of a case-history or biography, it may be called empirical evidence.

More exactly, of course, the existence of a trait may be established with the aid of statistical techniques that determine the degree of coherence among the separate responses. Although this employment of statistical aid is highly desirable, it is not necessary to wait for such evidence before speaking of traits, any more than it would be necessary to refrain from speaking of the habit of biting finger-nails until the exact frequency of the occurrence is known. Statistical methods are at present better suited to intellective than to conative functions, and it is with the latter that we are chiefly concerned in our studies of personality.

5. Traits are only relatively independent of each other. The investigator desires, of course, to discover what the fundamental traits of personality are—that is to say, what broad trends in behavior do exist independently of one another. Actually, with the test methods and correlational procedures in use, completely independent variation is seldom found. In one study, expansion correlated with extroversion to the extent of $+.39$; ascendance with conservatism, $+.22$; humor with insight, $+.83$; and so on. This overlap may be due to several factors, the most obvious being the tendency of the organism to react in an integrated fashion: when concrete acts are observed or tested, they reflect not only the trait under examination but also, and simultaneously, other traits. Several traits may thus converge into a final common path. It seems safe, therefore, to predict that traits can never be completely isolated for study, since they never show more than a relative independence of one another.

In the instance just cited, it is doubtful whether humor and insight (provided their close relationship is verified in subsequent studies) represent distinct traits. In the future, it may be possible to agree upon a certain magnitude of correlation, below which it will be acceptable to speak of separate traits, and above which only one trait will be recognized. If only one trait is indicated, it will presumably represent a broadly generalized disposition. For example, if humor and insight cannot be established as independent traits, it will be necessary to recognize a more inclusive trait and name it, perhaps, "sense of proportion."

6. *A trait of personality, psychologically considered, is not the same as moral quality.* A trait of personality may or may not coincide with some well-defined, conventional social concept. Extroversion, ascendance, social participation and insight are free from preconceived moral significance, largely because each is a word newly coined or adapted to fit a psychological discovery. It would be ideal if we could, in this way, find our traits first and then name them. But honesty, loyalty, neatness and tact, though encrusted with social significance, *may* likewise represent true traits of personality. The danger is that, in devising scales for their measurement, we may be bound by the conventional meanings and thus be led away from the precise integration as it exists in a given individual. Where possible, it would be well for us to find our traits first and then seek devaluated terms with which to characterize our discoveries.

7. *Acts, and even habits, that are inconsistent with a trait are not proof of the nonexistence of the trait.* The objection most often considered fatal to the doctrine of traits has been illustrated as follows: "An individual may be habitually neat with respect to his person and characteristically slovenly in his handwriting or the care of his desk."

In the first place, this observation fails to state that there are cases frequently met where a constant level of neatness is maintained in all of a person's acts, giving unmistakable empirical evidence that the trait of neatness is, in some people at least, thoroughly and permanently integrated. Not everyone will show the same degree of integration in respect to a given trait. What is a major trait in one personality may be a minor trait, or even nonexistent, in another personality.

In the second place, there may be opposed integrations—that is, contradictory traits—in a single personality. The same individual may have traits *both* of neatness *and* of carelessness, of ascendance *and* of submission, although these will frequently be of unequal strength.

In the third place, there are in every personality instances of acts that are unrelated to existent traits, the product of the stimulus and the attitude of the moment. Even the characteristically neat person may become careless when he is hurrying to catch a train. But to say that not all of a person's acts reflect some higher integration is not to say that no such higher integrations exist.

8. *A trait may be viewed either in the light of the personality that contains it or in the light of its distribution in the population at large.* Each trait has both its unique and its universal aspect. In its unique aspect, the trait takes its significance entirely from the role it plays in the personality as a whole. In its universal aspect, the trait is arbitrarily isolated for study, and a comparison is made between individuals in respect to it. From this second point of view, traits merely extend the familiar field of the psychology of individual differences.

CHAPTER 9

Geneticism *versus* ego-structure

This essay brings together trait theory and motivation theory. It argues that acquired traits may become the primary motivational units in a life. The ego, thus constituted, develops a "go" of its own.

The essay (here condensed) appeared in a symposium published in the *British Journal of Psychology* (1946). It is in part a reply to Cyril Burt, who in the same *Journal* had criticized my position and defended instincts as the permanent motivational units in human personality.

Broadly speaking, British psychologists have been more partial than American psychologists to doctrines of instinct. And so, in a sense, this essay is an argumentative epistle to colleagues across the sea.

There are two ways of looking at motivation. *Geneticism* stresses the importance either of what is "given" in human nature or of early learned formations. Instinct theory, orthodox Freudianism, stimulus-response psychology are all of this type. For several decades this psychological orientation has prevailed.

The alternative view, defended in this essay, calls for emphasis on *ego-structure*.

Geneticism regards a man's motives, say, at the age of fifty, as elaborated, conditioned, sublimated or otherwise modified editions of a primary material. This material may be labeled instincts, or drives, or id (whose structure, Freud says, "never changes"). Geneticism says, in effect, that the passionate devotion of a pianist to his instrument is an elaboration of his original grasp reflex—plus, perhaps, a continuing, instinctive need for mastery.

Granted that there is a continuous evolution of manual dexterity from the digital grasp to fluent technique, one may well doubt that the energy sustaining the present musical passion has any relation to the aboriginal energy of the grasp or to the clamor of the infant for self-assertion. The subforms of the present pattern formerly served one function in the life; but the contemporary disciplined passion for music serves a wholly different function. *Historical continuity does not mean functional continuity*.

It is encouraging to note that the anachronistic fallacy in motivation theory is not now as dominant as it used to be. The past has begun to lose its appeal to many theorists and the present correspondingly to gain. Gestalt psychology illustrates the trend. To advocate "insight" and "belongingness" is to advocate current, and even momentary, dynamisms. The discovery of the motivational character of persistence in interrupted tasks, and of other closure-activities, has led to an emphasis upon the immediate situation. The field-theory of Lewin, with its topological representation, makes it almost impossible to include genetic factors in the representation of field forces. Again, a rebirth of introspective studies brought in the "feel" of motives as parts of the self. Koffka began to speak of the ego as a region of the personality having to do with states of tension and self-reference, which are so characteristic of motivated behavior.[1] Virtually nothing in the writings of Köhler, Koffka, Lewin and others of the Gestalt persuasion suggests that what we do today is a necessary product of unchanging id, eternal instincts or early conditioning. Belongingness, the field, the ego and closure are the characteristic motivational concepts.

Furthermore, a shift has definitely occurred in psychoanalysis. Currently, psychoanalysts are inclined to ascribe much more *momentum* to the ego than did Freud. I have commented elsewhere on this development.[2] Here I will only illustrate it by a quotation from Heinz Hartmann: ". . . Adaptation to reality—which includes mastery of it—proceeds to a large extent from the ego and in particular from that part of the ego which is free from conflict; and it is directed by the organised structure of ego-functions (such as intelligence, perception, etc.) which exist in their own right and have an independent effect upon the solution of conflicts."[3]

Outside psychoanalytic circles, the powerful therapeutic movement called non-directive therapy is gaining ground with a distinctly anti-genetic platform. The patient is allowed to re-structure and re-plan his life with as little or as much reference to past motives and influences as he himself feels to be relevant. It turns out that he, unlike the geneticist, is normally interested more in the future than in the past. Indeed, if we pause to think about it, any personal problem has an *effective* relation only to one's future, since it is in the future that all problems must be solved. The ego, in taking command, projects itself forward into the future and recasts its motives largely in terms of intentions and plans.

Ego-structure

Few writers on war neuroses or morale have been able to avoid using the concept of the ego. Writings dealing with theory, like those dealing with therapy, have reintroduced the very term that long ago fell into disuse. Over and over we have read of the "firm ego-structure" and the "weak ego-structure." The former, it is often said, resists fear, whether immediate or repressed; the latter succumbs to the traumatic conditions of battle.[4] Prisoners best able to resist the tortures of a concentration camp are those who have firm purposes and strong political convictions.[5]

One may ask, "Did not Freud acknowledge ego-strength in the ability of a patient to hold his impulses in check and to steer a safe course between the tyrannies of the id, the superego and the harsh environment?" He did, but he also claimed that the ego has no energy of its own. It is passive; it is the mere rider on the horse.

War studies show indisputably, I think, that, far from being a passive agent, the ego is a dynamic process of great positive power. What but a motivational structure of immense momentum could handle the fatigue, fear, anger, apathies, disgust and conflicts aroused by wartime conditions? Morale ascribed to ego-strength is not passive; it is a matter of powerful, dominant interests, capable of promoting activity so vital that lesser, segmental, impulsive activities are inhibited effectively and without serious repression.

A few passages from one of the books on psychiatric combat casualties indicate that the primary purpose of treatment is to restore normal ego-strength (that is, normal and current interests and motives) in order to offset the ravages of segmental and impulsive fears and conflicts. "As the ego becomes stronger, the therapist demands increasing independence and activity from the patient."[6]

A soldier—or civilian—is abnormal if he cannot proceed according to the lights of his ordinary, daily motivation. Horribly shocked, he becomes fearful, uncontrollably hostile or apathetic. In any case, he finds that he cannot absorb and handle the traumatic conditions. The provocation is great: "It is difficult to describe the intensity of these hostile feelings before which the ego recoils and withdraws."[7] Yet, normally, even these incredibly severe strains are handled adequately by an ego that is so firmly attached to its present projects that it refuses to regress or to split. And, even when the break comes, the physician knows there is a *norm* for each person to which he must be helped to return. After treatment, the physician writes with gratification: "The ego now seemed in full control."[8]

It is an interesting discovery that, unless the ego resumes control soon, there is special danger of malignant repression, chronicity and rigidity. In terms of theory, this finding seems to mean that the ordinary pattern of interests that comprise morale normally balances the life but that, if denied dominance for too long a time, it may yield permanently to regressive mechanisms. Hence, it was up to the war psychiatrist to "put pressure on the ego" to make it assume control as soon as possible.[9]

Is this ego-structure, which is emphasised so much during wartime, a mere matter of instincts, or of early training, or of constitutional make-up? That it may be historically conditioned by these factors no one can deny, but is it historic in essence? We have no data to show, for example, whether an optimum degree of security in early life correlates with ego-strength. We do know that wartime writers have emphasized, rather, the role of group-identification and of ideological conviction. Both make for resistance to combat neurosis. Both reflect the high importance of *contemporary* loyalty. The man who wants *now* to stand with his outfit, to support his commander, to win a victory for democracy, is the man who stands the strain. Even if it turns out that this man was also characteristically breast fed, secure within the family, father-identified or mesomorphic, the psychiatrist finds that ordinarily he cannot appeal to, or employ, these factors. He invokes only the most recent, adult, motivational structure. Childhood security may or may not be a factor in resistance to breakdowns (I suspect the correlation is low), but ideological strength and loyalty are factors of proven importance. "If the soldier could feel that the pain, the sacrifices, and death were dedicated to a larger purpose with which he was identified, his capacity to ward off anxiety would thereby increase."[10]

Functional Autonomy

Functional autonomy is merely a shorthand phrase designed to call attention to some of the considerations I have just reviewed. It marks a shift of emphasis in the theory of motivation from geneticism in its various forms to the present "go" of interests that contemporaneously initiate and sustain behavior.

It is not necessary for me to repeat the lines of evidence I have adduced.[11] They include such diverse considerations as the high correlation between skills and interests; conative perseveration, or the haunting urgency with which tasks accepted by the individual are held in mind until completed; and the obvious dynamism of sentiments which are so individual in character that they bear no ascertainable resemblance to underlying instincts. Patriotism, stamp collecting, religion are themselves the needs of a given person—often his *ultimate* needs.

In my earlier exposition, however, there was one defect, which I have tried subsequently to remedy.[12] My picture of derived motives led some readers to accuse me of allowing for a complete anarchy among motives. A motive (I seemed to be saying) might evolve, severing itself from its root-forms, and lead a wholly independent existence, devoid not only of historical ties but also of relationship to anything else in the personality. Such a loose conception is, of course, untenable. Though motives may often be (and, I argue, usually are) independent of their origins, they are obviously not independent of the contemporary ego-structure in which they are now embedded.

Let us take an example. During World War II, a fairly large number of illiterates turned up in the American draft. The men, Negro and white, were sent to special training centers where, with the aid of ingenious methods of instruction, most of them acquired within eight weeks a degree of literacy equal to that of four years of schooling.[13] They were highly motivated to learn, the chief incentives being to correspond by post with the folks at home; to avoid the shame of using an X in place of a signature when others were watching (as in signing the payroll); and to do what was expected of them. When these men left the special training unit, and especially after they were discharged from the army and returned home, these three incentives were completely eliminated. Yet many of the men, perhaps most, had acquired an interest in reading. The interest was a product of the three motives; but, since all three became demonstrably inactive, its subsequent existence must have been autonomous of these origins. The interest in reading, we conclude, brought them *new* sources of satisfaction. It played a revised role in the economy of their lives. Not only is the ego-structure somehow served by this new skill and interest; the skill and interest are now a *part* of the ego-structure itself. Literate interests now help to *constitute* the personality.

To say that some instinct must be sustaining the new literate interests is to invoke a remote abstraction. Even McDougall, I suspect, would grant that the interest in this case is merely an aspect of the generalized sentiment of self-regard. If so, his statement of the matter would be close to my assertion that the new interest now finds itself part of the essential economy of the ego. With the sentiment of self-regard, the doctrine of functional autonomy has much in common. The chief difference is that the latter sees no necessity for invoking the energies of underlying, hypothetical instincts. An ego-structure (sentiment of self-regard) is quite sufficient to keep an individual on the move. It seems to me unnecessary to seek its dynamics, as McDougall does, in the twin and abstract propensities of self-assertion and submission.[14]

Mr. Burt's Criticisms

Cyril Burt, who has criticized the theory of functional autonomy on several counts, is no doubt still unpersuaded. I hope, however, that he may find my relating of functional autonomy to ego-structure somewhat more to his liking than the earlier version of the theory he has criticized. In any case, his objections are all closely reasoned and well taken.

First: Mr. Burt starts with the evolutionary argument. "When the ape evolved into man, what freak of innumerable mutations obliterated all traces of the instinctive mechanisms, handed down throughout the ages through all our mammalian ancestors? Surely the 'higher brain centres' have been merely 'superposed' upon the lower, not suddenly inserted into their place."[15]

Phylogenetic continuity, I grant, may not be denied. The appetites of men and animals are much alike and rest on identifiable mechanisms that are closely similar. Yet these drives and these mechanisms comprise only a fraction of the vast motivational structure of human beings. Do we not know that the "superposed" higher brain centers in many ways regulate and dominate the lower? Since this is so, we have a right to expect a shift in emphasis and dominance of mechanisms, as well as phylogenetic continuity.

Second: he argues that drives are, after all, instincts and that once this is admitted, the argument is surrendered to the instinctivist. Here a serious misunderstanding exists.

Drives are primarily viscerogenic states of excess or deficit stimulation—what Woodworth calls conditions of "tissue change." Besides the obvious pressures that arise in body cavities, blood stream and autonomic organs, we may include among drives the irritation of proprioceptors and sensitivity (with a customarily adient response) to external stimulation. This equipment and the attendant initial responses, let us concede, are innate, unlearned, universal. They account for the "absolutely dependable motives" that Klineberg finds to be the possession of every individual in every culture. What is more, their physiological foundations are clearly identifiable.[16]

If instincts are defined in this way, then, of course, instincts exist. But the doctrine of instinct generally smacks more of the pull and less of the push. It stresses the innateness of the *purpose;* and most lists of instincts exceed by far the range of physiologically grounded drives or "absolutely dependable motives" that can be universally established.

Though drives are instinctive, they don't carry us far with our theory of motivation. They account well enough for the maintenance of physiological equilibrium and for initial and vague contacts with the environment. They furnish a fairly adequate picture of *infant* motivation, but a poor picture of adult motivation. Lust and the "activity drive," even hunger and elimination, are so regulated by acquired habits and sentiments that they do not for long operate as simon-pure drives but soon take their place as dynamisms in the ego-structure. The drive-force becomes fused with, and modified by, psychogenic accretions. Tastes often become inseparable from the drives.

Mr. Burt dislikes this view. He fears, to take the example of hunger, that we should "have to abandon any notion that there might be a biological purpose in eating, because there must be as many purposes in eating as there are types of objects to eat." [17] But I see no real difficulty here. We can take the purpose of eating at its face value and acknowledge that hunger and other "absolutely dependable" drives have a uniform significance for all creatures, without denying the obvious fact that differing tastes, modes and manners do affect the operation of the drive and form (from the individual's point of view) a highly integral part of the total motive.

To admit drives in the sense here defined is not to open the door to such alleged instincts as acquisitiveness, gregariousness, appeal, parental behavior, submission or self-assertion. These concepts are not in the least comparable with drives, but are abstractions from learned human behavior and ascribed without evidence to the primordial horme.

Third: my critic wonders, naturally enough, why some acquired patterns of activity and interest become autonomous and others not. Since he doubts that a satisfactory answer is forthcoming, he suggests that any adult interest is, after all, secretly fed by the springs of some instinct or other. He believes that the concept of "instinctive reinforcement" is more helpful to the teacher or therapist than the theory of "functional autonomy," for in the former case one invokes deeper dynamisms and escapes the perils of rationalization.[18]

In attempting to answer the question why some acquired motivational patterns become autonomous and others do not, I shall have to invoke the concept of ego-structure. To take an example, one individual finds that the cause of the labor movement, let us say, becomes his passion. Everything connected with the rights of the workingman takes on an urgency. Another individual, with perhaps similar upbringing, remains cool and indifferent to the issue. My first comment on this puzzling problem is that *all* theories of motivation fail to provide a full solution. Instinctive reinforcement applied to the riddle is certainly vague. Even assuming that in one case a bit of the parental instinct is inolved and in the other case not, the question of *why* this selectivity exists between two individuals remains unanswered. The conditioned reflex theory likewise finds no solution, at least so far as the *present* absorbing role of the interest in the personality is concerned. Freud might invoke in the case of the labor enthusiast a hypothetical reaction-formation—say, a repressed hatred of the father—but he would have difficulty in either proving his point or changing the man's interest when this alleged reinforcement is uncovered.

From the point of view of functional autonomy, I would approach the problem by saying that this mature interest, like all others, is now a part of the individual's style of life; it *is* his present egostructure. It brings satisfactions, not to this or that instinct, but to his total blended system of current sentiments, aspirations and intentions. It is not a channeling of the parental instinct, nor is it sublimated aggression (at least, not necessarily). It is *he*. There are, of course, genetic reasons why he evolved this particular zeal; but now the ego-structure, in its present economy, consists of a blending of this powerful motive with many others not sharply separated from it. Taken together they comprise the congruent pattern of the current ego-structure in which all dynamism resides.

Fourth: Mr. Burt worries lest, by taking motives at their face value, I open the door to all the misleading rationalizations of which every skilled psychologist is properly wary. Yes, there may be such a danger. We cannot always believe an individual's account of his own motives, for people have differing degrees of insight into their own ego-structures. What is more, in many cases there *are* infantile reasons for a current intense or obsessive interest. Undoubtedly *some* labor fanatics are merely expressing a neurosis. But without careful diagnosis we cannot tell, and there is certainly no reason to assume that *every* current interest is merely a mask for hidden instincts or early repressions.

I am inclined to believe that Mr. Burt will agree with me on this point, for he too seems impatient with the archaisms of psychoanalysis and with the everlasting recounting of stories of early life to the exclusion of a current, cross-sectional analysis of motives.[19]

Mr. Burt, I believe, is on solid ground when he says that, in individuals who have partly regressed or never risen above infantile level, one may look for the dominance of repressed innate tendencies. Whatever these genetic tendencies are, it is chiefly in neurotic or infantile personalities that they hold sway.[20] Normal people are not prisoners of the past. I would applaud Mr. Burt's concluding statement in the symposium, "Is the Doctrine of Instincts Dead?": "In studying the more normal adult the assessment of acquired interests, motives, and ideals may be far more important; here indeed, lies a field of research which, as is generally conceded, has been sadly neglected hitherto." [21]

Fifth: Mr. Burt wonders why habits-on-the-make should show so much functional autonomy, and why habits already formed recede in motivational force. He would think that the opposite condition ought to prevail.[22] My answer is that in learning a habit (driving a car, for example) the individual is distinctly *ego-involved.* He has accepted the task, and its accomplishment is important to his self-esteem. While this condition lasts, there is a peculiar urgency about acquiring the skill. When the skill is once acquired, it is relegated to the level of instrumentality and is called upon in the service of some more ego-involved motive.

Finally: Mr. Burt's sharpest shafts, like those of other critics, are reserved for my contention that an unavoidable corollary of the doctrine of functional autonomy is the resulting uniqueness of mature patterns of motives. Since this is a question of some moment, I shall devote the following section to it.

The Uniqueness of Personality

Mr. Maberly has presented persuasively the clinical point of view. He stressed the importance of evaluating any bit of behavior in the light of the individual's total motivational pattern as it exists at any given moment. Anyone who deals with personality in the concrete is likely to agree cordially with Mr. Maberly's emphasis. Mr. Burt apparently agrees with it, for he too writes of the need for obtaining a synoptic view of the individual with the aid of "imaginative insight." Yet, at the same time, Mr. Burt seems to land himself in something of a contradiction, for he affirms that it is the bounden duty of the scientist to occupy himself with *universals,* even in dealing with personality.

Let us look first at Mr. Burt's definition of personality, which I find to be excellent. For him, personality is the "entire system of relatively permanent tendencies, both physical and mental, that are distinctive of a given individual, and determine his characteristic adjustments to his material and social surroundings." [23]

Words like *distinctive* and *characteristic* should make Mr. Burt very chary of exalting universals to the extent that he does. He would have us study also the ego-sentiment, including the ego-ideal—which, he admits, is a qualitative matter and can best be "stated primarily in words." But all this evidence of Mr. Burt's sensitivity to the never-repeated patterns of personality does not quite fit with his scientific conscience, as expressed in his plans for the assessment of personality. He wants to find a small number of independent factors similar to "key-elements in chemistry." He favors the factorial approach. I doubt that he can easily reconcile this methodological preference with his own definition of personality.

Mr. Burt presents the dilemma, and his preference, in the following analogy: "Every man's face is absolutely unique; yet should we argue that the 'common' features—the eyes, the nose, the mouth— are not 'true' features at all? We may agree that a list of facial measurements would be no substitute for a photographic reproduction of an individual face in all its concrete completeness. But equally a set of portraits, however life-like, could not by themselves suffice for scientific purposes." [24]

It is true that every man has a nose, two eyes, a mouth and a chin, and that these are common and measurable features. It is also true that no method of measuring emotional expression of the face has been evolved, let alone the permanent configuration or set that *is* the person's face.

Yet, Mr. Burt insists, "psychology, as a science, deals with universals, not with particulars." I am tempted to reply—tartly, perhaps, but also justly—that as long as psychology deals only with universals and not with particulars, it won't deal with much, least of all human personality. His definition of psychology as science is far more rigid and narrow than his definition of personality. The consequence can only be that psychology as science is frankly and woefully inadequate to deal with personality, its natural subject matter. I wonder whether Mr. Burt really wants to accept this conclusion, to which he has inevitably committed himself.

Psychology, it seems to me, must be equipped to deal with the *whole* of personality, defined as Mr. Burt has defined it. What is "distinctive," what is "characteristic" must be included. The doctrine of functional autonomy helps to express the uniqueness of motives that confer distinctiveness to a person's characteristic adjustments.

Our difficulty here lies in the cultish conception of science, which bedevils most of us simply because of the incalculable prestige of those disciplines that have dealt so successfully with *inanimate* nature. If we no longer rivet our attention to their methods—so well adapted to their subject matter, but not to ours—and if we ask what the *aims* of science are, the dilemma can be resolved. Science aims to achieve powers of understanding, prediction and control above the level of unaided common sense. From this point of view it becomes apparent that only by taking adequate account of the individual's total pattern of life can we achieve the *aims* of science. Knowledge of general laws —including, let me repeat, the law of functional autonomy—quantitative assessments and correlational procedures are all helpful; but with this conceptual (nomothetic) knowledge must be blended a shrewd diagnosis of trends within an individual, an ability to transcend the isolated common variables obtained from current measuring devices and to estimate the ego-structure of the individual. Unless such idiographic (particular) knowledge is fused with nomothetic (universal) knowledge, we shall not achieve the *aims* of science, however closely we imitate the methods of the natural and mathematical sciences.[25]

Mr. Burt has earlier given a conspectus of methods and principles involved in assessing personality. The test-situations he has employed in his own original investigations are lifelike and situational. He believes that the proper manner of treating the data obtained is by correlational techniques. He advocates the use of variables that have been established by previous correlational studies, such as: a general factor of emotionality; certain bipolar dimensions, including introversion, cheerfulness, social responsiveness and their opposites; special factors or needs resembling McDougall's catalogue of instincts; and a measure of integration or consistency in the individual's life. He would then add (in order to repair the ravages of analysis) a "synoptic character sketch," which "calls quite as much for the imaginative insight of the artist as for the tabulated measurement of the scientist." [26]

I deplore his sharp separation of the "insights of the artist" and the "measurements of the scientist." Cannot a psychology of personality in the future do a better job of understanding, prediction and control by fusing these two modes of knowledge? Mr. Burt comes close to doing so himself in his matching studies. He demonstrates, as other studies have done, that the more information derived from many sources goes into a sketch, the more easily is it matched with a criterion. It is not, however, the mere array of psychometric scores that makes matching successful; it is, rather, the *patterning* of the variables that turns the trick.[27] In short, successful scientific prediction requires knowledge of the essential relations that comprise the unique ego-structure of the individual.

But how, concretely, shall we overcome the opposition between "science" and "art," and bring them into a single psychological discipline? Though the question cannot be answered fully for many, many years, I offer one illustration. Mr. Burt seeks a few "key-qualities." He thinks their discovery will enhance our powers of predicting an individual's behavior. So do I. But the key-qualities we seek must, I submit, be *personal*, not universal. Each life seems to have a limited number of themes, a handful of ascertainable values and directions—true key-qualities. In finding them, there is an opportunity for analysis and even quantification (on a strictly intra-individual level); it is not merely by "imaginative insight" that we make our study of unique and individual traits. Life-history techniques, matching, personal structure analysis (that is, the search for personal but not universal factors) and other methods are already available; others will be invented.

Exclusive reliance on factorial dimensions is not acceptable, for two reasons. *First:* the resulting factors are completely limited by the specific kinds of tests that happened to be thrown into the matrix. One cannot draw out more than one puts in. *Second:* the resulting factors are a peculiar hash of the personalities of all participants and do not necessarily represent the living ego-structure of any single participant.

In making these criticisms, I am not repudiating the use of nomothetic factors, nor of test-scales, ratings and dimensions. More of my own research and writing has been devoted to this type of approach to personality than to any other. The resulting "common traits," I find, have utility for *comparative* purposes, for approximations to the modes of adjustment that similarly constituted individuals in similarly constituted societies can be expected to acquire, and for the training of the young psychologists in respect to a common language and in the use of analytical procedures. What I argue is that, as psychologists, we must include many other procedures in our store of tools. We must acknowledge the roughness and inadequacy of our universal dimensions. Thereby shall we enhance our own ability to understand, predict and control. By learning to handle the individuality of motives and the uniqueness of personality, we shall become better scientists, not worse.

Summary

Various forms of geneticism have long dominated theories of personality. There has been an overemphasis on constitutionalism, instincts, an unchanging id and childhood habits. But, especially under the impact of the war, a desirable shift of emphasis to the contemporary motivational structure of the ego has now occurred. One theory, in line with this modern trend of emphasis, is the doctrine of functional autonomy, which holds that, while the transformation of motives from infancy onward is gradual, it is none the less genuine. Just as we learn new skills, so also we learn new motives.

A consequence of this view, disturbing to those who define science rigidly as the study of universals, is that the motivational structure of adult lives is essentially unique. Egos have infinite variety. Methods are now developing that will enable psychology to catch up with and deal more adequately with this unassailable fact. The bifurcation of scientific and clinical psychology is false and undesirable, as is an oversharp distinction between the methods of science and the methods of art.

Since Mr. Burt's views on personality are well known, I have stated my own in comparison with his. As I see it, in many respects our views are substantially identical. My definition of personality agrees with his. Together we repudiate the theory that "concatenated reflexes" constitute personality. We both wish to study the total person, and we both regard the rubrics of abnormal psychology as inadequate to the task. We agree that goal-striving is the essence of personality and that assessment is practicable and desirable. In other respects we likewise see eye to eye.

There are two chief differences. *First:* in my opinion, personality is a post-instinctive phenomenon, and reliance upon McDougallian instincts leads us into an anachronistic conception of adult motivation. Though viscerogenic drives exist throughout life (usually in an overlaid fashion), the postulation of other instincts not only seems unnecessary but fits badly with the known facts concerning the contemporaneity and individuality of the ego-structure.

Second: it seems to me improbable that a small number of uniform factors like "key-elements in chemistry" will account for the infinite variety of normal adult motivational patterns. I see more hope in the endeavor to find unique key factors (central traits) that animate an individual life. Common (that is, comparable) traits, whether called factors, dimensions or what not, have a certain utility; but they are at best rough approximations of what goes on in a given life and must be used guardedly.

Mr. Burt holds that the "scientific" study of personality demands the use of common variables exclusively. I argue that it is possible, by broadening our theory and our procedures, to avoid the sharp bifurcation of scientific and clinical psychology. Though less developed at the present time, idiographic methods of study are basically more important—and are no less "scientific"—than nomothetic methods.

REFERENCES

1. K. Koffka, *Principles of Gestalt psychology*, New York: Harcourt, Brace, 1935.

2. See Chapter 5 of the present volume.

3. H. Hartmann, "Ich-psychologie und Anpassungsproblem," *Int. J. Psycho-Anal.*, 1940, 21:214-16.

4. J. Dollard, *Fear in battle*, New Haven: Institute of Human Relations, 1943.

5. B. Bettelheim, "Individual and mass behaviour in extreme situations," *J. Abnorm. Soc. Psychol.*, 1943, 38:417-52.

6. R. R. Grinker and J. P. Spiegel, *War neuroses*, Philadelphia: Blakiston, 1945, p. 94.

7. *Ibid.*, p. 96.

8. *Ibid.*, p. 105.

9. *Ibid.*, p. 113.

10. *Ibid.*, p. 119.

11. Especially in *Personality: a psychological interpretation*, New York: Holt, 1937, Chap. 7. See also my "Motivation in personality: reply to Mr. Bertocci," *Psychol. Rev.*, 1940, 47:533-54; and Chapter 12 of the present volume.

12. "Motivation in personality: reply to Mr. Bertocci," *op. cit.*

13. P. Witty, "New evidence on the learning ability of the Negro," *J. Abnorm. Soc. Psychol.*, 1945, 40:401-4.

14. W. McDougall, *Outline of psychology*, New York: Scribner, 1923, p. 428.

15. C. Burt, *Brit. J. Educ. Psychol.*, 1943, 13:3.

16. O. Klineberg, *Social psychology*, 1940, pp. 160 f.

17. C. Burt, *op. cit.*, p. 5.

18. *Ibid.*, p. 10.

19. *Ibid.*, p. 11.

20. *Ibid.*, p. 14.

21. *Ibid.*, p. 14.

22. *Ibid.*, p. 11.

23. C. Burt, *Brit. J. Educ. Psychol.*, 1945, 15:107. In all essential features this definition is identical with my own; see G. W. Allport, *Personality: a psychological interpretation*, *op. cit.*, p. 48.

24. C. Burt, *Brit. J. Educ. Psychol.*, 1943, 13:7.

25. The point stated here so briefly I have argued more fully in the following publications: *The use of personal documents in psychological science*, New York: Social Science Research Council, 1942, Bull. 49. "The psychologist's frame of reference," *Psychol. Bull.*, 1940, 37:1-28; "Personalistic psychology as science: a reply," *Psychol. Rev.*, 1946, Vol. 54.

26. C. Burt, *Brit. J. Educ. Psychol.*, 1945, 15:110 f.

27. Cf. N. Polansky, "How shall a life-history be written?" *Char. & Pers.*, 1941, 9:188-207.

PART III: *Normative problems in personality*

CHAPTER 10

Personality: normal and abnormal

It is sometimes said that science is "value-free," that it makes no assumptions regarding good or evil. Science produces technology (including the H-bomb) and lets others worry about the ethics involved.

Whether any science can be entirely value-free is a question. One thing at least is certain: psychologists, by the nature of their profession, are persistently haunted by problems of value. Especially in the fields of therapy, guidance and consultation, a psychologist cannot escape them.

The four following chapters wrestle with common normative dilemmas confronting psychologists. In sequence, the essays attempt to answer the following questions:

What is a normal, sound, healthy personality?

By what guiding principle shall we try to resolve conflicting desires in the person and in society?

What are the requirements for a fully mature democratic personality?

Under what psychological conditions can love be maximized, hate minimized?

The present chapter is an address delivered at the Fifth Inter-American Congress of Psychology at Mexico City in December 1957. It first appeared in *The Sociological Review* (1958).

The word *norm* means "an authoritative standard," and correspondingly *normal* means abiding by such a standard. It follows that a normal personality is one whose conduct conforms to an authoritative standard, and an abnormal personality is one whose conduct does not do so.

But having said this much, we immediately discover that there are two entirely different kinds of standards that may be applied to divide the normal from the abnormal: one statistical, the other ethical. The former pertains to the average or usual, and the latter to the desirable or valuable.

These two standards are not only different but, in many ways, stand in flat contradiction to each other. It is, for example, *usual* for people to have some noxious trends in their natures, some pathology of tissues or organs, some evidences of nervousness and some self-defeating habits; but, though usual or average, such trends are not healthy. Or again, society's authoritative standard for a wholesome sex life is, if we are to accept the Kinsey Report, achieved by only a minority of American males. Here too the usual is not the desirable; what is normal in one sense is not normal in the other sense. And certainly no system of ethics in the civilized world holds up as a model for its children the ideal of becoming a merely average man. It is not the actualities, but rather the potentialities, of human nature that somehow provide us with a standard for a sound and healthy personality.

Fifty years ago this double meaning of *norm* and *normal* did not trouble psychology so much as it does today. In those days psychology was deeply involved in discovering average norms for every conceivable type of mental function. Means, modes and sigmas were in the saddle, and differential psychology was riding high. Intoxicated with the new-found beauty of the normal distribution curve, psychologists were content to declare its slender tails as the one and only sensible measure of abnormality. Departures from the mean were abnormal and for this reason slightly unsavory.

In this era there grew up the concept of "mental adjustment," and this concept held sway well into the decade of the '20s. While not all psychologists equated adjustment with average behavior, this implication was pretty generally present. It was, for example, frequently pointed out that an animal who does not adjust to the norm for his species usually dies. It was not yet pointed out that a human being who does so adjust is a bore and a mediocrity.

Now times have changed. Our concern for the improvement of average human behavior is deep, for we now seriously doubt that the merely mediocre man can survive. As social anomie spreads, as society itself becomes more and more sick, we doubt that the mediocre man will escape mental disease and delinquency, or that he will keep himself out of the clutch of dictators or succeed in preventing atomic warfare. The normal distribution curve, we see, holds out no hope of salvation. We need citizens who are in a more positive sense normal, healthy and sound. And the world needs them more urgently than it ever did before.

It is for this reason, I think, that psychologists are now seeking a fresh definition of what is normal and what is abnormal. They are asking questions concerning the *valuable*, the *right* and the *good* as they have never asked them before.

At the same time, psychologists know that, in seeking for a criterion of normality in this new sense, they are trespassing on the traditional domain of moral philosophy. They also know that, by and large, philosophers have failed to establish authoritative standards for what constitutes the sound life—the life that educators, parents and therapists should seek to mold. And so psychologists for the most part wish to pursue the search in a fresh way and, if they can, avoid the traditional traps of axiology. Let me briefly describe some recent empirical attempts to define normality and afterward attempt to evaluate the state of our efforts to date.

Naturalistic Derivations of "Normality"

Two proposals have recently been published that merit serious attention. Both are by social scientists, one a psychologist in the United States, the other a sociologist in England. Their aim is to derive a concept of normality (in the value sense) from the condition of man (in the naturalistic sense). Both seek their ethical imperatives from biology and psychology, not from value-theory directly. In short, they boldly seek the *ought*—the goal to which teachers, counselors and therapists should strive—from the *is* of human nature. Many philosophers tell us that this is an impossible undertaking. But, before we pass judgment, let us see what success they have had.

E. J. Shoben asks: what are the principal psychological differences between man and lower animals? [1] While he does not claim that his answer is complete, he centers upon two distinctively human qualities, and he makes the extra-psychological assumption that man *should* maximize those attributes that are distinctively human. The first quality is man's capacity for the use of propositional language (symbolization). From this particular superiority over animals, Shoben derives several specific guidelines for normality. With the aid of symbolic language, for example, man can delay his gratifications, holding in mind a distant goal, a remote reward, an objective to be reached perhaps only at the end of one's life, or perhaps never. With the aid of symbolic language, he can imagine a future for himself that is far better than the present. He can also develop an intricate system of social concepts that leads him to all manner of possible relations with other human beings, far exceeding the rigid symbiotic rituals of, say, the social insects.

A second distinctive human quality is related to the prolonged childhood in the human species. Dependence, basic trust, sympathy and altruism are absolutely essential to human survival, in a sense and to a degree not true for lower animals.

Bringing together these two distinctive qualities, Shoben derives his conception of normality. He calls it "a model of integrative adjustment." It follows, he says, that a sense of *personal responsibility* marks the normal man, for responsibility is a distinctive capacity derived from holding in mind a symbolic image of the future, delaying gratification and being able to strive in accordance with one's conceptions of the best principles of conduct for oneself. Similarly, *social responsibility* is normal; for all these symbolic capacities can interact with the unique factor of trust or altruism. Closely related is the criterion of *democratic social interest,* which derives from both symbolization and trust. Similarly, the *possession of ideals* and the necessity for *self-control* follow from the same naturalistic analysis. Shoben points out that a *sense of guilt* is an inevitable consequence of man's failure to live according to the distinctive human pattern, and so in our concept of normality we must include both guilt and devices for expiation.

Every psychologist who wishes to make minimum assumptions and to keep close to empirical evidence, and who inclines toward the naturalism of biological science, will appreciate and admire Shoben's efforts. Yet I imagine our philosopher friends will arise to confound us with some uncomfortable questions. Is it not a distinctively human capacity, they will ask, for a possessive mother to keep her child permanently tied to her apron strings? Does any lower animal engage in this destructive behavior? Likewise, is it not distinctively human to develop fierce in-group loyalties that lead to prejudice, contempt and war? Is it not possible that the burden of symbolization, social responsibility and guilt may lead a person to depression and suicide? Suicide, along with all the other destructive patterns I have mentioned, is distinctively human. A philosopher who raises these questions would conclude, "No, you cannot derive the *ought* from the *is* of human nature. What is distinctively human is not necessarily distinctively good."

Let us look at a second attempt to achieve a naturalistic criterion of normality. In a recent book entitled *Towards a measure of man,* Paul Halmos prefers to start with the question, "What are the minimum conditions for survival?" [2] When we know these minimum conditions, we can declare that any situations falling below this level will lead to abnormality, and tend toward death and destruction. He calls this criterion the *abnorm* and believes that we can define it, even if we cannot define normality, because people in general agree more readily on what is bad for man than on what is good for him. They agree on the bad because all mortals are subject to the basic imperative of survival.

The need for survival he breaks down into the *need for growth* and the *need for social cohesion*. These two principles are the universal conditions of all life, not merely of human life. Growth means autonomy and the process of individuation. Cohesion is the basic fact of social interdependence; it involves, at least for human beings, initial trust, heteronomy, mating and the founding of family.

Halmos believes that, by taking an inventory of conditions deleterious to growth and cohesion, we may establish the *abnorm*. As a start he mentions, first and foremost, disorders of child training. "Continued or repeated interruption of physical proximity between mother and child," he says, or "emotional rejection" of the child by the mother, is a condition that harms survival of the individual and the group. In his own terms, this first criterion of abnormality lies in a "rupture in the transmutation of cohesion into love." Most of what is abnormal he traces to failures in the principle of cohesion, so that the child becomes excessively demanding and compulsive. Here we note the similarity to such contemporary thinkers as Bowlby, Erikson and Maslow.

Halmos continues his inventory of the abnorm by accepting syndromes that psychiatrists agree upon. For instance, it is abnormal (inimical to survival) if repetition of conduct occurs irrespective of the situation and unmodified by its consequences; it is abnormal if one's accomplishments constantly fall short of one's potentialities; it is abnormal if one's psychosexual frustrations prevent both growth and cohesion.

It is well to point out that the basic functions of growth and cohesion postulated by Halmos occur time and time again in psychological writing. Bergson, Jung and Angyal are among the writers who agree that normality requires a balance between individuation and socialization, between autonomy and heteronomy. There seems to be considerable consensus in this matter. Let me quote from Werner Wolff, one of the founders of this Society whose recent death has brought sorrow to us all:

"When an individual identifies himself to an extreme degree with a group, the effect is that he loses his value. On the other hand, a complete inability to identify has the effects that the environment loses its value for the individual. In both extreme cases the dynamic relationship between individual and environment is distorted. An individual behaving in such a way is called 'neurotic.' In a normal group each member preserves his individuality but accepts his role as participator also." [3]

While there is much agreement that the normal personality must strike a serviceable balance between growth as an individual and cohesion with society, we do not yet have a clear criterion for determining when these factors are in serviceable balance and when they are not. Philosophers, I fear, would shake their heads at Halmos. They would ask, "How do you know that survival is a good thing?" And, "Why should all people enjoy equal rights to the benefits of growth and cohesion?" And, "How are we to define the optimum balance between cohesion and growth within the single personality?"

Halmos himself worries especially about the relation between abnormality and creativity. It was Nietzsche who declared, "I say unto you: a man must have chaos yet within him to be able to give birth to a dancing star." Have not many meritorious works of music, literature and even of science drawn their inspiration not from balance but from some kind of psychic chaos? Here, I think, Halmos gives the right answer. He says in effect that creativity and normality are not identical values. On the whole, the normal person will be creative; but if valuable creations come likewise from people who are slipping away from the norm of survival, this fact can only be accepted and valued on the scale of creativity, not properly on the scale of normality.

Imbalance and Growth

In this day of existentialism, I sense that psychologists are becoming less and less content with the concept of adjustment and, correspondingly, with the concepts of "tension reduction," "restoration of equilibrium" and "homeostasis." We wonder if a man who enjoys these beatific conditions is truly human. Growth, we know, is due not to homeostasis but to a kind of "transistasis." And cohesion is a matter of keeping our human relationships moving, not in mere stationary equilibrium. Stability cannot be a criterion of normality, for stability brings evolution to a standstill, negating both growth and cohesion. Freud once wrote to Fliess that he finds "moderate misery necessary for intensive work."

A research inspired by Carl Rogers is interesting in this connection. One series of patients manifested before treatment a zero correlation between their self-image and their ideal self-image. Following treatment the correlation was +.34—not high, but approaching the coefficient of +.58 that marked a healthy, untreated group.

Apparently this magnitude of correlation is a measure of the satisfaction or dissatisfaction that normal people have with their own personalities.[4] A zero correlation between self and ideal-self is too low for normality; it leads to such anguish that the sufferer seeks therapy. At the same time, normal people are by no means perfectly adjusted to themselves. There is always a wholesome gap between self and ideal-self, between present existence and aspiration. On the other hand, too high a satisfaction indicates pathology. The highest coefficient obtained, +.90, was from an individual clearly pathological. Perfect correlations we might expect only from smug psychotics, particularly paranoid schizophrenics.

And so, whatever our definition of normality turns out to be, it must allow for serviceable imbalances within personality, and between person and society.

Approaches to Soundness

The work of Barron illustrates an approach dear to the psychologist's heart. He lets others establish the criterion of normality—or, as he calls it, *soundness*—and then proceeds to find out what "sound" men are like. Teachers of graduate students in the University of California nominated a large number of men whom they considered sound, and some of the opposite trend. From testing and experimenting with these men, whose identities were unknown to the investigators, certain significant differences appeared.[5] For one thing, the sounder men had more realistic perceptions; they were not thrown off by distortions or by surrounding context in the sensory field. Further, on check lists they stood high on such traits as integrated pursuit of goals, persistence, adaptability and good nature. On the Minnesota Multiphasic Personality Inventory they were high in equanimity, self-confidence, objectivity and virility. Their self-insight was superior, as was their physical health. Finally, they came from homes where there was little or no affective rupture—a finding that confirms Halmos' predictions.

Most authors do not have the benefit of professorial consensus on soundness. They simply set forth in a didactic manner the attributes of normality, or health, or soundness, or maturity, or productivity, as they see them. Innumerable descriptive lists result. Perhaps the simplest of these is Freud's: he says the healthy person will be able to "love" and to "work." One of the most elaborate is Maslow's schedule of qualities, which includes, among others: an efficient perception of reality, philosophical humor, spontaneity, detachment and an acceptance of self and others. Such lists are not altogether arbitrary, since their authors base them either on a wide clinical experience, as did Freud, or on a deliberate analysis of case materials, as did Maslow.[6]

So many lists of this type are now available that a new kind of approach is possible—namely, the combining of these insightful inventories. From time to time I have assigned this task to my students, and while all manner of groupings and re-groupings result, there are recurrent themes that appear in nearly all inventories. If I were to attempt the assignment myself, I should probably start with my own list of three criteria, published twenty years ago, but I would now expand it.[7]

The three criteria I originally listed were:

Ego-extension—the capacity to take an interest in more than one's body and one's material possessions. The criterion covers, I think, the attributes that Fromm ascribes to the productive man.

Self-objectification, which includes the ability to relate the feeling tone of the present experience to that of a past experience, provided the latter does in fact determine the quality of the former. Self-objectification also includes humor, which tells us that our total horizon of life is too wide to be compressed into our present rigidities.

Unifying philosophy of life, which may or may not be religious, but in any event has to be a frame of meaning and of responsibility into which life's major activities fit.

To this inventory I now would add:

The capacity for a warm, profound relating of one's self to others, which may, if one likes, be called "extroversion of the libido" or *Gemeinschaftsgefühl*.

The possession of realistic skills, abilities and perceptions with which to cope with the practical problems of life.

A compassionate regard for all living creatures, which includes respect for individual persons and a disposition to participate in common activities that will improve the human lot.

I am aware that psychoanalysts are partial to the criterion of "ego-strength": a normal person has a strong ego, an abnormal person a weak ego. But I find this phrase ill defined and suggest that my somewhat more detailed criteria succeed better in specifying what we mean by ego-strength.

The weakness of all inventories, including my own, is that the philosopher's persistent questions are still unanswered. How does the psychologist know that these qualities comprise normality, that they are good and that all people should have them? Before I attempt to give a partial answer to our irritating philosopher friend, let me call attention to one additional psychological approach.

Continuity of Symptom and Discontinuity of Process

I refer to a fresh analysis of the problem of continuity-discontinuity. Is abnormality merely an exaggerated normal condition? Is there an unbroken continuity between health and disease? Certainly Freud thought so. He evolved his system primarily as a theory of neurosis, but he and his followers came to regard his formulations as a universally valid science of psychology. Whether one is normal or abnormal depends on the degree to which one can manage his relationships successfully. Furthermore, the earlier enthusiasm of psychologists for the normal distribution curve helped to entrench the theory of continuity. The strongest empirical evidence in favor of this view is the occurrence of borderline cases. Descriptively there is certainly a continuum: we encounter mild neurotics, borderline schizophrenics, hypomanics and personalities that are paranoid, cycloid, epileptoid. If scales and tests are employed, there are no gaps; scores are continuously distributed.

But—and let me insist on this point—this continuum pertains only to symptoms, to appearances. The *processes,* or mechanisms, underlying these appearances are not continuous. There is, for example, a polar difference between confronting the world and its problems (which is an intrinsically wholesome thing to do) and escaping and withdrawing from the world (which is an intrinsically unwholesome thing to do). Extreme withdrawal and escape constitute psychosis. But, you may ask, do not we all do some escaping? Yes, we do; and what is more, escapism may not only provide recreation but also have a certain constructive utility, as it has in mild daydreaming. The process of escape can be harmless, however, only if the *dominant* process is confrontation. Left to itself, escapism spells disaster. In the psychotic, this process has the upper hand; in the normal person, confrontation has the upper hand.

Following this line of reasoning we can list other processes that intrinsically generate abnormality, and those that generate normality. The first list deals with catabolic functions. I would mention:

> Escape or withdrawal (including fantasy)
> Repression or dissociation
> Other "ego-defenses," including rationalization, reaction
> formation, projection and displacement

Impulsivity (uncontrolled)
Restriction of thinking to concrete level
Fixation of personality at a juvenile level
All forms of rigidification

The list is not complete, but the processes in question are intrinsically catabolic. They are as much so as are the disease mechanisms responsible for diabetes, tuberculosis, hyperthyroidism or cancer. A person suffering only a small dose of these mechanisms may appear to be normal, but only if the *anabolic* mechanisms predominate. Among the latter I would list:

Confrontation (or, if you prefer, reality testing)
Availability of knowledge to consciousness
Self-insight, with its attendant humor
Integrative action of the nervous system
Ability to think abstractly
Continuous individuation (without arrested or fixated development)
Functional autonomy of motives
Frustration tolerance

I realize that what I have called processes, or mechanisms, are not in all cases logically parallel. But they serve to make my point—that normality depends on the dominance of one set of principles, abnormality upon the dominance of another. The fact that all normal people are occasionally afflicted with catabolic processes does not alter the point. The normal life is marked by a preponderance of the anabolic functions, the abnormal by a preponderance of the catabolic.

Conclusion

And now, is it possible to gather together all these divergent threads and to reach some position tenable for psychology today? Let us try to do so.

First, I think, we should make a deep obeisance in the direction of moral philosophy and gracefully concede that psychology by itself cannot solve the problem of normality. No psychologist has succeeded in telling us why man ought to seek good health rather than ill, or why normality should be our goal for all men, and not just for some. Nor can psychologists account for the fact that meritorious creativity may be of value even if the creator himself is by all tests an abnormal person. These and a variety of other conundrums lie beyond the competence of psychology to solve. That moral philosophers have not agreed among themselves upon solutions is also true, but we gladly grant them freedom and encouragement to continue their efforts.

At the same time, the lines of research and analysis I have here reviewed are vitally related to the philosopher's quest. After all, it is the psychologists who deal directly with personalities in the clinic and laboratories, in schools and industry. It is they who gather the facts concerning normality and abnormality, and try to weave them into their own normative speculations. A fact and a moral imperative are more closely interlocked than traditional writers on ethics may think. Among the facts that psychology can offer are the following:

Investigations have told us much concerning the nature of human needs and motives, both conscious and unconscious. A grouping of these needs into the broad categories of growth and cohesion is helpful. Much is known concerning the pathologies that result from frustration and imbalance of these needs. It would be absurd for moral philosophers to write imperatives in total disregard of this evidence.

We know much about childhood conditions that predispose toward delinquency, prejudice and mental disorder. A moralist might do well to cast his imperatives in terms of standards for child training. I can suggest, for example, that the abstract imperative *respect for persons* should be tested and formulated from the point of view of child training.

By virtue of comparative work on men and animals, we know much about the motives common to both—but also, as Shoben has shown, about the qualities that are distinctively human. Let the philosophers give due weight to this work.

While I have not yet mentioned the matter, psychology, in cooperation with cultural anthropology, has a fairly clear picture today of the role of culture in defining and producing abnormality. We know the incidence of psychosis and neurosis in various populations; we know what conditions are labeled abnormal in some cultures but regarded as normal in others. We also know, with some accuracy, those conditions that are considered abnormal in all cultures. These facts are highly relevant to the deliberations of the moral philosopher.

Following the lead of Halmos, we may say that biologists, psychologists and sociologists know much about the conditions of individual and group survival. While these facts in themselves do not tell us why we *should* survive, they provide specifications for the philosopher who thinks he can answer this riddle.

Still more important, I think, is the empirical work on consensus that is now available. We have noted Barron's method of determining the attributes of men judged to be "sound" as distinguished from those of men judged to be "unsound." While the philosopher is not likely to accept the vote of university professors as an adequate definition of soundness, he might do well to heed opinions other than his own.

Another type of consensus is obtained from the inventories prepared by insightful writers. These authors have tried, according to their best ability, to summarize as they see them the requirements of normality (or health, or maturity). They do so on the grounds of extensive experience. As we survey these inventories, we are struck both by their verbal differences and by an underlying congruence of meaning that no one has yet succeeded fully in articulating. Here again, the philosopher may balk at accepting consensus; yet he would do well to check his own private reasoning against the conclusions of others no less competent—and probably more clinically experienced —than he.

He would also do well, I think, to explore the goals of psychotherapy as stated or implied in leading therapeutic systems. If he were to comb the writings of behavioristic therapists, for example, he might reasonably conclude that *efficiency* (the ability to cope with problems) is their principal goal. Those who advocate non-directive therapy clearly prize the goal of *growth*. The desideratum for Goldstein, Maslow and Jung is *self-actualization;* for Fromm, *productivity;* for Frankl and the logotherapists, *meaningfulness* and *responsibility.* Each therapist seems to have in mind a preponderant emphasis, which, in terms of value theory, constitutes for him a definition of the good way of life and of health for the personality. While the emphases differ and the labels vary, there seems to be a confluence of these criteria. Taken together, they remind us of the tributaries to a vast river system, none the less unified for all its variety of source and shape. This confluence is a factor that no moralist can afford to overlook.

Finally, the distinction between the anabolic and catabolic processes in the formation of personality represents a fact of importance. Instead of judging merely the end-product of action, the moralist might do well to focus his attention upon the processes by which various ends are achieved. Conceivably the moral law could be written in terms of strengthening anabolic functions in oneself and in others, while fighting against catabolic functions.

It is true that the preferred method of moral philosophy is to work "from the top down." Apriorism and reason are the legitimate tools of philosophy. Up to now, this method has yielded a wide array of moral imperatives, including the following: So act that the maxim of thy action can become a universal law. Be a respecter of persons. Seek to reduce your desires. Harmonize your interests with the interests of others. Thou art nothing; thy folk is everything. And thou shalt love the Lord thy God with all thy heart, and with all thy soul, and with all thy mind . . . and thy neighbor as thyself.

We have no wish to impede this approach from above, for we dare not block the intuitive and rational springs of ethical theory. But—and this is my point of chief insistence—each of these moral imperatives, and all others that have been or will be devised, can and should be tested and specified with reference to the various forms of psychological analysis that I have here reviewed. By submitting each imperative to psychological scrutiny, we can tell whether men are likely to comprehend the principle offered; whether and in what sense it is within their capacity to follow it; and what the long-run consequences are likely to be. We will also learn whether there is agreement among men in general, and among therapists and other meliorists, that the imperative is indeed good.

One final word. My discussion of the problem of normality and abnormality has, in a sense, yielded only a niggardly solution. I have said, in effect, that the criterion we seek has not yet been discovered, nor is it likely to be discovered by psychologists working alone, nor by philosophers working alone. The cooperation of both is needed. Fortunately, psychologists are now beginning to ask philosophical questions, and philosophers are beginning to ask psychological questions. Working together, they may ultimately formulate the problem aright—and conceivably solve it.

In the meantime, the work I have reviewed in this essay represents a high level of sophistication, far higher than that which prevailed a short generation ago. Psychologists who, in their teaching and counseling, follow the lines now laid down will not go far wrong in guiding personalities toward normality.

REFERENCES

1. E. J. Shoben, Jr., "Toward a concept of the normal personality," *Amer. Psychologist*, 1957, 12:183-89.
2. P. Halmos, *Towards a measure of man: the frontiers of normal adjustment*, London: Routledge & Kegan Paul, 1957.
3. W. Wolff, *The threshold of the abnormal*, New York: Hermitage House, 1950, pp. 131 f.
4. Cited by C. Hall and G. Lindzey, *Theories of personality*, New York: John Wiley, 1957, pp. 492-96.
5. F. Barron, *Personal soundness in university graduate students* (Publications of Personnel Assessment Research, No. 1), Berkeley: California University Press, 1954.
6. A. H. Maslow, *Motivation and personality*, New York: Harper, 1954, Chap. 12.
7. G. W. Allport, *Personality: a psychological interpretation*, New York: Holt, 1937, Chap. 8.

CHAPTER 11

Circles of interest and the resolution of conflict

Under the leadership of Pitirim A. Sorokin, a group of scientists held a symposium at the Massachusetts Institute of Technology in the fall of 1957. Their essays dealt with the relationship between various sciences and the realm of values.

The following essay was prepared for this occasion and makes a brief reference to others in the symposium.

Modern psychological research supports the principle of "maximum inclusion of interests," which is the subject of this essay. The principle has been championed by many philosophers from antiquity to the present day; and investigations conducted in industry, in the classroom, in therapy—in all settings where conflict is studied—give empirical support to this central ethical imperative.

The essay was first published in *New knowledge in human values*, edited by Abraham H. Maslow, under the title "Normative compatibility in the light of social science" (1959).

Several distinguished scientists have made the point that, although moral values cannot be derived from natural data or from science, they can in some sense be validated (confirmed or disconfirmed) by the activity of science. This point has been made by both natural scientists and social scientists. I find myself in full agreement.

Likewise, I agree with Maslow when he says that the validating capacity of social science is still somewhat feeble. Its data and methods are coarse and imprecise. One critic complained that "social science is nothing but journalism without a date line." However that may be, I offer this essay in support of the proposition that modern social science, for all its imperfections, can now aid us in selecting from among the moral imperatives prescribed by various philosophers as guides to social policy. It can do so by helping us test broad types of ethical theory in the light of our modern knowledge of human nature and human collectivities.

By way of illustration, and without offering detailed evidence at this time, let me mention some of the broad types of ethical theory that seem to fare badly when they are exposed to social-scientific analysis:

Theories of renunciation or asceticism, to give one example, make the error of assuming that men seek a life that is one-sided rather than one that is full and abundant. According to this view, morality is largely a matter of repression or negation—a denial of much or most of man's endowment for growth. We cannot, of course, deny that this path of life, with its implied beatific vision, may be well suited for a few; but it is doomed to failure if it is prescribed for the masses of mankind.

Authoritarian morality, of which we have seen much in our day, defines goodness merely in terms of obedience. The adult, with all his potentialities for growth, is kept at the childhood level. While it is easy for many people to adopt the authoritarian code in order to "escape from freedom," the result, we know, is stultification, tyranny and war—and thus the destruction of virtually all values.

Legalistic theories prescribe morality in terms of "thou shalts" or "thou shalt nots." The psychological error here is that the letter of the law, being inflexible, does not guide men in the novel and changing encounters of daily life.

Utopian theories are inept, not because they counsel perfection—all morality does that—but because they plot no pathway from today's quandaries to the ultimate beatitude they depict.

Utilitarian ethics—in fact every version of *hedonism*—fixes men's minds on a will-o'-the-wisp. Happiness can never be a tangible goal; it can only be a by-product of otherwise motivated activity. We may add that, in the mid-nineteenth century, ethical hedonism (*laissez faire*) was given an explicit trial in the social policies of Britain and America, where it succeeded in creating moral dilemmas, not in solving them. Its failure was experimentally demonstrated, much as the failure of authoritarian morality has been demonstrated in our own day.

With these negative examples before us, we may ask: what type of ethical theory does social science find most congruent with recent researches on human nature and on human aggregates?

Before answering this question, let us remind ourselves that all theories of moral conduct have one primary purpose: they set before us some appropriate formula for handling conflict—conflict between warring interests in one individual, or conflict among individuals. In testing rival ethical theories, therefore, it is necessary to know a good deal about the interests of men—about the motives that are likely to come into conflict within the individual or between persons or groups of persons.

Desires Versus Demands

While our present interest is in validatable moral theory, not in motivation, let me refer to one relevant finding concerning motivation, which comes from industrial research. Summarizing a number of studies of motivation and morale in industry, Likert concludes that workers have, in effect, two primary sets of interests. They want *ego-recognition*—a broad motivational category that includes credit for work done, economic security, praise and many other means of building self-esteem. But they also, and no less urgently, want *affiliation with the group*—a dimension that includes pleasant relations with the foreman, a sense of participation in teamwork and, above all, the satisfaction of conducting themselves in terms of the values and normative expectations prevailing within the group of co-workers.[1]

The point is important. In industry, and probably in any form of human association, men wish to preserve their self-esteem—their self-love—and simultaneously wish to have warm, affiliative relations with their fellows. No one seems initially to want to hate. Hatred grows up as a consequence of blocked self-esteem and blocked affection.

It has been further discovered that high production, high morale and successful relations can be achieved only when formulae are discovered that permit the adequate expression of these two sets of interests on the part of all participants. The movement called human relations in industry teaches this lesson over and over again —in terms of labor-management councils, group decision, the retraining of foremen and basic changes in managerial philosophy.[2] In former days industry ran almost entirely on the basis of punishment—or, we may say, subtraction. Workers were asked to give up their identity, their pride, their social impulses during the hours they were earning a living. Today, the saying is, "The whole man goes to work." Realizing this fact, certain industries now have counselors on personal and family problems. Through improved communication the individual is given a means of participating in his own destiny. His private life and his work life are integrated; the interests of management and employees come together to a greater degree than formerly. I am not saying that utopia is achieved in industry, but only that experimentation has already gone far enough to demonstrate the validity of ethical theory that advocates the resolution of conflict through the harmonious integration of interests.

This approach to morality does not aim at the reconciling of conflicting *demands*. Demands are usually nothing more than ways and means prematurely conceived to be the only channels for the realization of desires. All theories of the enlargement of interests stress the distinction between demands and desires—that is to say, between instrumental and intrinsic values—and insist that the moral individual himself must at every step distinguish between his demands and his desires. E. B. Holt calls the process *discrimination;* Ralph Barton Perry calls it *reflection.*[3]

To illustrate the distinction; let us borrow a classic incident from Mary Follett.[4] It seems that, in a certain part of Vermont, dairy farmers who lived up the hill from the railway station and those who lived down the hill from the station both claimed the right to unload their milk supply first at the platform. Their demands were irreconcilable, and for a long time a feud prevailed. Finally they perceived their error. Their root-desire was not, as they thought, to unload first. This was a demand. The underlying desire of each faction was that it not be kept waiting. Profiting from this discriminative insight, they joined forces on a Saturday afternoon and lengthened the railway platform. Thereafter they were both able to unload "first."

Although the illustration may seem a bit pat, it does contain the paradigm for moral action: Two or more conflicting sets of apparent purposes collide. They are analyzed reflectively and so purged of preconceived ways and means. The root-desires themselves are then brought to fulfillment through the invention of a larger framework, which renders them compatible. In Weisskopf's term, a *union upward* is achieved.

The Principle of Enlargement of Interests

Wartime research is filled with examples of our principle. Let me cite one study, drawn from Stouffer's investigation of the American soldier.[5] Men in combat, we should expect, would show the maximum of destructive, self-preserving motivation. A number of them were asked, "When the going was tough, how much were you helped by thoughts of hatred for the enemy?" Roughly a third said such thoughts "helped a lot." But when they were asked, "When the going was tough, how much did it help you to think that you couldn't let the other men down?" approximately two-thirds said that it "helped a lot." Thus the affiliative motive, even under extreme stress, seems to hold twice as many men to their task as does the motive of hate. The point to note is that an enlargement of interest systems to include one's comrades is, even in the time of physical combat, a natural bent of man.

Successful psychotherapy offers a basic illustration of the principle. The most elementary formula for encouraging a patient is to assure him that "lots of people suffer from your difficulty." Most patients brighten when they know that they are not alone in their misery. Such assurance does not, of course, solve the patient's problem, but even this imaginative integration of interests proves helpful. True neuroses, we know, are best defined as stubborn self-centeredness. No therapist can cure a phobia, obsession, prejudice or hostility by subtraction. He can assist the patient to achieve a value-system and outlook that will blanket or absorb the troublesome factor.

The successful resolution of *social conflict* proceeds always along the same lines. Take the issue of desegregation, a problem of the first magnitude not only in this country but in the world at large. On the social level, it is a matter of bringing resistant provincial interests in line with more inclusive national and world values. On the personal level, it is a problem of enlarging the outlook of individuals who live now according to an exclusionist formula that secures for them self-esteem at the expense of dark-skinned people. At present, these individuals are willing to form no inclusive unit with the federal majority in this country or with the world majority; nor will they form inclusive units with the Negro minority in their midst. They are not able even to resolve the moral dilemma in their own breasts. In all directions the principle of inclusion fails.

At the moment this particular problem is most acute in the United States and in South Africa. Although I have not the space to diagnose the situation in detail, let me say briefly that, so far as South Africa is concerned, the chief blunder of the Nationalist Party government, morally and politically, lies in its failure to consult with the Bantu peoples concerning their own destiny. The master group *tells* the servant group, who outnumber the masters three to one, that they have nothing to contribute to the life of the multiracial society except manual labor. Thus cultural pride, love of homeland and all other normal human aspirations and abilities of the Bantus are excluded from the existing matrix of values. The policy of *apartheid* extends to housing, transportation, schools, public assemblies, recreation and politics, so that there is no legal opportunity to become acquainted. And, needless to say, the precondition of all normative compatibility is communication.

Both South Africa and the United States are exciting test cases for social science at the present time, the one following officially a policy of *excluding* interests, the other an official policy of *inclusion*. The world is watching the outcome.

We could pile up evidence from areas of conflict I have not yet touched upon—from family, classroom, neighborhood, municipality and deliberative assemblies. But I shall limit myself to one question that cuts across all these areas: how far is it possible for people, especially for children, to learn the moral principle of discrimination and inclusion?

The Process of Enlargement in Childhood

A study by Piaget and his associates is enlightening.[6] These investigators find that children around six and seven years of age, living in the city of Geneva, are unable to think of themselves as *both* Genevese and Swiss. Given a crayon and asked to draw two circles, one for Geneva and one for Switzerland, they ordinarily draw the circles side by side. They insist that if they are Genevese, they cannot simultaneously be Swiss. As for foreign lands, the children suffer from even greater cognitive impoverishment. Concerning Italy they know only that their father visited Italy, or that an aunt comes from there. Even loyalty to the homeland does not yet exist. The child's affective reactions are wholly egocentric: "I like Lausanne because I ate chocolate there." "I like Bern because my uncle lives there." In Piaget's term, these children have not yet commenced the process of "decentering" from the unit of self to any larger social unit.

Ages eight and nine are transitional. Although the child draws a circle for Geneva properly inside the circle for Switzerland, he still has difficulty translating spatial enclosure into terms of social enclosure. He may say, for example, "I'm Swiss now, so I can't be Genevese any longer." True, the concept of the homeland is gradually growing, but in a self-centered way. The child says, "I like Switzerland because I was born there." As for foreign lands, he knows of their existence but commonly views them with scorn. The French are dirty; the Americans want war; and people living in other lands all wish, of course, that they were Swiss. The child at this age has taken bits of conversation from his home and school and fitted them to this own affective self-centeredness.

Only at the ages of ten and eleven do we find that decentering has made appreciable progress. Egocentricity begins to give way to the principles of reciprocity and inclusion. The child of ten or eleven understands his dual membership, in a smaller and a larger political unit. He also gives fewer personal reasons for his affective attachment to his homeland. Switzerland now becomes the land of the Red Cross; it is the country without war. Further, the child understands that members of other countries are as attached to their own lands as he is to his; this is the principle of *reciprocity*. But cognitive reciprocity does not necessarily mean that the child is capable of seeing good in all the peoples he knows about. He may still despise them. Whether the child outgrows his affective provincialism along with his cognitive provincialism seems to depend largely on the attitudes he learns from his parents.

Now, this study teaches us certain lessons. For one thing, it shows that maturation and time are needed to achieve a decentering from the unit of self to a progressively larger social unit. Further, this process may be arrested at any stage along the way, especially in its affective aspects. It is significant that Piaget gives no evidence that his children, at least up to fourteen years of age, discern the possibility of membership in any supranational grouping. Decentering has not reached the point where the child feels himself as belonging to the European region or to the United Nations; certainly none mentions his membership in the inclusive collective of mankind. Even if, in later years, such a cognitive enlargement takes place, the chances are that the corresponding affective enlargement will be lacking. We may then say that adults in all nations are still incompletely decentered. Cognitively they may stumble at the threshold of supranational chambers, but affectively they fail to enter.

Resolving International Conflicts

A study conducted in Belgium by de Bie shows how few adults are concerned with identification across national boundaries. Even those of a higher level of education have little sense of international relationships. Membership in any unit larger than the nation simply is not a psychological reality. Let international problems be handled by our leaders, they say.[7] But most, though not all, leaders themselves lack affective, or even cognitive, decentering beyond the sphere of purely national interests.

In its *Tensions and technology* series, UNESCO has recently published a volume entitled *The nature of conflict*, surveying much relevant research. In summing up the results, R. C. Angell concludes that interacting nations will enjoy peace only when they become parts of a social system that embraces them.[8] It is not necessary to destroy national loyalties, only to include them. In Angell's words, "The social system which is painfully coming to birth will grow out of national states, but their structures will not be annihilated in the process." J. C. Flugel has made the same point: "We must probably agree that intra-group behavior is on the whole far more moral than inter-group behavior; and in so far as the latter is moral it is often because the groups in question are for certain purposes themselves members of a larger group, so that it can at bottom be reduced to behavior of the intra-group variety." [9]

Such conclusions are based on a considerable amount of historical and contemporary research. This research, broadly speaking, indicates the relative futility of the moral creeds and strategies that are hortatory, authoritarian, hedonistic, legalistic or utopian. To abolish war, some of these theories have said: *Let us give up our prejudices, our malice and our fear. Let us remove barriers to trade, to communications and travel. Let nations surrender land, money, aspirations, armaments, pride and sovereignty.* Though it is necessary that some of these subtractions take place, they will not do so if the approach is negative. Each and every local interest, deplored by us as making for international discord, serves a legitimate purpose so long as no social system exists to transcend nationhood. To state the case psychologically, individuals who favor the conditions making for war do so because they have no embracing circle of loyalties or expectations that would render these present conditions maladaptive to their purposes. Conflicts of value are never solved by the process of direct collision or defeat, nor by the double-edged subtraction that comes through compromise, but only through a process of inclusion and decentering.

Although the subtractive, authoritarian, legalistic and utopian moralities still prevail, we view with hope certain signs of progress. The United Nations, of course, is organized for the express purpose of resolving conflict through the enlargement of interest systems. True, its major activities seem for the present to be hopelessly blocked by a centering on national interests. There are even signs of regress in the present violent upsurge of national, religious and linguistic provincialism. So we must count our gains humbly: evidences of regional grouping and of increased student and personnel exchanges (though evaluative studies of this policy seem to show somewhat less gain than we might hope).[10] We note progress against illiteracy— progress that eventually may establish a firmer ground for communication. International meetings of scientists and other scholars are all to the good; so, too, the Olympic games. But perhaps our firmest gain is the widening circle of enlightenment and discussion that our common problems have evoked.

Returning to Piaget's research for a moment, we can surely say of the average adult that cognitively and affectively he is potentially capable of considerable decentering. The average man has no difficulty at all thinking of himself as a member at one and the same time of his family, neighborhood, town, state and nation. Along the way he manages to include his church, lodge and friendship circles. The principle is thus established that larger loyalties do not clash so long as they allow for the maximum possible inclusion of smaller loyalties. Trouble, to be sure, arises when values conflict at the same level: a bigamist cannot comfortably apportion his loyalty between two wives, nor can a traitor serve two countries. But it is clearly within the capacity of men to continue the decentering process illustrated by Piaget's children and to go well beyond them. Empirically we can point, as Sorokin and Maslow have done, to individuals who have already realized this capacity.[11] Unfortunately, they are still relatively few in number.

Nothing that I have said is intended to detract from the positive values of rivalry, or of pride in one's kin and kind. Rival scientists struggle vigorously to prove their respective theories against their opponents, but they do so within the frame of loyalty to science as a whole. What is good in free enterprise comes from competition regulated by common loyalty to the rules of the game. One's pride in one's way of life is not incompatible with an attitude of "let both grow together until the harvest." To critics who reply that conflict is the essence of existence—that "to live is to struggle; to survive is to conquer"—we reply that we aim not to eliminate struggle but to establish it within a framework that will actually lead to survival in a fully human sense, not to extermination in a strictly literal sense.

Preparing the Individual

The root of the matter, of course, lies in the posture of the individual's mentality. Psychologists today like to speak of "cognitive style." Now, the style of mind that welcomes rivalry within the constraints of potential inclusion is marked by a kind of *tentativeness*.

It does not insist upon the absolute validity of its equations; it prefers a way of life without prescribing it for all; it possesses humor; it maintains its loyalties within an expanding and yet discriminating frame. Its judgments are tentative, its religion heuristic, its ultimate sentiment compassion. There are people with this outlook; and it is they who, in this period of rapid social change, give the world such stability as it possesses. Our problem is to increase their numbers.

On this particular problem I shall say only one thing at this time. The cognitive style I have defined is the precise opposite of the prejudiced style of life. The past decade or so has produced hundreds of studies of the sources and correlates of prejudice.[12] If the prejudiced style of life can be learned—and certainly it is not innate—then surely the tentative style (in Gandhi's term, the *equiminded* outlook) can also be acquired. There is no simple formula for teaching it, but the books lie open for those who can adapt current research to educational policy for the home, school and church. In the home there is much to be said for the method of the family conference wherein all the members, from the oldest to the articulate youngest, can seek a rational, inclusive plan for the fulfillment of their interests. In schools, I suggest that we discard if necessary up to 10 per cent of the present content and replace it with suitably chosen instruction and experience in the principle of integration of interests. The lesson should include classroom and playground activities, as well as studies in neighborhood, national and international experiments in inclusion. In my opinion, our knowledge to date warrants this deliberate change in educational policies.

Final Word

But, of course, our knowledge, solid as some of it is, has many deficiencies. Let me conclude by stating explicitly four implications of my remarks for a possible research program:

First: at the level of the individual person, we need to know much more about the frame of mind that I have called tentative or equiminded, for to me it seems to be the very essence of altruism. Research by Sorokin and by Maslow has given us valuable insights, but much more of the same order is needed.

Second: a problem of joint concern to psychology, anthropology and philosophy confronts us. The moral guideline we have laid down requires discrimination between root-desires and demands, between intrinsic values and instrumentals. It seems probable that the root-desires (not the demands) of men in all countries are very similar and therefore not incompatible. Hence, I advocate cross-cultural investigations that will compare men's motives in many lands, but always with a view to distinguishing their root-desires from their demands.

Third: how can we develop symbols of inclusion that will assist children, and citizens, and statesmen to look beyond the confines of egocentricity? Without images it is impossible to form attitudes. Our symbols today are overwhelmingly local and nationalistic. We continue to view our membership circles, as did Piaget's children, as lying side by side, not as concentric. We have few symbols of inclusion; but even if effective supranational symbols existed, they would have no magic property. Men's choices can be only among sequences they have known, and so our problem of training involves also the giving of experience, especially in childhood, that will enlarge the cognitive style and turn the mind automatically toward the integrative mode of handling conflict.

Finally: continued philosophical research is needed concerning the principle of enlargement of interests. The harmonious realization of abilities, interests and purposes is, of course, a familiar theme in philosophies as diverse as those of Plato, Spinoza, Kant, Dewey and Perry—to name but a few. What philosophy must now do, with the aid of social science, is to specify which inclusive sets of interest can best be achieved by which available techniques—in industry, in education and in statecraft. Philosophy has the further critical task of refining the principle and examining instances where it may not fully apply. I am aware that not all conflicts are easily brought under our formula. Yet the philosophical task, I am convinced, is one of refinement, not of refutation, for the principle of maximal inclusion has the overwhelming testimony of social science in its support.

REFERENCES

1. R. Likert, *Motivational dimensions in administration,* Ann Arbor: University of Michigan Press, 1951.

2. The story is told in F. Roethlisberger and W. J. Dickson, *Management and the worker,* Cambridge: Harvard University Press, 1939; and in S. D. Hoslett, *Human factors in management,* New York: Harper, 1946.

3. E. B. Holt, *The Freudian wish and its place in ethics,* New York: Holt, 1915; R. B. Perry, *Realms of value: a critique of human civilization,* Cambridge: Harvard University Press, 1954, Chap. 6.

4. See M. P. Follett, *Creative experience,* New York: Longmans, Green, 1924; and *The new state,* New York: Longmans, Green, 1920.

5. S. A. Stouffer *et al., The American soldier,* Princeton: Princeton University Press, 1949, II, 178.

6. J. Piaget and A. Weil, "The development in children of the idea of the homeland and of relations with other countries," *Int. Soc. Sci. Bull.*, 1951, 3:561-78.

7. P. de Bie, "Certain psychological aspects of Benelux," *Int. Soc. Sci. Bull.*, 1951, 3:540-52.

8. R. C. Angell, "Discovering paths to peace," in *The nature of conflict*, New York: UNESCO, 1957, Chap. 4.

9. J. C. Flugel, "Some neglected aspects of world integration," in T. H. Pear (ed.), *Psychological factors of peace and war*, Hutchinson & Co., 1950, Chap. 6.

10. *J. Soc. Issues*, 1956, Vol. 12, No. 1; *Ann. Amer. Acad. Pol. Soc. Sci.*, 1954, Vol. 295.

11. P. A. Sorokin, *Altruistic love: a study of American good neighbors and Christian saints*, Boston: Beacon, 1950; A. H. Maslow, *Motivation and personality*, New York: Harper, 1954. See also P. A. Sorokin (ed.), *Forms and techniques of altruistic and spiritual growth*, Boston: Beacon, 1954.

12. G. W. Allport, *The nature of prejudice*, Cambridge: Addison-Wesley, 1954.

CHAPTER 12

The psychology of participation

American psychology bears the stamp of American democracy. Its assumptions, its directions of research, its applications are consonant with the American creed. We cannot escape this value frame, nor do we wish to do so. On the contrary, it is a valid concern of psychology to identify those qualities of a citizen which prepare him to play his role in a participant democracy.

This essay is the chairman's address to the Society for the Psychological Study of Social Issues, delivered at Columbia University in September 1944 and published in the *Psychological Review* (1945). It bears an Author's Note:

"Were it customary for the Chairman to dedicate his address, I should offer my remarks in honor of John Dewey. He more than any other scholar, past or present, has set forth as a psychological problem the common man's need to participate in his own destiny."

John Dewey has shown that psychological theories are profoundly affected by the political and social climate prevailing in any given time and place. For example, an aristocracy produces no psychology of individual differences, for the individual is unimportant unless he happens to belong to the higher classes.[1] Dualistic psychology flourishes best when one group holds a monopoly of social power and wishes to do the thinking and planning, while others remain the docile, unthinking instruments of execution.[2] And apologists for the status quo are the ones who most readily declare human nature to be unalterable.

"The ultimate refuge of the stand-patter in every field," he declares, ". . . has been the notion of an alleged fixed structure of mind." [3] It was no accident that psychological hedonism flourished as a justification for nineteenth-century *laissez faire;* or that reflexology, blended with dialectical materialism, dominated Russian psychology after 1917. All of us watched with dismay the abrupt perversion of German psychological science after 1933.[4] With such evidence before us, can we doubt that American psychology too bears its own peculiar stamp of political and social dependency?

It is not my purpose to determine whether social and economic determinism has been decisive in the history of psychology, or whether the facts about human nature must be true regardless of any politico-ethical frame that we may hold. Dewey boldly declares that democracy and sound psychology are forever coextensive, that it is impossible to have one without the other. He would frankly banish all psychological postulates that are not democratically oriented.[5] Alluring as this whole problem is, let us limit our consideration to one distinctive, culturally conditioned feature of American psychology.

A Motorized Psychology

The genius of American psychology lies in its stress upon action—or, in slightly dated terminology, upon the motor phase of the reflex arc. Of all the schools of psychological thought we might name, only behaviorism, in both its muscle-twitch and its operational versions, is primarily American. Functionalism is American (rather than German or British) chiefly in its motor emphasis. Capacity psychology and mental testing in America deal primarily with accomplishment, activity and performance. The individual differences that are said to be a typical American interest have to do chiefly with measurable operations. We seldom record, for example, an individual's unique and subjective pattern of thought-life.

Of the many potential lines of development laid down in James's *Principles* over fifty years ago, the threads that were picked up were the radical motor elements. In the hands of Holt, Washburn and Langfeld, they led to a *motor theory of consciousness;* in the hands of Dewey, to a psychology of *conduct, adjustment* and *habit.* James himself established *pragmatism,* a doctrine that invites attention almost exclusively to the motor consequences of mental life. When James waxed ethical, as he frequently did, his moral advice was generally: "If you really care about something, you should *do* something about it." Even Josiah Royce, whose thought is often said to be the opposite of James's, agreed (like a good American) with his emphasis on *action*. Loyalty, said Royce, "is complete only in motor terms, never in merely sentimental terms. It is useless to call my feelings loyal unless my muscles somehow express this loyalty. . . . Nobody can be effectively loyal unless he is highly trained on the motor side." [6]

Returning on every ship from Europe, in the first decades of this century, were fresh young American *Doktoranden*. Their intellectual luggage was filled with European theories and concepts. But when unpacked at our motor-minded laboratories, these importations looked alien and were promptly subjected to a strenuous course in Americanization. *Feelings of innervation,* for example, were promptly dubbed outlandish. *Innervation* would do; feelings were *de trop.* *Ideo-motor* theory arrived and, though given a hospitable welcome by James, made little headway. *Ideas,* as the sovereign source of movement, smacked too much of the divine rights of Herbart. When *ideas* were offered to American psychologists, they commonly replied, "Keep them: stimulus and response will do quite nicely, thank you." *Empathy* arrived in a portmanteau packed in Munich. It was embedded in a whole self-psychology and in an epistemology of *Wissen von fremden Ichen.* Everything went into the ash can, save only a greatly oversimplified version of what Lipps originally intended. *Motor mimicry* was all we wanted. What would we be doing with a "mental act that held a guarantee of the objectivity of our knowledge"?

Importations in the psychology of thought were so roughly handled that they scarcely survived at all. What was *unanschaulich* in Würzburg became *anschaulich* at Cornell. To think without images seemed mildly treasonable; but to think *with* them gradually became unpatriotic. Better to think with our larynx, hands and viscera—or better still, in recent years, with our action currents. To explain volition in Würzburg, an impalpable decision factor, a *Bewusstheit,* was needed. But it all became so much simpler in Berkeley —a mere matter of rat vibrissae quivering with VTE at a choice point in a maze.

Other transformations were equally drastic. Of the countless dimensions for the study of personality proposed by Stern, the IQ alone was picked up. Wertheimer died perplexed by the selective attention Americans were paying to the visible, tangible portions of his work.[7] The entire *Geisteswissenschaft* is known in this country chiefly through an absurd little pencil-and-paper test leading to the inevitable profile. Small wonder that Spranger exclaimed, "Die grösste Gefahr Deutschland's ist die Amerikanisierung." [8]

One might think that phenomenology, since it derives from *Akt* psychology, might take hold in this country. But *mental* acts are not popular; it is *motor* acts that count. Or one might suppose that Americans would take to *intentionality,* a concept dealing with the orientation of the subject toward an object from which one might predict his future action. But such a concept is still too subjective; it is hard for us to even understand what it means. *Attitude* we will admit—if it can be operationally defined—but intentionality is just too Central European.

In short, we Americans have motorized psychology. Our theories of human nature transform meditative functions into active functions. The process clearly reflects the demand of our culture that inner life issue quickly and visibly into tangible success—that closures be reached both overtly and swiftly.

Do I seem to deplore the one-sidedness of our approach? I do not mean to. Quite the contrary: it is our way of going at things. Our preference for action, for objectivity, has carried us to new levels of attainment and will carry us still further. In the future, European models will be followed even less than formerly. What we produce must be indigenous within our culture and must harmonize with our active orientation. Especially in social psychology, I think, our derivations from Europe are virtually at an end. What may have been valid in Wundt, Durkheim, Le Bon, Tarde and Pareto will find better expression in the fresher, behavioral approach of America.

It will do so, that is, if our psychology of social action expands to give fuller play to the activities of the total organism than has been customary in the past. Even though subjective categories do not appeal, we need to find better ways of linking our psychology of action to the central regions of personality. Up to now, little progress has been made in this direction.

Motor Activity and Higher Mental Processes

True, American psychologists have to their credit the discovery that motor activity plays a pivotal role in higher mental functions. Take, as an example, *learning*: we have repeatedly insisted that learning is not passive absorption but an active response. In the classic experiment by Gates, learning scores jumped 100 per cent when four-fifths of the subject's time was devoted to recitation rather than to passive reading.[9] Haggard and Rose, reviewing many learning studies, including those that have to do with the simple conditioning of reflexes, report that in all cases learning seems to be facilitated if the subject himself overtly takes part, perhaps by turning the switch that rings the conditioning bell, or by drawing a line to accompany the apparent movement of the autokinetic phenomenon, or even by clenching his fist while memorizing nonsense syllables. These authors generalize these studies under a *Law of Active Participation:* ". . . When an individual assumes an active role in a learning situation (a) he tends to acquire the response-to-be-learned more rapidly, and (b) these response-patterns tend to be more stably formed, than when he remains passive."[10]

How to permit such helpful motor activity in a classroom where fifty pupils are busy learning is a large-sized pedagogical problem. "The chief source of the 'problem of discipline' in schools," says Dewey, "is that the teacher has often to spend a larger part of the time in suppressing the bodily activities" of the children.[11] The situation is wholly abnormal: the teacher tries to divorce bodily activity from the perception of meaning, yet the perception of meaning is incomplete without full manipulation and adequate bodily movement.

Memory for material learned in school and college is notoriously poor, so poor that educators are forced to console themselves with the wistful adage that education is "what you have left when you have forgotten all you learned in school." Perhaps a few studious attitudes, a few analytical habits are left; but should content disappear from the mind as rapidly as it does? We know that content acquired through personal manipulation does not seem to evaporate so rapidly. I recently asked 250 college students to write down three vivid memories of their schoolwork in the eighth grade. Afterward I had them indicate whether the memories involved their own active participation in the events recorded. Were they reciting, producing, talking, playing, arguing; or were they passively listening, watching, not overtly involved? Three-quarters of the memories were for situations in which the subject himself was actively participating, even though the percentage of time actually spent in participation in the average eighth grade room must be small.

We may mention also the problem of voluntary control. Although America has contributed little enough to the psychology of volition, what it has contributed is typical—namely, the finding of Bair[12] and others that a large amount of excessive, and apparently futile, motor involvement is necessary before one can gain control voluntarily over a limited muscular segment of the body. We know that a considerable overflow of effort is needed before fine skills can be differentiated, and before the individual can develop any satisfactory degree of self-determination.

In the realm of modern therapy, self-propelled activity plays an increasing part as the "Rogers technique" becomes more and more widely applied.[13] Analogously, the Kenny treatment for infantile paralysis requires the patient to take more and more responsibility and to be more and more active. Otherwise, it is discovered, the suggestions given by the therapeutist will not accomplish their purpose.[14] Angyal refers to the universal experience of psychiatrists that healthy ideas can be easily conveyed to the patient on the intellectual level without the slightest benefit accruing. The difficulty is to induce a state in which the idea "permeates the personality and influences the behavior." [15] In World War II we learned the importance of reconditioning at the front—that is, of allowing the patient himself quickly to work out his *own* relations with the terrifying environment that shocked him.

Facing the problem of re-education in postwar Germany, Lewin pointed to the impossibility of ideological conversion until the requisite experience is available: "To understand what is being talked about, the individual has to have a basis in experience." No amount of verbal defining will convey the meaning of such concepts as "his Majesty's loyal opposition" or "fair play." To most Germans, loyalty is identified with obedience; the only alternative to blind obedience is lawless individualism and *laissez faire*.[16]

One of the chief problems confronting military government is to keep the inhabitants of liberated countries active in shaping their own destiny.[17] Handouts beget apathy, and apathy prevents an interest in one's own future. How much better it was for Parisians to retake their own city than for the Allies to have done all the work, handing over the finished product. In his excellent book *Mental hygiene*, Klein expresses the point: "Without action there is no shift from the wish to the deed. There is motive, but no purpose. There is yearning without striving; hence the potential self-improvement dies stillborn." [18]

Activity Versus Participation

Facts of this sort prove to us that people must be active in order to learn, and to store up efficient memories, to build voluntary control and to be cured when they are ill or restored when they are faint. But implied in much American work is the proposition that one activity is as good as any other activity. It is *random* movement, according to much of our learning theory, that brings the organism to an eventual solution. And, according to one experimentalist, "If the body muscles are tense, the brain reacts much more quickly and intensely, if they are relaxed, it may react weakly or not at all." [19] The implication seems to be that tenseness of any kind makes for mental alertness. Activity as such is approved.

Random movement theories of learning, muscular tension theories of efficiency, speed theories of intelligence and motor theories of consciousness do not make a distinction that seems to me vital—

namely, the distinction between mere *activity* and true, personal *participation*.

Before we examine this distinction as it affects psychological theory and practice, I should like to point out that the selfsame distinction occurs in the economic and social life of the common man. Take, for example, Citizen Sam, who moves and has his being in the great activity wheel of New York City. He spends his hours of unconsciousness somewhere in the badlands of the Bronx. He wakens to grab the morning's milk left at the door by an agent of a vast dairy and distributing system, whose corporate maneuvers, so vital to his health, never consciously concern him. After paying hasty respects to his landlady, he dashes into the transportation system, whose mechanical and civic mysteries he does not comprehend. At the factory he becomes a cog for the day in a set of systems far beyond his ken. To him, as to everybody else, the company he works for is an abstraction. He plays an unwitting part in the "creation of surpluses"; and, though he doesn't know it, his furious activity at his machine is regulated by the "law of supply and demand," "the availability of raw materials" and "the prevailing interest rates." Unknown to himself, he is headed next week for the "surplus labor market." A union official collects his dues; just why, Sam doesn't know. At noontime that corporate monstrosity, Horn and Hardart, swallows him up, much as he swallows one of its automatic pies. After more activity in the afternoon, he seeks out a standardized daydream produced in Hollywood to rest his tense but *not* efficient mind.

Sam has been active all day, immensely active, playing a part in dozens of impersonal cycles of behavior. He has brushed against scores of corporate personalities, but has entered into intimate relations with no single human being. The people he has met are idlergears like himself, meshed into systems of transmission and far too distracted to examine any one of the cycles in which they are engaged. Throughout the day Sam is on the go, implicated in this task and that —but does he, in a psychological sense, *participate* in what he is doing? Although constantly *task-involved*, is he ever really *ego-involved*?

This problem is familiar to all of us, and one of the most significant developments of the past two decades is its entrance into both industrial and social psychology. The way the problem has been formulated by industrial psychologists is roughly this: the individual's desire for personal status is apparently insatiable. Whether we say that he longs for prestige, self-respect, autonomy or self-regard, a dynamic factor of this order is apparently the strongest of his drives. Perhaps it is an elementary organismic principle, as Angyal [20] and Goldstein [21] would have it; perhaps it is, rather, a distillation of more primitive biological drives, with social competitiveness somehow added to the brew. For our purposes, the distinction does not matter.

The industrial psychologist has discovered that when the work-situation in which the individual finds himself realistically engages the status-seeking motive—when the individual is busily engaged in using his talents, understanding his work and having pleasant social relations with foreman and fellow-worker—then he is, as the saying goes, "identified" with his job. He likes his work; he is absorbed in it; he is productive. In McGregor's term, he is industrially *active*. That is to say, he is participant.[22]

When, on the other hand, the situation is such that the status-motive has no chance of gearing itself into the external cycles of events, when the individual goes through motions that he does not find meaningful, when he does not really participate—then come rebellion against authority, complaints, griping, gossip, rumor, scape-goating and disaffection of all sorts. The job satisfaction is low. In McGregor's term, under such circumstances the individual is not active; he is industrially *reactive*.

In the armed forces, in federal employment, in school systems, the same principle holds. Ordinarily, those at the top find that they have sufficient comprehension, sufficient responsibility and sufficient personal status. They are not the ones who gripe and gossip. It is the lower-downs who indulge in tendency-wit against the brass hats, complain, go AWOL, become inert or gang up against a scapegoat. In actual combat, all the energies, training and personal responsibility of which a soldier is capable are called upon; egos are engaged for all they are worth. Men are then active; they have no time to be reactive—nor have they reason to be.

Accepting this analysis as correct, the problem before us is whether the immense amount of reactivity shown in business offices and factories, in federal bureaus and in schools, can be reduced, as it is when men at the front are using all their talents and are participating to the full in life-and-death combat.

We are learning some of the conditions in which reactivity does decline. Friendly, unaffected social relations are the most indispensable condition. Patronizing handouts and wage-incentive systems alone do not succeed. Opportunities for consultation on personal problems are, somewhat surprisingly, found to be important;

and group decision, open discussion and the retraining of leaders in accordance with democratic standards yield remarkable results. One of Lewin's discoveries in this connection is especially revealing: people who dislike a certain food are resistant to pressure put upon them in the form of persuasion and request; but when the individual himself as a member of a group votes, after discussion, to alter his food-habits, his eagerness to reach this goal is independent of his personal like or dislike.[23] In other words, a person ceases to be reactive and contrary in respect to a desirable course of conduct only when he himself has had a hand in declaring that course of conduct to be desirable.

Such findings add up to the simple proposition that people must have a hand in saving themselves; they cannot and will not be saved from the outside.

In insisting that participation depends upon ego-involvement, it would be a mistake to assume that we are dealing with a wholly self-centered and parasitic ego which demands unlimited status and power for the individual himself.[24] Often, indeed, the ego is clamorous, jealous, possessive and cantankerous. But this is true chiefly when it is forced to be *reactive* against constant threats and deprivations. We all know of "power-people" who cannot, as we say, "submerge their egos." The trouble comes, I suspect, not because their egos are unsubmerged, but because they are still reactive toward some outer or inner features of the situation that are causing conflicts and insecurity. Reactive egos tend to perceive their neighbors and associates as threats rather than as collaborators.

But, for the most part, people who are participant in cooperative activity are just as much satisfied when a teammate solves a common problem as when they themselves solve it.[25] *Your* tensions can be relieved by *my* work, and my tensions by your work, provided we are co-participants. Whatever our egos were like originally, they are now, for the most part, socially regenerate. Selfish gratifications give way to cooperative satisfaction when the ego-boundaries are enlarged.

A revealing study by Leighton conducted at a Japanese relocation center during World War II makes this point clear.[26] When the Japanese were asked to pick cotton at nearby ranches to help save the crop, very few responded. The reason was that they were expected to donate all wages above $16.00 a month to a community trust fund, to be used for the common good. There was as yet insufficient community feeling; the over-all trust fund seemed too big, too distant, too uncertain. All that happened was endless argument for and against the trust fund, while the cotton stood in the fields. At this point, the schools asked to be allowed to go picking and to use the money for school improvements. This request was granted, and soon church groups, recreational societies and other community units showed themselves eager to go on the same basis. The project was a success.

What we learn from this study is that self-interest may not extend to include an object so remote and impersonal as a community trust fund, but may readily embrace school improvements and church and recreational centers. For most people there is plenty of ego-relevance to be found in teamwork, provided the composition of the team and its identity of interest are clearly understood. Thus Americans will endorse international cooperation in time of peace (and not only in time of war), provided they continue to see its relevance to their own extended egos, and provided they feel that in some way they themselves are participating in the decisions and activities entailed.

Nearly everyone will bear testimony to the superior satisfaction that comes from successful teamwork as contrasted to solitary achievement. Membership in a group that has successfully braved dangers and surmounted obstacles is a membership that is ego-involved, and the egos in question are not parasitic but socialized.

An important by-product of participation, as I am using the term, is the reduction of stereotypes. Sam's mind, we can be sure, is a clutter of false stereotypes concerning the dairy company, the transportation system, the abstract corporation for which he works and the economic laws and federal regulations that determine much of his routine, to say nothing of the tabloid conceptions begotten in Hollywood and by advertisers. If he really participated in his employment, his notions of "the Company," of surpluses and of labor unions would become realistic.

Participant Democracy

Even in a presidential election, only about three in every five eligible voters go to the polls. In a primary, the ratio is more likely to be one in every four. Yet voting is the irreducible minimum of participation in political democracy. People who do not vote at least once in four years are effectively nonparticipant; those who vote only in a presidential election—that is to say, at least a third of all voters —are scarcely better off. If we wished to complicate matters, we might ask whether those who go to the polls are really participating with the deeper layers of personality or whether their voting is, so to speak, a peripheral activity instigated perhaps by fanfare or by local bosses. It would not be hard to prove that participation in political affairs, as well as in industrial, educational and religious life, is rare. In this respect, most people resemble Citizen Sam.

Two social psychologists have concerned themselves deeply with this problem. They see that increasingly, since the days of the industrial revolution, individuals have found themselves in the grip of immense forces whose workings they have no power to comprehend, much less to influence. One of the writers, John Dewey, states the problem this way: "The ramification of the issues before the public is so wide and intricate, the technical matters involved are so specialized, the details are so many and so shifting, that the public cannot for any length of time identify and hold itself. It is not that there is no public, no large body of persons having a common interest in the consequences of social transactions. There is too much public, a public too diffused and scattered and too intricate in composition." [27]

Dewey spent many years seeking remedies for this situation. Chiefly he laid emphasis upon the need for face-to-face association, for evolving democratic methods within school and neighborhood so that citizens may obtain in their nerves and muscles the basic experience of relating their activities in matters of common concern. Some political writers, such as Mary P. Follett,[28] have held that the solution lies in reconstituting political groups on a small enough scale so that each citizen can meet face-to-face with other members of a geographical or occupational group, electing representatives who will in turn deal face-to-face with other representatives. Though the town may no longer be the best unit for operation, the spirit of the town meeting is thus to a degree recaptured. "Democracy," says Dewey, "must begin at home and its home is the neighborly community." [29]

Central to Dewey's solution also is freedom of publicity. To obstruct or restrict publicity is to limit and distort public opinion. The control of broadcasting and of the press by big advertisers is an initial source of distortion. Other groups need freer ventilation for their views in order to reduce rigidity, hostility and reactivity.

The second social psychologist, F. H. Allport, states the problem rather differently. He asks how an individual enmeshed within innumerable cycles of activity, all imposed upon him from without, can retain his integrity as a person. Like Sam, he finds himself a cog in countless corporate machines. State, county and federal governmental systems affect him, as do economic cycles, the impersonal systems known as private enterprise, conscription in wartime and social security. So, too, do city transportation, milk production and delivery, consumption, housing and banking. But he does not affect them. How can he?

F. H. Allport points to an inherent contradiction that seems to lie in Dewey's position.[30] The latter hopes that the individual will participate in every public that his own interests create in common with others. That is to say, Sam should join with others who are affected by the same municipal, banking, transportation, feeding and housing cycles. Together they should work out common problems. But Sam would be a member of hundreds of segmental types of public; and in dashing from one "common interest" meeting to another, he would not find his interests as an individual truly fulfilled. He would still be a puppet of many systems. As complexities increase under modern conditions, total inclusion of the personality in specialized publics becomes increasingly difficult to achieve.

Like Dewey, F. H. Allport has given various suggestions for the solution of the problem, but chiefly his emphasis has been upon the creation of a scientific spirit in the common man, encouraging him to call into question the corporate fictions and the sanctity of the economic cycles that, unthinkingly, he takes for granted. By questioning the transcendental reality commonly ascribed to nationhood, to "consumer competition" and to institutional fictions, and by substituting direct experience with the materials affecting his life, the individual can eventually work out a measure of integrity and wholeness within himself.[31]

Both Dewey and F. H. Allport seem to agree that the only alternative to a keener analysis of the behavioral environment and more active participation in reshaping it is to give way progressively to outer authority, uniformity, discipline and dependence upon the leader. This battlefield exists here and now within each of us. The answer to growing complexity in the social sphere is either renewed efforts at participation by each one of us, or else a progressive decline of inert and unquestioning masses, submitting to government by an elite that will have little regard for the ultimate interest of the common man.

Drawing together the threads of this problem, we are confronted with the following facts:

First: since the industrial revolution, there has been increasing difficulty on the part of the ordinary citizen in comprehending and affecting the forces that control his destiny.

Second: potentially the individual is a member of many, many publics, defined as groups of people having a common interest—as, for example, voters, motorists, veterans, employers, consumers or coreligionists.

Third: no public includes all of an individual's interests.

To these facts, we add our earlier conclusions:

Fourth: activity alone is not participation. Most of our fellow citizens spin as cogs in many systems without engaging their own egos even in those activities of most vital concern to them.

Fifth: when the ego is not effectively engaged, the individual becomes reactive. He lives a life of ugly protest, finding outlets in complaints, in strikes and above all in scapegoating. In this condition he is ripe prey for a demagogue whose whole purpose is to focus and exploit the aggressive outbursts of nonparticipating egos.

Toward a Solution

It is risky indeed to suggest in a few words the solution of such an immense social problem. Certainly it will require the combined efforts of educators, statesmen and scientists to rescue the common man from his predicament. But, from our preceding discussion, one line of thought stands out as particularly helpful.

Is it not true that all of us find coercive demands upon our motor systems imposed by the corporate cycles in which we move, generally *without* serious frustration resulting? Speaking for myself, only the outer layers of my personality are engaged in my capacity as automobile owner, insurance holder, Blue Cross member, consumer of clothing and patron of the local transit system. Perhaps I should be more interested in these cycles; but one must choose, and other things are more important to me. In this age of specialization, all of us are willing to delegate expert functions to experts. We simply cannot be bothered about the innumerable technical aspects of living that are not our specialty. In matters of broad political or ethical policy-making, the story is different; we cannot so easily avoid responsibility. Political reforms making possible good schools, recreation and health are presumably the concern of all people. National policy in securing a lasting peace is a matter of great moment for each one of us. But even among these broad social and political issues I find some that excite me more than others.

Thus I cannot share Dewey's dismay at our failure to create innumerable self-conscious publics wherever there are common interests. These publics need operate only on the broadest policy-forming level, and a relatively few members of a group can often serve adequately as representatives of others who are like-minded. I do not mean that a few public-spirited citizens should do all the work. There should be wider distribution of responsibility. But talents differ, and what warms one ego chills another.

Assuming that the major fields of activity open to all normal people are the economic, the educational, the recreational, the political, the religious and the domestic, we might assert that a healthy ego should find true participation in all of them. Or, allowing one blind spot to the bachelor, the constitutional hater of sports or of politics and the agnostic, there is still need for a balanced diet of participation in, say, five fields.

Against some such norm we might test our present situation. Do we find Citizen Sam truly participating in some *one* political undertaking? In some *one* of his economic contacts—preferably, of course, in his job, where he spends most of his time? Is he really involved in *some* religious, educational and recreational pursuits, and in family affairs? If we find that he is not actively involved in all these areas of participation, we may grant him a blind spot or two. But unless he is in some areas ego-engaged and participant, his life is crippled and his existence a blemish on democracy.

In brief, it is neither possible nor desirable that all of our activities and contacts in our complex social order should penetrate beneath the surface of our personalities. But unless we try deliberately and persistently to affect our destinies at certain points, especially where broad political policies are concerned and in some of the other representative areas of our life, we are not democratic personalities. We then have no balance or wholeness, and society undergoes proportionate stultification.

New Directions for Social Psychology

Returning to our starting point, my contention is that the earlier emphasis of American psychology on motor activity as such is now changing into an emphasis upon ego-involved participation. As time goes on, it will mark increasingly the essential differences that exist between movement initiated at the surface level and that initiated at the deeper levels of personality.[32] To do so will not be to abandon our dependence on the social climate in which we work. Quite the contrary: at last the genius of American psychology will be brought into line with the century of the common man.[33]

What, concretely, are the roles that psychologists will play in this process? Several can already be fairly well defined:

To those who serve in some consulting or guidance capacity, Citizen Sam will come as a client. He will have this symptom or that —perhaps resentment, depression, bewilderment or apathy. Among college students, one study suggests that 20 per cent are apathetic, complaining that they have no values whatever to live by. It calls for great therapeutic skill to lead such clients to commit themselves unreservedly to something. I have suggested that a balanced personality needs deep-rooted participation in all or most of the six spheres of value: political, economic, recreational, religious, educational and domestic. But commitments cannot be too comprehensive. It is not politics or economics as a whole that evokes participation, but merely some one limited and well-defined issue in the total sphere. The democratic personality needs to influence *some* but not all of the factors that influence him in representative fields of his activity.

The consultant may go one step further. Sam should not only feel that he is a citizen participating at crucial points in common activities; he should be oriented as well, toward the inner crises such as will occur in middle age, when his vitality recedes and his furious activity can no longer be sustained, when he faces old age and death itself. Sam, if I may put it this way, needs to find that metaphors and images are ultimately more important than motor gyrations. The consulting psychologist has responsibility for encouraging subjective richness in personality. For, in the broader sense, participation extends beyond the days when active citizenship is possible. The ego needs to be wholesomely attached to life, even after efficiency of action declines.

Industrial psychologists and group workers have already found a rewarding line of work in educating management, foremen and employees about the conditions that increase efficiency through participation in the job. The same type of effort is also yielding returns in other directions, especially in recreational and educational enterprises.

As teachers, both in college and in adult centers, we have a job to do in encouraging the participation of the public in the progress of science itself. The layman now finds it impossible to keep pace with science. Dazed by the benefits of television, auto, airplane and vitamins, all of which regulate his life, he stands on the side lines and cheers as the procession of science goes by. He has little real contact with the material from which his life is fashioned. Exhibitions, demonstrations and simplified experiments will help him understand.[34] But the layman needs even more: he needs to know how to *control* the applications of science. While bestowing upon him many blessings, science has also given its bounty to tyrants and to the self-appointed elite, with the result of fabulous fortunes for the few, slums and squalor for the many, violent wars and suffering beyond endurance. The common man has not chosen these consequences. He was never consulted, was never participant in guiding the applications of science.

Half a century ago, psychologists characteristically ascribed to the personality certain governing agencies: the will, the soul, the self, the moral sentiments or some other ruling faculty. Subsequent emphasis upon the motor processes, especially in America, resulted in a kind of entropy for personality. Being deprived of its self-policing functions, personality seemed to dissolve into endless cycles of motor activity controlled by stimulus or by habit. Like a taxicab, its successive excursions had little relation to one another. Then, gradually, some principles of self-regulation returned to psychology, a bit timidly and not too clearly, under the guise of *integration, vigilance* and *homeostasis.*

Ego-functions, too, were introduced, to provide for a recentering of personality with an increase in its stability. Ego-functions, as I have shown elsewhere, are of many kinds, and the ego is susceptible of many definitions.[35] Perhaps the most important distinction concerns *reactive* ego-functions, which are resistant, contrary and clamorous, as opposed to *active* ego-functions, which find full expression in participant activity. When participating, the individual discovers that his occupational manipulations grow meaningful; his community contacts are understood and appreciated. He becomes interested in shaping many of the events that control his life.

Participation, as opposed to peripheral motor activity, sinks a shaft into the inner subjective regions of the personality. It taps central values. Thus, in studying participation, the psychologist has an approach to the complete person.

Random movement, derived from the sensori-motor layer of the personality, has too long been our paradigm for the behavior of man. It fails to draw the essential distinction between aimless activity and participation. The concept of random movement denies dignity to human nature; the concept of participation confers dignity. As American psychology increasingly studies the conditions of participation it will elevate its conception of human nature, an event, we can be sure, that will at last gratify the man in the street.

In focusing upon problems of participation social psychology will also be advancing democracy, for, as Dewey has shown, the task of obtaining from the common man participation in matters affecting his own destiny is the central problem of democracy.

REFERENCES

1. J. Dewey, *Psychology as philosophic method*, Berkeley: University Press, 1899.

2. J. Dewey, *Human nature and conduct*, New York: Holt, 1922, p. 72.

3. J. Dewey, "The need for social psychology," *Psychol. Rev.*, 1917, 24:273.

4. F. Wyatt and H. L. Teuber, "German psychology under the Nazi system—1933-1940," *Psychol. Rev.*, 1944, 51:229-47.

5. G. W. Allport, "Dewey's individual and social psychology," in P. A. Schilpp (ed.), *The philosophy of John Dewey*, Evanston: Northwestern University Press, 1939, Chap. 9, especially pp. 281, 283, 290.

6. J. Royce, *Race questions, provincialism, and other American problems*, New York: Macmillan, 1908, pp. 239, 241.

7. W. Köhler, "Max Wertheimer: 1880-1943," *Psychol. Rev.*, 1944, 51:143-46.

8. Cf. E. Spranger, *Kultur und Erziehung*, Leipzig: Quelle & Meyer, 1923, p. 199.

9. A. I. Gates, "Recitation as a factor in memorizing," *Arch. Psychol.*, 1917, Vol. 6, No. 40.

10. E. A. Haggard and R. J. Rose, "Some effects of mental set and active participation in the conditioning of the autokinetic phenomenon," *J. Exp. Psychol.*, 1944, 34:56.

11. J. Dewey, *Democracy and education*, New York: Macmillan, 1919, p. 165.

12. J. H. Bair, "Development of voluntary control," *Psychol. Rev.*, 1901, 8:474-510.

13. C. R. Rogers, *Counseling and psychotherapy*, Boston: Houghton Mifflin, 1942.

14. C. Bohnengel, "An evaluation of psycho-biologic factors in the re-education phase of the Kenny treatment for infantile paralysis," *Psychosom. Med.*, 1944, 6:82-87.

15. A. Angyal, *Foundations for a science of personality*, New York: Commonwealth Fund, 1941, p. 326.

16. K. Lewin, "The special case of Germany," *Publ. Opin. Quart.*, 1943, 7:555-66.

17. G. W. Allport, "Restoring morale in occupied territory," *Publ. Opin. Quart.*, 1943, 7:606-17.

18. D. B. Klein, *Mental hygiene*, New York: Holt, 1944, p. 319.

19. A. G. Bills, *The psychology of efficiency*, New York: Harper, 1943, p. 23.

20. A. Angyal, *op. cit.*

21. K. Goldstein, *Human nature in the light of psychopathology*, Cambridge: Harvard University Press, 1940.

22. D. McGregor, "Conditions of effective leadership in the industrial organization," *J. Consult. Psychol.*, 1944, 8:55-63.

23. K. Lewin, "The dynamics of group action," *Educ. Leadership*, 1944, 1:195-200.

24. H. D. Spoerl, "Toward a knowledge of the soul," *The New Phil.*, 1944, 47:71-81.

25. H. B. Lewis, "An experimental study of the role of the ego in work. I. The role of the ego in coöperative work," *J. Exp. Psychol.*, 1944, 34:113-26

26. A. H. Leighton, *et al.*, "The psychiatric approach in problems of community management," *Amer. J. Psychiat.* 1943, 100:328-33.

27. J. Dewey, *The public and its problems*, New York: Holt, 1927, p. 137.

28. M. P. Follett, *Creative experience*, New York: Longmans, Green, 1924.

29. J. Dewey, *The public and its problems*, op. cit., p. 213.

30. F. H. Allport, *Institutional behavior*, Chapel Hill: University Press, 1933, Chap. 5.

31. F. H. Allport, "The scientific spirit and the common man," *Proc. Conf. on Sci. Spirit & Dem. Faith*, New York: 2 West 64th St., 1944.

32. See Chapter 5 of the present volume.

33. C. J. Friedrich, "The role and the position of the common man," *Amer. J. Sociol.*, 1944, 69:421-29.

34. F. H. Allport, "The scientific spirit and the common man," *op. cit.*

35. See Chapter 5 of the present volume.

CHAPTER 13

A basic psychology of love and hate

The human hunger to give and to receive love is insatiable. No one ever feels that he can love or be loved enough. Yet this root fact of human nature is seldom acknowledged or studied by psychologists.

The present essay attempts to explain the curious neglect. It examines the evidence and proposes a theory to advance our understanding of affiliative motives and of their pathological distortion into hate.

Originally an address at the Conference on Educational Problems of Special Culture Groups, held at Teachers College, Columbia University, in September 1949, the essay was printed in its present form in *Explorations in altruistic love and behavior,* edited by Pitirim A. Sorokin (1950).

While it is inevitable that self-love should be positive and active in every man, it is not inevitable, and it is very far from necessary, that it should be sovereign with him.
—Theophilus Parsons

A persistent defect of modern psychology is its failure to make a serious study of the affiliative desires and capacities of human beings. If I am not mistaken, only two sustained theories concerning their nature have been developed. Both seem to me somewhat abortive. One is the approach of those writers who postulate a *gregarious instinct.* This pallid conception turned out to give us little more than a name and, at the hands of McDougall and Trotter, led nowhere in particular except into a curious kind of British chauvinism. The other approach is that of Freud, who, with an oddly limited perspective, contrived to reduce affiliative motives to sexuality—a blunder that even the ancient Greeks, with their distinction between *eros* and *agape,* knew enough to avoid.

The "Flight from Tenderness"

Why psychologists, by and large, have side-stepped the problems of human attachment is an interesting question. Ian Suttie speaks of it as their "flight from tenderness." He believes that, in repudiating theology, modern mental science overreacted and deliberately blinded itself to the tender relationships in life so strongly emphasized by Christianity.[1] Somehow it feels more tough-minded to study discord. The scientist fears that, if he looks at affiliative sentiments, he may seem sentimental; if he talks about love, he may seem emotional; and if he studies personal attachments, he may appear personal. Better leave the whole matter to poets, saints or theologians.

Besides overreacting against theology, the psychologist has, of course, a well-grounded suspicion of hypocrisy and of rationalization. Protestations of friendliness, he knows, do not always signify friendliness; they are often a mask for more basic conditions of bitterness and hate. His fear of appearing pious is not altogether a matter of yielding to a currently fashionable scientific taboo. He knows the error that lies in rationalized accounts of human motivation.

But there is yet another reason, still more fundamental, for this flight from tenderness. Desires for affiliation are—as I shall try to show—the inescapable groundwork of human life. As such they are quite naturally overlooked, for normally we do not perceive groundwork at all; we notice only the superimposed figures. The white page of the book I am reading fails to interest me; it is merely the necessary ground for the black type that I perceive. And is it not always the waterspout, rather than the otherwise calm surface of the sea, that rivets our attention? Alfred North Whitehead has pointed out that we do not even have words with which to describe what is always with us; we tend to take the ubiquities of our lives for granted and never feel the need to discuss them. It is for this reason, I think, that we pay so little attention to the prior state of concord that alone confers meaning on discord. Even the expressions of the human face illustrate the principle I am discussing: the emotion of love brings a wholly relaxed, "neutral" set to the musculature of the face. By contrast, anger, jealousy and hate are well-figured expressions. In the human face, as in life itself, it is far easier to identify and to fix for study the manifestations of intolerance and hate than the manifestations of love and tolerance: these are taken for granted.

In their theories of motivation, psychologists have been misled by this figure-ground relationship. They see antagonism as more salient and exciting than good will—and, of course, it is. Hostile emotions are warlike emotions, stimulating to the possessor and visible to the observer. Frustration and aggression interest the psychologist, but not friendship and trust. Yet it is unescapably true that hostility derives its very existence from the prior groundwork of affiliative desire with which it so sharply contrasts. Unless one first loves, one cannot hate. For hatred is an emotion of protest, directed always toward real or imagined obstructions that prevent one from reaching objectives that are positively valued—that is, loved.

The Trend in Research Findings

Although psychologists are backward in their conceptualizations of the affiliative needs of mankind, they have recently shed considerable empirical light on the nature of these needs. Modern techniques of research in the study of human relations are being profitably employed in many different kinds of groups—in the classroom, in the community, in industry. It is pleasing to watch the results of research converge. A common thread seems to run through every set of findings; before long, we may hope, this thread will lead to unifying theory.

In industrial research, investigations have been particularly fruitful. They have made it clear that management has been guilty in the past of disastrous blunders in its relations with employees. For one thing, management formerly assumed that men could be best motivated by fear and punishment. If employees came late to work, fines were levied; if they spoiled material or disobeyed rules, they paid more fines. Afraid of losing their jobs, they toed the line at the command of foremen who, more likely than not, were saturated with an authoritarian view of their own status. The policy worked so badly that industries began to give rewards and to make concessions. But these inducements had the flavor of patronage and raised the workers' expectations, rather than their morale. Psychologically, the blunder was that the rewards did not grow directly out of the workers' own activity, but were arbitrary in character, being conferred by the employer rather than generated by the work process. Rest periods, bonuses and badges are extrinsic to the work situation. Industry then tried to improve matters through time and motion studies; but such "efficiency management" does not touch the human problem. Finally, in despair, industry often multiplied its efficiency and personnel departments until the plant developed a Goliath of bureaucracy—all to no avail. Industrial relations were not improved.

Then came the modern period of research. It did not take long to discover the source of the trouble. Workers, it turns out, like jobs that are free from condescension and overclose supervision, give free play to their talents, give credit for work done, allow them to participate in decisions affecting themselves, bring together small teams of congenial co-workers and permit personal growth and advancement.

Whether investigations are conducted in factories, in business offices, in schools, in camps or in the armed forces—the same pattern of findings always emerges. People want to remain integrated human beings in a work situation, as well as at home. It is the whole individual who goes to school, to work or to war. He desires congenial, informal relations with his fellows and wants to participate in his own destiny. And he will not for long tolerate patronage.

The common thread that emerges seems to have two interwoven strands. People in any form of human association wish to preserve their self-esteem—their self-love, if you wish—and simultaneously to have warm, affiliative relations with their fellows. No one seems initially to want to hate. But hatred, none the less, grows up in many lives as a consequence of blocked self-esteem and blocked affiliation.

I dip again into research. Stouffer's extended study of the motivation of soldiers in combat in World War II revealed that the affiliative motive, even under extreme stress, seems to hold twice as many men to their task as does the motive of hate. The only reported form of help that exceeded the desire not to let other men down was religious. Fully three-quarters of the soldiers reported that prayer "helped a lot"—and prayer obviously reflects some deep affiliative (certainly not a destructive) desire.[2]

For the moment, these few examples drawn from modern research may serve our purposes.[3] They indicate that men are basically eager for friendly and affiliative relations with others, provided these relations preserve their own sense of integrity and self-esteem. Thus a double finding must be taken into account in our theorizing: people want close, warm, loving relationships with their fellows—but, at the same time, they are exceedingly sensitive to slights to their *amour-propre*. Indignity to one's self-esteem quickly generates hatred.

Here, then, is our dilemma: neither our economic nor our political life is arranged to accommodate this dual pattern of need. Except in limited ways, chiefly within the family, opportunities are not provided for the expression of the craving for love—to give and to receive. Nor is the maintenance of self-respect a serious concern of our economic and political institutions. Since the affiliative needs are so badly met, we must not be surprised to find reactivity, hostility and anxiety as the most common by-products of our social relationships. Though people want love above all else, prejudice and hostility take command of their lives. One study establishes the fact that group prejudice is an appreciable factor in the mental life of perhaps four-fifths of the American population.[4] Yet the affiliative need remains somehow basic.

Such being our quandary, it behooves us to study far more closely than we have in the past the place of love and hate in human personality, and to pay particular attention to the swift and easy manner in which hostility comes so readily to take over the management of a life.

The Nature of Love and Hate

Up to now, it is the philosophers who have formulated our major theories of love and hate. We think first, of course, of Empedocles, the pre-Socratic, who tells us that love and hate are cosmic forces—the only cosmic forces that exist. They act upon the material elements of the earth, from which they fashion harmonious and inharmonious creations. From the time of Empedocles onward, we find the history of philosophy haunted by the dialectic of love and hate. Always hate has been regarded as a less desirable emotion than love, as a disruptive and dangerous emotion unless mastered. When the Christian religion came along, it gave absolute sanction to love and absolute dissanction to hate. Perhaps it was the very severity of this sanction that led science, as Suttie suggests, to avoid the subject.

Though many philosophers have emphasized equally, as did Empedocles, the forces of love and of hate in the process of life, there is a distinct tendency among many of them to regard hatred and its attendant aggressions as somehow more fundamental. The influential Hobbes did so. To him, mortals are by their very nature impelled to seek honor, precedence, glory. We are driven above all else by "a perpetual and restless desire of power after power that ceaseth only in death." This "state of nature" leads all men to aggress against each other, to condemn their fellows and to find them offensive. Hate, aversion and suspicion are far more easily engendered than are love and loyalty, for are not man's two fundamental passions vainglory and fear? To be sure, laws, customs and religion may keep an uncertain and uneasy control over us by invoking fear; but against this restraint our vainglory presses hard. Since, according to Hobbes, everyone wishes others to value him as highly as he does himself, a cycle of fierce competition is inaugurated. Men are truly equal in one respect: they are all highly satisfied with themselves.

A more modern writer, the French biologist Felix Le Dantec, goes still further: he declares egoism to be the only keystone in our social edifice. He who professes fondness for his fellows is a hypocrite. Machiavelli, La Rochefoucauld, Schopenhauer and Nietzsche all see irrevocable egoism in human nature. For them, only one form of love ultimately exists—self-love. If this basic assumption is sound, the outlook for improving human relations is dim. Rationalize our self-love as we will, we remain frauds. Human relations cannot be improved; they can only be prettified.

Now, nothing could be more important than to know whether this view of human nature is right or wrong. Some moralists, of course, have declared it wrong. Hume, for example, poured his scorn on the principle "that all benevolence is mere hypocrisy, friendship a cheat, public spirit a farce, fidelity a snare." To Hume there is a basic sociality in man that engenders a capacity for genuine sympathy and benevolence. Shaftesbury, Adam Smith and Kropotkin agree. But it gains us little to cite venerable authorities pro and con. What is more important is that nowadays we have become wholesomely critical of our own motives. We do not wish to prate of love if self-love is at the root of our behavior, or if sympathy is merely a mask for aggression. For this grace of self-criticism we have largely Freud to thank.

But Freud's picture of human motivation, though not so simple as Hobbes's, is basically similar: all of us have a primal instinct making for death and destruction. Aggressive urges are therefore as natural as the outpouring of hot lava from a volcano. Paralleling this destructive urge are the life instincts, whose representative is the sexual drive. Taken by itself, this drive may be regarded as constructive and binding in social relationships. In fact, the best we can hope for is that a child's sex life will so develop that the libidinal striving will somehow neutralize the destructive forces in his life.

But, alas, the two instincts (destruction and sex) often fuse. Aggression is intimately bound up with each stage of developing sexuality and, in Freudian theory, seems necessary in order that the sex impulses reach their aim. The fusion is so marked that all our benign human relations, including good leadership, good will, religion and our virtues generally, can be viewed best as mere "sublimations"—mere incidents, mere by-products—of sex and aggression. There is little indication in Freud, just as there is little in Hobbes, that the affiliative desire may be basic in the constitution of human nature.

Yet is it not obvious that, from the very moment of its inception, the business of life calls for adherence, for mutuality? *In utero* the mode of life is symbiotic: the associative relationship reigns supreme, and there is no evidence whatever of destructive instincts. After birth the affiliative attachment of the child to its environment still remains dominant—in nursing, playing, resting. The social smile early symbolizes his contentment with people. Toward his entire environment he is positive, approaching nearly every type of stimulus, every type of person. From no human being does he by instinct withdraw. His life is marked by eager adience. To be sure, in the process of relating himself positively to his environment, the child may do damage and may unwittingly violate the rights of others. A two-year-old is, in one sense of the word, very destructive. But his depredations are psychologically irrelevant to what he is trying to do. From his point of view, he is greedily ingesting his environment, eagerly affiliating with it—nothing more.

When negative emotions of fear and anger arise, they owe their whole existence to the interruption of this zeal for approach. Affiliative tendencies, when threatened or frustrated, give way to alarm and defense. Suttie puts the matter picturesquely: "Earth hath no hate *but* love to hatred turned, and hell no fury but a baby scorned." [5]

So obvious is the priority of affiliative groundwork that one must perform contortions in order to give equal footing to the alleged aggressive instincts. Some psychoanalysts achieve the feat by assuming that eating, perhaps the most conspicuous of an infant's activities, is a destructive act—"oral aggression," it is called. Our primordial ancestors, writes one Freudian, "were cannibals." "We all enter life with the instinctive impulse to devour not only food, but also all frustrating objects. Before the infantile individual acquires the capacity to love, it is governed by a primitive hate relationship to its environment." [6] This statement precisely reverses the order of love and hate in ontogenetic development. Furthermore, it inverts the meaning of the act of feeding. When I devour roast beef, it is not from hate but from love. Acts of incorporation into myself are, from my point of view, affiliative.

The truest statement that can be made of a normal person is that he never feels that he can love or be loved enough. He always wants more love in his life. One reason why religion is an almost universal attachment of mankind is that religion maintains the basic love relationship of the individual with some embracing principle. The major religions represent not only a free, indestructible attachment to one's Creator, but likewise the unattained ideal of the brotherhood of man. When we imagine a perfect state of being, we invariably imagine the unconditional triumph of love.

But the desire for love, when rejected or threatened, turns to anxious fear. No one can remain indifferent if the bid he is making for affiliation is rebuffed. A recent study of delinquent boys shows that in virtually every case of incorrigible delinquency there was gross emotional inadequacy in the home. The boys were rejected by their parents or had parents incapable of providing affectional security. Their bid for affiliation was blocked; and, only half-aware of their misery, they turned as a means of defense to antisocial acts.[7] During the war a thirteen-year-old boy, rejected at home, "spat on the American flag and announced that the other boys were fools to believe in our government, that he was for Hitler and Nazism, and intended to become a traitor. 'I hate all Americans,' he added."[8] Children deprived of secure affection often rant against "dirty niggers," "Jew bastards" and other minority groups.

Misanthropy—I think we may now generalize—is always a matter of frustrated affiliative desire and the attendant humiliation to self-esteem. What is so fascinating psychologically is the displacement that frequently occurs in the resulting hatred. Few of the children in the research I have cited are aware of the source of their distress. Their hatred and aggression are fixed on irrelevant objects. That the process of displacement is subtle, a California research study on anti-Semitism abundantly shows. College girls high in prejudice, it was found, ordinarily profess complete love and respect for their parents—more so than do tolerant girls. But deeper study shows that their lives are marked by much buried hostility toward their parents. In spite of appearances, they do not have a free affiliative relation in the home; and, surprising as it may seem, their anti-Semitism reflects this situation.[9]

A study among war veterans has a similar result. In this investigation, a significant relation was discovered between the recollection of love and affection enjoyed in childhood and the present tolerance for minority groups. Veterans who reported that their parents were lacking in affection toward them were found far more often among the intolerant.[10] Granted that retrospective reports of affection in childhood are not fully reliable, this stricture does not affect the proposition before us. The very fact that the men in this study *reported* basic love disturbance shows that somehow in them a bitter wound existed, and this wound had a demonstrable relation to their later intolerance.

It is necessary here to add the caution that not all hatred is displaced. Conceivably, members of a minority group may be genuinely frustrating agents and may be hated or despised directly for the obstructions they create. Not all victims of prejudice are lily-white in their innocence; but, if we look closely at the process, we find that in almost every case they attract additional displaced animosity for which they are not conceivably to blame.

Hatred is a normal enough response whenever intensely held, positive values are threatened or destroyed. The threatened values may be self-love, or the desire to be loved, or altruistic love. The point is, as Suttie said, "There is no hatred but love to hatred turned." It is an error, therefore, to regard the numerous hostile sentiments of men as merely the outpouring of aggressive instincts. Since hate is a contingent phenomenon, it is, theoretically at least, avoidable. Actually, in proportion as man's affiliative needs are met, aggression and hostility disappear. To know this fact is the first requirement for improving human relations.

Are Love and Hate Instincts?

Since hatred is a contingent phenomenon, it is not proper to argue, as the Freudians do, that it stems from an instinct of aggression or of destruction. To be sure, hostility is a normal—seemingly almost a reflex—capacity of men when severe frustration blocks the affiliative trend in their behavior. But a capacity, though native, is not itself a drive in the sense that it must find an outlet for its energy.

But how do matters stand with what I have called the affiliative desires? I realize that I may seem to imply that here, at last, is the root instinct of life. If hate exists only when affiliation is threatened, must we not therefore assume that the affiliative need itself is primordial instinct? Psychological literature has many references to this possibility—to the instinct of gregariousness, to the parental instinct, to the "wish" for response, to the "need" for affiliation.

While I would agree to endorse a postulation of this order if it seems logically necessary, I feel compelled to point to the essential emptiness of all instinct formulae. An "instinct of love" could mean nothing more than that the nature of human life seems to require strong personal attachments. Regarding the nature of this need in the individual case, it says nothing. Nor does it allow for the myriad transformations that a person's attachments undergo, including the subtle interplay of self-love and socialized love. The really important questions concerning love—and concerning hate—are postinstinctive questions. It is always our contemporary attitudes, our present loyalties and aversions, that rule our behavior; not, as Freud and others maintain, unchangeable instinctual forces.[11] I do not believe that we can view the myriad forms of attachment and repulsion in the ever growing personality as merely so many channels of outlet for the permanent instincts of sex and aggression, or of gregariousness and love, or of anything else.

Motivation—it seems obvious to me—is always a contemporary process directed toward the future, comprising attitudes, beliefs and forms of adjustment that, in the individual's mind, bind him successfully to his world. There is a concrete character in motivation to which instinct doctrines cannot do justice. Starting fairly early in our lives, we are propelled, I maintain, not by instincts but by *interests*.

In the earliest months of life, a child develops systems of positive attachments. He loves his own mother, not someone else's. His initial, undifferentiated adience is quickly polarized by objects. He develops attachments to groups of which he is a member: his family, his church, his ethnic group—and later his lodge, his office and his own offspring. The love and loyalty are concrete. They are fashioned into sentiments, and these sentiments are learned. To say that a person's positive attachments are nothing but an adventitious channeling of an instinct is simply not helpful. It is the sentiments that are the ongoing, postinstinctive motives of the developing personality.

Hatred too is concrete. When a Negro child makes friendly advances to a white child and suffers a rebuff, and the humiliation turns into hate, shall we say that the instinct of aggression has become channelized? Or shall we say that a very particular attitude of resentment is built up, which becomes dynamic in its own right because the child must thereafter adjust to this new phase of his experience? The hatred did not exist until it was learned. Always the growing child learns specific sets of ideas concerning specific sets of people and builds his sentiments accordingly. It is these sentiments (not instincts) that thereafter guide his behavior. And these postinstinctive units in personality are basic to the understanding of human relations, for they alone specify the course that the individual will take.

Let me repeat that, if we wish, we can speak of an affiliative need or instinct and in this way universalize the phenomena we are discussing. It seems to me, however, a somewhat hollow procedure; for, in so doing, we are likely to overlook the fact that each person's life history is unique and that his motives are not strictly commensurable with those of other individuals. It is always the focalized forms of affiliation that concern us in dealing with concrete human beings.

How these postinstinctive units are developed is, of course, the riddle of learning—a subject we cannot here explore. We know that attitudes take shape partly under the pressure of conformity and imitation. We know that parents are the chief influences, but that educators likewise do their part, for good and for ill. We know that displacement and generalization loom large in the process. We know, too, that a curious projectivity marks all hostile attitudes: the person we dislike is almost always regarded as wholly to blame. It seldom occurs to us that the basis for our hate may lie wholly within ourselves, that we may be merely scapegoating the individual we dislike. No person ever asks to be cured of his prejudice. Hate behaves like jaundice: the sufferer overlooks the state of his own liver; it is the world *out there* that appears maliciously yellow.

Some hostility, as I remarked earlier, can be logically justified when the hated individual or group has deliberately obstructed our path. But it seems to be one of the hardest tasks in the world to persuade an individual to sift his hostile attitudes and to separate correctly the causes that lie *out there* from the causes that lie *in here*.

In the view of motivation that I am here proposing, the important thing is the person's systematized design for living. This design—not his hypothetical instincts—is the dynamic force in his life. Whenever an adjustment confronts him, he will make it with his *present* equipment—with his current prejudices, attitudes and sentiments. It is to the credit of most neo-Freudians that they see this point: they recognize that the ego is not a servant of the id, as Freud declared. Rather, one's *present* philosophy of life may hold the key to one's conduct. One person views the world as a jungle, where men are basically evil and dangerous; another views it as a friendly place inhabited by potentially congenial fellow beings. Each acts according to his own present belief.

This postinstinctive view of motivation has two great merits. First, it assures us that improvement in human relations is possible. We are not doomed by our inherent nature to do something—pro or con—with our "instinctual" aggression; we don't have to worry about it. Our behavior results from the sentiments and prejudices we have learned. But improved education can make for better learning, and suitable therapy can make for relearning.

The second merit is that we can now grapple fruitfully with the hardest problem of all: how the affiliative needs of an individual can be reconciled with his self-love and self-esteem.

Self-Love and Altruism

The issue may be formulated as follows: *how far have the individual's affiliative desires become extended?* Does his picture of his own security and personal integrity include only a few or many affiliative relations? Does he say, as did E. M. Forster's Englishman in India, "We must exclude someone from our gathering, or we shall be left with nothing"? How many we invite to our gathering is purely a matter of our past learning. We may fashion a tiny island of security embracing a small affiliated circle, or a larger island where our self-esteem is identical with the interests of an extended circle. Some individuals are so well socialized that they feel actually stronger when they reach further in their attachments, when they invite more and more people to their gathering.

If I read the course of ontogenetic development aright, the sequence of stages is approximately as follows: There is, first of all, the symbiotic phase that I have described. After this period of dependence and security with the mother, the child enters vigorously into affiliative relations with his environment. His curiosity and friendly interest know no bounds. Such frustrations as he suffers are but ripples in the onrushing tide. Around the age of two or three, when restrictions increase, frustrations grow more severe and help to intensify the growing sense of selfhood that marks the child off more sharply from his social and physical environment. Though he normally continues for many years to have warm and positive emotional identification with his parents, he learns also to be clamorous for his rights and quick to resent slights to his *amour-propre*. Self-love becomes a prominent factor in his life—perhaps the most prominent. But, often, the welfare of others is likewise an authentic concern.

It is at this point, however, that life histories markedly diverge. Some children never seem to lose the egocentricity of their early orientation; life revolves entirely around their own interests as conceived by themselves. In other children, the introceptive, enlarging process takes hold. Just how it comes about that some youths remain essentially infantile in their self-love, while others merge their developing ego-awareness with interests that reach far beyond their own hedonistic demands, is something we do not yet know. For our purposes it may be enough to note that individuals come to have different ranges of values—all emerging from an initial affiliative thrust at the start of life, then deflected by early egotism, but finally crystallized in narrow or in broad sentiments of greater or lesser degrees of socialization.

Hobbes was certainly not entirely wrong. Vainglory, pride and insatiate self-love are found in most mortals, even where a broadly socialized structure of values exists. This fact appears in all the relevant researches I have cited. People want congenial associations, but of the sort that maintain their own self-esteem. Very few individuals are saintly enough or humble enough to maintain friendly regard for individuals who offend their self-love. At the same time, myriad patterns develop, and myriad combinations of self-love and altruism. A really mature person has a wide range of socialized interests; and his altruistic sentiments, whatever they may be, are no less genuine components of his nature than are his narrower patches of pride and egotism.

Although loving regard is seldom able to survive when self-esteem is wounded, sometimes it does; and our theory must cover this fact. Forgiveness, though surely less common than resentment, may follow upon an offense to one's ego, and the preceding love may continue unabated. A serene and highly developed personality may forgive even when forgiveness is not sought. It is possible, likewise, for some personalities to distinguish sharply between *deed* and *doer,* to hate the evil while holding the perpetrator in true esteem. It is generally true that these charitable virtues stem only from an essentially religious philosophy of life, developed to a high degree and now functionally autonomous within the personality. In these cases of extreme affiliativeness, we are dealing with an extension of the ego to a very marked degree. The autonomy of the sentiment thus developed represents a genuine transformation of the proud, clamorous ego so characteristic of personality in its early juvenile years. But saints are rare among us.

The Economy of Hate

Why is it that, in our society today, relatively few people seem able to enlarge their scope of affiliation to include the larger gathering? The prejudiced or exclusionist style of life appears to predominate.

The answer to this question seems to have something to do with the principle of least effort. There is a marked short-run economy in holding a negative view of other people. If I can reject foreigners as a category, I shan't have to bother with them, except to keep them out of my country. If I can then ticket all Negroes as constituting an inferior and objectionable race, I conveniently dispose of a tenth of my fellow citizens. If I can put the Catholics into another category and reject them kit and caboodle, my life is still further simplified. To pare down again, I slice off the Jews, the Democrats and the members of labor unions. As for experts, professors and reformers, they are easily exiled along with all the other "communists." Soon there isn't much left for me to worry about except my own group on Suburban Heights—and I can proceed at leisure to destroy them one by one through gossip. I shall probably do so, depending on the extent of emotional deprivation in my own life.

That this easy, exclusionist style of life is exceedingly common is shown not only by recent studies in the *extent* of prejudice but also by the strikingly high correlation that exists among various *forms* of prejudice. A person who is anti-Negro is usually anti-Semitic, antilabor, antiforeigner. Conversely, if a person's self-esteem and his esteem for others have blended, he is likely to be friendly with members of all groups.

Perhaps the biggest obstacle to the improvement of human relations is the amazing ease with which the human mind creates categories. To categorize human groups is a simple, socially sanctioned way of sorting one's emotions and integrating one's behavior. The process is especially clear-cut in wartime. To make a fair-minded statement about the enemy in time of conflict is regarded as treason, or at least as weakness; and to criticize one's own side is taboo. We are expected to divide our sentiments sharply between institutional friend and institutional foe. To the out-group we ascribe all vices, all evil intentions, all atrocities; to the in-group belong all virtues. By this simple device the in-group flourishes, and our lives are economically arranged.

In peacetime the process is more subtle; but even here we tend to view those who are not in our orbit as ominously outside. An interesting lesson can be found in the word *rival*. In Latin, *rivales* meant two neighboring communities on the two banks of a common stream. Even in Shakespeare's English, rival meant companion.[12] But to us it means opponent, one whom we contend against. Unless a person is clearly *for* me I come to regard him as a competitor. People who live on two sides of a stream (or an ocean) might be friends—but more often they are rivals.

The categorizing effect is seen in the responses of American troops in World War II when they were asked about their attitudes toward foreign populations. Interestingly enough, almost all questions that referred to members of other groups *as individuals* fetched a friendly enough response. Thus, the soldiers on the whole liked the German people, Englishmen, and civilians "back home." But when categorical questions were asked about Germany or Britain as a country, or about Negroes, Jews or labor groups "back home," negative prejudice was apparent. For example, although the attitude toward English civilians was usually friendly, the categorical cleavage between national groups appeared in answers to the question, "Do you think England is doing her share in helping win the war?" The same question was asked about the United States. Seventy-eight per cent of the American troops said that the United States was doing *more* than its share; only 5 per cent said that England was doing so.[13]

So easy and socially approved is this black-white arrangement of groups in our thinking that one is tempted to ask, "Why challenge it?" The answer is that, in a shrunken world, such categorizing is a peril. Contacts between *ins* and *outs* are becoming more frequent; and whenever conflicts occur—in strikes, in riots or in war—they are too deadly to tolerate. Further, our democratic ethic tells us that the exclusionist philosophy of life is somehow subpersonal; it is less than mankind is capable of.

We have not yet learned how to control or to change the exclusionist philosophy of life, but progress is certainly being made in understanding its essential nature. I have already referred to the investigations at the University of California that show a definite connection between disturbance in a child's affiliative relationships with his parents and bigotry in his outlook upon minority groups.

The youthful (and older) authoritarian personality is one that feels insecure and threatened; as a result, it creates safe little islands of self-esteem. Mental hierarchies are formed, with most groups standing below one's own. Human relationships are regarded chiefly in terms of power, not of love. Institutional securities are prized. Patriotism is important, as are the church, the sorority, and any other established in-group. Much that happens outside this circle seems alien and menacing. Any sort of ambiguity or indefiniteness is troublesome—and democracy is replete with indefinite situations. The exclusionist personality wants his categories fixed and clear; he believes "there is only one right way to do a thing"; his mind is rigid. He will not extend his circle of affiliation. As a result he is suspicious, provincial, hostile.[14]

Of course we cannot say that personalities fall neatly into two groups: the bigoted and the tolerant, or the democratic and the authoritarian. No one, least of all the average American, has a wholly consistent pattern of affiliation and hostility. A foreign student in this country recently remarked, "When it comes to minorities, you Americans talk like heaven and feel like hell. I wonder, when the time comes, whether you will act more as you talk or more as you feel." And what a tangle of conflicts the white Westerner is! Often he is fair-minded and compassionate, following political, ethical and religious codes that are unexcelled in their universalistic ideals of respect for the person. On the other hand, he is often smug, self-righteous and insufferably patronizing in his dealing with the majority of the inhabitants of the earth, who happen to have skins of different pigmentation and older, if less technical, civilizations.

The Outlook

What are the chances for widening the scope of affiliative sentiments within our preferred political structure, democracy? I find two contrasting views. E. M. Forster wrote in 1938: "Two cheers for democracy—one because it admits variety, and two, because it permits criticism. Two cheers are quite enough; there is no occasion to give three. Only Love, the Beloved Republic, deserves that." Precisely the opposite view is found in the concluding sentence in the 1950 research report *The authoritarian personality*: "If fear and destructiveness are the major emotional sources of fascism, *eros* belongs mainly to democracy."

Overlooking the too narrow implications of the term *eros*, it seems self-evident that the chances for human beings to broaden their affiliative relations are better under democracy than elsewhere. Yet Forster, too, is right in saying that, though democracy allows diversity and criticism, it has not yet found methods for releasing the potential of love in human relations. History does not indicate that it will ever do so unaided. Even organized religion today would seem to require technical assistance.

To me, the most hopeful sign lies in the developments within modern social science. Research in personality and in human relations is teaching us much concerning the nature of affiliation and hostility. Though theory lags, there is hope that serviceable inductive generalizations, properly tested against philosophy and the wisdom of the ages, will soon emerge. In fact, I venture even now to list principles that seem to me already fairly established:

It is the nature of human life to crave affiliation and love, provided such attachments are not inimical to one's sense of personal security and self-esteem. Love that entails forgiveness likewise exists, but is more rare.

When the bid for affiliation is rebuffed or self-esteem is wounded, ordinarily a secondary hostility develops. This hostility is often displaced upon irrelevant "enemies."

The operations of both affiliative and hostile motives are properly regarded, not as manifestations of instincts, but as expressions of the learned sentiment structure of the individual.

Each person, through circumstance and training, develops an exclusionist, an inclusionist or a mixed style of life that guides his own human relations.

There is a short-run economy in the exclusionist style of life—that is, in a sentiment structure narrowly built around a limited conception of self-interest and a small "safety island" of affiliation. Yet a person who experiences his own integrity only in opposition to other people, who feels secure only by undermining the security of others, can scarcely be said to have a significant purpose or integrity of his own.

There is no inherent limitation in the nature of man or in the nature of learning that requires self-esteem to be secured only through the exclusionist style of life. Personal integrity is entirely compatible with a wide circle of affiliation.

Finally, to implement these principles in action, we must maximize situations in which the individual (child or adult) can participate fully and on terms of equal status in projects of joint concern to him and his associates. By so doing, we shall realize affiliation, safeguard self-esteem and reduce hostility. Whenever this formula is applied, it goes far in improving human relations in home, school, factory and nation—and between sets of "rivals" who live on the two banks of the stream of life.

REFERENCES

1. I. Suttie, *The origins of love and hate*, London: 1935.
2. S. A. Stouffer *et al.*, *The American soldier: I, combat and its after-math*, Princeton: Princeton University Press, 1949, p. 174; see also Chapter 11.

3. For additional evidence along the same lines see Chapter 12 of the present volume; K. Lewin, *Resolving social conflicts*, New York: 1948; and F. J. Roethlisberger and W. J. Dickson, *Management and the worker*, Cambridge: Harvard University Press, 1939.

4. G. W. Allport and B. M. Kramer, "Some roots of prejudice," *J. Soc. Psychol.*, 1946, 22:9-29.

5. I. Suttie, *op. cit.*, p. 23.

6. E. Simmel, *Anti-Semitism, a social disease*, New York: 1946, p. 41.

7. E. Powers and H. Witmer, *An experiment in the prevention of delinquency*, New York: Columbia University Press, 1950.

8. S. K. Escalona, "Overt sympathy with the enemy in maladjusted children," *Amer. J. Orthopsychiat.*, 1946, 16:333-40.

9. T. W. Adorno, E. Frenkel-Brunswik, D. J. Levinson and R. N. Sanford, *The authoritarian personality*, New York: Harper, 1950.

10. B. Bettelheim and M. Janowitz, *Dynamics of prejudice*, New York: 1950.

11. See G. W. Allport, *Personality: a psychological interpretation*, New York: Holt, 1937, Chap. 7.

12. Well, good-night.
    If you do meet Horatio and Marcellus,
    The rivals of my watch, bid them make haste.

                                                    Hamlet, Act I, Scene I

13. S. A. Stouffer *et al.*, *op. cit.*, II, 627.

14. H. W. Adorno *et al.*, *op. cit.*, *passim*.

PART IV: *Group tensions*

CHAPTER 14

Prejudice in modern perspective

During the past two decades we have learned much about the causes of human prejudice, about its nature and evil consequences. In these twenty years, more research, more writing and more objective analysis have occurred than in all previous centuries taken together.

The creed of brotherhood is ancient; it has long been present in all the great religions of the world. But the pathway to this high goal has only recently become a concern of social and psychological science. The three following essays deal with selected aspects of the problem. The issues receive fuller consideration in *The nature of prejudice* (1954).

The first essay deals with racial tensions. In two lands—South Africa and the United States—the conflict is especially acute. There are important differences between these two countries, but the underlying causes and manifestations of their prejudice are the same. What we learn in one land has considerable applicability to the other.

An invitation to give the twelfth annual Alfred Hoernlé Memorial Lecture in Durban, South Africa, in July 1956 provided the occasion for this essay. The South African Institute of Race Relations sponsored the lecture and published it in pamphlet form at its Johannesburg headquarters in 1956.

Between 1913 and 1920, R. F. Alfred Hoernlé lectured in philosophy at Harvard University, adding strength and luster to a department already famous for its scholars and teachers. I had the privilege of studying with him the thought of Descartes and Spinoza and the philosophic mood of the Enlightenment. As is the case with all great teachers, he influenced his students not only by what he said but even more by what he was. We knew him to be a truly international personage. Our student gossip mistakenly identified his birthplace as England, as Germany, as France, as Belgium, as South Africa. One of our number suggested that he might have come from Tristan da Cunha. But to our minds he was also an authentic Bostonian, so well did he fit into our special corner of New England.

For many decades I have admired him as a cosmopolitan scholar who offered us a compassionate conception of man and an idealism with firm terrestrial roots. Therefore I know that you will understand my sense of pride and gratitude in being invited to pay my personal tribute to his memory in the land of his adoption.

It is in his own broad, synoptic spirit that I venture upon my assignment. My desire is to bring the perspectives of social philosophy and of social science to bear upon man's agelong struggle with the disorder of bigotry, which lies deeply embedded in his own nature. You will forgive me if, as a visitor to South Africa, I make few direct references to problems in the Union. I think you will agree with me that, by dealing with issues which transcend national boundaries, we can on this occasion more fittingly honor Alfred Hoernlé as a figure of world significance.

Prejudice and Loyalties

One sometimes hears people of unquestionable sincerity ask, "Isn't prejudice, after all, a good thing?" I have met the query both in the United States and in the Union of South Africa. Really, I suspect, the questioner is asking, "Isn't loyalty to one's own group and to one's cherished values a good thing?" To this question, the answer is, of course, emphatically yes. In a world where the cement of positive values is badly loosened, we welcome any evidence of loyalty; for loyalty, as Josiah Royce taught us, is intrinsically a virtue. From this point of view, even the spectacular rise of nationalism today is not necessarily evil; it becomes so only when it arbitrarily circumscribes the domain of loyalty. Alfred Hoernlé himself examined the sentiment of patriotism and found it altogether good, provided only that it is neither aggressive nor exclusive.[1] Like Royce, he would require of our personal attachments only one condition—that they give due respect to our neighbor's loyalties. Only one virtue stands higher than our separate and special devotions, and that is loyalty to the concept of loyalty itself.

When a man asks, "Isn't prejudice a good thing?" he is probably confusing prejudice with particular loyalties. The very ease of this confusion places upon us an obligation to define *prejudice* carefully.[2] Prejudice, I hold, is an almost universal psychological syndrome marked by two—and only two—essential features. The first is the affective disposition that makes us lean toward or away from an object. Spinoza rightly speaks of both "love prejudice" and "hate prejudice." We can be prejudiced for or against an object. This ingredient by itself does not distinguish prejudice from any liking or disliking.

The second ingredient is more crucial—the basing of love or

hate on beliefs that are wholly or partially erroneous. To take an example: belief in witchcraft, today as in the past, rests upon a wrong diagnosis of our distress. Our cows do go dry; disease does torment us; a vague *ufufunyane* affects our nerves—but the cause is not witches. In the world at large, many such false diagnoses lead us to accuse whole nations, races or cultures of evil intentions and witch-like attributes that they do not in fact possess.

The commonest form of erroneous belief is the overgeneraliza-tion which holds that *all* members of a group possess some alleged characteristic. We say that Jews as a group are dishonest; Americans as a group are materialistic; or Africans as a group are like children. These assertions, and others like them, are either demonstrable ex-aggerations or total falsehoods. Any negative attitude based on such errors entails prejudice.

I am not, of course, implying that human antagonisms are always based on an error. Some, on occasion, may be based on a true op-position of values in which prejudice plays no part. One is not prejudiced against a gangster who invades one's premises and threatens one's life; this is a realistic conflict, and antagonism is based on a correct appraisal of facts. It is still too early to attempt an esti-mate of the amount of human conflict that is realistic and the amount that is imaginary. We now know, however, that if we can lead men to correct their erroneous appraisals of human groups, they tend to abandon long-standing antagonisms. They cease to fear what is not fearful and to hate what is not hateful. No longer do they tilt at windmills. Rather, they reserve their animus for real problems and real enemies.

A crisp but satisfactory definition of prejudice is one derived from the writings of St. Thomas Aquinas: *Prejudice is thinking ill of others without sufficient warrant.* Our examples of witch-hunting, anti-Semitism and anti-Americanism fit the definition well. If you happen to prefer slang to the discourse of the angelic Thomas, I recommend as an equivalent definition: *Prejudice is being down on something you are not up on.*

So much for the term itself. The question still remains: is pre-judice an evil thing in human relationships? Might it not be argued that partisanship, even if based on error, is necessary to the achieve-ment of desirable goals? And that prejudice against prejudice is merely the currently fashionable bigotry of the liberal? I am, as you can see, committed to answer the charges that we are all creatures of prejudice, that nothing can be done about it and that, anyway, prejudice is sometimes a good thing.

Value and Disvalue

There are, I think, two modes of reasoning which lead us to the conviction that, while prejudice is a common enough pattern of mental existence, it is not inevitable—and that it is invariably an evil. The first mode of reasoning is employed by deductive theories of value; the second is more pragmatic in character and is closely meshed with the operation of social science itself.

Philosophers ordinarily employ the deductive mode. They ask, in effect: what ethical goal, if consistently followed, would prove most viable for mankind? That is to say, what goal would lead to the maximum fulfillment of men's interests, or to the greatest possible happiness for the greatest possible numbers of human beings. All ethical inquiry seeks rules that, if followed, would be fecund for the maximization of human values. The search led Kant to the conclusion that man may *never* treat another human being as a means to an end. It led Royce to affirm loyalty to loyalty as the supreme imperative. It led Hoernlé to conclude that what he called "the liberal spirit" is most conducive to safeguarding and promoting *quality* in human life. Any social order is evil, writes Hoernlé, "in which, from the nature of its internal arrangements, any group of its members is, in principle, condemned to stunted bodies and to stunted minds." [3]

Philosophic reasoning of this type leads to the conclusion that prejudice is indefensible, since it can never lead to an increase in value over a wide range of human concerns. By its very nature, it hinders loyalties, constricts man's reason and sows disvalue.

The deductive approach is manifested also in the ethical imperatives of religion. Starting with a universalistic outlook, all the great religions of the world establish rules that would make life maximally livable for mankind. To Christians, *Love thy neighbor as thyself* is perhaps the most familiar rendering of this golden rule, but every great religion has a precise equivalent. Mahatma Gandhi sought long and hard for a term in English that would represent the exact opposite of prejudice. The term he chose was *equimindedness*, a condition of spiritual generosity wherein one's own firmly held beliefs permit others to hold equally firm beliefs of a different order. A Christian equivalent is the moving injunction of Jesus to His disciples: "Let both grow together until the harvest." [4] We do not know our ultimate worth to the harvester; but we can, if we will, grow together peaceably until the day of reckoning arrives.

Unfortunately, we may not assume that all religious reasoning is of this equiminded order. While every major religion endorses the golden rule and extols the values of brotherhood, each has generated contradictory, if minor, principles whose consequences are divisive and ethnocentric. Forgetting the universalistic implications of their monotheism, certain Moslems believe that destruction of the infidel is a high duty. Christianity, through its doctrines of election, revelation and theocracy, opened the door for a special and self-serving interpretation of God's plan for His creation. The special dogmas of election and revelation invited men to set themselves at the summit of God's supposed hierarchical arrangement for the human race. Theocracy made it possible to enforce this arrangement. Until the seventeenth century, it was never doubted that the State should implement the reasoning of its theologians. In certain lands today, the tie between theology and politics is still close.

Bigotry is thus a paradoxical product of Christianity. To justify bigotry, theologians are often forced back upon certain obscurities in the Book of Genesis. The story of the tower of Babel, for example, they interpret to mean that equimindedness is not only impossible but clearly opposed to God's will. Especially interesting to psychologists is the manner in which adherence to the bigotry-inspiring portions of the Old Testament is reconciled with the clear imperatives of equimindedness in the New. A historical example is the serpentine reasoning of Menno Simons, the Anabaptist theologian of the sixteenth century, who wrestled with St. Paul's injunction: "Therefore judge nothing before the time, until the Lord come" [5]— a precept identical with Christ's command: "Let both grow together until the harvest." Menno Simons interpreted the Pauline text to mean: "None may judge unless he have the judging word on his side." [6]

Here is the trap into which every religious bigot falls. Claiming to have the "judging word" on his side, he finds that he can conveniently violate the universalistic imperatives of his religion. Accordingly, he reverses the humility of Job and says, in effect, to the Lord, "Thy ways are, after all, only the same as my ways."

No need to dwell longer on deductive answers to the question: is prejudice an evil? I have tried to indicate that all the synoptic philosophies of man and all the great religions concur in their answer: only a condition of mind that is prejudice-free can consistently augment human values. I have also sounded the warning that it is all too easy to argue from selected and partial premises to a conclusion that justifies particularistic prejudices. Bigotry, one may say, is the result of ethical reasoning wherein an ontological premise is secretly abandoned in favor of a hidden premise of self-interest.

How does social science stand in relation to this matter? First, of course, some social scientists are philosophically or religiously inclined. They accept the universalistic view and lead their scientific lives in accordance with this commitment. A few are not so universalistic; they proceed from partisan premises. One thinks of the meretricious Nazi and Communist scientists who have contrived to prove what their leaders desire them to prove. Both these groups, however different their premises, are deductive in practice.

But for the most part, I suspect, social scientists are *inductive* by temperament. They ask, "Cannot science shed light on man's quest for an adequate ethics, and help build sound standards for moral conduct?" They say, in effect, "Let's look at man's social behavior and see why so much of his conduct is self-defeating and unproductive of what he himself considers to be good."

Inductive studies show, for one thing, that many of our thought-models become set early in life and that they prove maladaptive to our adult needs. Scientific concepts such as *stereotype, rationalization, defense mechanism, cognitive rigidity* and *semantic therapy* are testimony to the new type of insight we have gained. As contributors to this enlightenment we think of such writers as Walter Lippmann, Stuart Chase, Korzybski, Freud, Moreno, Wittgenstein, Richard Thouless, Trigant Burrow and Cantril. The exposure to ourselves of our own prejudices, though only the first step toward cure, is a significant achievement.

But the work of social science does not stop with a mere challenge. It offers means for clarifying our values and for implementing them in a rational way. Until relatively recent years, for example, it was thought that the only way to conduct an industry or business was on an essentially punitive basis. Harshness and hierarchy dominated the practices of management. Workers were nameless; they were hired or fired on whim. Placements in jobs were haphazard, and praise was an unused incentive. Above all, the worker did not participate in the many decisions affecting his destiny. This dark age of industry is, of course, far from ended; but in many shops and offices we see wholesome results that come from applying social science. When workers are no longer nameless, nor punished, nor patronized, nor overlooked; when it is realized that the whole man goes to work, carrying with him his deep need for affection, his hopes, fears and troubles; when industry meshes into his life so that he feels participant in his own destiny; when his purposes are making use of his abilities; when his aspirations are socially understood and approved—then the whole productive process improves.[7]

Social science has played a significant part in bringing about this new stage in the industrial revolution. It is by no means a matter of teaching management superficial tricks for manipulating workers. On the contrary, social science demonstrates to the employer that he cannot achieve his own purposes unless he ceases to use his workers as targets for his own private anxieties and hostilities. It teaches him self-knowledge and, in this way, knowledge of others. It teaches him a new conception of human relations. In so doing, it reveals prejudices for what they are—a prime source of suffering and disvalue.

Moving to the field of race relations, think what would happen to our prejudices if we were to admit to our minds the following fairly certain scientific discoveries:

Racial membership accounts for only a negligible fraction of human attributes. For complexion, hair form and shape of shinbone —yes. For intelligence, temper, talent, outlook, virtue and worth— not at all.

There are no instinctive aversions of human races one toward another. All such aversions are built into children, and only with considerable difficulty.

In almost every case where segregation is practiced, the financial loss is enormous, thus lowering the standards of nourishment, shelter, health, recreation and freedom for all groups concerned. Prejudice sows only economic disvalue.

Most hostility arises not from unacceptable characteristics in other people, but from our private emotional disorders for which the hated group is not responsible.

When people live in such a way as to have equal-status contact with one another in the pursuit of common objectives, they ordinarily cease to perceive one another as threats and are likely to develop a tolerance and liking for one another.

These are but a few of the almost certain scientific laws that bear on our racial relationships. A prejudiced person who can be brought to admit these laws to his mental store will find his previous creed of exclusiveness untenable.

To restate my point: The net effect of modern science is to show that prejudice can never maximize value. While it may make for short-run emotional gains for the individual, in the long run it is uneconomic, fecund for violence and for war, trivializing to human reason and stultifying to both its possessor and its victim. It is impossible to see how value—define it as you will—can be enhanced through prejudice. Social science therefore joins its answer to that of philosophy and religion: prejudice is not, never has been and never will be a good thing in human society.

This being the case, we must next inquire: what can social science contribute to the *conquest* of prejudice in modern life?

Group Differences

The most logical place to start is with the factual study of group differences. We have already observed that the distinction between realistic conflict and prejudice lies chiefly in the erroneous beliefs, especially the overgeneralizations, on which prejudice is based. To distinguish fact from falsity, we need an accurate perception of peoples and their institutions, and an understanding of their real purposes and capacities. The first duty of the social scientist is to discover what *truth* lies behind such concepts as "mind of the nation" or "ethnic character." Like the medical diagnostician, he may start by asking embarrassing questions: *Are* Armenians a bad credit risk? *Are* Jews clannish and exclusive? *Are* Africans inherently stupid and unteachable? (It so happens that the answer to these questions is almost certainly no.)

Even though our methods of research are imperfect, such scientific evidence as we have regarding these and similar allegations is far sounder than the guesswork and anecdotalism customarily employed to support prejudiced accusations. Yet the social scientist who insists upon discovering the objective facts concerning group differences runs the risk of opprobrium. Some sentimentalists prefer on a priori grounds to deny the existence of racial or national differences; bigots are certain that they know all the differences in advance. But the social scientist wards off these attacks as best he can and affirms that his first logical duty is to *find out the facts*.

We cannot here survey all the results that are coming to light.[8] Research has still far to go. But, as I read the preliminary results, there seems to be little justification for most of our racial accusations. Differences that are expected to appear fail to do so, or else they are of a trivial order.

Let us take one sample finding of a positive difference. It concerns the incidence of alcoholism among ethnic groups in the United

States. After making a comprehensive survey, one sociologist concludes: "In statistics of admissions for alcoholic disorders to various hospitals in this country the Irish have consistently had rates two to three times as high as any other ethnic group." [9] In one institution, for example, the rate of admission for the Irish is fifty times that of the Jews.[10] Here is a factual ethnic difference; yet it is pure prejudice to say, "I don't like the Irish because they drink too heavily." For even among the Irish, the rate of alcoholic psychosis is only about 25 in any group of 100,000 Irishmen. The only realistic statement of personal preference that could be made, therefore, is somewhat as follows: "Since I don't like heavy drinkers, I probably would not like approximately 1 per cent of the Irish."

What a world of difference it would make in our human relationships if we could learn to say *one per cent* instead of *all*; this *Irishman* instead of *the Irish*; and *he* or *she* instead of *they*.

Techniques for the study of national and ethnic differences are rapidly developing. Vital statistics of the sort just cited are one source of information; international public opinion polls are another. Cross-national studies using scaling techniques are entering the scene. This topic is too specialized for further discussion here, but I do wish to sound two warnings:

First: in uncovering differences in the character of peoples, we must not forget to look also for similarities—for what Kluckhohn calls "cultural universals." [11] While differences readily strike the eye, the existence of a common ground in all cultures and in all branches of the human family is a more pervasive fact. It is true that each group has some defining attribute that makes it a group. Polish people speak Polish; most Africans have dark complexions; most Moslems hold the Koran in high regard. But these valid *defining* attributes (technically called J-curve attributes) are few.[12] Our error is to assume that all other alleged attributes are also of this order, as when we say that Poles as a group are stupid, Africans are childlike and Moslems are bloodthirsty.

Second: we must not assume that even validly discovered differences justify hostility. People can differ from us without menacing us. Suppose, for example, that one group turns out to be shorter than we in stature, less educated, less humorous, more irascible, more suspicious, even less trustworthy. Are we justified in hating members of this group or in regarding them as a threat? Do not the same differences exist within our own families? Some brothers and sisters are ill-favored compared with others; but they are often loved in spite of their oddity.

While the study of group differences is rapidly expanding, we still stumble at thresholds. Unless I am mistaken, there are few studies under way in South Africa of the beliefs, capacities, aspirations and hopes of the several ethnic groups composing the Union. Assertions are rife; data are few.

Phenomenological Studies

Besides the factual appraisal of group differences, what has social science to offer? Well, for one thing it teaches us the manner in which we *perceive* other groups of people. This area of investigation is *phenomenological*. Some years ago Dr. Malherbe reported an early study of this type: In a public service examination, candidates were instructed to "underline the percentage that you think Jews constitute of the whole population of South Africa: 1 per cent, 5 . . . 10 . . . 20 . . . 25 . . . 30 . . . per cent." When tabulated, the modal estimate turned out to be 20 per cent. The true answer is just a little over 1 per cent.[13]

This neat little experiment shows how our fears and hostility tend to inflate our perceptions out of all proportion to the facts. The American public, we know—and probably also the public of South Africa—tends to overestimate the size of the Communist party in its own land.[14]

A particularly important line of phenomenological investigation concerns the effect of equal-status contact upon our perceptions. Several studies have demonstrated that equal-status contact between groups leads to mutual regard and respect. This favorable effect is greater if members are working together for common objectives and if law and custom sanction this type of contact.[15]

Examples of this research, neat in design and convincing in result, are the two large-scale studies of public housing projects conducted respectively by Deutsch and Collins, and by Wilner, Walkley and Cook.[16] In both studies, integrated and segregated occupancy patterns were investigated. (In the former study, Negroes constituted approximately 50 per cent of the integrated housing units; in the latter they constituted 10 per cent.) From both investigations the same basic findings emerged: white people living closer to Negroes felt more friendly to them; proximity brought favorable attitudes. And what for our present purpose is most important, proximity tended to change perceptions. People living in segregated units tended to see the Negroes as a dirty people, aggressive, hostile, dangerous, not to be trusted. People living in integrated units more often reported that the Negro inhabitants of the projects were much the same as white people. Unfavorable stereotyped attributes vanished on closer acquaintance. Segregation, we may now reasonably conclude, makes for mystery, stereotypy and unfriendliness.

The phenomenological approach is broader than I have yet indicated. For example, there is the well-known tendency in man to perceive a living human agent as the cause of his miseries. Belief in witchcraft, still widespread, locates the cause of one's sufferings in a malign human agency. But it is not only among primitive people that the anthropomorphizing tendency exists. We find the same disposition in our own society, although the witches we accuse are more likely to be collective than single. Is my business shaky? *They* are to blame. Is my job insecure? *They* want to take it from me. Am I worried about my immoral impulses? Well, just look at *them*. *They*, of course, are the Jews or Bantus, Catholics or men from Mars, according to the fixations of our fantasy.

Psychodynamic Research

Which brings us to psychodynamics, an area of investigation in which marked advances have been made. Psychodynamics focuses attention upon the type of person who, because of his own needs and structure of character, is prone to develop strong prejudices. Bigotry stands revealed as one of the psychological crutches adopted by people who are crippled in their encounters with life. The crippling may have occurred in childhood, or it may come from feelings of insecurity and wounded pride in adult years. In any case, prejudice exists in many lives because it fulfills a protective and even sedative function for its bearer. The first major series of researches establishing this fact was published as recently as 1950 under the title *The authoritarian personality*. This pioneer production has since been followed by many additional studies dealing with character-conditioned prejudice.[17]

To my mind, the crux of this extensive work is its demonstration that bigotry is an easy and natural style of life to adopt. Most people are buffeted by the anxieties of existence—the normal fears of death and disaster, augmented by economic insecurity, affectional deprivation and feelings of guilt. This total "existential anxiety" fuses with the irritations of daily life. The resulting complex may lead one to seek human agents to explain his distress: it is *they* who are to blame. A punitive and exclusive style of life gradually evolves. One feels secure only in the bosom of his own group. There his pride is fed by myths of superiority, and there his two fiercely possessive needs—property and sex—are focused. There he finds social support for his prejudice; religion, literature, humor, tradition and the usages of language help sustain his exclusionist mode of life.

We owe to MacCrone some of our understanding of this life-style. He demonstrates the interlocking of suspiciousness, exclusive-ness and ethnic hostility in human lives, and their blending with rigid religious ideology. He also offers us a theory of "ethno-erotism," which relates this disorder to a fixation of man's capacity-for-love exclusively upon his immediate in-group.[18] In still another sense, it is wise to note the erotic complications in prejudice. To a surpris-ing extent, sex-conflict and guilt seem to enter the process. It is comforting to think that the demon of impulse resides not in our own breasts so much as in the lascivious black man, or Italian, or French-man, or Jew. As Goethe says, we never feel so free from sin as when we expatiate upon the sinful deeds of others.

Since the clamorous needs of the body and the ego, and the insistent goads of fear and anxiety, dispose us to develop a prejudiced pattern of life, we need no longer wonder at the ubiquity of our problem. We marvel, rather, at the frequency with which we en-counter equiminded mortals. We should be asking: how is it that so many people develop self-insight, self-criticism and a universalistic ethic to counteract the bent toward bigotry? Up to now, psychology has given less attention to the tolerant personality than to the intol-erant.

Genetic Studies

Basic to the study of both types is the study of child develop-ment, including teaching at home, in school and in the culture at large. In this area, too, there is progress to report.

Children, we know, manifest no prejudice whatever in the early years of life. Such awareness of race difference as exists is for the most part neutral or friendly, though sometimes marked by puzzle-ment. A little boy of four was playing for the first time with a little black girl. He said to her, "You are very nice." Then screwing up his eyes with intense effort, he added, "But I can't quite see you." There was a perceptual adjustment to be made, but the simple fact of skin color was not for him a cause for dislike.

Certain styles of child training, we now know, lead more surely than others to the production of prejudice. Broadly speaking, chil-dren who feel a warmth and security in their parents—children who know that, however badly they misbehave, they are still loved—are less prone to prejudice in later years than are children who encounter at home a rejective situation, where discipline is both harsh and capricious. It is ominous for the future of a child when the discipline he receives is based on the emotional needs of the disciplinarian rather than on any consideration of the child's own needs.[19]

Sociocultural Studies

Hastily I move on to the perspectives of sociology, anthropology and economics.

We are familiar with the Marxist theory that holds all prejudice to be rooted in an exploitation. The theory holds that ruling groups devise an ideology to justify and maintain the "surplus value" accruing to dominant groups from the ill-paid labor of subordinate groups. It seeks the roots of prejudice in one and only one human passion: greed. Herein lies its one-sidedness, for we know that prejudice also draws nourishment from fear and insecurity, from feelings of inferiority and pride, from frustration and irritability, from deprivation of love and from the sheer need to conform. Yet greed surely is to be reckoned with, as are all the economic trappings of prejudice that it brings in its train.

Economics teaches us also to look to the ecological structure of a region in order to understand the immediate nature of group conflicts, and to look to the cycles of depression and prosperity for upswings and downswings in prejudice. Above all, economics confronts us with a supreme paradox of prejudice. Through greed, men seek to reap economic profit from their prejudices, but they are betrayed by these same prejudices into behaving in most uneconomic ways. Segregation and discrimination—fruits of prejudice—turn out to be economically debilitating.[20]

From sociology and anthropology we learn additional facts to correct and supplement our psychological analysis. These social sciences warn us that prejudice is not always a crutch employed by immature or crippled personalities. It may be a phenomenon of sheer conformity, barely skin-deep. But whether it is skin-deep or bone-deep, we cannot understand prejudice unless we know its social context. What strata exist in a given society? Which are traditionally regarded as high in status, and which low? Does the culture offer a ritualized target for aggression, such as formally sanctioned anti-Semitism, a dogma of white supremacy or a belief in witchcraft? Answers to these and similar questions are needed if we are to achieve adequate perspective.

Research in sociology and in anthropology has resulted in several important laws. Let me cite three:

In a heterogeneous society there is more group prejudice than in homogeneous societies. South Africa, for example, which has several "perceptual points for alarm," harbors more prejudice than, say, St. Helena or Sweden, both remarkably homogeneous societies.

Prejudice is greater whenever there are severe barriers to communication between groups. This law has as its reciprocal the law of contact: prejudice lessens whenever there is equal-status contact between members of groups in the pursuit of common objectives.

Assuming that there is germinal prejudice against a certain group, this prejudice will become stronger in proportion to the size of the group in the total population. Only about one thousand people from India live in the United States, but there are about thirteen million Negroes. The former group is overlooked; the latter is a target for much prejudice and discrimination. If the number of Indians were to rise to the proportion obtaining in Natal, there is no doubt that fear, suspicion and dislike would rise accordingly.

Yet it would be an error to assume that the mere density of a group in the total population brings about prejudice against it. In South Africa, for example, I find myself quite overwhelmed by South Africans. I am not for this reason prejudiced against them. Populational density, I suggest, is never a causal factor, but rather a multiplier of whatever prior prejudices exist.[21]

Historical Horizons

We have not yet spoken of the perspective of history. The truth of the matter is that, without the lens of history, we fumble along in shortsighted confusion. Take, for example, that stubborn prejudice bequeathed to us from antiquity: anti-Semitism. Only history can show us how, throughout the ages, Jews have been forced to occupy a position "at the fringe of stable values" as money-lenders, entertainers and entrepreneurs; and how such marginal people are regarded by conservatives in every era as agents of threat.

Again, without a knowledge of the Civil War in the United States and the Anglo-Boer War in South Africa, and of the heartbreaks and bitterness engendered by each, it would be impossible to understand the present family quarrels in the two lands. Only with the aid of this perspective can we come to see that, in both countries, the black man is to a certain extent an innocent bystander. He is caught, through no fault of his own, between two bitter trains of memory.

Besides adding to our knowledge of specific prejudices in specific eras, history teaches us that the official morality of a nation—what we may call its stateways—has always exerted an influence of major importance. One can point to countless violations of the spirit of the Magna Charta, the Fourteenth Amendment to the Constitution of the United States and the Charter of the United Nations, but it is impossible to deny that these statements of policy have a continuing and meliorative effect upon human relationships.

Speaking for myself, I cannot yet decide which is a more important factor in the creation of bigotry: stateways or folkways— folkways being defined here to include child training and the individual's style of life. If we are dedicated to the reduction of prejudice, is it better to fight the battle on the political front or in the home, classroom and church? Fortunately, this question need not be answered in terms of either-or. Each of us may work according to his lights and his talent. There is plenty to be done at both ends.

Finally, a lesson of history which I consider the most important of all: history helps us to determine whether we are, in fact, waging a losing battle. The prejudiced style of life is so easy to develop, so natural, so ubiquitous and, in many places, so solidly supported by the social and political structure that one could easily despair. We are tempted to say that there is no solution to our dilemma; in Sartre's words, "No exit." Among white South Africans I have encountered this pessimism. Black South Africans, too, assume the impasse. One tribe has an imaginative explanation for the situation: it holds that God Himself is good, wishing the whole human race well, but that unfortunately He has a half-witted brother who constantly interferes with His plans. It is this half-witted brother who has taken charge of relationships within the human family.

But to despair is to misread the long lesson of history. Relationships within the human family have always been strained and often fratricidal. No story is more depressing than the history of the Christian Church, which for the most part has disregarded its Founder's injunction, "Let both grow together until the harvest." Yet, during the sixteenth century and even earlier, golden words were spoken in defense of religious liberty and toleration; in the nineteenth century, many of these words were realized in practice; and in the twentieth century, we begin to descry a genuine purging of the religious conscience from much of its bigotry.

Similarly, stateways, if viewed in historical perspective, reveal slow but true advance. The progress is signalized in recent years by the United Nations' Declaration of Human Rights. Especially striking is the banding of private citizens for the extension of racial sanity and the reduction of prejudice. The South African Institute of Race Relations is an example. Comparable organizations exist in the United States for the same purpose; many are international in scope.

I have already drawn special attention to one recent historical thread: the perspective on the causes and cures of prejudice disclosed by modern social science. Its discoveries have no magical power, but they do bring a cleansing spirit and new hope into the oppressive caves of human ignorance and hate. The current outpouring of research and books; the training of younger people who, in increasing numbers, are dedicating themselves to the betterment of human relationships—these are signs of progress. At long last, in every land, enlightened men and women are determined that man's intelligence shall be brought to serve the cause of man's redemption. They see more clearly than ever before that living together as a single human family is the only future mankind can have.

Thus, viewing the matter in historical perspective, we detect a new spirit in the land. Whether it will spread rapidly enough to avert disastrous clashes of nation and race we cannot yet predict. We can say only that the age-old disorder of prejudice is beginning to yield to diagnosis and treatment, much as other endemic diseases have yielded. The more we learn of its nature, the more we discover about modes of possible cure.

The road ahead looks discouraging, but it is marked with these beacons of hope. We have, therefore, abundant reason to keep faith with all humane prophets of equimindedness in the past. They labored—and so must we—to bring rationality and compassion to bear upon our common problem.

REFERENCES

1. R. F. A. Hoernlé, *Race and reason,* Johannesburg: Witwatersrand University Press, 1945, pp. xxii, xxxii.

2. Elsewhere I have considered the problem of definition in greater detail; see G. W. Allport, *The nature of prejudice,* Cambridge: Addison-Wesley, 1954, Chap. 1. Here I summarize briefly the conclusion reached.

3. R. F. A. Hoernlé, *South African native policy and the liberal spirit,* Johannesburg: Witwatersrand University Press, 1945, p. 112.

4. St. Matthew 13:30.

5. I Corinthians 4:5.

6. Menno Simons, "A foundation and plain instruction of the saving doctrine of Christ" (trans. by I. D. Rupp), *On the ban: questions and answers,* 1550, Lancaster: Elias Baar, 1863.

7. The story of this modern chapter in the industrial revolution has been told many times. A significant publication is F. J. Roethlisberger and W. J. Dickson, *Management and the worker,* Cambridge: Harvard University Press, 1939. One may also consult S. Chase, *The proper study of mankind,* rev. ed., New York: Harper, 1956; likewise, Chapter 12 of the present volume.

8. For discussions of methods, findings and theory in this area of research see G. W. Allport, *The nature of prejudice, op. cit.,* Chaps. 6, 7, 13; see also A. Inkeles and D. J. Levinson, "National character: a study of modal personality and sociocultural systems," in G. Lindzey (ed.), *Handbook of social psychology,* Cambridge: Addison-Wesley, 1954, Vol. II, Chap. 26.

9. R. F. Bales, "Cultural differences in rates of alcoholism," *Quart. J. Stud. Alcohol,* 1946, 6:484.

10. H. W. Haggard and E. M. Jellinek, *Alcohol explored,* Garden City: Doubleday, Doran, 1942, p. 252.

11. C. Kluckhohn, "Universal categories of culture," in A. L. Kroeber (ed.), *Anthropology today,* Chicago: Chicago University Press, 1953.

12. See G. W. Allport, *The nature of prejudice, op. cit.,* Chap. 6.

13. E. G. Malherbe, *Race attitudes and education,* Johannesburg: South African Institute of Race Relations, 1946. Second Annual Hoernlé Memorial Lecture.

14. S. A. Stouffer, *Communism, conformity and civil liberties,* New York: Doubleday, 1955.

15. Cf. G. W. Allport, *The nature of prejudice, op. cit.,* Chap. 16.

16. M. Deutsch and M. E. Collins, *Interracial housing,* Minneapolis: University of Minnesota Press, 1950; D. M. Wilner, R. P. Walkley and S. W. Cook, *Human relations in interracial housing,* Minneapolis: University of Minnesota Press, 1955.

17. T. W. Adorno, E. Frenkel-Brunswik, D. J. Levinson and R. N. Sanford, *The authoritarian personality,* New York: Harper, 1950. More recent summaries of the topic may be found in H. J. Eysenck, *The psychology of politics,* London: Routledge & Kegan Paul, 1954; and in G. W. Allport, *The nature of prejudice, op. cit.,* Chaps. 25-27.

18. I. D. MacCrone, "Ethnocentric ideology and ethnocentrism," *Proc. S. A. Psychol. Assoc.,* 1953, 4:21-24.

19. G. W. Allport, *The nature of prejudice, op. cit.,* Chap. 18.

20. See, for example, E. de S. Brunner, "Problems and tensions in South Africa," *Pol. Sci. Quart.,* 1955, 70:368-86.

21. The factor of density and other sociocultural principles here mentioned are discussed in greater detail in G. W. Allport, *The nature of prejudice, op. cit.,* Chap. 14.

CHAPTER 15

Techniques for reducing group prejudice

Can social science help us reduce bias through a more effective use of law, of the classroom, of mass media, of individual therapy? The question is audacious, for prejudice is deeply ingrained and will not yield easily to remedial treatment. Yet in recent years a good deal has been discovered that can serve as a guideline for the reduction of prejudice.

This survey of the subject is based on the Leo. M. Franklin Memorial Lecture, delivered at Wayne University in April 1951, and published in its present form in P. A. Sorokin (ed.) *Forms and techniques of altruistic and spiritual growth* (1954).

All sorts of methods have been tried in the attempt to change ethnic attitudes for the better. Roughly they seem to fall under the following headings (although each could be extensively subdivided): legislation, formal educational methods, contact and acquaintance programs, group retraining (group dynamics), mass media, exhortation and individual therapy.

Millions of dollars are being spent annually in the attempt to reduce group conflict and prejudice by these methods. Is the money well spent? Or should some of the money and effort spent in one direction be diverted to another, more successful direction? These are entirely practical questions, but their answer cannot be found except through painstaking research devoted to the evaluation of present action programs.

Let it be said at the outset that we are today only just starting the needed evaluative research. The studies summarized in this essay are of a pioneer character, and, while they yield many valuable indications concerning the merits and limitations of action programs, they cannot yet be considered final or definitive. They do, however, blaze a trail of progress.

Can We Expect Change?

First, it is proper to ask ourselves: is it reasonable to expect any single action program to achieve an appreciable change in the prejudices that people carry with them? One estimate says that group prejudice plays an appreciable part in the lives of four-fifths of the

American adult population.[1] Can we reasonably expect to alter this ominous proportion?

Certain weighty considerations prompt us to say no. A mounting array of evidence tells us that a person's whole life economy may be erected on prejudice. The habits of categorizing, projecting and scapegoating may be too ingrained to be disturbed. To change the attitudes would require a recentering of the whole personality. There is no medicine strong enough to counteract the functional significance of prejudice in certain lives. Moreover, prejudiced attitudes receive such continual support from the social environment that isolated target-programs seem insufficient and feeble. The child, for example, cannot possibly escape the ethnic, religious and class membership of his parents—and this anchorage is so firm that a few hours of "social science studies" in school are unlikely to affect the basic structure of his attitudes. Also, the sanctions of his gang and his neighborhood are likely to hold him within the prevailing framework of prejudice, even though films or specially prepared Sunday school lessons spray him with the message of tolerance.

But there are arguments on the other side. Not only a prejudiced outlook, but all of its ingredients, are learned. What is learned can theoretically be unlearned; or at least the learning can, from the start, be prevented.

Moreover, Americans seem to have inexhaustible faith in the changeability of attitudes. The Goliath of advertising in this country is erected on this faith. And we are equally confident in the powers of education. We brush aside aristocratic slogans, such as "blood will tell," "you can't change human nature" and "instincts of the herd," and set out to slay any attitudinal dragon that we decide to eradicate. This extreme faith in environmentalism may not be justified, but the faith itself is a factor of prime importance. If everyone expects attitudes to change—through education, publicity or therapy—then, of course, they are more *likely* to do so than if no one *expects* them to change. Our gusto for change will bring it about, if anything can. The result may yet surprise us.

The Research Approach

We have reached a point where we can begin to submit this dispute to objective tests. Efforts to improve human relations are as old as the hills. What is new is the ability and the will to evaluate the success of these efforts.

True, methods for measuring change are still in their infancy, and the more we attempt to apply them, the more complexities come to light.[2] The following instance indicates some of the difficulties:

In 1950 the National Association of Colored Graduate Nurses disbanded after forty-two years of independent existence. It did so because Negro nurses were at last welcomed to membership in most local chapters of the American Nurses' Association. Here is an example of attitude change resulting in the termination of one form of segregation. But to what was it due? Did it come about through the crusading efforts of certain Negro and white nurses? Was the present trend in FEPC legislation, or the tenor of recent Supreme Court decisions, a factor? Did the good will and brotherhood propaganda of various national bodies play a part? Or was the change a result of all these and many additional pressures? Some cause or causes had an effect, but it is not easy to trace the sequence.

There are three ideal essentials for evaluation research:

First: there must be an identifiable program to be evaluated (a course of instruction, a law, a moving picture, a new type of contact between groups). This factor is called the *independent variable.*

Second: there must be some measurable indices of change. Attitude scales might be administered before and after the program, or interviews conducted, or indices of tension within the community computed (for example, the number of group conflicts reported to the police). Such yardsticks are known as the *dependent variable.*

Third: less vital but still important is the use of *control groups.* When the independent variable is applied, we should like to prove that the measured change is unquestionably a result of this fact. We can do so best if we have a control group of people (matched for age, intelligence and status) who are not submitted to the impact of the independent variable. If they too show an equivalent amount of change, we cannot conclude that our independent variable was effective. Some other influence, as yet unidentified, must have been reaching both groups.

The need for a control group is not often realized by investigators. In one survey of eighteen evaluations of college programs in intercultural education, it was revealed that only four had employed controls.[3] And even when used, controls are not always effective. Suppose two groups of students are being investigated—one receiving a course of instruction, the other acting as a control. If the students gossip outside of school, the lessons learned by one group may be passed along informally to the other. In such a case, the experimental group "contaminates" the control.

A problem also arises in selecting the time when the effects of a program should be evaluated. It is ordinarily easiest to do the evaluating (testing, interviewing, etc.) immediately after the close of the program. But even if we find change at this point, who knows whether it will endure? And, if no change is found, who knows whether the program may not have "sleeper effects" and first show its influence months or even years later? Perhaps the ideal plan is to measure the effects immediately and then *again* after a lapse of a year.

Enough has been said to show that the field of evaluative research has many obstacles. It is difficult to keep the independent variable uncontaminated; it is hard to devise suitable measures of change; and when the findings are in, one cannot always interpret them with confidence, for all sorts of unwanted variables have intruded themselves into the design. The hurly-burly of everyday life in a complex community is very different from the test tube in a chemical laboratory. Yet, in spite of these difficulties, there are scores of evaluative studies that pretend to tell how effective some one type of program has been with a specified population.[4]

All organizations devoted to the betterment of group relations— and there are thousands of them—can be classified as either public or private. The former include the so-called mayor's committees, governor's committees and civic unity committees, established either by the city or state executive or by legislative ordinance. Public agencies likewise include city, state and federal commissions empowered to enforce anti-discrimination laws—sometimes all relevant laws, sometimes only specific laws, such as those dealing with housing or fair employment practices. Often a public agency is simply a fact-finding body, a notable example being the President's Committee on Civil Rights, whose incisive report in 1947 became a rallying point for the forces of tolerance.

Public efforts come to a focus in legislation. I shall try, first, to summarize available evidence and opinion regarding this technique for reducing prejudice. The story is complex, and my comments will necessarily be condensed.[5]

Legislation

Laws against discrimination are of three types: *civil rights* legislation, *employment* legislation and *group libel* legislation. Against all of these is advanced one customary argument: "But you can't legislate against prejudice." Toward the close of the nineteenth century, the Supreme Court of the United States declared that it was hopeless for laws to expect to counter "racial instincts."

This argument is weak in two respects. *First:* we know that segregation and other anti-minority laws increase prejudice against groups. Most historians agree that the legal establishment of second-class citizenship for Negroes in the South has stimulated racism, contempt and abuse. A white child who sees segregation legally enforced is very unlikely to grow up with ideas of equality and friendliness. If legislation can thus increase prejudice, why can it not *diminish* prejudice?

Second: legislation favorable to minority groups never aims to reduce prejudice directly. Its intent is to equalize advantages and lessen discrimination. As a by-product, people gain the experience of working or studying side by side; and such equal-status contact makes indirectly for lessened prejudice. Increasing the skills of minority groups, raising their standard of living, improving their health and education—such measures may have a similar indirect effect. Further, the establishment of a legal norm for behavior creates a public conscience and a standard for expected behavior that lessens *overt* signs of prejudice. Legislation aims at controlling, not prejudice, but only its open expression. Yet, when expression changes, thoughts, in the long run, are likely to fall into line.

When discrimination is reduced, prejudice tends to lessen. The vicious circle begins to reverse itself. The legal termination of bias in employment, housing and the armed forces has the result, evidence shows, of raising the respect one ethnic group holds for another. Experience tells us that the difficulties of integrating hitherto segregated groups are ordinarily less than anticipated. But it often takes a law or a strong executive order to start the process moving. The *principle of cumulation,* as Myrdal calls it, holds that raising the Negro plane of living will lower prejudice on the part of the white, and that this in turn will again raise the Negro plane of living. Benign circles of this order can be established under the initial prompting of law.

To sum up: While it is true that most Americans will not obey laws of which they disapprove strongly, most of them, deep inside their consciences, do approve civil rights and anti-discrimination legislation. They often approve even while they squeal in protest. Laws in line with one's conscience are likely to be obeyed; when not obeyed, they still establish an ethical norm that holds before the individual an image of what his conduct should be. The goad of the

law often breaks a vicious circle, so that a process of healing can start
to occur. Forces in the individual and in the community that have
nothing whatever to do with the law are thus liberated. It is not true
that legislation must wait on education, at least not on complete and
perfect education. For legislation itself is one root of the educational
process.

Formal Educational Programs

It is not possible to report all of the available evaluative studies
of educational programs. These programs range widely in type, and
a number of them are omnibus, containing many varieties of teaching techniques.

Some evaluations are concerned with the impact of special and
limited programs. The latter may be classified under six headings:
the *informational approach,* which imparts knowledge by lectures and
textbook teaching; the *vicarious experience approach,* which employs
movies, drama, fiction and other devices that invite the student to
identify with members of an out-group; the *community study-action
approach,* which calls for field trips, area surveys and work in social
agencies or community programs; *exhibitions, festivals and pageants,*
which encourage a sympathetic regard for the customs of minority
groups and our Old World heritage; the *small group process,* which
applies many principles of group dynamics, including discussion, so-
ciodrama and group retraining; and the *individual conference,* which
allows for therapeutic interviewing and counseling.

We are not yet able to say categorically which of these six approaches brings the greatest return. While it is fairly certain that
desirable effects appear in approximately two-thirds of the experiments, and ill effects very rarely, we still do not know for sure what
methods are *most* successful. The trend of evidence, as Cook points
out, seems to favor indirect approaches—that is, programs which do
not specialize in the study of minority groups as such, or focus upon
the phenomena of prejudice as such. The student seems to gain
more when he loses himself in community projects, when he participates in realistic situations and develops, as William James would
say, *acquaintance with* the field rather than *knowledge about* it.

The informational approach. This tentative conclusion clearly
puts the informational approach on the defensive. Traditionally it
has been thought that planting right ideas in the mind would engender right behavior. Many school buildings still display the So-

cratic motto, *Knowledge Is Virtue*. But the student's readiness to assimilate and to use knowledge, it is now pretty well agreed, depends upon his attitudes. Information seldom sticks unless mixed with attitudinal glue. Facts themselves are inhuman; only attitudes are human. Purely factual training often has one of three equally abortive results: it is soon forgotten, or it is distorted in such a way as to rationalize existing attitudes, or it is allowed to sit in one corner of the mind, isolated from the main determinants of living conduct.

This segregation of knowledge from conduct is revealed in certain investigations that have tested both beliefs and attitudes. Authoritative instruction may have the power of correcting erroneous beliefs without appreciably altering attitudes. Children may learn the facts of Negro history without learning tolerance.

Yet there is an argument to be made on the opposite side. Perhaps students may, in the short run, show no gains or twist the facts to serve their prejudices. But in the long run, accurate information is probably an ally of improved human relations. To take one example: Myrdal has pointed out that there is no longer any intellectually respectable "race" theory that can justify the position of the Negro in this country. Since people are not wholly irrational, the fact that scientific evidence fails to support the theory of racial inferiority can scarcely fail *gradually* to penetrate into the marrow of their attitudes.

The fundamental premise of intercultural education is, in effect: *no person knows his own culture who knows only his own culture.* A child who grows up to believe that the sun rises and sets on his own in-group, and who views foreigners as strange beings from the outer darkness, is a child lacking perspective on the conditions of his own life. He will never see the American way for what it is—one of many alternative patterns of living that men have invented for their needs. Without intercultural information obtained at school, a child cannot acquire this perspective, for most children come from homes and neighborhoods where they have no opportunity to learn about out-groups in an objective way. Thus, while the teaching of correct information in the school does not automatically change prejudice, it may be an indispensable condition of change.

But may not scientific and factual instruction contain information *unfavorable* to minority groups? Yes, it is conceivable that the incidence of evil traits may be higher in one group than in another. If so, this information should not be suppressed. If we are going after the truth, we must go after the whole of it—not merely after the part that is flattering to minorities. Enlightened members of minority groups favor the publication of *all* scientific and factual findings; for they are convinced that, when the whole truth is known, it will show that most of the common stereotypes and accusations are false. If a small percentage of the accusations prove to be justified, the explanation of the findings probably lies in the adverse conditions under which many minority groups live. Properly understood, this finding will improve perspective and motivate reform. For example, the fact that *some* members of persecuted groups may *sometimes* develop ego-defenses is a fact not to be suppressed but to be faced and sympathetically understood.

How shall I sum up? Information does not necessarily alter either attitude or action. Its gains, according to available research, seem slighter than those of other educational methods employed. At the same time, there is virtually no evidence that sound factual information does any harm. Perhaps its value may be long delayed, and may consist in driving wedges of doubt and discomfort into the stereotypes of the prejudiced. It seems likely, too, that the greater gains ascribed to action and project methods require sound factual instruction as underpinning. All in all, we do well to resist the irrational position that invites us to abandon entirely the traditional ideals and methods of formal education. Facts are not enough, but they still may be indispensable.

Direct versus *indirect approaches.* A related question arises concerning the merits of focusing attention directly upon intergroup problems. Is it well, for example, for children to discuss the "Negro problem," or is it better for them to learn facts through more incidental methods? Some people think that courses in English or geography supply a better context for intercultural studies than do courses focused directly on social issues.

There surely is no call to sharpen in the child's mind a sense of conflict. Yet we cannot be categorical about the matter. While a child may, through indirect methods, learn to take cultural pluralism for granted, he is still perplexed by visible differences in skin color, by the recurrent Jewish holidays, by religious diversity. His education is incomplete unless he understands these matters. Some degree of directness would seem to be required. And with older and more sophisticated people there may be even greater value in a direct approach, particularly with advanced students who are prepared to face issues head-on.

In an experiment devoted to three modes of teaching one-week seminars, Rabbi Kagan reports greatest gains by the direct method.[6]

To one group of Christian students he taught Old Testament literature, avoiding any mention of Christian-Jewish friction or of present-day problems. In this indirect method, he merely stressed the positive contribution of Jews to biblical history. A second group was taught the same subject, but with frequent, direct reference to the problem of prejudice, allowing catharsis and a recounting of personal experiences in the class. A third group was taught by the indirect method, but the instruction was supplemented by personal conferences covering the student's experiences and allowing catharsis. This method Kagan called *focused interview*. Before-and-after tests were administered to all students by a Christian colleague.

The author concludes that the indirect method resulted in no significant change, but that the direct method was markedly effective and the focused interview yielded positive results. On the whole he favors the direct method group. It is important to add that a few extremely anti-Semitic students in the population were unchanged by any of these methods of approach.

It seems probable that the relative success of the direct method in this research was due to the composition of the group. The students were of high school age and were selected for their interest in religious matters. Most of them were thus probably prepared to face issues frankly and to shift their attitudes in a favorable direction. The evidence, therefore, remains uncertain. Only in the future can we decide with what groups and under what circumstances direct or indirect methods are to be preferred.

The approach through vicarious experience. Some evidence indicates that films, novels and dramas may be effective if they induce sympathetic identification with minority group members. While we are not yet certain of the facts, it seems likely that strategies of realistic participation constitute too strong a threat to some people. A milder invitation to identification at the fantasy level may be a more effective first step. Perhaps in the future we shall decide that intercultural programs should *start* with fiction, drama and films, and move gradually into more realistic methods of training.

Most of the remaining methods in intercultural education call for active participation on the part of the student. He makes field trips into the neighborhoods where minorities live; he participates in festivals or community projects with them. He develops an *acquaintance with*, not merely *knowledge about*, them. Most investigators favor the participation method above all others. It is considered good for both young and old; it can be adapted to the school program and also for use with adults. Let us consider this important technique further.

Contact and Acquaintance Programs

Contact brings friendliness: this assumption lies at the basis of many so-called action programs. The assumption, however, is stated too broadly. We know that, while some kinds of contact make for mutual understanding and friendliness, the reverse is also true. Contacts are not helpful between people of unequal status or between people who equally *lack* status (poor whites and poor Negroes). Residential contacts are unhelpful if these are perceived in terms of threatening invasion.

Yet studies are accumulating to show that, under certain conditions, increased contact does make for lessened prejudice. We can state the situation in the form of a tentative law: *prejudice tends to diminish whenever members of different groups meet on terms of equal status in the pursuit of common objectives.*

The law, it will be noted, contains two propositions: the contact must be one of equal status, and the members must have objective interests in common. While it may help to place members of groups side by side on a job, the gain in tolerance is greater if these members regard themselves a part of a team. Lewin has pointed out that many committees on race or community relations do not really engage in common projects of mutual interest. They merely meet to talk about the disease. Lacking a definite objective goal, such good-will committees often experience frustration and irritation.[7]

It follows from this law that enforced segregation should be abolished. Otherwise, equal status contacts cannot take place; until they take place, cooperative projects of joint concern cannot arise. And until this condition is fulfilled, we may not expect widespread resolution of intergroup tensions. Hence the attack on segregation must continue. Gandhi, it will be remembered, called for elimination of untouchability as the *first* point in his program. Without this gain, he felt, no other improvement in Hindu life could be achieved.

A final word of caution concerning the law. It would be easy to point to apparent exceptions, but these exceptions are usually not actual test cases. For example, it may be found that boys in a mixed school are as prejudiced against Negroes as are boys in an all-white school. Apparently, equal-status contact does not have the expected result. But status is a subtle thing, and minority groups in a school system do not always enjoy true equality. Furthermore, contact alone is not enough. The contact must lead to further action in the pursuit of common ends. In many schools, this form of mutuality does not occur.

Last but not least, this law, like all social laws, can claim to hold only when other things are equal. It is quite possible that counter-currents may set the law temporarily in abeyance. For example, if economic conditions should suddenly become stringent for both Jewish and gentile doctors, and if conditions led them to perceive each other as rivals, their former cooperativeness in pursuit of common ends might cease. But the existence of counter-tides does not mean that there are no lawful currents.

Group Retraining

One of the boldest advances in modern social science is the deliberate formation of groups for the express purpose of changing the members' outlook. People band together voluntarily in programs of group dynamics because they are dissatisfied with their skill in human relations. They wish to study techniques of democratic leadership. True, they do not join the retraining group expressly to get rid of their prejudices, but they may soon learn that it is their own attitudes and biases that are blocking their effectiveness as foremen, teachers or executives.

Unlike the citizen who reads a pamphlet or listens to a sermon on Brotherhood Sunday, the individual who submits himself to a retraining program is in it up to his eyes. He may be required to act out the roles of other people—employees, students, Negro servants—and he learns through such psychodrama what it feels like to be in another's shoes. He also gains insight regarding his own motives, anxieties and projections. Sometimes the training program is supplemented by private sessions with a counselor, who helps him further along the road of self-examination. As perspective grows, a deeper understanding of the feelings and thoughts of others develops.[8]

Evaluations of this type of training have shown that the gains are greater if social support is maintained. For example, in a study designed to increase skills in community relations work, it was found that if, after training, workers return to localities where no other members of the training team live, they tend to be less effective. They become discouraged and overwhelmed by the mores. On the other hand, two or more people who have been retrained give each other the needed support and carry through their newly acquired insights and skills more effectively.⁹

Not all retraining is of this direct, self-conscious, self-critical type. It may be more objectively centered. An example is the retraining that comes to people who band together to investigate group relations in their city or region. The experience of designing the study, framing questions, conducting interviews and computing the discrimination indices (in housing, employment and education) is highly beneficial. The follow-up activities are even more so; for as people work to improve the situation, further gains in knowledge, community skills and sympathy are bound to result.¹⁰

Another example of outwardly centered retraining is found in connection with the technique known as *incident control*. Its purpose, as in any group retraining, is to break down inhibition and rigidity in several individuals at once, so that they may become more effective in the pursuit of common ends. In this particular case, those who submit to training wish to develop a skill for use in everyday life—skill in answering the bigoted remarks that stain our national habits of conversation. What does one say, for example, to a stranger in a public place who has let fall a venomous comment on the Jews that reaches uninvited the ears of many bystanders? Of course, there are many situations where propriety would have us keep silent; but there are other situations where silence would lend consent, and here our sense of justice prompts us to speak up. Research shows that a calm voice, marked by obvious sincerity and expressing the view that such comments are un-American, has the most favorable effect on bystanders. But it is not easy to summon the courage to speak at all, let alone to find the right words and to control one's voice. Hours of practice under supervision in a group setting are required.¹¹

Some of the retraining programs discussed thus far have a marked limitation. They are designed to free the tolerant person of his inhibitions and to provide him with skills, if he wants them. But it is clear that full-scale group retraining cannot be used with people who resist both the method and its objectives. Yet, with patience and tact, groups or classes formed for other purposes may be led by easy stages into practicing the techniques of group dynamics.

Furthermore, partial use may be made of these techniques of group dynamics without going the whole way. School children, for example, can easily be led into role-playing.¹² By playing the part of a child in an out-group, the juvenile actor may begin to appreciate, through his own sensations, the suffering and defensiveness engendered by discrimination. A related technique has been employed by Axline, who reports that play therapy in a group of young children results in the amelioration of serious racial conflicts within the group.[13] Three or four children, white and colored, are put together in a play situation with dolls and miniature house furnishings. This arrangement offers opportunities for the projection of conflicts and nascent hostility. It was found that, as the play progresses, accommodation sets in and a lasting friendly adjustment between the Negro and white playmates is established.

Mass Media

There are good grounds for doubting the effectiveness of mass propaganda. People whose ears and eyes are bombarded all day with blandishments of special interests tend to develop a propaganda blindness and deafness. And what chance has a mild message of brotherhood, sandwiched in between layers of war, intrigue, hatred and crime? Furthermore, pro-tolerance propaganda is selectively perceived. Those who do not want to admit it to their sanctuaries of belief find no trouble in evading it. Usually those who admit it do not need it. But this general pessimism should not block our search for more detailed knowledge. After all, we know that advertising and films have molded our national culture to a considerable degree. May they not profitably be used in the task of remolding it?

Research, though still somewhat meager, suggests even now certain tentative laws: [14]

1. While a single program—a film, perhaps—shows only a slight effect, several related programs produce effects even greater than could be accounted for by simple summation. This principle of *pyramiding stimulation* is well understood by practical propagandists. Any publicity expert knows that a single program is not enough; there must be a campaign.

2. Propaganda must cope, however, with the law of *specificity of effect.* In the spring of 1951, a motion picture theater in Boston ran the film, *The Sound of Fury.* The picture concluded with the clearly stated moral that conflicts can be solved only through patience and understanding, not through violence. The audience, deeply moved by the dramatic story, applauded the moral. Later in the same program, a newsreel depicted Senator Taft speaking on international relations. He made the identical point—that conflict can be solved only through patience and understanding, not through violence. The same audience hissed. What they had learned in one context did not carry over to another. Several researches confirm the conclusion; opinions may change, but the change tends to be limited to a narrow context and to generalize very little if at all.

3. Propaganda must also cope with *attitude regression*. After a period of time, opinions tend to slip back toward their original configuration—but not all the way.

4. This regression, however, is not universal. Studying both the short-run and long-run effect of indoctrination films in the army, Hovland and his associates found that, while attitude regression was common enough, in some people a reverse trend occurred.[15] *Sleeper effects* came to light. These delayed effects occur in "die-hards" who at first resist the message of the film but later accept it. The sleeper phenomenon is noted especially among well-educated people whose initial opinions are contrary to those held by most other educated people. The authors suggest that these individuals have predispositions favoring the propaganda message but must first overcome some inner resistance to it. The moral seems to be that pro-tolerance propaganda reaching people who are ambivalent in their attitudes may have long-range effects, especially among the better educated portions of the population.

5. Propaganda is more effective when there are no *deep-seated resistances*. Research shows that people who are on the fence are more likely to be affected than those who are deeply committed.

6. Propaganda is more effective when it has a *clear field*. The monopoly of propaganda that exists in totalitarian lands forces a monotonous barrage upon the defenseless citizen, and he cannot long maintain his powers of resistance. Counterpropaganda, if it is permitted, throws the individual back upon his own resources of judgment and frees him from a one-sided view of reality. In the light of this principle, it may well be argued that pro-tolerance propaganda is needed—not only for its positive effects but also as an antidote to agitators who work on the other side.

7. To be effective, propaganda should *allay anxiety*. Bettelheim and Janowitz found that propaganda striking at the roots of a person's frame of security tends to be resisted.[16] Appeals geared into existing systems of security are more effective.

8. A final principle concerns the importance of *prestigeful symbols*. A Kate Smith can sell millions of dollars in war bonds over the radio in a single day. An Eleanor Roosevelt or a Bing Crosby

have prestige for great masses of people. Their espousing of tolerance helps to win many fence-straddlers.

Exhortation

We do not know the effects of preachment, admonishment or ethical pep talks. Religious leaders have exhorted their followers for centuries to the practice of brotherly love. The cumulative effect seems slight; yet we cannot be too sure that the method is futile. Without such constant admonishment, matters might be much worse than they are.

A reasonable guess might be that exhortation helps strengthen the good intentions of those already converted. And this achievement is not to be scorned, for without religious and ethical reinforcement of their convictions, the already converted might not maintain their efforts toward the betterment of group relations. For the character-conditioned bigot, however, and for the conformist who finds his social environment too powerful, hortatory eloquence is likely to have small effect.

Individual Therapy

Theoretically, perhaps the best of all methods for changing attitudes is individual psychotherapy. The person who, in distress, seeks the aid of a psychiatrist or counselor is usually desirous of change. He is likely to be ready for a realignment of many of his basic orientations toward life. While it is safe to say that a patient never comes to a therapist for the express purpose of changing his *ethnic* attitudes, these attitudes may assume a salient role as the course of treatment progresses, and may conceivably be dissolved or re-structured along with the patient's other fixed ways of looking at life.

No conclusive study has been made of this hypothesis, although various psychoanalysts have reported their clinical experience.[17] This experience is particularly cogent, for most patients think of psychoanalysis as a "Jewish movement" and this fact alone is almost certain to stir up such anti-Semitic prejudice as may exist. The course of the treatment may be somewhat as follows: Early in the course of his analysis, the patient enters the phase known as negative transference. He blames the analyst for the suffering the therapeutic process causes, and hates him for his position of dominance and advantage, for being *pro tem* a parent-substitute. Sometimes the analyst is a Jew; even if he is not, the patient thinks of psychoanalysis as a Jewish movement. This circumstance elicits his private anti-Semitic feelings, which more likely than not explode in his outbursts against the analyst. As the treatment progresses, and as the patient gains insight into his whole pattern of values, the anti-Semitism may abate. Indeed, in principle we should expect that, whenever prejudice of any sort intersects with a neurosis, amelioration of the neurosis will result in a reduction of the prejudice.

Psychoanalysis is only one mode of treatment. Almost any prolonged interview with a person concerning his personal problems is likely to uncover all major hostilities. In talking about them, the patient often gains a new perspective. And if in the course of the treatment he discovers a more generally wholesome and constructive way of life, his prejudice may abate. For example, one student engaged in research was conducting a long interview with a woman concerning her experience with, and attitudes toward, minority groups. There was no therapeutic intention whatsoever. In the course of the interview, the woman told of her anti-Semitic feelings. Pursuing her whole past experience with Jews and with neighborhood anti-Semitism, she gradually gained greatly in self-insight. At one point she exclaimed, "The poor Jews, I guess we blame them for everything, don't we?" Unless she had fixed her attention for considerable time (about three hours) on this feature of her belief system, she would not have tracked it down to its sources and placed it in rational perspective in her life.

The frequency of transformations under therapeutic or quasi-therapeutic conditions is unknown. More research is needed. But even if individual therapy proves to be the most effective of all methods—and because of its depth and interrelatedness with all portions of the personality, it should be—the proportion of the population reached will always be small. We cannot psychoanalyze each and every bigot.

Catharsis

Experience shows that in certain situations—especially in individual therapy and in group retraining sessions—an explosion of feeling often occurs. When the subject of prejudice comes up for discussion, a person who feels his views are under attack or disapproved may need the purging that comes with such explosion.

Catharsis has a quasi-curative effect. It temporarily relieves the tension and may prepare the individual for a change of attitude. It is easier to mend an inner tube after the air has been released. Blake's poem expresses this relation between catharsis and tension:

> I was angry with my friend;
> I told my wrath, my wrath did end.
> I was angry with my foe;
> I told it not, my wrath did grow.

Yet not every expression of hostility has a cathartic effect. Only under special circumstances does a person who "blows his top" then become willing and able to understand the other side of the argument. While he remains at all tense and aggrieved, he cannot and will not listen.

In an eastern city, a number of unpleasant instances of ethnic conflict had occurred. Aroused citizens put pressure on the local police force to introduce a course of instruction dealing with the backgrounds of group antagonism and the policemen's role in preventing and handling outbreaks. The police officers who attended this compulsory course were resentful, for the very circumstances under which it was arranged cast reflections upon their competence and fairness. This sense of injustice, together with their own prejudices against certain minority groups, created a condition of tension that made instruction difficult—almost impossible. Whenever an objective point was made concerning Negroes in the community, some police officer would be sure to respond with a story of a vicious Negro who bit him while being arrested.

Under such conditions of injured self-esteem it is unlikely that existing prejudice can be changed. No one can be taught who thinks himself under attack. The course of instruction encountered stereotypes, caustic anecdotes and expressions of hostility from the police. None of the instruction seemed to register; it provoked only a torrent of abuse, directed partly against the teacher and partly against the minority groups under discussion. Often the class would complain: "Why does everyone pick on the police?" "We've never had any trouble. Why do we need this course?" "Why don't the Jews mind their own business? If they find a dead cat in the ash can, they call it anti-Semitism." "The Negro leaders ought to control their people and not set them against the police."

The course lasted for eight hours. The first six were largely occupied with this type of catharsis. The instructor offered no counterarguments and listened as sympathetically as possible to the hostile outbursts.

Gradually, a change seemed to occur. For one thing, the class became bored with its own complaining. The attitude seemed to be, "We've had our say; now we'll listen to what you have to say on the subject." Furthermore, so many obvious overstatements had been made in anger that a certain sheepishness crept in. The man who asserted, "We've never had any trouble; there is no problem here," was soon recounting several incidents of conflict that he had encountered and, as a policeman, did not know how to handle. A man who at first railed against Jews tried in later remarks to make amends.

Catharsis, then, may occasionally be effective because one's irrational outburst shocks one's own conscience. When the immediate tensions have been released, the individual is freer to reconstruct his perception of the total situation. Even while expressing hostility, he may be developing private plans for future conduct that will be more acceptable to the community at large. Thus a given official might have been thinking, especially toward the end of the course, "Well, I certainly have blown my top. Damn it, I had a right to; it's terrible the way we're picked on. Everybody's got prejudices. But it *is* tough on the minorities in this community. I don't want any trouble in my district. I'd better look out for so and so; he's likely to make trouble, the way he hates Negroes and Jews. I guess I'll. . . ." And here he begins to construct in imagination a plan for future handling of the problem in his precinct.

It cannot be proved that such mental processes occur following catharsis, but the impression of observers of this particular course of instruction was that during the last two hours, when the antagonism had worn out, the lessons commenced to register and the gain in self-insight was appreciable.[18]

Catharsis itself is not curative. The best that can be said for it is that it prepares the way for a less tense view of the situation. Having had his say, the aggrieved person may be more ready to listen to the other point of view. If his statements have been exaggerated and unfair—as they usually are—the resulting shame mollifies his anger and induces a more balanced point of view.

It is not recommended that every program start off by inviting catharsis. To do so would create a negative atmosphere at the outset. When catharsis is needed, it will come without special invitation.

This is most likely to occur when prejudiced people feel that they themselves are under attack. When this situation prevails, no progress can be made until catharsis is allowed. With patience, skill and luck, the leader may at the right moment guide the catharsis into constructive channels.

Final Word

The improvement of human relations is a broad subject—considerably broader than the scope of this essay. Our aim has been to pass in review a large variety of recent research in the area of ethnic antagonism. From it we have learned two things: *First:* there is an immense amount of activity and interest in applying scientific methods to the discovery of effective techniques for reducing prejudice. *Second:* present indications favor certain techniques over others, and indicate to some extent the specific conditions when we would do well to select one technique and not another.

While I sincerely believe in the value of the work reviewed, I have no desire to oversimplify the problem of building altruistic character. The issue is so complex, and the need so great, that every resource must be called upon. It would be a grave error to think that we have devised a bag of tricks, which, if adroitly manipulated, will conjure up a good neighbor. But it would be an equally grave error to assume that the plodding and serious investigations here reported have nothing to contribute to the improvement of human relationships. Education and religion, mass media and legislation, child training and psychotherapy—these and all other channels of human effort must be followed if we are to produce a race of men who will seek their individual salvation, not at the expense of their fellows, but in concert with them.

REFERENCES

1. G. W. Allport and B. M. Kramer, "Some roots of prejudice," *J. Psychol.*, 1946, 22:9-39.
2. Technical discussions concerning the measurement of attitudes, of prejudice, of group tension are omitted. The reader is referred to M. Jahoda, M. Deutsch and S. W. Cook, *Research methods in social relations,* New York: 1951.
3. L. A. Cook (ed.), *College programs in intergroup relations,* Washington: American Council on Education, 1950.
4. Surveys of these evaluational studies have been reported by O. Klineberg, *Tensions affecting international understanding: a survey of research,* New York: Social Science Research Council, 1950, Bull. 62, Chap. 4; R. M.

Williams, Jr., *The reduction of intergroup tensions: a survey of research on problems of ethnic, racial, and religious group relations,* New York: Social Science Research Council, 1947, Bull. 57; A. M. Rose, *Studies in the reduction of prejudice,* Chicago: American Council on Race Relations, 1947 (mimeographed).

5. For fuller accounts of the relationship between legislation and prejudice containing evidence for the statements made in the present discussion, see: J. H. Burma, "Race relations and anti-discriminatory legislation," *Amer. J. Sociol.,* 1951, 56:416-23; W. Maslow, "The law and race relations," *Ann. Amer. Acad. Pol. Soc. Sci.,* 1946, 244:75-81; T. S. Kendler, "Contributions of the psychologist to constitutional law," *Amer. Psychologist,* 1950, 5:505-10; M. Deutscher and I. Chein, "The psychological effects of enforced segregation—a survey of social science opinion," *J. Psychol.,* 1948, 26:259-87.

6. H. E. Kagan, *Changing the attitudes of Christian toward Jew,* New York: 1952.

7. K. Lewin, "Research on minority problems," *Tech. Rev.,* 1946, 48: 163-64, 182-90.

8. An elementary exposition of "group dynamics" is given by S. Chase, *Roads to agreement,* New York: 1951, Chap. 9.

9. R. Lippitt, *Training in community relations,* New York: 1949.

10. M. H. Wormser and C. Selltiz, *How to conduct a community self-survey of civil rights,* New York: 1951.

11. A. F. Citron, I. Chein, and J. Harding, "Anti-minority remarks: a problem for action research," *J. Abnorm. Soc. Psychol.,* 1950, 45:99-126.

12. G. Shaftel and R. F. Shaftel, "Report on the use of 'practice action level' in the Stanford University project for American ideals," *Sociatry,* 1948, 2:243-53.

13. V. M. Axline, "Play therapy and race conflict in young children," *J. Abnorm. Soc. Psychol.,* 1948, 43:279-86.

14. A bibliography of research is contained in the monograph by J. T. Klapper, *The effects of mass media,* New York: Columbia University Bureau of Applied Social Research, 1950 (mimeographed).

15. C. I. Hovland *et al., Experiments on mass communication,* Princeton: 1949.

16. B. Bettelheim and M. Janowitz, "Reactions to fascist propaganda: a pilot study," *Publ. Opin. Quart.,* 1950, 14:530-60.

17. See N. W. Ackerman and M. Jahoda, *Anti-Semitism and emotional disorder,* New York: 1950; R. M. Lowenstein, *Christians and Jews: a psychoanalytic study,* New York: 1950; E. Simmel (ed.), *Anti-Semitism: a social disease,* New York: 1948.

18. This case is recounted more fully in G. W. Allport, "Catharsis and the reduction of prejudice," *J. Soc. Issues,* 1945, 1:1-8.

CHAPTER 16

Religion and prejudice

We all know some religious people who are bigoted against various ethnic and religious groups. But we also know others who sincerely practice brotherhood. In both types of people, religion seems to be largely responsible—for their prejudice, or for their tolerance.

This essay first dips into the history of the Christian church and finds that, while the opposed strands of bigotry and tolerance have always been with us, in recent years the clash has grown acute.

The essay then offers a functional analysis of the two forms of religiosity. *Extrinsic* religion is a self-serving, utilitarian, self-protective form of religious outlook, which provides the believer with comfort and salvation at the expense of out-groups. *Intrinsic* religion marks the life that has interiorized the total creed of his faith without reservation, including the commandment to love one's neighbor. A person of this sort is more intent on serving his religion than on making it serve him. In many lives, both strands are found; the result is inner conflict, with prejudice and tolerance competing for the upper hand.

Originally presented as the Ratcliff Lecture at Tufts University in April 1959, the essay was first published in *The Crane Review* (1959).

Brotherhood and bigotry are intertwined in all religion. Plenty of pious people are saturated with racial, ethnic and class prejudice. At the same time, many of the most ardent advocates of racial justice are religiously motivated. Like Gandhi they labor for equimindedness within the whole human family. This is the paradox I wish to explore.

The paradox is one to haunt both the psychologist and the clergy. Within the past decade, social and psychological scientists have made great advances in understanding the dynamics of prejudice, although they tend to overlook the tie with piety. Usually they are content merely to point to the common finding that, on the average, churchgoers are more intolerant than non-churchgoers. As for the clergy, can any minister fail to spot both bigotry and anti-bigotry in his own flock? Can he fail to sympathize with the plight of the Christian clergy in Little Rock, which has been so well described by Campbell and Pettigrew in their recent book *Christians in racial crisis?* [1]

Let me first briefly outline the nature of the problem in historical terms, for I urgently desire to emphasize its pervasive and apparently permanent character. In the concluding sections I shall try to unravel the paradox from a psychologist's point of view and point the road to a solution.

I

In the Christian religion, and to a varying degree in other religions, there are three intrinsic sources of bigotry.

The first is the doctrine of *revelation:* truth once revealed cannot be tampered with. This doctrine has a curious consequence for successive generations of believers: it leads to a rigidity that the original Scriptures do not warrant. Take, for example, St. Paul's injunction, "Therefore judge nothing before the time, until the Lord come." [2] St. Paul seems here to be enlarging on the words of Christ: "Let both grow together until the harvest." [3] Later believers have difficulty with these permissive sentiments. How can one be tolerant of those who depart from the revealed formula for salvation? Menno Simons, the Anabaptist, worried about the matter, and his narrow solution is typical of all the centuries. He simply reinterpreted St. Paul to mean, "None may judge unless he have the judging word on his side." [4] In effect, Simons—like many men of piety—interposed his right to judge according to his own view of the revelation. Since all sects and creeds claim to have the judging word on their side, the door swings wide to bigotry. Unbelievers are sharply judged here and now.

The second intrinsic source of bigotry lies in the doctrine of *election.* Whatever theological justification the doctrine may have, the view that one's own group is chosen (and that other groups are not) leads forthwith away from brotherhood and into bigotry. It does so because it feeds one's pride and hunger for status—two important psychological roots of prejudice. Some groups have claimed to be the lost tribe of Israel; the claim enhances the status of the members and consigns all "gentile" groups to a position of inferiority. A cardinal example of election is based on certain obscurities in the Book of Genesis. Noah, it seems, cursed Ham and declared that his children should forever be "the servants of servants." Legend has it that the children of Ham are the black race. By this sleight of hand, many white people in South Africa and in our own Southern states declare that they are divinely elected to the position of permanent white supremacy.

Thus the doctrines of revelation and election provide open channels to prejudice—but do they *necessarily* have this end-result? If so, we should have to despair of many religions. The Roman Catholic Church holds firmly to the revelation that it alone is the True Church, divinely established and protected from error. The Jewish religion could not exist at all without its revelation that the Jews are God's chosen people. Does it follow that Roman Catholics and Jews and comparable bodies are destined to bigotry?

Speaking to this very point, Bishop Lesslie Newbigin of the Anglican Church writes: "We must claim absoluteness and finality for Christ and His finished work; but that very claim forbids us to claim absoluteness and finality for our understanding of it." [5] Revelation and election, being divinely ordained, are not susceptible to human interpretation. Only God knows His plan for the human race. It is not for us to judge those who do not share our understanding of this plan.

This more relaxed interpretation of revealed religion and election requires a subtle mind, one that can embrace absolutes and at the same time judge nothing "until the Lord come." It may take a long time for the masses of religious people to acquire this delicate balance. As matters stand, we can safely say that the majority of the people will continue to regard religious outsiders with condescension and even with contempt. This will be true among Jews, Catholics, Fundamentalists—and even among liberal Christians, who often hold to a special version of revelation and election akin to intellectual snobbery.

The third intrinsic source of bigotry in Christian history— *theocracy*—has lost much of its power. It is the view, prevalent for many centuries, that rulers are divinely ordained to enforce through civil and military power the currently fashionable interpretations of revelation and election. This doctrine of divine rights and divine obligation drove the Western world into centuries of persecution and bloody bigotry under the banner of Holy Zeal. It took a very long time for the West to rid itself of physical coercion as a device for enforcing the judging word. Not only the rulers themselves, but also the people—even many saintly people—felt that it was the duty of civil authority to enforce agreement with the then prevailing interpretations of election and revelation.

One thinks of St. Augustine's appeal to the emperor to crush the Pelagians, who disputed his views on the damnation of unbaptized infants. Of the persecution of the Jews by St. Ambrose, St. Gregory of Nyssa and St. John Chrysostom.[6] Of the fanaticism of Pope

Urban II, who launched the Crusades, wherein political and economic gain at the expense of the "unspeakable Turk" was sanctified in the frenzied battle cry, "Deus vult." Of Pope Sixtus IV, who, while building the Sistine Chapel, authorized Spain's sovereigns to make a ruthless inquisition. Of the thousands of Jews burned at the stake in 1485, when Tomas de Torquemada took over the management of the Inquisition. Of St. Bartholomew's Eve in 1572, when twenty to thirty thousand Huguenots were massacred.[7] Of Pope Innocent VIII, who in the fifteenth century anathematized all who refused to believe in witchcraft.[8] Of the inconclusive savagery of the wars of religion, which subsided only toward the close of the seventeenth century.

When Protestantism arrived on the scene, it behaved no better, for it was founded on the same three pillars of bigotry: revelation, election and theocracy. It is the parodox of Protestantism that, except at high moments of its history, it has not lived by its primary tenet—that the channel of revelation is personal. Although the individual is told to seek revelation, he is expected to reach the "right" answer from his communion with the Scriptures and the Holy Spirit. Death at the stake was the punishment for Servetus, who, according to Calvin, misinterpreted the promptings of the Holy Spirit. Under Protestantism, heresy remained for a long time a capital crime, though its definition shifted capriciously through the evolution of sects and through the theocratic reigns of assorted sovereigns.

Queen Elizabeth I required every Roman Catholic to attend the Church of England. During much of the eighteenth century, the saying of the Roman Mass in England was punishable by "perpetual imprisonment"; and, as late as 1825, foreigners who wished to become English citizens had to take the Sacrament of the Lord's Supper from a minister of the Anglican Church.[9] The General Court of Massachusetts decreed in 1647 that "no Jesuit or spiritual or ecclesiastical person (as they are termed), ordained by the pope of the see of Rome, shall henceforth come into Massachusetts. Any person not freeing himself of suspicion shall be jailed, then banished. If taken a second time he shall be put to death."

II

The history of bigotry is tiresome and painful to recount. But unless we have it in mind, we shall not be able to understand the nature of our present problem. The horrors are not by any means all in the past. But what is new is our comprehension of some of the psychodynamic factors that add fire and flame to theological dispute.

Anti-Catholicism in the United States, like anti-Negro prejudice, has often drawn on the appetite for sexual disclosures. Incited by stories of immorality in convents, a mob in Charlestown, Massachusetts, on August 11, 1834, burned the Ursaline Convent. One influential political party, the Know-Nothings, rose to considerable power in the mid-nineteenth century largely on the basis of such legends. Later in the century the American Protective Association flourished, sustained by anti-Catholic periodicals. Typical among such periodicals was *Watson's Magazine,* not only anti-Catholic but anti-Negro and anti-Semitic as well. Its logic is illustrated by the following typical quotation: "Heavens above! Think of a Negro priest taking the vow of chastity and then being turned loose among women who have been taught that a priest cannot sin. It is a thing to make one shudder." Similarly, the "libertine Jew" was said to have a "ravenous appetite for the forbidden fruit—a lustful eagerness enhanced by the racial novelty of the girls of the uncircumcised." [10] This combination of the sexual and the religious is receiving considerable attention in contemporary psychology.[11]

In the present century, no less than in the past, political self-interest has sparked religious persecution. We think of the Jewish pogroms of Czarist Russia and of the slaughter of Muslim by Hindu and of Hindu by Muslim only a decade ago. A kind of religious rapture intoxicated the Nazis: " 'Hitler is a new, a greater, a more powerful Jesus Christ. Our God, our Pope, is Adolph Hitler.' So rhapsodized Nazi leader Binve. And not to be outdone in ecstatic homage, Propaganda Minister Goebbels in an address at Berlin, instructed the regimented German nation: 'Our leader becomes the intermediary between his people and the throne of God. . . . Everything which our leader utters is religion in its highest sense, in its deepest sense, and in its deepest and most hidden meaning.' " [12]

Even these few examples show us why many thoughtful people today discredit religion. A college student summed up a common judgment: "Religion has tried for centuries to establish a brotherhood of man. It has had its day. . . . The problems religion tries to solve need solving, but religion has failed." A second student speaks of organized religion as "another schism in a divided world—a curse." [13]

III

The history we have reviewed up to now is one-sided. We should not forget that even in times of persecution there have been great-souled prophets who, often to their peril, spoke out against bigotry and preached the Gospel of equimindedness. Socrates did so. So too did Christ—many centuries ahead of His church.

Early in the Christian era the voices were timid and clouded. Tertullian, for example, asserted that God did not wish to be worshiped unwillingly; salvation could not be coerced but must be freely appropriated. And it was Tertullian who so brilliantly perceived the dynamics of scapegoating: "They take the Christians to be the cause of every disaster to the state, of every misfortune to the people. If the Tiber reaches the wall; if the Nile does not reach the fields; if the sky does not move, or if the earth does; if there is a famine, or if there is a plague—the cry is at once 'The Christians to the lions.'" [14] Yet it was also Tertullian whose rigid interpretations of election and revelation led him to speak so fiercely against recusants that he has been called the first Christian bigot.

Toward the end of the fifth century, Pope Gelasius I likewise opposed coercion and questioned the right of any emperor to interpret the Sacrifice of the Cross or to prescribe how its benefits shall be spread among mankind. St. Ambrose, too, opposed the emperor's right to interpret the Christian trust, but he did not hesitate to denounce the Jews. In the thirteenth century Raymond Lully dared to oppose both the Crusades and the rising Inquisition. And a century later Cardinal Cusa suggested that human transcripts of the divine will are always contaminated by the blindness of self-interest of mortal men. He proposed a parliament of religions to which even the Muslims should be invited. But such voices were feeble and sporadic.

The Reformation added its pleas, even while it took over the three pillars of bigotry. In 1554, Sebastian Castellio issued his manifesto advocating religious toleration. Christianity, he insisted, is beneficence; persecution is its antithesis, and if persecution belongs to religion, religion is a curse to mankind. At the height of witch-burning, Montaigne expressed his misgivings in golden words: "After all, it is rating one's conjectures at a very high price to roast a man alive on the strength of them." Also in the sixteenth century, Schwenkfeld taught that a sense of divine immediacy should keep us from hatred: the Holy Spirit has sevenfold gifts, and we should acknowledge their diversity among men of all kinds. Irenicism, a search for peaceful unity among churches, grew on this foundation, as did modern Quakerism. But the full flower of this sixteenth-century spiritualism was slow in being achieved. As Bainton remarks, "The best things on religious liberty were said in the sixteenth century but not practiced until the nineteenth." [15]

But advocates of equimindedness were seldom wholehearted. Milton advanced the principle of religious freedom but would have denied its benefits to Catholics and atheists—a position held likewise by John Locke. Cromwell declared for freedom of conscience but denied it, for political reasons, to Catholics, Anglicans and Baptists.

But slowly there arose strong champions of the separation of church and state. Preliminary skirmishes were fought by dissenters in Holland and by Roger Williams in the New World. The decisive turning point came, of course, when James Madison wrote and Congress adopted the First Amendment to the Constitution of the United States: "Congress shall make no law respecting the establishment of religion, or prohibiting the free exercise thereof. . . ." For the first time in the history of the Western world, men canceled the claim of divine sanction for the state, and therewith the possibility of official persecution for religious deviance. This decisive step has been called by one of America's foremost jurists, David Dudley Field, "the greatest achievement ever made in the course of human progress."

The First Amendment eliminated the possibility of theocracy in America, and its repercussions were so wide that today heresy or any other form of religious deviance is seldom if ever punished as a legal crime in any country of the world. The theocratic pillar of bigotry is gone, and the other two pillars are weakening. It is this fact that helps create the current crisis, with its potential for profound change.

Only in certain markedly orthodox sects today do we find the doctrines of revelation and election explicitly used to justify anti-Negro, anti-Jewish, anti-Gentile or any other prejudice. Yet if explicit theological justification is rarer than it was, an analogous psychological process is still at work.

IV

Let us take a not uncommon form of the religious-prejudice syndrome. A certain child, let us say, is taught the usual adult complex of ideas. Christ came into the world to save all men—black, brown and white—but dreadful things will happen if any but a white man should move into the neighborhood. He is taught that his family's church is the best and that all others are inferior. He learns that the Heavenly Father grants favors when asked, but especially to a child who belongs to the elect.

Now, suppose this teaching is absorbed by a child who has deep psychological needs engendered by insecurity, inferiority of status, suspicion and distrust. He may never think explicitly of the doctrines of revelation and election; yet his background prepares him for the same type of reasoning that has marked bigotry throughout the course of history: "God is partial to me. Through prayer I can conjure His special favor. Since God is created in my image, His role is to confer security and other benefits upon me. My economy of living is one of exclusion—of barring from my presence out-groups, which threaten my comfort. My religion and my prejudice both serve my exclusionist style. They are islands of safety in a threatening world. They are custom-tailored lifejackets to be donned in frightening waters." In such a life, religion is not the cause of ethnic prejudice, nor is prejudice the cause of the religion. Both strategies are protective; both confer security, a sense of status and of encapsulation.

This syndrome appears to be exceedingly common; many investigations show that, on the average, churchgoers and professedly religious people have considerably more prejudice than do non-churchgoers and nonbelievers. Today, as in former times, countless people assume that the Almighty meant to arrange the human family in a hierarchical order, with themselves at the top. And some will still cite Holy Scripture to prove their point.

In the case we have described, it is clear that religion is not the master-motive in the life. It plays an instrumental role only. It serves and rationalizes assorted forms of self-interest. In such a life, the full creed and full teaching of religion are not adopted. The person does not serve his religion; it is subordinated to serve him. The master-motive is always self-interest. In such a life-economy, religion has extrinsic value only. And it is *extrinsic* religion, thus defined, that we find most closely associated with prejudice.

V

But now we turn to the opposite, or *intrinsic,* type of religious sentiment. It too gets an early start in life. The child's mind is, as in the other case, early tuned to the favors that God can render—a gift of skates for Christmas, or cancellation of an appointment with the dentist. It is hard at the start for any child to avoid a self-centered and family-centered view of religion. But there is an early difference: the youngster we are now describing has the benefit of basic trust and security within his home. He does not need to look on people as threats to his well-being. He does not need to use religion as a talisman. He does not become fixated on an immature level of development. At adolescence he can take the leap that Piaget calls *reciprocity*, the ability to perceive that others too have convictions and preferences (for their own religion, culture and race) that are analogous to—and, from their point of view, as reasonable as—his own.

The youth we describe is not crippled by his fears and anxieties. He has them, to be sure, but he accepts them as normal afflictions of the human race. It is a sound principle of psychology that the acceptance of one's anxieties makes for a compassionate understanding and acceptance of others.

Advancing thus into maturity, the individual does not necessarily lose his religious faith, nor even his belief in revelation and election. But dogma is tempered with humility: in keeping with biblical injunction, he withholds judgment until the day of the harvest. A religious sentiment of this sort floods the whole life with motivation and meaning. It is no longer limited to single segments of self-interest. And only in such a widened religious sentiment does the teaching of brotherhood take firm root.

I do not wish to imply that people are wholly intrinsic or wholly extrinsic in their religious outlook. Gradations occur along a continuum. Extrinsic religionists have moments when the universalism of the Christian teaching breaks through to them, causing them perhaps to doubt their own stand on such issues as Negro segregation. Intrinsic religionists too may have their lapses, as when they slip into snide and socially fashionable anti-Semitism.

Yet, in principle, the distinction is crucial. Unless we accept it, we shall fail to explain the age-old paradox that troubles us all: how does it come about that religious people tend to be more prejudiced than nonreligious people, while at the same time most of the fighters for equality and brotherhood throughout the centuries have been religiously motivated? We think of Pope Gelasius, Castellio, St. Francis, Schwenkfeld and Roger Williams; in more recent days, of Gandhi, Father Huddleston, Martin Luther King and Albert Schweitzer; and of countless active members of the American Friends Service Committee, the Catholic Interracial Councils, the Unitarian Service Committee and other religious groups too numerous to mention.

VI

The relationship between religion and prejudice hinges on the type of religion that the personal life harbors. When it is extrinsic, the tie with prejudice is close; when intrinsic, prejudice is restrained. Now that religious bodies are becoming self-critical and alert to the issue, they would do well to employ this central fact to guide their policies and plans for the future. Their problem, if I may venture to state it for them, is how to transform the prejudice-linked, extrinsic style of religion held by most of their members—whatever the religious body may be—into intrinsic religion, where the total creed of equimindedness becomes woven into the fabric of personality itself.

REFERENCES

1. E. Q. Campbell and T. F. Pettigrew, *Christians in racial crisis*, Washington: Public Affairs Press, 1959.

2. I Corinthians 4:5.

3. St. Matthew 13:30.

4. Menno Simons, "A foundation and plain instruction of the saving doctrine of Christ" (trans. by I. D. Rupp), *On the ban: questions and answers*, 1550, Lancaster: Elias Barr, 1863. And see Chapter 14, p. 223, of this volume.

5. Rt. Rev. L. Newbigin, "The quest for unity through religion," *J. Rel.*, 1955, 35:17-33.

6. The history of anti-Semitism in the Catholic church is told by M. Hay, *The foot of pride*, Boston: Beacon, 1950, reissued in 1960 as a Beacon Paperback under the title, *Europe and the Jews*. In one of the sermons of the golden-mouthed St. John Chrysostom (whom Cardinal Newman called "a sensitive heart . . . elevated, refined, transformed by a touch of heaven"), we read: "The synagogue is worse than a brothel . . . it is the den of scoundrels and the repair of wild beasts . . . a criminal assembly of Jews . . . a house worse than a drinking shop . . . a den of thieves; a house of ill fame, a dwelling of iniquity, the refuge of devils, a gulf and abyss of perdition. . . . As for me, I hate the synagogue. . . . I hate the Jews for the same reason," pp. 27 ff.

7. For convenient accounts of these and many similar episodes, see G. Meyers, *The history of bigotry in the United States*, New York: Random House, 1943. See also R. H. Bainton, *The travail of religious liberty*, Philadelphia: Westminster, 1951.

8. H. Kramer and J. Springer, *Malleus Maleficarum* (trans. by M. Summers), London: Pushkin Press, 1948, p. xx. See also A. Huxley, *The devils of Loudon*.

9. M. Freedman (ed.), *A minority in Britain*, London: Valentine, Mitchell, 1955, p. 39 f.

10. G. Meyers, *op. cit.*, pp. 252, 259 f.

11. G. W. Allport, *The nature of prejudice*, Cambridge: Addison-Wesley, 1954, Chap. 23.

12. G. Meyers, *op. cit.*, pp. 389 ff. A useful account of the mixing of political bias with Protestant bigotry is R. L. Roy, *Apostles of discord*, Boston: Beacon, 1953.

13. G. W. Allport, J. M. Gillespie, and J. Young, "The religion of the post-war college student," *J. Psychol.*, 1948, 25:3-33.

14. Tertullian, *Apology*, Chap. 40, in Migno: *Patrologia Latina*, Vol. 1, Col. 542.

15. R. H. Bainton, *op. cit.*, p. 253. Other sources regarding the growth of religious toleration are K. S. Latourette, *A history of Christianity*, New York: Harper, 1953; and W. K. Jordan, *The development of religious tolerance in England*, 4 vols., Cambridge: Harvard University Press, 1932-40.

PART V: *Perception and social programs*

CHAPTER 17

Social service in perspective

A psychologists's interests often range widely. He is sometimes concerned with the way people perceive their worlds—that is to say, how they define the situation they are in. He may also be concerned with the process of communication—including rumor, public opinion and persuasion—and may want to know how these and other psychological factors can lead to improvement in the human condition. Part V deals with these topics.

My earliest years of teaching were in the Department of Social Ethics at Harvard University. This in part explains my interest in applying psychological principles and methods to the professional field of social work.

The essay was read at a conference held as part of the Bicentennial Celebration of Columbia University from June 2-5, 1954. It is reprinted here from a volume of proceedings entitled *National policies for education, health, and social services* (1955), where it appeared under the title, "The limits of social service."

A century ago both Thoreau and Emerson spoke out sharply regarding the limits of social service—of "philanthropy," as they then called it. In *Walden*, Thoreau criticized the tendency of the would-be benefactor to project his own ailments onto others. Because he himself suffers a stomach-ache he thinks that the whole world has been eating green apples. Thoreau advised the benefactor to cure himself, to grow cheerful, to abandon his melancholy projections and thus to permit the victims of his "charitable" impulses to do the same.

Emerson pointed to a different shortcoming. In *Self-Reliance* he wrote: "I tell thee, thou foolish philanthropist, that I grudge the dollar, the dime, the cent I give to such men as do not belong to me and to whom I do not belong." Where no spiritual affinity exists, charity is in vain. Emerson deplored the thousandfold impersonal relief societies devoted to distributing "alms for sots."

When we think back on the unwisdom of nineteenth-century benevolence, we applaud these thrusts of criticism. But we recognize the critics' error. Thoreau and Emerson were presuming to condemn all social service because they mistook momentary limitations for ultimate limits. They could not foresee the enlargement of horizons and improvement in practice that would come through the labors of

Octavia Hill, Arnold Toynbee, Jane Addams, Richard Cabot, Mary Richmond and many other thoughtful leaders. Nor could they predict the future influence of psychological science and psychiatry upon social service. They could not foretell the evolution of public policy as guided by Bismarck in Germany, by the Fabians and the Labor Party in Britain and by the New Deal in the United States.

We therefore take warning. It would be folly to set dogmatic and premature limits upon the sciences and arts that comprise social service. Unlike Thoreau and Emerson, we know that its methods and its philosophy are still evolving. Present faults and shortcomings surely exist, but most of them, we suspect, are removable. As such they constitute *limitations* in social service but not *limits*. In the course of our discussion we shall hit upon boundaries beyond which neither public nor private social work may proceed. But for the most part we shall be concerned with limitations that can in principle be overcome.

Evaluating Social Service

The brightest feature of the present situation is the spirit of self-objectification, self-scrutiny and self-criticism that marks contemporary social services. We are less inclined than formerly to mistake our good intentions for good results, or our own professional growth for growth in our clients. We have reached a stage of wholesome skepticism. Today the question is whether social service, in any of its philosophies and methods—public or private; family-centered, community-centered or person-centered; manipulative or interpretative; based on psychoanalytic theory, economic theory, religious theory or no theory—does in fact achieve the results we aim to achieve.

It is now thirty years since leaders of social service began to call for an evaluation of results. To some extent the impetus came from donors who rightly wondered whether society actually benefits from their financial support of social work. But chiefly, I think, the impetus for evaluation has come from ardent workers who wish to know whether their efforts are truly in the public interest or reflect merely pleasant conceits of their own. Among the early voices raised in behalf of evaluative research were those of Porter R. Lee, Dr. Haven Emerson and Dr. Richard Cabot.[1] Two of the earliest investigations were those of Miss Theis, who followed the later careers of nearly eight hundred foster children, and of the Gluecks, who traced five hundred former inmates of the Concord Reformatory.[2]

The former study made us hopeful concerning the policies and practices of child-placing agencies, while the latter thrust us into a state of despair regarding the outcome of our efforts to rehabilitate delinquents. No subsequent evaluation of penal practices has in any respect restored our hope. But when evaluative results turn out to be negative, we are not entitled to say, "Nothing can be done." Rather, we feel goaded to restate our aims, alter our approach and redouble our efforts. For example, we might decide to study the few cases of successful reformation, and re-tool our practices by them.

Deeply disturbed by this failure with adult delinquents, Dr. Richard Cabot, shortly before his death in 1938, established and subsidized the Cambridge-Somerville Youth Study, perhaps the most elaborate evaluative investigation yet attempted. The study was action research; it instituted a program of long-continued treatment of pre-delinquent children for the express purpose of discovering whether such social service could check later delinquency. Specially established action research of this type has marked advantages over the cursory evaluative investigations that are all we can expect from agencies busy with daily demands. The financial resources are more adequate; research specialists are employed; and the important condition of having a control group can be observed. The three hundred boys in treatment were matched at the outset of the study with an equal number of controls. It was thus possible to estimate accurately the amount of change that occurred as a result of treatment rather than as a result of gradual maturing in the average community setting, where schools, churches and assorted social agencies are likewise engaged in the building of character. The treatment plans were badly interrupted, however, by the coming of the war; many of the boys entered service at the age of seventeen, the very time when the most effective casework might have been done.

The results of this elaborate study, as set forth by Powers and Witmer, are not as conclusive as we might wish.[3] In general terms, the study showed that, by police standards, approximately the same number of treatment and control boys turned out to be delinquent. Thus, in a sense, even five to seven years of casework, commencing between the ages of six and ten, proved ineffective. This pessimistic generalization, however, masks certain subsidiary findings of potentially great importance. There is some evidence, for example, that treatment boys, though they tangled with the courts as often as control boys, did not continue into careers of serious and aggravated criminality. There is also evidence that those who benefited most from the program were boys who, like their parents, were genuinely fond of the counselor; were relatively free from severe neurotic or pathological traits; and seemed to need most of all guidance and example in making up for minor defects in the home. At the same time, the study found that caseworkers were rarely, if ever, able to provide full and sufficient emotional anchorage for a boy whose own parents rejected him. Social service—at least of the type we are here discussing—seems unable to compensate for wretched emotional situations in the home. This example shows that evaluative research can help us determine the limits of an agency's work and identify the types of cases that can and cannot be rehabilitated.

It also came to light in the Cambridge-Somerville Youth Study that certain types of caseworkers seemed to have greater success than others. Specifically, the warm or friendly or informal workers, who to some critics seemed actually "unprofessional" in their approach, apparently had more success than the highly trained, diagnostic-minded, theoretically oriented workers. While too few cases are involved in this comparison to justify a generalization, the finding is potentially of great significance. If substantiated, it will cause us to examine sharply some of our current presuppositions regarding the selection and training of personnel—indeed, our whole philosophy of the "professional approach."

While I have used for illustrative purposes a study in the field of delinquency prevention, I could point to numerous areas that have recently yielded to evaluative penetration. The advances have been impressive. In 1952, David G. French published his book *Measuring results in social work,* a survey that places the whole subject in excellent perspective. One merit of the book is that it sets forth a detailed proposal for an Institute for Research in Social Work, which would supply agencies and programs with expert assistance in conducting evaluative investigations. Meanwhile, an avalanche of special and limited evaluative studies have been tumbling from the press.[4]

The trend toward social evaluation reaches far beyond casework. It embraces psychotherapy, health education, recreational programs; the effects of study in foreign lands, of summer camps, of programs for the reduction of ethnic prejudice; the efficiency of information services, even of general education in our colleges; and many other socially relevant policies and practices.

In the field of social service, anecdotal proof of success has given way. We can no longer say that failure to assess our efforts is in principle a major limitation. The chief obstacles in evaluation now are scant funds and a shortage of technical skills. Evaluation is not a job for amateurs; it requires shrewd planning, inventiveness, technical training and great caution in interpreting results. But these barriers are not insurmountable. If progress in the next twenty-five years matches progress in the past, we shall soon have this important instrument well under control.

The Goals of Social Work

One cardinal requirement for successful evaluation forces us to pause and take stock. Every evaluator agrees that we cannot measure progress unless we know our objectives, and these objectives must be stated in accessible (that is, operational) terms. We are thus brought face to face with the question of the goals of social service. While the question is familiar, it is none the less true that only a tiny fraction of the mountainous literature on social service is concerned with its *raison d'être*, with its philosophical guidelines and moral objectives. Such formulations as we do encounter are often too general or too vague to help the evaluator.

It may well be that—in certain respects, at least—we face an insoluble problem. If we accept as our goal "growth in personality" (and this is a goal upon which, I suspect, most of us would agree), how can we measure progress? How long after a program of treatment shall we attempt to determine growth? And what is our *criterion* for "growth in personality" or "improvement in character" —or, for that matter, for "self-reliance," "wholesomeness," "good citizenship," "happiness" or even "normality of adjustment"?

Occasionally our stated objectives are less elusive. When we say, for example, that our goal is economic rehabilitation of a client, we can set a reasonable criterion, such as holding a job steadily for a year. We can then determine what proportion of our clients reach this criterion of success. Even more general objectives, which may appear at first like clouds of vapor to a social scientist, can be and have been reduced to accessible operations. I have in mind the criterion of "movement," deemed desirable in certain casework philosophies; Hunt and Kogan have captured this will-o'-the-wisp and, with considerable success, impounded it for reliable measurement.[5]

It remains true, however, that our deepest concerns and highest ideals are not likely to lend themselves to exact measurement. And so we are faced here with the necessity for compromise. Measurement we surely want, but not if it tempts us to state our aims and objectives in brittle or trivial terms. Where meaningful and concrete operations are statable, let us use them in our evaluative procedures; but let us not assume that our total philosophy is reducible to criteria of this order.

Social service now proceeds under a wide variety of philosophies. While we hear a good deal about the need for "a single integrative professional philosophy," such articulate axiology as exists—and there is not a great deal of it—is far from receiving unanimous endorsement. Scientific humanism, as represented by Bisno, asks social service to adhere to a philosophy of science that is empirical in outlook, pragmatic in method, relativistic respecting values and negative toward all absolutes.[6] Some form of the philosophy of self-realization is, I suspect, more widely endorsed. For example, Richard Cabot, Mary Richmond and many like-minded workers hold that the supreme test of social service is "growth in personality": [7] does the personality of clients change, and change in the right direction? ("Right direction" is determined always by reference to the unique potentialities of the individual in relation to the rights and privileges of others.) The emphasis of Roman Catholic social service is somewhat different. It advocates bringing man under the sway of reason, in order that this distinctive human faculty may assist man, who is made in the image of God, to "find his way back to God." [8]

Is such disagreement on basic philosophy a serious limitation? The matter can be argued both ways. On the one hand, it could be said that social service, lacking a single ethical direction, slips easily into adulation of techniques. It does so because science and technology are the idols of our society and, lacking an explicit conscience of its own, social service unconsciously adopts the idolatry of the day. Four hundred years ago Rabelais warned us that "science without conscience spells only the ruin of the soul." We have minimized the warning of Rabelais and have lived rather by the faith of Karl Pearson, who, in his *Grammar of science*, prophesied that the gradual spread of scientific objectivity to the common mind will cure us of all passionate prejudices and improve our human relationships. Yet up to now science has brought only slight visible improvement in this regard. Like social service, it seems to require a doctrine of man, and a firm ethics by which to test its practices.

On the other hand, it may be argued that agreement on matters of such ultimate importance is impossible to achieve and not really desirable. Final truth we cannot know; human wisdom evolves best through diversity. A rough proximate agreement is all we need, and this we have already achieved. We know that social service aims to insure the survival and smooth functioning of the group; also, that in a democracy it aims to contribute to the fullness of individual life by helping to remove limitations that impede self-reliance. Sophisticated philosophers may try, if they will, to order these proximate goals under a framework of ultimates; but the harder they press their logic of values, the greater will be the resulting disagreement. Their final formulations will be as diverse as positivism and Thomism, humanism and existentialism, quietism and socialism. Why worry about the matter, when a rough working basis is already at hand?

What shall we say about this dispute? My own inclination is to concede that agreement on ultimates is neither possible nor, at this time, desirable. Yet if we are content with only a crude working basis, we may easily be trapped by the ideology of engineering and find ourselves preoccupied with techniques and gadgets, thus embracing, without fully knowing it, a directionless and conscienceless scientism. The safeguard, I think, is to foster continuous consideration of the aims of social service and the frames of axiology into which it may fit. Students should receive nutritive doses of ethics in schools of social work and should be encouraged to debate the matter in order to develop their own views. No one is bound to accept the final philosophy of another, but a philosophy of some kind he must have. It is, I believe, a serious shortcoming of social service that it pays too little attention—in its curricula of training and in later professional years—to its goals, objectives, policies and ethical premises, and to philosophies of life under which the daily activities of social workers may be ordered.

Public and Private Service

Modern social work developed from the attempt to offset the pauperizing effects of almsgiving and indiscriminate charity. It soon became apparent that private efforts, as represented in the Charity Organization movement, were hopelessly inadequate to repair the ravages caused by the industrial revolution and by the long period of *laissez faire* that accompanied it. Action by the state became imperative; and gradually, throughout the Western world, the ideals of social insurance, social security and governmental assistance to the sick, the aged, the unemployed and the young became accepted practices.

In a democracy, having a free economy and reasonable opportunities for upward mobility, as well as respect for the dignity of the individual, the ideals and aims of governmental and private social service are essentially the same. Whatever the division of functions, both forms of service wish to reduce unnecessary suffering, preserve a basic social order and maximize the opportunities of individuals to develop their potentialities.

Unless I am mistaken, the division of function that has occurred follows essentially the arrangement predicted and approved by Sidney Webb forty years ago.[9] This author employs the metaphor of the extension ladder. Public welfare services are charged with filling the gaps that exist in the basic economic and institutional structure of society. They provide means by which individuals obtain physical care, decent housing and protection against disability and poverty in old age, even though they cannot pay for such services in a competitive market. Thus public agencies provide a standardized form of assistance to all who meet certain specifications.

It is commonly agreed that the function of private social service, on the other hand, is to help individuals make the most of the resources of society, including the benefits that the government provides. Relieved of many of the burdens of economic relief, private social service has turned more and more to the understanding and treatment of personality. The ideal of "casework above the poverty line" emerged in the First World War, when the home service rendered by the Red Cross to the families of men on military duty demonstrated that human needs are by no means always economic. As early as 1909, Richard Cabot had written that he could see no reason why social work should be done only with the poor.[10]

This ideal of professional service above the poverty line has spread so widely that today we find a large percentage of the services privately rendered paid for by the client. This trend seems to hold not only for casework and guidance services but also for recreational and group work. A decreasing proportion of the funds raised by Community Chests go into direct relief and a larger proportion into administration, organization and even research. The trend is made possible by the creation of what has come to be called the "welfare state," in which unemployment benefits, industrial safety, health services, child care and social security are recognized matters for public rather than private responsibility.

Originally Sidney Webb held that voluntary agencies are superior to public authorities in three main features: (1) invention and experimentation with new services and new methods, (2) ability to give special and individualized care to particular cases and (3) freedom to bring religious or other moral influences to bear on clients. On the whole, it has been felt that voluntary agencies maintain high standards, which act as a model and monitor for public service. Today these distinctions are less sharp than formerly. Excellent casework is now done by civil service appointees, and public officials may be as imaginative and experimental as private workers. Nearly all of our personnel in public service is trained in private schools of social work, where the ideals and methods of voluntary agencies prevail.

Whatever their functions may be, the spread of public agencies has been continually and vigorously fought by economic and political conservatives. They profess to see in it the undermining of initiative, as well as threatening dislocations caused by excessive taxation, bureaucracy and loss of freedom. A century ago, conservatives objected to the elimination of the workhouse test for relief and held firmly to the principle of "less eligibility." Unless a pauper is stigmatized, they argued, we shall all lose our sense of shame and gladly become paupers. No battle was ever lost more decisively. Conservatives have been losing ground for decades—to such an extent, in fact, that we are now obliged to ask whether there is not some validity in their position. We need not include here conservatives whose transparent motivation is the preservation of their own privilege and status.

The plain fact is that the scope of social service has expanded, and is still expanding, at a spectacular rate. Private social services now receive and spend approximately one and a half *billion* dollars a year. In one cluster of 117 cities, gifts to Community Chests more than doubled between 1941 and 1954.[11] Government expenditures have mounted at a still more rapid rate. Two and a half billion dollars is the annual outlay of states, while the federal government spends many more billions on its social services, including programs for health and welfare, veterans' benefits and social security. In all, the total annual expenditure is over thirteen billion dollars, and ever rising.[12]

The reason for this mounting outlay is not increased destitution, but, rather, a change in the public's attitude toward social responsibility. Problems that received no attention a few decades, or even a few years, ago, now are accepted as legitimate and pressing obligations of society. The conservative's alarm merits fresh attention. Are we growing reckless and extravagant in our outlay? Do individuals cease to exert themselves and weakly prefer public bounty? Are we all passengers on the gravy train?

The danger, if I may venture an opinion, does not lie in the expansion of social services, or even in the fraction of the national income invested in them. The philosophy of both public and private service, and of their interrelationships, is essentially sound. The danger is more subtle: we might phrase it in terms of the growing insistence upon "rights" and the diminishing emphasis upon "duties." Take the social worker's own mental attitude, for example. His profession sensitizes him to the injustices he encounters. He is led to demand basic rights for dependent children, for victims of desertion, for the aged, for minority ethnic groups. It is proper that he should do so. But there is a reciprocal question: in fighting for rights, are social workers—and American citizens generally—aware of the duties they in turn owe to their community and their state? We greedily scramble for our share of public benefits, but pay our taxes reluctantly, and sometimes not at all. Almost half of us do not vote. Very few participate in civic affairs. Do social workers, in dealing with clients, try to inculcate in them an awareness of their duties? Or do they merely intensify the sense of "rights," already so prominent in the American's mind? In the Japanese culture, we are told, heavy emphasis is placed upon the sense of obligation, far less on rights. In our culture the burden of emphasis is precisely reversed.

Another example: unless I am mistaken, most young people training for the profession of social service prefer to work for private agencies and shun opportunities for public service. This is true, I think, even though half the openings in social service today occur in public agencies and a large number of scholarships and other inducements are offered by public agencies, including the Veterans Administration, the National Mental Health Foundation and state welfare departments.[13] The reason for this disaffection is fairly apparent. It is felt to be somehow less pleasant to be bound by public bureaucracy than by private bureaucracy. It is disagreeable to be exposed to political control and the hazards of McCarthy-like persecutions. Yet how are we to build and maintain our public services, if we as citizens shun them? The basic philosophies of public and private agencies do not greatly differ. What we need is a more cordial and equal relationship between them, and in particular a higher sense of obligation to public service, an area that will continue to grow by leaps and bounds.

While I am deploring overemphasis upon private and proprietary conceptions of social service, let me bemoan also our national provincialism. When we view the world situation as a whole, we are forced to conclude that some of our refined distinctions and preoccupations look like fancy embroidery. We quarrel, for example, over the hairlike boundary between casework and psychotherapy, while most of the world has never heard of either. In most countries of the earth, the poor survive only with the help of the poor. The professions of social work and psychiatry are totally unknown. Voluntary service is nonexistent. Most countries have no public assistance, no social security, no community resources to which the needy can be referred. Sickness, poverty and desolate old age are so familiar that the people, submerged in despair, ignorance and apathy, are benumbed. In these countries, social service for the present can mean only the launching of some vast social change that will lift the masses to the point at which individual problems can be perceived and differential treatment become possible.

It is a limitation of American social service that, lacking world perspective, it cosily believes that the United States lives safely on an island, unaffected by the misery of other nations. Their revolt into communism and into other desperate experiments can easily cause a world conflagration that will wipe out the painful gains of social service in the United States. I suggest that those of us who are engaged in social service are living, to some extent, in a fool's paradise. It would seem to be high time for us to concern ourselves more actively with the new international ethics of mutual aid.[14]

Professionalism

A dilemma of a different order confronts us when we consider the motivation that sustains social service. Unless there are elements of love, compassion and a desire to share one's own life-benefits with others, the whole process of social service is likely to be a husk. At the same time, it is fatal if these altruistic impulses are concentrated into fitful ecstasies and allowed undisciplined expression. Nor is it enough for the social worker to engage in the immediately rewarding contacts of good casework. The needed discipline requires also a long-range focus, sustained by a social and personal philosophy tempered by patience, a sense of political strategy and all other virtues of sturdy citizenship. Discipline requires also freedom from self-deception.

I realize that in these days of strict self-scrutiny, social workers are expected to examine their own motives. They are, for example, supposed to be aware of the dangers of projection—the same pitfall Thoreau denounced when he accused philanthropists of surrounding others with the remembrance of their own cast-off griefs and despair, and mistakenly calling the process "sympathy." Most social workers today agree that their professional equipment requires, first of all, a fundamental security in themselves, and, secondly, an ability to understand that other people have different needs and ways of thought.[15]

But projection is only one form of self-deception. There is also the bias of optimism, which often leads a worker to put a too rosy complexion on his relationships with a client. Technically we speak of a "parataxic dyad" whenever a worker or his client (or both) seriously misperceives the attitude of the other respecting their relationship. In a study of delinquency prevention, Teuber and Powers discovered that, in about a third of the cases, the counselor or the boy was ignorant of the other's true attitude. A counselor, for example, might describe a boy's attitude toward him as trusting and affectionate, while the boy really believed that the counselor was a paid detective, hired to spy on bad boys. Instead of affection and trust, the boy felt fear and hostility in the relationship. In parataxis it is usually the worker who takes the rosier view of the state of rapport and overestimates the therapeutic value of his efforts. In the Teuber-Powers study, it turned out that parataxis was greater, and rapport less, in cases where the worker approached his task with rigid ideas concerning what constituted admissible and inadmissible professional practices. The dyadic relationship, in general, was much better among workers who adhered to a "friendship theory" of social service.[16]

The "friendship theory" has met strenuous objections. Its opponents argue convincingly that we do not choose clients on the same basis that we choose a friend. There are insuperable barriers of age, of contrasting educational and economic status, and of lifelong differences in habits of thought. Still worse, clients demand of the caseworker far more patience, objectivity and self-control than do friends.

Here, then, is the dilemma. The basic motives for social service can only be charity, compassion and tolerance—all of which are central ingredients in friendship. At the same time, we are rightly warned that these virtues may lead us into sentimentality and unwisdom. Only strict objectivity and a professional view of our roles will save us; yet professionalism may freeze the heart, lead to parataxis in our relationships and betray us into harmful excesses of specialism.

Specialism is a peculiar hazard in social service, medicine, the ministry or any other profession devoted to helping people in distress. Distress defies job analysis. We know how, in medicine, the decline of the general practitioner has created problems for many a sick person whose real difficulties elude the succession of specialists he visits. In social work, the problem is growing acute. Increasing emphasis on defining "agency function" can lead to a rat-race of referrals, sometimes demoralizing to the client and hence unethical. Even if referrals themselves do not damage the client, he may find at the end of his trek that there is no rubric for his distress and therefore no agency to help him. An unmarried girl in a certain town could find no help: she was seven months pregnant, and the only appropriate agency had a rule that no applicant more than six months pregnant could be accepted. Good casework, the agency said, could not be done at this late stage of pregnancy. But is good casework an end in itself? Are we wrong in assuming that social service exists to aid mortals in distress, not to sharpen skills or gratify the professional self-image of the worker?

Another peril of excessive professionalism is overemphasis upon diagnosis. Ever since the ideal of "social diagnosis" was set before us forty years ago in Mary Richmond's epoch-making book, *What is social case work?* it has seemed self-evident that it is folly to launch into a program of treatment without knowing the nature of the problem and its roots. No one wishes to retard the development of diagnostic methods; yet we do well to keep their limits in mind.

In the first place, a worker—whether in a public or a private agency—may be so preoccupied with diagnosis that, by placing his client under a lens, he sets up a relationship that endangers his ultimate chances of helping him. Even in medicine, successful therapy may be blocked by excessive shunting of the patient from laboratory to laboratory, and the therapeutic relationship in social work is even more delicate and easily torn. A client who discovers that he is regarded as a specimen, an exercise in diagnosis and manipulation, draws back from the friendly relation that, in most cases, is the essential condition of helping him.

In the second place, it is simply not true that successful treatment invariably presupposes accurate diagnosis. Many a client, like many a medical patient, has with friendly support and encouragement mastered his trouble without enjoying the luxury of a diagnosis.

Finally, diagnoses are likely to be little more than coarse classifications. Certainly the present rubrics of psychiatry and of psychology are not final. It is not particularly helpful to decide that a certain client had unfortunate conditioning, or feels rejected, or harbors resentment against authority figures. All these diagnoses may be true, but one cannot pluck out the root causes one by one. Better to view the person himself, in all his maladaptive complexity, and the immediate environment he faces, as the "cause" of his trouble. Best work with him where he stands.

Let me repeat: I am not arguing against diagnosis, but I am pointing to the fact that excessive emphasis upon diagnosis, as one aspect of excessive professionalism, may constitute a serious limit to the effectiveness of social service.

Another dogma of social service may prove a handicap if it is carried to an extreme—the dogma that help should be offered only to those individuals and families who express a conscious need for help. Granted that the chances for effective work are greater with those who present a "growing edge" to the social worker, I question whether such initiative is a *final* measure of ability to profit from an agency's service. I have heard of an agency that rejected a dependency case because the five-year-old child in question had expressed no "felt need." Such extremes engender countermovements: we hear nowadays about "aggressive casework"—first practiced on a large scale, I believe, by the Cambridge-Somerville Youth Study—and about "reaching the unreached." Without presuming here to judge the merits of these new movements, I venture merely to point out the need for sensible balance in settling this matter of policy in social service.

My remarks on certain aspects of professionalism in social service may seem excessively critical. If so, I can only plead that my subject calls for a certain acidulousness. And if my criticism is in part justified, it points to a wholly understandable weakness. Social service is a young profession. In setting its standards and defining its policies, it is very likely to overshoot the mark, to exalt its insight into the realm of dogma—and then, perhaps, to oscillate between extreme positions. In time we can expect a better equilibrium to be achieved, but only if we recognize dogmas and excesses for what they are.

The Foundations in Psychology

Social service is what Auguste Comte called "concrete" science—that is to say, it borrows and applies theories and principles derived from the more basic "abstract" sciences. The laws and formulations of biology, sociology and psychology supply the foundations for the practices of social service, as they do for education, therapy and all other skills in human relations.

One weakness of social service lies, I think, in its faddist tendency—its tendency to borrow too heavily from some theory currently fashionable in the underlying "abstract" sciences. Early in the present century, we know there was an almost total blindness to psychological laws of motivation and learning, as well as dense disregard for psychiatric principles. It was thought that the capacity for normal living could be restored merely by observing one sociological law—that the family is the primary unit of human association, survival and adjustment. Somewhat later the biology of tonsils became an obsession; social workers stood their charges in line outside tonsillectoria, hoping for biological magic to restore a capacity for normal living. But these fevers were as nothing compared with the awesome regard for the human psyche that settled upon us during the 1920s.

At first William Healy, Ernest Southard, Richard Cabot, Adolf Meyer and Mary Jarrett pushed us gently toward the psychiatric point of view. Then, suddenly, depth psychology descended upon us! Our watchwords became "transference," "countertransference," "attitude therapy," "rebirth," "clarification" and "insight development." We were supposed to "support neurotic equilibrium" and to re-create in our client "a sense of the security and emotional dependency of the childhood period." (These quotations, incidentally, are all from the recent literature of casework.)

It would be most unbecoming for a psychologist to criticize social work for giving enthusiastic if belated recognition to the basic importance of the human psyche. I do, however, wish to point out that the enthusiasm has generally been directed toward *psychiatry* (the art of treating sick people), rather than toward *psychology* (the science of the normal mind). Psychology is a less vivid, more mundane and more time-consuming subject for study. Like psychiatry and psychoanalysis, it is fallible. Yet it offers principles of learning, motivation, social interaction, leadership, group dynamics, thought-processes, personality growth, assessment and diagnosis—principles that ought not be overlooked in favor of easier and more dramatic formulations, even though these too have great merit.

If social service follows the best thinking available in psychology and psychiatry—and I would not have it do otherwise—it will be subject to the limitations of this best thinking. Psychology, psychoanalysis and psychiatry are in a stage of rapid development. It would be unreasonable to expect social service to advance more rapidly than they. But because the change is so rapid, caution and balance are necessary in appraising dicta that may be more fashionable than true.

Let us consider one example. Freud, seconded by Rank, Bowlby and Melanie Klein—all of whom have had a marked influence upon social work—tells us that the essential foundations of character are established by the age of three. This proposition is startling. It may be true. But as yet it is unproved. A great many social workers, however, accept it as if it were gospel.

Such a fatalistic and dispiriting view leaves only a few relatively mean functions for the social worker to perform. He can, to be sure, enter the family constellation and help steer its prevailing neurosis. In a self-sacrificing mood, he might offer himself as a scapegoat and try to channel the mother's aggression from her long-suffering husband and children. At best a "limited therapy" might be undertaken with a client, provided there are vestiges of warmth and security in early childhood upon which to build. But for infants wholly deprived and therefore irretrievably warped, nothing can be done in later life except to distract them from their errant ways with such ingenuity as the worker can muster.

Within this framework of thinking, there is little merit in friendliness or in spiritual support unless there is also a suitable early soil on which to build, and unless the personality of the client can be suitably matched to the personality of the worker. But by the time depth diagnosis is accomplished, and the matching of the neurosis of the client with that of the worker is completed, all human impulses to sympathy and understanding may have evaporated.

Recent researches have, indeed, indicated the importance of early years in the formation of character. But these researches are as yet of limited scope, and do not justify a sudden and complete revising of the whole philosophy of social service. While Freudian and Rankian theories undoubtedly contain valuable truths, I venture to believe that they contain no more truth than certain opposing theories —those which maintain that personality is subject to constructive influences all through life; that it possesses inherent resources for growth and change at every period; and that no character is conclusively set at the age of three, or thirteen, or thirty.

If we knew the full truth about the foundations of human nature, we should have to include within our view the limitations that heredity sets upon our efforts. At present, psychology, psychoanalysis and social work all proceed with an environmental bias (though for psychoanalysis the environment is of little consequence after the infant years). The social worker secretly knows that nature sets ironclad limits to his labors, through constitutional defects, perverse temperament and mental inadequacy. But until we understand human genetics better than we do, we cannot say how serious these limits may be. Meanwhile, it seems sensible to continue to attack human problems with an environmental bias, remaining ready to correct our bias if and when it becomes necessary to do so.

I am sure that those who engage in social service, as well as those charged with the curricula in our schools of social work, would reply that no school of psychological thought today is followed blindly, but that the insights gained are synthesized and adapted to the realities of casework. Certainly the admirable effort spent on devising "an integrated program of professional education for social work" reflects a commendable breadth of view.[17] My fear is not directed primarily toward the unbalanced curricula of instruction, though more varied psychology, more philosophy and ethics, and more concern with public policy are certainly needed. I am worried, rather, that individual social workers, confronted by the tangled skein of a human life, might oversimplify what they learn and gravitate toward pet psychological formulas in order to "understand" the problems presented. It takes detachment, maturity and wide study of psychology not to compress a given life into an easy, and probably erroneous, formula.

In no field of human endeavor is it more essential to balance science and art. On the one hand, a client is a representative of the human species, and universal laws of health and disease, instincts and impulses, frustration and resentment, ego-defense and prejudice, reason and the irrational are likely to apply. General laws of economics, cultural expectation and taboo, family structure and the role requirements of our society are likewise relevant to each concrete case. At the same time, every individual is an idiom unto himself. His course of becoming is unlike any other. His problems and his assets are his alone; so, too, his suffering and his bid for affection.

The busy social worker is likely to let the particular be overwhelmed by the general. It is easier to conjure with the principles of psychoanalysis than to make a separate study of development and growth in each individual. It is easier to recall the general principles of criminology than to understand the particular malefactor. It is simpler to categorize in terms of neuroses and therapeutic roles than to comprehend and treat personal patterns of trouble. The balancing of general knowledge against a knowledge of the particular poses a harder problem for social service, I suspect, than for any other occupation.

This problem is directly related to the issue previously mentioned: the need for balance between the "professional" theory and the "friendship" theory of social service. Friendship is precisely that human relationship in which the particular takes precedence over the general. Yet, as we have seen, social service cannot be exclusively a relation of friendship, for the relationship from the beginning imposes certain restrictions. One member of the dyad is, by definition, older, or wiser, or stronger, or more resourceful. The other is the weaker, the suitor, suffering from adversity. Yet little can be done for the client unless some of the virtues of friendship, along with the perception of the particular and the art of individualizing, are well represented.

In short, it is the fate of social service to seek broad and accurate foundations for its policies and practices, but it should balance its dependence upon the general with a regard for the particular. Such a dexterous balance is difficult to achieve. Many of our current disputes over the "true function" of social service arise, I feel, from denying its essential and unavoidable versatility. Who can say whether the social worker is an "adjustment adviser," a "teacher," a "resource person," a "big brother" or a "psychotherapist"? If he places the need of the client first, he will be all these things at different times and under different circumstances. Only when we mistakenly place "agency function" or one-sided theories of science first do we find ourselves quarreling over the precise role or attitude that is, or is not, appropriate to social service.

Before leaving the relationship between social service and social science, I should like to protest the present one-sidedness in their communication. Why should social service do all the borrowing? Why should not the bulging files of social agencies be made to yield their buried knowledge to help build a more comprehensive psychology of motivation, of learning, of personality growth and of human relations? There are mountains of case records awaiting analysis and inductive handling. Our files are for the most part graveyards of *knowledge*. They should, rather, become treasure-troves for the development of new *principles* of human nature and of social relations.

Social Change and Public Apathy

An atomic war may force all of us who survive to forage for edible weeds and a cave to dwell in. One spasm of international madness could, at a single sweep, destroy the intricate fabric of social service and turn its fine philosophy into an absurdity. Even short of an atomic war, we rightly fear what may happen to the values of our unique democratic society as communism spreads more widely in the world. Already we see how its grim pressure is strain-

ing our historical conceptions of civil liberties, of individual rights
and of mutual trust and respect. The extension of public service,
which we welcome, can conceivably slide into the crude statism of
Stalin or, more likely, the subtler but equally destructive statism of
Hitler. Our demagogues are pushing hard. We feel ourselves on the
defensive before titanic forces of social change.

The ideals and practices of social service are among the finest
fruits of the orchard of democracy. Their existence depends upon
maintaining the soil, the roots and the main trunks of our way of
life. It is fatal blindness if social service does not realize this fact
and act in accordance with it. Today the social worker who does
not labor to preserve the foundations of democracy is like a squirrel
nibbling fruits others have planted in an orchard now withering.

Here I am speaking from the "structural" point of view. Sociologists and historians often tell us that, as individuals, we are
nearly helpless before the sweep of social change. It is the total frame
in which we live that conditions our acts. Social service as we know
it will survive only so long as it is maintained by political democracy
and economic free enterprise—and by our subtly evolved sense of
social responsibility, based on a delicate blend of protectiveness toward and autonomy for the individual person. The structural argument is harsh. It holds that this intricate framework is subject to
historical changes, no matter what you and I may will to do.

The same argument also takes another form, drawing not on the
inevitabilities of social change but upon the now familiar creed of
natural selection. It asks whether social service is viable from the
point of view of nature. Evolutionists from Herbert Spencer to
Raymond Pearl have warned us that arrogant interference with nature's law can bring misery, if not actual destruction, to the human
race. From their point of view, the protection and unnatural preservation of the inept fills the earth with misfits whom nature, left
to herself, would promptly dispatch. Like medicine and public
health, social service conspires to negate nature.

This issue has been tiresomely debated, though it has never been
definitely settled. One thing only is clear: we have decided deliberately to disregard the simple logic of natural selection. We have
asserted, once and for all, that nature's coarse standards are not a
proper measure of man's worth or of his right to survive. In place
of "rugged individualism," our society has chosen "socialized individualism." We may be wrong, but we shall have to make the best
of it. As we reap the consequences in terms of high birth rates,
increasing maladies of old age and overpopulation, we shall have to

learn gradually to solve the problems that medicine and social service may have caused in our society.

In this matter, social service has contracted to transcend its own limits. It hopes that, by adapting to altered conditions, it can continue to work out its ideals. A cataclysm might prove fatal; but short of that, we shall endeavor to adjust to—and, when possible, guide and direct—social change. So far as the specter of natural selection is concerned, we believe that here too the strategies of intelligence will enable us to meet and master whatever dislocations may result from abandoning the jungle theory of survival in favor of higher ethical ideals.

I do not mean to imply that these commitments are conscious and deliberate on our part. Few people think about the philosophy that underlies their support of social service. The public gives generously to private philanthropy and votes decisively for an extension of state and federal benefits, yet the social worker knows that he cannot count on consistency in the public's attitude. While wanting more state and federal services, people are definitely antagonistic toward paying taxes. While wanting freedom for themselves, many people are ready to deny it to others. While wanting better opportunities for their children than they themselves enjoyed, people hold to resistant and stagnant ideologies of child training, from which neither social workers nor educators can successfully convert them. While deploring the contagion of delinquency in society, neither the public nor its legislative representatives will sanction the drastic types of reform we know to be needed. All in all, public attitudes are conservative—far more so, as a rule, than the attitudes of those who are active in social welfare. It is, therefore, a major frustration of our calling that those who are engaged in its practice will be limited, and often defeated, by public ignorance and apathy.

Self-confidence and Its Enemies

Since social service is severely restricted—by social structure on the one hand, and by public apathy on the other—it seems ungracious to blame it for feelings of inadequacy. Yet this is, I think, one of its defects, the final defect of which I wish to speak.

Social service lacks self-confidence; it lacks a firm sense of conviction in its own goals.[18] In part, our confidence is weak because we feel at a disadvantage in a society where competitiveness and aggressiveness reap conspicuous rewards, while the ideals of cooperation, to which social service is committed, represent a minority point of view. In part, our low confidence is engendered by the very atmosphere of doubt in which we live, by the same atmosphere that causes us to engage in wholesome self-scrutiny, self-evaluation and self-criticism.

But self-assessment should take into account assets as well as liabilities. Among its assets social service can reckon its recent achievement of the status of a full-fledged profession. The two major characteristics of any profession, writes Dean Ralph Tyler, are its use of technics derived from general principles and its possession of a code of ethics.[19] I have already mentioned the present alertness of social work in deriving its procedures from underlying sciences. I have, to be sure, criticized a certain one-sidedness in the derivations now popular, but the trend in general is wholesome. And social service is making good progress in the formulation of an explicit code of ethics.[20] Thus the advance to professional status, in both public welfare and private social work, is clear and gratifying.

Still, some of us, caught in the current atmosphere of doubt, tend to lack courage. We are not as certain as we once were that our efforts will succeed. Who can be? Yet the existentialists remind us that men can be half-sure without being half-hearted. Accepting our doubt, and admitting every hazard, we are still free to elect and pursue our option. Living requires that we know the worst and make the best of it. Some of us would benefit from a generous injection of this type of existentialist courage.

But we need not rest content with a philosophy of make-the-best-of-it. Deep inside, each of us knows that the spirit behind social service knows no limits. This spirit, the finest fruit of Judeo-Christian ethics, is eternally sound. How ironical it is that the scriptural word "charity," as used by St. Paul, has in our profession become a sign of opprobrium rather than of inspiration! The motive behind social work always has been, and will continue to be, *caritas*, and this motive is infinitely valid.

The root problem of social service is how to express the impulse of charity effectively with the technical skill and flexible intelligence required by complex modern conditions. The chief lesson we learn from the nineteenth century is that good intentions are not enough. Nowadays we know a great deal more about sound means of fostering growth in personality, about the basis of human motivation, about a proper relationship between public and private effort. When we reflect on our progress in theory and in practice, we have every right to reassert our faith and stiffen our courage. There are plenty of obstacles in our path and many trends that need correcting; but, barring global catastrophe, we can expect continued development in the right direction.

Social service has a greater clarity of perspective than does politics or commerce. It can therefore press for the stabilizing reforms that are needed to make life rich, meaningful and just in a system of free initiative and individual liberty. By asserting its convictions more loudly than it has, social service can make itself not only the servant but also the prophet of democracy. And today, as never before, democracy needs both servants and prophets.

Social service has limits and limitations. But it has also the saving virtue of self-criticism, and is daily growing in shrewdness and sense of strategy. Its foundations are eternally valid. The balance, therefore, is in its favor.

REFERENCES

1. Dr. Cabot's presidential address to the Fifty-eighth National Conference of Social Work in 1931 is an important historical landmark. In it he reviews the handful of evaluative studies available at that time and pleads with unmatched eloquence for a continuing program of evaluation in all social agencies. R. C. Cabot, "Treatment in social casework and the need of criteria and of tests of its success or failure," in *Proceedings of the national conference of social work,* Chicago: University of Chicago Press, 1931.

2. S. van S. Theis, *How foster children turn out,* State Charities Aid Association, 1924. S. Glueck and E. T. Glueck, *Five hundred criminal careers,* New York: Knopf, 1930. See also E. T. Glueck, *Evaluative research in social work,* New York School of Social Work, 1936.

3. E. Powers and H. Witmer, *An experiment in the prevention of delinquency* (Foreword by G. W. Allport), New York: Columbia University Press, 1951.

4. Among representative evaluative studies I would call attention to the following:

G. W. Allport, *The nature of prejudice,* Cambridge: Addison-Wesley, 1954, Chaps. 29-31.

S. Axelrad, J. Frings and E. Herzog, *A study of short term cases,* New York: Research Department, Jewish Family Service, 1951.

I. A. Berg, "Measures before and after therapy," *J. Clin. Psychol.,* 1952, 8: 46-50.

M. Blenkner, "Obstacles to evaluative research in casework," *Social Casework,* 1950, 31: 54-60, 97-105.

C. F. Cannell, F. G. Wale and S. B. Withey, "Community change: an action program in Puerto Rico," *J. Soc. Issues,* 1953, Vol. 9, No. 2.

H. S. Coffey, M. Freedman, T. Leary and A. Ossorio, "Community service and social research—group psychotherapy in a church program," *J. Soc. Issues,* 1950, Vol. 6, No. 1.

H. J. Eysenck, "The effects of psychotherapy: an evaluation," *J. Consulting Psychol.,* 1952, 16:319-24, No. 5.

S. Glueck and E. T. Glueck, *Unraveling juvenile delinquency,* New York: Commonwealth Fund, 1950.

W. Healy and A. F. Bronner, *Treatment and what happened afterward,* Boston: Judge Baker Guidance Center, 1939.

P. Hoch (ed.), *Failures in psychiatric treatment,* New York: Grune and Stratton, 1948.

J. McV. Hunt, "The problem of measuring the results of psychotherapy," *Psychol. Ser. Cen. J.,* 1949, 1:122-35, No. 4.

L. S. Kogan, "Evaluative techniques in social casework," *Soc. Ser. Rev.,* 1952, 26:305-09, No. 3.

L. S. Kubie, "Objective evaluation of psychotherapy: roundtable," *Amer. J. Orthopsychiat.,* 1949, 19:463-91.

H. H. W. Miles, E. L. Barrabee and J. E. Finesinger, "Evaluation of psychotherapy with a follow-up study of 62 cases of anxiety neurosis," *Psychosom. Med.,* 1951, 13:83-105.

R. E. Perl and A. J. Simon, "Criteria of success and failure in child guidance," *Amer. J. Orthopsychiat.,* 1942, 12:642-58.

H. A. Rashkis and D. A. Shaskan, "The effects of group psychotherapy on personality inventory scores," *Amer. J. Orthopsychiat.,* 1946, 16:345-49, No. 2.

G. J. Rich, "Preschool clinical service and follow-up in a city health department," *Amer. J. Orthopsychiat.,* 1948, 18:134-39, No. 1.

S. B. Sells, "Problems of criteria and validity in diagnosis and therapy," *J. Clin. Psychol.,* 1952, 8:23-28.

R. I. Watson, "Research design and methodology in evaluating the results of psychotherapy," *J. Clin. Psychol.,* 1952, 8:29-33.

5. J. McV. Hunt and L. S. Kogan, *Measuring results in social casework: a manual on judging movement,* New York: Family Service Association, 1950.

6. H. Bisno, *The philosophy of social work,* Washington: Public Affairs Press, 1952, p. 92.

7. R. C. Cabot, *The meaning of right and wrong,* New York: Macmillan, 1933. M. Richmond, *What is social case work?* New York: Russell Sage Foundation, 1922.

8. M. J. McCormick, *Diagnostic casework in the Thomistic pattern,* New York: Columbia University Press, 1954, pp. 13, 51.

9. S. Webb, "The extension ladder theory of the relation between voluntary philanthropy and state or municipal action," *The Survey,* 1914, 31: 703-07.

10. R. C. Cabot, *Social service and the art of healing,* New York: Moffat, Yard and Co., 1909.

11. *Trends in giving,* Community Chests and Councils of America, 345 East 46th Street, New York 17, New York, Table 12.

12. R. H. Kurtz (ed.), *Social work year book, 1954,* New York: American Book-Stratford Press, 1954, p. 221.

13. See *Social work fellowships and scholarships in the United States and Canada,* Council on Social Work Education, 345 East 46th Street, New York, New York.

14. A good place to start our self-education in this regard is with the valuable reports of the Economic and Social Council of the United Nations,

such as the "Programme of concerted practical action in the social field of the United Nations and specialized agencies," Report E/CN.5/291, March 2, 1953. Also significant is the work of private international organizations, such as the International Conference of Social Work with its many branches, the International Federation of Social Workers and the International Committee of Schools of Social Work.

15. Cf. V. P. Robinson, *A changing psychology in social casework,* Chapel Hill: University of North Carolina Press, 1930, p. 180.

16. H. L. Teuber and E. Powers, "Evaluating therapy in a delinquency prevention program," in *Psychiatric Treatment,* Vol. 21, *Proc. of the Assoc. for Research in Nervous and Mental Disease,* Baltimore: Williams and Wilkins, 1953, Chap. 12.

17. Report of Annual Meeting–1952, New York, American Association of Schools of Social Work, 1 Park Avenue, New York 16, New York.

18. L. H. Towley has made this point forcefully in his address "Professional responsibility in a democracy," in *Education for social work: proceedings annual program meeting,* New York: Council on Social Work Education, 1953, pp. 10-21.

19. R. W. Tyler, "Distinctive attributes of education for the professions," *Soc. Work J.,* April 1952, p. 5.

20. "A proposed code of ethics for the social worker," *Soc. Work J.,* April 1949.

CHAPTER 18

Perception, proception and public health

An exciting development in recent years is the joining of forces between the medical and the social sciences. The points of contact are numerous and the results beneficial. We are now becoming familiar with the social structure of hospitals, with the role of the family and of cultural background in cases of illness, and with the importance of the patient's attitude toward his physician and nurses. We are exploring ever more deeply his attitude toward medication and surgery, toward life and death.

This essay focuses attention on certain important points of contact between the psychology of perception and the practical work of public health practitioners. It introduces the new but, I trust, useful concept of "proception."

The Health Education Monographs first published the essay in 1958 under the title "Perception and public health." It was the second annual Dorothy B. Nyswander Lecture, delivered at the School of Public Health at Berkeley, California, in May 1958.

During the past decade, the outlook and duties of health education have changed significantly, principally in the direction of closer cooperation with psychological and social science.[1] At the beginning of that period, terror of infectious diseases was still uppermost. Since these specific scourges had specific causes, research in public health meant chiefly finding the antitoxin or antibiotic that would defeat the invading microbe. This work required little cooperation or knowledge on the part of the ordinary citizen. He was not deeply involved in sanitary engineering, water purification or rodent control. But he did develop, thanks to public health education, a "bacterio-technological perspective on illness."[2] He became vaccine conscious, as the recent rush of the public for Salk vaccine shows. Miracle cures he now understands; and his faith in them is still growing.

But where is the vaccine to prevent mental breakdowns? to lead people to early examinations for cardiac and cancer conditions? to abolish harmful practices of eating, sleeping and recreation? to control alcoholic and other addictions? to eliminate reckless automobile driving? to establish wholesome practices of child training? Health workers agree that we have now entered an era when the human factor—the whims, values and perceptions of the ordinary citizen—must be considered before further progress can be made. Future advances will require the consent and cooperation of people: the *public* part of public health will increasingly concern us.

It is not possible to review in a single essay all the exciting advances in social science that have potential value for future progress in public health. Many of these developments are already familiar, perhaps especially those concerned with opinion and communication, with leadership and group process, and with the differing ethnic and regional requirements of public health work. I shall concentrate, rather, on the less often considered question of perception and public health—in practical terms, the question: *Does the receiver hear and comprehend the health message as the health educator intends?*

The Paradox of Perception

A traveler to Naples tells the following story: Arriving at his hotel overlooking the fabulously beautiful bay, his cab driver burst forth in rapture. Although the driver had seen the lovely view a thousand times, he cried out, *"Come e bello, come e bello!"* The traveler agreed with his ecstatic driver and entered his hotel. There the innkeeper confided that he was having much trouble with a rich American oil magnate who had come to Naples to escape boredom in his retirement. This American, after glancing at the view, had merely sniffed, "Just trees and water and a city—I've seen them thousands of times." Hiring a taxi, he drove to Pompeii and returned full of wrath. "I've seen enough good houses in my lifetime," he said, "without going to look at a lot that are in ruins." The oil magnate retreated to his only solace, a concoction made of schnapps and champagne. A few weeks later he developed delirium tremens and was shipped back to the United States.

The story illustrates our first principle: *environment may be less a matter of physical surroundings than of perception.* Two men in the same geographical spot do not live in the same environment. It is for this reason that a health worker, even though he does not alter his approach in the slightest degree as he goes from house to house, may be perceived as threatening or consoling, as a friend to be welcomed or as a pest to be avoided. The worker thinks that he plays a steadfast professional role; but he doesn't. Like the Bay of Naples, he is two things to two perceivers—and ten things to ten perceivers.

But here we run into the prime paradox of perception: there *is*, after all, a Bay of Naples. The process of perceiving is subjectively swayed, but it is objectively anchored. Perception is governed by both outer and inner factors; in the language of Plato, "The light within meets the light without." What we see and hear is, therefore, both veridical and distorted, both true and false.

The fact that we perceive the world around us fairly accurately is due to the evolution of sensory and brain processes well tuned to outer reality. Eyes perceive color, line and shape with exquisite fineness; ears register accurately a wide range of air vibrations. The skin, less perfect in sensitiveness, still mediates evidence of shape and the finer gradations of temperature. The reason for this mirroring ability is undoubtedly its "functional usefulness." The organism has a better chance of survival if the sensory equipment is finally accurate. As Woodworth maintains in a recent book, the first and foremost motive in life is man's pervasive need to handle his world competently.[3] For Woodworth, the process of perception is the fundamental dynamism serving this fundamental motive.

Yet, by following the same line of reasoning, we can say the perceptual process must *depart* from true mirroring in order to be of maximum use to us. Not every tree in the forest comes into perceptual focus; only the one we are chopping. Not every object on the dinner table is perceived with clarity; only the bite we are about to put into our mouths. If you hear a babble of vague conversation, how quickly *your* name stands out if it is mentioned. Selective perception is as much a functional necessity as is veridical perception.

In coping with our world, it would not be enough to follow only "the light without." We have first to select what we shall see; in so doing, we become hypervigilant toward some cues and indifferent or actively defensive toward others. We perceive in order to cope, but coping means more than passive mirroring. It means fulfilling our needs; it means finding safety and reassurance, love and self-respect, freedom from worry, opportunities for growth—and, ultimately, a satisfying meaning for our existence. Our coping may thus be best served by disregarding some stimuli entirely, by modifying our interpretation of others and by blending incoming meanings with our past habits, our present needs and our future directions.

The point is illustrated in a recent health investigation conducted by Dr. Dorrian Apple of the Boston University School of Nursing. Her problem was to determine when people "perceive" sickness—that is to say, what configuration of experience tells a person that he, or someone else, is sick. The answer, she found, is that the symptoms must be *actively present* now; they must be *acute and well-defined;* and they must lead to an *impairment of activity*. These criteria are additive, and a really sick person will show all three conditions. Thus a man with a present fever and a head cold, unable to go to work, is perceived as sick. But a man with a vague and chronic discomfort in the chest who suffers no interruption in his daily duties is seldom seen as sick.[4] From the health worker's point of view, of course, the latter may be far more seriously ill and may need medical attention more urgently. But how shall the health worker deal with a sick person who perceives no sickness?

And when a person does perceive that he is ill, how greatly his perceptual field changes. Objects previously of interest lose their demand; the health visitor is no longer perceived as a busybody but as an angel of mercy; bodily functions loom large; minor as well as major discomforts fill the horizon. As Charles Lamb observed: "How sickness enlarges the dimensions of a man's self to himself! He is his own exclusive object. Supreme selfishness is inculcated upon him as his only duty."[5] In illness the "bacterio-technological perspective" of which we have spoken melts away. The sick person cannot take an impersonal, aseptic view of the health worker, even though he may pretend to do so. He is sensitized, as is the child, to his own fears and to signs of love and support from those who care for him. Small matters arouse aggression or querulousness, ill humor or shame. An inadvertent frown on the face of the examining doctor or health worker may be perceived as a prophecy of doom.[6] A proud adult may even view his illness as a reflection on his heredity and therefore as a disgrace to his family. Clearly the perceptual worlds of health and disease are not the same.

Percept or Procept?

Before examining the application of modern perceptual research to health education, may I invite your close attention to a current technical issue in the psychology of perception?

Up to now I have been employing the term *perception* broadly, as indeed many psychologists today do. There is good reason for this broad usage. Psychologists have always known that perception is the process of adding meaning to sensory input. It is the process that creates a stable environment out of what would otherwise be a chaos of unsorted sensory impressions. Perception is the stabilizer of our mental life. Yet, while this fact has been known, psychologists' curiosity until recently has been restricted to a few standard laboratory problems. Size and depth, localization and movement were studied on the assumption that somehow the structure of the outer world is cast in a veridical manner upon our sense organs, with a few minor exceptions known as "illusions."

Then, suddenly, less than two decades ago, psychologists grew excited by the discovery (though they should have known it all along) that perception is not simply the faithful translation of outer configurations into inner experience. Perception is profoundly influenced by two additional factors: social and cultural custom, and the personality of the perceiver. We sense what the outer world offers, yes; but we sense it through social and personal lenses. So startling was the discovery that it became known as the "new look" theory of perception (deriving its nickname from the then current fashion in women's clothes).

This theory says, in brief, that unless the external stimulus is unusually strong and compelling, what we perceive is a blend of the external message and our own subjective meanings. Innumerable experiments have by now established the fact that the words we hear or the sights we see—at least when they are not compellingly clear and well structured—are influenced by subjective conditions. Among these conditions, various investigators have identified the influence of hunger, thirst, fear and hate; of deep-lying interests and values; of traits of temperament; and of one's total character-structure and way of looking at life.[7]

The specific influence of social and cultural customs also shapes our perception of words, of time and of worth. Examples of so-called *social perception* are to be found in Benjamin Paul's book *Health, culture and community.* An American physician in a village in India, for instance, will be perceived as a powerful and revered figure if he pronounces the confident words, "The patient will recover." In Chile the same degree of confident prediction may make the physician seem arrogant and hence not to be trusted.[8] In India a cow that falls sick on the streets of a city may be perceived as an object of compassion, whereas a dying man who falls on the same street is avoided, because to touch him would bring defilement.

The enthusiasm of psychologists for these "new look" discoveries led them to use the concept of perception somewhat promiscuously. But a specialist is known by the words he uses carefully. And among the careful words for the psychologist should certainly be *perception*.

Even if used scrupulously, however, the concept of perception inevitably covers the energy from the stimulus, the receptor activity, a sensory core projected and organized through expectancy and inten-

tion, blended with subtle muscular adjustments and capped by a
lightning process of categorization, made possible by bewilderingly
swift associations with past experience—the whole baffling sequence
occupying only a split second and resulting in a firm, well-con-
figurated experience of objectified meaning. Even the most careful
use of the term must cover all these interlocking processes.

At the same time, *perception* should not be extended to cover
other so-called higher mental operations. It should not be stretched
to include the judgment, reflection, evaluation or emotional response
that follow rapidly on a percept; nor should it cover the trains of
memory, imagination and motor performance that ensue. Strictly
speaking, a percept is a quasi-sensory organization—though involving
central as well as peripheral processes—located "out there." It is a
complex interpretation of sensory experience, but it is not coextensive
with the whole of mental life.

Suppose you ask a sample of people: *Would you agree that the
world is a hazardous place and that men are basically evil and
dangerous?* About half the replies are likely to be yes and about
half no. Now, do those who reply affirmatively really *perceive* the
world as threatening and *perceive* men as evil, or do they merely
judge them to be so? Neither term is entirely satisfactory. To
judge is to make an intellectual assertion; but a person who gives
an affirmative answer probably has such a deep-seated suspicious
outlook that he actually *sees* malice in people's faces, much as did
H. A. Murray's children after they had played a scary game of
"murder." [9] A person with such a deep suspicion might, on opening
the door to a health worker, actually *see* the visitor as having a hostile
face and menacing manner. At the same time, not every distrustful
attitude is a perception. In his extensive analysis of research and
theories of perception, F. H. Allport has shown that very often what
is called a percept is, in reality, the judgment of a percept or a response
to a percept.

The truth of the matter is that psychologists today are in a
predicament. While the classical account of perception is not adequate, it does offer us at least two concepts directly pertinent to our
problem. One of these is *apperception,* a recognition of the role of
past experience and association in shaping a present percept. The
other is the concept of *set,* a recognition of the incontestable fact that
a person will for the most part perceive what he is at this moment
"tuned" to perceive. But these concepts antedate depth psychology.
They seem a trifle intellectualistic and fail to allow for the fact that
perceptions may be rooted in deeper layers of personality, in what

Tolman calls our "belief-value matrix." Not long ago Postman help-fully proposed that the concept of *perceptual response disposition* (really a modern version of set) may help us account for all the clearly identifiable factors that enter into the "subjective" shaping of perception. And by distinguishing "perceptual response disposi-tions" from "mnemonic response dispositions," we can avoid con-fusing perception proper with the total process of cognition.[10]

This type of discussion is important for the psychologist who wishes to avoid terminological promiscuity and hopes for a model by which he can distinguish one cognitive process from another. But what of the health worker? He too is a behavioral scientist—or, as Dr. Griffiths has expressed it more accurately, a *practitioner* of be-havioral science.[11] As such, he needs a new concept that will by-pass the fine distinctions so important for the psychologist—a concept that will enable him to deal with the *integrated* disposition of a person to perceive, pay attention to, extract meaning from, feel, think about and respond to a situation, and to hold it in memory. It is this larger unitary process of the human organism that we seek to christen, for it is this more molar disposition with which the health worker must deal.

Borrowing from the philosopher Justus Buchler, I propose that the term we need is *proception*.[12] The term recognizes the fact that each individual carries with him his past relations to the world—his cumulated experience—and at the same time is strongly propelled into the future. Every human being has "proceptive directions," which are his potentialities for seeing, hearing, doing, thinking, making and saying. These potentialities are derived in part from his own temperament and in part from the culture and situation in which he has acquired his proceptive directions. The term designates the total process of personally relevant behavior from input to act. Unlike *percept,* the term *procept* gives full weight to cumulative habit, emotional direction and all other forms of "gating" that the complex psychophysical dispositions of the individual exert upon his behavioral sequence. It is wholly in keeping with modern research in neurophysiology to suggest that the procept "gates" (that is, opens and closes pathways to) the percept.

Why do I deal with this terminological issue in an essay on public health? I do so partly to fortify the health educator in his future encounters with psychologists. If a critical laboratory psychologist says to you, "Look, you are using the term 'perception' too broadly, and I find this a sloppy practice," the proper reply is, "Well, in the first place, many of you psychologists are equally sloppy;

but in the second place, if it pleases you better, I'll speak when appropriate of proception, rather than of perception." This sophisticated reply will probably bewilder your critic. It will surely shut him up.

But there is a still better reason for this terminological digression. The health worker of the future cannot overlook the dynamic propulsion that causes one individual to accentuate, another to reject and a third to distort a given health message. Its reception will vary according to the nationality, the class membership, the ethnic group and, above all, the personality and present situation of the client. By suggesting the concept of "proception," I hope to fix your attention upon this variable of prime importance and to allow you no escape from it. *Perception* you might be tempted to shrug off as a problem for the psychologist; *proception* is clearly the concern of both pure and applied behavioral scientists.

Proceptive Types

We must next ask whether there is such a thing as basic proceptive types. Without using this particular label, many of the "new look" researches are converging on precisely this problem. It is characteristic of these investigations that they first demonstrate some inner consistency among an individual's perceptions (considered in the narrow sense) and then discover that these ways of perceiving are linked to the person's needs, his "directive states," his character structure or his whole "cognitive style."

Thus, for example, Witkin and his collaborators describe two basic and contrasting proceptive types (admitting, of course, that many people fall between the extremes). One type they label *field-dependent;* the opposite, *field-independent.* First they study certain elementary perceptual tendencies by placing a subject in a chair that can be mechanically tilted. The chair is in a room whose walls, ceiling and floors can likewise be tilted. The subject is asked to adjust a movable rod so that it stands vertically. Field-dependent subjects tend to adjust the rod so that it remains parallel to the tilted walls of the room. Field-independent subjects are able to disregard the visual field; they take their cues from their own sensations of gravitational pressure and locate the rod closer to the true vertical.

Thus far the experiment demonstrates nothing more than individual differences in a very limited perceptual task. But studying the same subjects further, it is discovered that field-dependent persons are limited in other ways by the perceptual context. They cannot, for example, easily analyze out a particular geometrical design that lies embedded in a complex visual pattern. Field-independent people seem more able to disregard the context and discriminate the needed detail.

These perceptual styles turn out to be merely a part of a wider proceptive syndrome. The field-dependent person is usually characterized by a general passivity in dealing with the environment, a certain unfamiliarity and distrust of his own impulses and a low degree of self-esteem. The independent or analytical perceptual performer is in general more active and independent in meeting the environment; he is higher in self-esteem and shows greater control and understanding of his own impulses.[13]

Let me mention very briefly several researches which have broadly confirmed Witkin's. In a series of experiments, Klein discovered what he calls "levelers" and "sharpeners," the former behaving much like Witkin's field-dependent cases and the latter showing the more highly differentiated ability of the field-independent type.[14] Even before the advent of the "new look," Goldstein identified "concrete" and "abstract" styles of cognitive operation which have much in common with Witkin's and with Klein's.[15] Ericksen overlaps this typology with his conception of *repressers* and *intellectualizers*.[16] Barron discovered that *simplicity* and *complexity* are basic proceptive dimensions.[17] Boldest of all is the work of our late friend and neighbor, Else Frenkel-Brunswik. She has related a purely perceptual tendency (called "intolerance of ambiguity") to the deepest proceptive layers of character structure, showing that people whose emotional lives are filled with prejudice and rigidity concerning their relations with other groups must also, by and large, have definiteness and structure in what they see and hear in the outer world.[18] There seems to be a relation here to the work of Hastings, who, using Dr. Knutson's *Personal Security Scale,* found that observers low in personal security tend to locate objects—if the objects have no firm anchorage in the environment—as closer to themselves than do people with a high sense of personal security.[19] It is as though anxious people are distrustful, apprehensive and insecure in handling even simple percepts. Postman and Bruner have discovered a kind of "perceptual recklessness" among persons under stress:[20] such persons seem to jump at premature hypotheses and demand a definiteness in the outer world that it may not in fact possess.

All this varied work, I am well aware, is not yet firmly collated; and some researches, as Postman and other critics have pointed out, are imperfect in design and execution. But one cannot help feel that important knowledge is emerging, establishing beyond doubt the dependence of perception upon broad underlying proceptive directions.

Now for further applications to public health. The health worker himself is a selected, well-educated, highly specialized person. In terms of these proceptive types, he is likely to be field-independent, an intellectualizer, a sharpener, an abstract thinker. But the people with whom he deals are likely *not* to be so, especially in times of illness, anxiety and strain. When a health worker calls on the distraught mother of a sick child, for example, the mother almost certainly is not listening, in a field-independent way, for coldly rational instructions. She is listening in large measure for approval of what she is doing, for reassurance and hope. She is field-dependent: the health worker is seen as a global agent of mercy. Unless the health worker somehow puts his instructions within this context, they are very likely to be unperceived, distorted or repressed.

Every health worker knows too that some people over-react to the educator's message, even to the point of hypochondria, whereas others turn a deaf ear and repress what they hear. Workers on cancer control will surely recognize the over-vigilant and over-defensive types. Since the health worker tends to dislike both hypervigilance and defensiveness, his own proceptive directions may lead him to assume erroneously that his client is an intellectualizer like himself.

Physicians, like all other health workers, have their own proceptive tendencies to guard against. It is a known fact, for example, that, in the field of mental health, patients who most nearly approach the therapist's own syndrome of proceptive dispositions are likely to receive from him the best treatment and most sympathy.[21]

Such class-anchored procepts are of great importance. For example, it is said that the main goal of public health work is "the inculcation in each individual of a sense of responsibility for his own health." This is a pleasant, middle-class, democratic-sounding axiom; it resonates sweetly among our own proceptive dispositions. But to some people, especially among what we call the "lower classes," such a maxim may not resonate at all. They may perceive it as a slap at their cherished domestic values. To them individual responsibility is a kind of self-centeredness; what is important is to take care of one's family in times of trouble and to be taken care of by them. Self-responsibility is isolationism; it is even disloyal.

A similar misunderstanding may attend our middle-class emphasis on preventive medical, dental and child guidance work—all of which demands present sacrifice for future good. The message of preventive medicine is less meaningful to people who, from economic necessity, have to live from day to day, seizing present gratifications where they can and leaving tomorrow's evil, as the Bible admonishes, to the morrow. . . . Likewise with "cleanliness": you and I are likely to see in a dirty house an index of moral turpitude, but those who live in such a house may view our concern for cleanliness as compulsive and downright neurotic. In this case, who is to say whose perceptions are correct? [22]

Ethnic Procepts

An exciting new field of research is the proceptive study of health problems in cross-cultural perspective. Take the case of pain. One might think that such an elementary perception would have no cultural variation. And the best scientific evidence does seem to indicate that the threshold of pain is more or less the same for all human beings, regardless of nationality, sex or age.[23] Can we, then, conclude that people perceive pain in the same way? In a limited and literal sense, yes; but we can also safely assert that they do not *proceive* it in the same way. Dr. Zborowski shows that, by and large, Italians regard pain as a physical misery to be complained about, to be relieved immediately and then to be forgotten. Jewish patients, on the other hand, often regard it as something to be complained about and also to be worried about, in terms of its significance for one's future and the future of one's family. Old-line Americans generally view it as something *not* to be complained about, but to be relieved scientifically with an optimistic expectation regarding the eventual outcome.[24]

In our own culture, then, and especially in foreign cultures, health workers must learn how to circumvent proceptive rigidities. In South Africa I found myself admiring the resourceful strategies of public health workers who, when confronted with cultural beliefs harmful to health, invented artful detours.

At one health station in Zululand, the nutritional state of expectant and nursing mothers was found to be deplorable. Milk was badly needed in their diet. The whole wealth of a Zulu homestead is in its cattle, so in most cases the needed nutrient is available. It is forbidden by taboo, however, to partake of milk from cattle belonging to another kin group; and the wife, of course, lives with her husband's kin group. Worse still is the belief that a pregnant woman who partakes of milk will bewitch the cow who gave it. Hence, of all people in the community, the married woman is most rigidly excluded from partaking of milk. The belief systems here are too deep for the health educator to challenge, but his imagination comes to the rescue. Powdered milk, because of its texture, is regarded by the tribe as a wholly different substance, hence prescriptions of powdered milk meet no resistance. Through this strategy, the health of the mothers is greatly improved.

Again, in Zululand tuberculosis is rife. It is possible with tact to persuade acutely affected cases to go to a sanitarium for treatment. But if the educational effort goes further and explains to the tribesmen that acute cases are carriers of the disease, resistance will arise. This explanation is proceived as an accusation of witchcraft, for a person who carries a disease must certainly be a witch. A father will insist on keeping his sick daughter at home, rather than accept the implication that she is an evil agent.[25]

A physician friend of mine found that Zulu mothers were giving their children an opium-laden nostrum as protection against bewitchment. Rather than counter the mothers' fixed belief in witchcraft prophylaxis, the physician persuaded them that the drug would be just as effective if it were poured into the child's bath water. He told no lie, aroused no resistance and improved the babies' health.

Such deceptions are occasionally necessary to circumvent proceptive rigidities. But there is an ethical hairline between beneficent deception and mendacious condescension; and this is a matter requiring constant moral vigilance. Kutner reports that one of the commonest complaints of surgical patients is, "They won't tell me anything" or "I want to ask them a question, but they are always too busy." And the research of Dr. Beryl Roberts concerning reasons women delay in seeking treatment for breast lesions has shocked me with evidence of indifference and intellectual patronage on the part of some physicians.[26]

Proceptive dispositions, cultural and personal, run deep, but not deepest. They are incident to the one basic desire of all mortal men: *the desire for meaning*. The health and suffering, the life and death of each individual are his own existential concern. The health worker should help, and not hinder, the person's quest for meaning in this sequence of mystery. To assume that the patient's perceptions are those of scientific medicine is certainly an error; but to assume that he neither wants nor deserves the truth is intolerable condescension. There is no solution to this ethical predicament of the health worker, except to develop sensitivity to each patient at each stage of growth, to respect him as a unique being-in-the-world and to advance his quest for meaning with all the skill at one's command.

Further Explorations

I feel I have touched only the fringes of my subject. I should like to trace an additional score of contacts between perceptual research and public health work, but shall content myself with a brief mention of two.

First: modern laboratory work on sensory deprivation has particular relevance. Until recently we have not known how important for our lives is the perceptual flood of sights, sounds, smells, touches, muscular strains and speech that engulfs us. Like fish, we live in an environmental water; and like fish, we are slow to discover this fact. Recent research has shown how profoundly disturbing it is for a subject, even a healthy college student paid twenty dollars a day for his pains, to lie in a room from which this perceptual bombardment is almost excluded. In this drastic isolation he develops a fierce hunger for perception—any kind of perception. He also develops hallucinations and loses an integrated image of himself and his body. He perceives his body as one thing, his "self" as another. Most remarkable of all, if his hunger for perception is in a small way appeased by the voice of the experimenter, he seems to develop unusual receptivity to the message. If, for example, the experimenter tries to persuade him that ghosts exist, he accepts the suggestion—and retains it even after he returns to normal life. All indications are that this planted idea has taken firm root.[27]

Obviously, this finding has a bearing upon the macabre problem of "brainwashing"; but it also has implications for the health worker. It clearly relates to the phenomenon Spitz has called "hospitalism." [28] Patients who have suffered even mild sensory deprivation through a long illness may develop unusual perceptual disturbances and suggestibility. In the same way, the apparent stupidity and deficiency in learning ability of some children and some primitive tribes may well be due to the relatively low level of perceptual bombardment from their impoverished environments.

Second—and finally: research in the critical area of child and parental guidance is of profound concern to health workers. Probably all of us are convinced that future advances in the physical and mental welfare of our nation require improvement in the attitudes and practices of parents, especially mothers. But one cannot change a mother's attitudes without realizing that she has her own proceptive biases, that she sees her child and her world in her own peculiar way.

Take the case of the young mother who applies excessive discipline too early in a child's life. She almost certainly is not intentionally cruel. Rather, she lacks the ability to proceive the child's destructive acts for what they are. Every exploring infant is destructive: he pulls off eyeglasses, spills his cup of milk and soils himself. A young mother may perceive these acts as aggressive on the part of the child and forthwith start her scolding, spanking and withdrawal of love. Some mothers proceive aggressive intent when the child is only two or three months of age and punish him accordingly. At the other extreme, there are mothers so patient or so blind that they do not undertake to socialize the child even when, a year or two later, his destructiveness does involve aggressive intent.[29] In either case, the health worker cannot expect to change the mother's socialization practices until he corrects her proceptions of her baby's behavior.

Final Word

The alert health worker, in short, has no choice: from now on, he must develop skill as an *oculist,* training himself to look *at* his spectacles and not merely *through* them—and to look both at and through the spectacles of the client with whom he deals.

He will soon discover that his habit of viewing sickness and health in a sharpened, field-independent way is not often his client's mode of perception, especially if the client is ill. He will discover that culture, social class and personality lay down stubborn proceptive dispositions that in part control what a person sees and hears, what he thinks and feels and what he does. Since, in the last analysis, every percept bears the imprint of the individual, no reliance on rules of thumb, routine curricula, or mass media can adequately guide health education. To sense and to nourish the growing edge of each individual in his present situation is the only formula for success.

There is another lesson that all of us who teach need to learn. We are habitually tempted to present to our students and clients a summary statement of our hard-won conclusions. We entrust our cryptic wisdom to a burnished lecture or a polished pamphlet, hoping thereby to bring our audience rapidly to our own level of knowledge. I try in a single essay to give the gist of my conclusions respecting proceptive processes—and I largely fail. A health worker may, at the clinic or on a doorstep, present his client with a finely wrought sonnet on sanitation or child care—but he too will largely fail. The sad truth is that no one learns by having conclusions presented to him. Learning takes place only when there is a need, a curiosity, an interest; an exploring, erring and correcting of errors; a testing and verifying—all carried through by the individual himself. In school, in college, in the clinic we cannot scamp the process.

It is hard to know how to present our invitation to learning to students or clients who, because of their own proceptive directions, have a need for safety, a need for simple and gratifying rubrics to reinforce their own prejudices; who are untrained in following evidence or logic; who are emotionally fearful and cognitively self-centered. It is usually approval they want and not fact; reassurance and not alarm; certainty and not challenge. Even those who, on the surface, appear objective and responsive often are not so; for them, too, the message is darkened, blurred and misshapen.

Discouraging as the outlook may be, it is still inescapably the moral duty of the health worker to advance the learning process, even in the most resistant cases, as best he can, so that the client may participate constructively in his own destiny and become creatively aware of factors making for sickness and for health.

The time has passed when we can impose a mere routine of sanitation, nutrition and hygiene, leading to a controlled, calculated, technically efficient life of conformity with our antiseptic cultural ideal. Such mechanical regulation leaves untouched the client's future role in managing his and his family's affairs. However important it may still be in certain respects to impose hygienic practices from the outside, our task now is increasingly to win the participation of the public in seeking sounder personal, domestic and civic values, so that the physical and spiritual welfare of our nation may increase.

REFERENCES

1. M. Derryberry, "Health education in transition," *Amer. J. Pub. Health,* 1957, 47:1357-66.

2. T. Parsons and R. Fox, Introduction to "Sociocultural approaches to medical care," *J. Soc. Issues,* 1952, 8:2.

3. R. S. Woodworth, *Dynamics of behavior,* New York: Holt, 1958.

4. D. Apple, "Definitions of illness," unpublished research from the Boston University School of Nursing.

5. C. Lamb, "The convalescent," in *The essays of Elia,* New York: Macmillan, 1905, p. 222.

6. H. D. Lederer, "How the sick view their world," *J. Soc. Issues,* 1952, 8:4-15.

7. For a recent review of the "new look" literature see N. Jenkin, "Affective processes in perception," *Psychol. Bull.,* 1957, 54:100-27.

8. B. D. Paul (ed.), *Health, culture, and community,* New York: Russell Sage Foundation, 1955, cf. pp. 112, 340.

9. H. A. Murray, "The effect of fear upon estimates of the maliciousness of other persons," *J. Soc. Psychol.,* 1933, 4:310-29.

10. For critical discussion of this issue see: F. H. Allport, *Theories of*

perception and the concept of structure, New York: Wiley, 1955; L. Postman, "Perception, motivation, and behavior," _J. Pers.,_ 1953, 22:17-31; and E. C. Tolman, "A psychological model," in T. Parsons and E. A. Shils (eds.), _Toward a general theory of action,_ Cambridge: Harvard University Press, 1951.

11. W. Griffiths, "Communication problems facing our profession," _Health Educ. Monogr.,_ 1957, 1:27.

12. J. Buchler, _Nature and judgment,_ New York: Columbia University Press, 1955.

13. H. A. Witkin _et al., Personality through perception,_ New York: Harper, 1954.

14. G. S. Klein, "Personal world through perception," in R. W. Blake and G. Ramsey (eds.), _Perception: an approach to personality,_ New York: Ronald Press, 1950.

15. K. Goldstein and M. Scheerer, "Abstract and concrete behavior: an experimental study with special tests," _Psychol. Monogr.,_ 1941, Vol. 53, No. 239.

16. C. W. Ericksen, "The case for perceptual defense," _Psychol. Rev.,_ 1954, 61:175-82.

17. F. Barron, "Complexity-simplicity as a personality dimension," _J. Abnorm. Soc. Psychol.,_ 1953, 48:163-72.

18. E. Frenkel-Brunswik, "Intolerance of ambiguity as an emotional and perceptual personality variable," _J. Pers.,_ 1949, 18:108-43. See also G. W. Allport, _The nature of prejudice,_ Boston: Addison-Wesley, 1954, Chap. 25.

19. P. K. Hastings, "A relationship between visual perception and level of personal security," _J. Abnorm. Soc. Psychol.,_ 1952, 47:552-60, No. 2. Supplement.

20. L. Postman and J. S. Bruner, "Perception under stress," _Psychol. Rev.,_ 1948, 55:314-23.

21. F. C. Redlich, A. B. Hollingshead and E. Bellis, "Social class differences in attitudes toward psychiatry," _Amer. J. Orthopsychiat.,_ 1955, 25:60-70.

22. For a discussion of the "belief-value matrix" in relation to social class, see O. G. Simmons, "Implications of social class for public health," _Human Organization,_ 1957, 16:7-10.

23. J. D. Harley, H. G. Wolff and H. Goodell, _Pain sensations and reaction,_ Baltimore: W. Wilkins Company, 1950, p. 122.

24. M. Zborowski, "Cultural components in responses to pain," _J. Soc. Issues,_ 1952, 8:16-30.

25. These instances are described by J. Cassel, "A comprehensive health program among South African Zulus," in B. D. Paul, _op. cit._

26. B. Kutner, "Surgeons and their patients: a study in social perception," in G. E. Jaco (ed.), _Patients, physicians and illness,_ Glencoe, Ill.: The Free Press, 1958. See also B. J. Roberts, "A study of selected factors and their association with action for medical care," unpublished thesis, 1956, Harvard Medical School Library.

27. D. O. Hebb, "The motivating effects of exteroceptive stimulation," _Amer. Psychologist,_ 1958, 13:109-13.

28. R. A. Spitz, "Hospitalism: a follow-up report," _Psychoanalytic Study of the Child,_ 1946, 2:113-17.

29. R. R. Sears, E. E. Maccoby and H. Levin, _Patterns of child rearing,_ Evanston, Ill.: Row, Peterson and Co., 1957, Chap. 7.

CHAPTER 19

The analysis of rumor

As old as human society itself, rumor has flourished in wars and depressions, in peace and prosperity.

Why do rumors spread? What motives do they satisfy? What basic laws govern the quantity of rumor in circulation and the distortions that individual rumors undergo in transmission?

The essay was written collaboratively with Leo Postman and appeared in the *Public Opinion Quarterly* (1946-47). It is, in effect, a condensation of our book, *The psychology of rumor,* which was published in 1947 and is now out of print.

Rumor became a problem of grave national concern in the frenzied years 1942 and 1943. At that time a high official in the Office of War Information gave a reason for rumor and a recipe for its control that were partially—but only partially—correct. "Rumor," he said, "flies in the absence of news. Therefore, we must give the people the most accurate possible news, promptly and completely."

It is true that rumor thrives on lack of news. The almost total absence of fear-inspired rumors in Britain during the darkest days of the blitz was due to the people's conviction that the government was giving full and accurate news of the destruction and that they therefore knew the worst. When people are sure they know the worst, they are unlikely to darken the picture further by inventing unnecessary bogies to explain their anxieties to themselves.

At the same time, it would not be hard to prove that rumor also flies thickest when news is most plentiful. There were few rumors about our desperate losses at Pearl Harbor until the papers themselves had published an official report on the disaster. Although there were scattered rumors of Hitler's death before the papers told of the assassination attempt in the summer of 1944, there were many more immediately afterward. The deluge of peace rumors in late April and early May 1945 coincided with the open discussion of the approaching collapse of Germany in the press. Similarly, a flood of rumors swamped the country during the final hours before V-J Day: premature stories of the war's end spread faster than they could be officially denied. One of the odd episodes in the history of rumor was the fact that, within a few hours after the release of the news of President Roosevelt's sudden death on April 16, 1945, tales spread regarding the death of many other notable persons, including General Marshall, Bing Crosby and Mayor La Guardia.

If public events are not newsworthy, they are unlikely to breed rumors. But, under certain circumstances, the more prominence the press gives the news—especially momentous news—the more numerous and serious are the rumored distortions this news will undergo.

The OWI official made his error in assuming that rumor is a purely intellectual commodity, something one substitutes, *faute de mieux,* for reliable information. He overlooked the fact that, when events of great importance occur, the individual never stops at a mere acceptance of the event. His life is deeply affected, and the emotional overtones of the event breed all sorts of fantasies. He seeks explanations and imagines remote consequences.

Yet the official did state, inexactly and too simply, a part of the formula for rumor-spreading and rumor-control. Rumor travels when events have *importance* in the lives of individuals and when the news received about them is either *lacking* or *subjectively ambiguous.* The ambiguity may arise if the news is not clearly reported, or if conflicting versions of the news have reached the individual, or if he is unable to comprehend the news he receives.

The Basic Law of Rumor

These two essential conditions—importance and ambiguity—seem to be related to rumor transmission in a roughly quantitative manner. A formula for the intensity of rumor might be written as follows:

$$R \sim i \times a$$

In plain words, this formula means that the amount of rumor in circulation will vary with the importance of the subject to the individuals concerned *times* the ambiguity of the evidence pertaining to the topic at issue. The relation between importance and ambiguity is not additive but multiplicative; if either importance or ambiguity is zero, there is *no* rumor. For instance, an American citizen is not likely to spread rumors concerning the market price for camels in Afghanistan because the subject has no importance for him, ambiguous though it certainly is. He is not disposed to spread gossip concerning the doings of the people in Swaziland, because he doesn't care about them. Ambiguity alone does not launch or sustain rumor.

Nor does importance. Although an automobile accident in which I lose my leg is of calamitous significance to me, I am not susceptible to rumors concerning the extent of my injury because I *know* the facts. If I receive a legacy and know the amount involved, I am resistant to rumors that exaggerate its amount. Officers in the higher echelons of the army were less susceptible to rumor than was GI Joe, not because coming events were less important to them, but because, as a rule, the plans and strategies were better known to them. Where there is no ambiguity, there can be no rumor.

Motives in Rumor-Mongering

This principle—that rumor does not circulate unless the topic has importance for the individual who hears and spreads the story—is linked to the *motivational factor* in rumor. Sex interest accounts for much gossip and most scandal; anxiety is the power behind the macabre and threatening tales we so often hear; hope and desire underlie pipe dream rumors; hate sustains accusatory tales and slander.

It is important to note that rumor is not a simple mechanism; it serves a complex purpose. The aggressive rumor, for example, by permitting us to slap at the thing we hate, *relieves* a primary emotional urge. At the same time—literally in the same breath—it serves to *justify* us in feeling as we do about the situation, and to *explain* to ourselves and to others why we feel that way. Thus rumor rationalizes even while it relieves.

But to justify our emotional urges and render them reasonable is not the only kind of rationalization. Quite apart from the pressure of particular emotions, we continually seek to extract *meaning* from our environment. There is, so to speak, intellectual pressure along with the emotional. To find a plausible reason for a confused situation is itself a motive; and this pursuit of a "good closure" (even without the personal factor) helps account for the vitality of many rumors. We want to know the why, how and whence of the world that surrounds us. Our minds protest against chaos: from childhood we are asking *why, why?* This effort after meaning is broader than our impulsive tendency to rationalize and justify our immediate emotional state.

The result of this demand for meaning is curiosity rumors. A stranger whose business is unknown to the small town where he takes up residence will breed many legends, each designed to explain to curious minds why he has come to town. An odd-looking excavation in a city inspires fanciful explanations of its purpose. The atomic bomb, only slightly understood by the public, engenders much effort after meaning.

When a person's emotional state is reflected, unknown to himself, in his interpretation of his environment, we speak of *projection*. He is failing to employ exclusively impartial and objective evidence in his explanations of the reality surrounding him.

In dreams, everyone projects. Only after we awaken do we recognize that our private wishes, fears or revengeful desires have been responsible for what came to pass in our dream-imaginations. The child asleep dreams of finding mountains of candy; the inferior youth asleep triumphs on the athletic field; the apprehensive mother dreams of the death of her child.

Daydreams too are projective. Relaxed on a couch, our minds picture events that actualize our hopes, desires, fears. We find ourselves in fantasy successful, satisfied or sometimes defeated and ruined —all according to our temperament or the type of emotion that is, for the time being, steering the associational train of thought.

Rumor is akin to the daydream at second hand. If the story we hear gives a fancied interpretation of reality that conforms to our secret lives, we tend to believe and transmit it.

In short, in a homogeneous social medium, rumor is set in motion and continues to travel by its appeal to the strong personal interests of the individuals involved in the transmission. The powerful influence of these interests harnesses the rumor largely as a rationalizing agent, requiring it not only to express but also to explain, justify and provide meaning for the emotional interest at work. At times the relationship between the interest and the rumor is so intimate that we must assume the rumor to be simply a projection of an altogether subjective emotional condition.

The Basic Course of Distortion

It is a notable fact that the same pattern of distortion is found both in the changes an individual's perceptions and memories suffer in the course of time and in the transformations a tale undergoes as it travels from person to person. This pattern of change in both social and individual memory has three aspects: *leveling, sharpening* and *assimilation*.

As a rumor travels, it tends to grow shorter, more concise, more easily grasped and told. In successive versions, more and more of the original details are *leveled* out; fewer words are used and fewer items are mentioned. In our laboratory experiments on rumor, we found that the number of details retained in transmission declines most sharply at the beginning of a series of reproductions. The number continues to decline, but more slowly, in each successive version. The same trend is typically found in individual retention, but "social memory" accomplishes as much leveling within a few minutes as individual memory accomplishes in weeks of time.

As leveling of details proceeds, the remaining details are necessarily *sharpened*. Sharpening denotes the selective perception, retention and reporting of a few details from the originally larger context. Although sharpening, like leveling, occurs in every series of reproductions, the same items are not always emphasized. Much depends on the constitution of the group in which the tale is transmitted, for those items will be sharpened which are of particular interest to the reporters. There are, however, some determinants of sharpening which are virtually universal: unusual size, for example, and striking, attention-getting phrases.

What is it that leads to the obliteration of some details and the pointing up of others? And what accounts for the transpositions, importations and other falsifications that mark the course of rumor? The answer is to be found in the process of *assimilation*, which results from the powerful attractive force exerted by habits, interests and sentiments already existing in the listener's mind. In the telling and retelling of a story, for example, there is marked assimilation to the principal theme. Items become sharpened or leveled to fit the leading motif of the story, and they become consistent with this motif in such a way as to make the resultant story more coherent, plausible and well rounded. Assimilation often conforms to expectation: things are perceived and remembered as they *usually* are. Most important of all, assimilation expresses itself in changes and falsifications that reflect the agent's deeply rooted emotions, attitudes and prejudices.

Leveling, sharpening and assimilation, even though distinguished for purposes of analysis, are not independent mechanisms. They function simultaneously, and they reflect the singular, subjectifying process that results in the autism and falsification so characteristic of rumor.

The Fusion of Themes in Rumor

To enumerate the emotions that launch and sustain rumors is a difficult task because the motivational pattern is always complex and often runs very deep. One scheme of classification, however, based on the dominant type of motivational tension reflected in rumors, was attempted during the war.[1] The analysis of one thousand wartime stories current in 1942 indicated that nearly all seemed to express either hostility, fear or wish. To sort rumors in terms of their motivational mainsprings was probably much easier in wartime than in peacetime; but even in wartime, the hate-fear-wish trichotomy is much oversimplified. A fear rumor (concerning an enemy atrocity, for example) may be sustained by elements of sexual interest, adventure and feelings of moral superiority. The complex of motives to which a rumor is assimilated is a personal matter, and to learn why a given individual falls for a certain story would require a clinical study of that individual. Because of the diversity of motivational blends that may nourish a rumor, any psychological classification will be inevitably oversimplified and crude.

Thus we must not expect to find any one rumor correlated with only a single emotion or with only a single cognitive tendency. Assimilation does not work on a unit basis. Even an apparently simple story may serve as explanation, justification and relief for a *mixture* of feelings.

Anti-Negro Rumors

A fusion of hatred, fear, guilt and economic bewilderment is found in the curious rumors of the "Eleanor Clubs," which circulated busily in Southern states in 1943. The theme of these stories was that large numbers of Negro women, especially domestic servants, were banded together under the spiritual sponsorship of Eleanor Roosevelt for the purpose of rebellion against the existing social order. Here the most obvious fusion is that of antagonism against New Deal liberalism with traditional anti-Negro feeling. But the complex of motives goes even deeper.

There were many versions of the rumors, in which the "Eleanor Clubs" were sometimes called "Daughters of Eleanor," "Eleanor Angel Clubs," "Sisters of Eleanor" and "Royal House of Eleanor."[2] These fanciful titles represent, of course, assimilation of the rumor to the stereotype concerning the religiosity of the Negro and his supposed flair for pompous institutional names. It was widely told that the motto of these groups was "A white woman in every kitchen in a year." A typical Eleanor story ran as follows: "A white woman was away for a while; and when she returned, she found her colored maid sitting at her dresser combing her hair with her comb." Others represented the Negro servant as bathing in her employer's bathtub or entertaining her friends in the parlor. One rumor had it that when a white lady called her cook to come and prepare dinner for her guests, the cook demanded, in turn, that the mistress be at *her* home by eight o'clock Sunday morning to fix breakfast for *her* guests. One Negro maid was reported to have offered to pay a white woman to wash her clothes. Occasionally the stories hinted at coming violence, charging that the clubs were saving ice picks and butcher knives for a rebellion.

All these versions, besides reflecting anti-Roosevelt and anti-Negro feeling, show a distinct fear of *inversion of status*. The colored people are represented, not merely as nursing resentment beneath the surface, but as being on the verge of revolt. They threaten to take over, to reverse the social scale. Why? Because the white rumor-spreaders find their feelings of economic and social insecurity to some extent explained and relieved by these stories. Suffering a vague anxiety, they justify their jitters by pointing to Negro aggression and derive a melancholy consolation from alerting one another to the menace.

But we must probe still further. A rumor of inversion of status admits in a circuitous way that a relationship other than the *status quo* between the races is conceivable. And, according to the American creed, the *status quo*, being essentially unjust, should not be permanent. Every American, as Myrdal points out, believes in and aspires to something higher than the present plane of race relations.[3] At heart he agrees with Patrick Henry, the slave owner, who as long ago as 1772 wrote: "I will not, I cannot, justify it." At the same time, most whites permit themselves only a squint-eyed insight into their moral dilemma. A century and a half after Patrick Henry, the conflict still persists. Were whites to face the issue squarely, they would be torn asunder by their conflicting loyalties—to the American creed, and to their convenient belief in white supremacy.

Rather than face this pointed and irreconcilable conflict between two cherished loyalties, many white people twist and squirm and rationalize. The guilt-evasion rumor is eagerly seized upon as a means of escape. If, as the Eleanor Club stories hold, the Negro is overly aggressive, illegally plotting and vulgarly menacing, then he has no *right* to equal status. He must expect no more consideration than we give to trespassers, marauders and blackmailers. He must be kept in his place; and if there are instances of injustice, do not our patience and indulgence more than make it up to him? After all, he is only an unruly child and must be treated as such—kindly but firmly. By this devious mental maneuvering, the bigot is able to escape his feelings of guilt.

Guilt-evasion is likewise detectable in innumerable rumors detailing incidents of the Negro's criminal and disloyal tendencies. One wartime story had it that Negroes were not being drafted as rapidly as whites because authorities were afraid to let them get their hands on guns. Even humorous yarns concerning Negro stupidity, gullibility and laziness have the same functional significance; so, too, the myriad tales of Negro sexual aggression. All of these tend to allay the white man's sense of guilt; for what can we do with a black man who is disloyal, criminal, clownish, stupid, menacing and immoral—except to keep him in his place, just as we are now doing? The ideal of equality may be all right in theory, the bigot concludes, but it was never meant to apply to criminals, imbeciles or black men.

The ultimate ally of anti-Negro prejudice is the sex rumor. Negroes are repeatedly represented as plotting to cross the color line and commit the sin of miscegenation. The stories invariably concern the relations between Negro men and white women, not the far more frequent liaisons of white man and Negro woman. There are stories of rape and attempted rape, and less lurid versions representing Negroes as approaching white women, following them on the streets, trying to hold their hands, and so on. One wartime story asserted that Negroes who were not drafted (the disloyalty theme) were saying to the white men who left for the war that they would "take care of" the white women back home. Though especially common in the South, Negro sex rumors are frequent also in the North. In a New England city, known for its relatively peaceful race relations, a local story circulated to "explain" why the washroom in a certain restaurant had been boarded up. The reason alleged—and wholly fictitious—was that two Negroes had taken a white woman into that particular washroom and raped her.

The motivational current here runs deep. In the American Puritan tradition, all matters pertaining to sex are likely to have a high emotional charge and, for this reason, to spill over easily into other regions of strong passion. Sex, as a proposition for topical interest, is a never failing target for rumor. Like the measurement of status, it is also a source of heavy guilt-feeling. To blame ourselves for our sexual sins, as for our sins against the American creed, is never agreeable; better, by far, blame someone else for his real or imagined lapses. The resemblance between the sex and the minority-group rumor is close—projection in the interest of guilt-evasion is common to both—and this resemblance facilitates fusion. Why not escape guilt by heaping the blame for our own sexual lapses upon the very same persons who threaten our social position?

Deep inside, many people feel insecure in their status, or in their economic future, or in their own sexual morality. All of these matters are intimate and central in their lives, and such intense and pivotal interests cannot well be kept separate: a threat to one is a threat to the others. Hence the Negro scapegoat is seen not only as socially arrogant but also as pressing upon us vocationally, and as sexually more potent and less inhibited than we. In him we perceive all the grabbing, climbing, lewd behavior we might indulge in if we let ourselves go. He is the sinner. Even if we are not blameless, his misdeeds—as recounted in rumor—are more overt and worse than ours. Why, then, should we feel guilt at our peccadillos?

While all this rationalizing is going on, we may, perversely enough, find the Negro's "animal" qualities darkly fascinating. If so, we must severely repress this satanic attraction and, through reaction formation—that is, by turning against the fascination that we disapprove of—fight the devil even harder.[4] We do so by adopting the most sacred of taboos: undeviating opposition to racial amalgamation. The very thought fills us with horror (or does it?). Were it violated, the way would be opened for a collapse of all our moral and economic standards. We would admit defeat at the hands of the black and evil stranger whom, in our unconscious, we regard in part as our own unhallowed alter ego.

Complicated as this analysis of anti-Negro rumors may be, it does not exaggerate the intricacy of the emotional and cognitive fusions that account for their appeal. It seems to be the rule that people *personify* the forces of evil and center them in some visibly different, near-lying *minority group*. The commonest, but by no means the only, "demons" today are "Communists," Jews and Negroes. Since the blame ascribed to them is certainly in excess of their just deserts, we technically call them *scapegoats*.

Case Studies in Rumor

Let us now examine in closer detail two samples of rumor-discourse. The fact that both samples seem out of date itself illustrates the ephemeral quality of rumor. "Propositions for belief" are likely to be short-lived, simply because the panorama of human interest changes rapidly. Much may be learned, however, from a study of standard examples drawn from different social atmospheres, even if they are dated.

The analysis of any given rumor can never be perfect, because the precise psychological and social conditions under which it is told are known only in part and often through inference alone. Further, no single story can be expected to illustrate all the principles of rumor; but the basic formula should be detectable in every case.

CASE ONE. Immediately following the San Francisco earthquake on April 18, 1906, the wildest rumors were afloat in the city. Four of these were recounted by Jo Chamberlain in the Baltimore *Sunday Sun* (March 31, 1946): (a) a tidal wave had engulfed New York at the same time as the San Francisco quake; (b) Chicago had slid into Lake Michigan; (c) the quake had loosed the animals in the zoo, and they were eating refugees in Golden Gate Park; and (d) men were found with women's fingers in their pockets, for they had not had time to take the rings off. In these last stories, the ghouls were always strung up to the nearest lamp post.

Comment: The suspicious reader may wonder whether these rumors, recounted forty years after their circulation, may not have suffered considerable additional sharpening and other distortion in the interim. An example, perhaps, is the word "always" in Rumor (d): it would certainly be difficult to prove that this ghoulish story *invariably* was accompanied by the denouement of summary justice. The rumors circulating after the catastrophe were, however, recorded at the time; and we may assume, for purposes of our analysis, that they did not differ greatly from those listed above.

1. One obvious principle illustrated in this series is the *fecundity of rumor*. Prodigious importance and vast ambiguity conspired in the manufacture of one wild story after another, many of which were merely slight variations of others. The chain of associations is simple: one big city has been destroyed, why not others? The fecundity makes for sharpening through a multiplication of catastrophes.

2. The disturbed population is trying to gauge the importance of the event as one phase of its *effort after meaning*. Metaphorically, people were saying "things just couldn't be more horrible." Having lost home and perhaps loved ones, they underlined their feelings of anxiety and desolation by adding the ravages of wild beasts or ghouls and the destruction of an additional metropolis or two. Through these embellishments, the sense of total disaster is metaphorically conveyed.

3. In their effort after meaning, people likewise drew many *inferences*—some plausible, some not. Among the more reasonable inferences is the possibility that the quake might have liberated

animals from the zoo. Whether there was a kernel of truth in this statement we do not now know; it is possible that the shattered cages permitted *some* animals to escape. But it is likely that, as the rumor spread, many qualifying phrases were leveled out, so that the extent of the stampede was sharpened. And it seems probable that *condensation* brought in the gruesome fate of the refugees. Imagination—in rumor as in dreams—often unifies discrete events, drawing simplicity out of multiplicity and a specious order out of confusion. In this case, animals were in Golden Gate Park, and refugees were in Golden Gate Park; the latter were condensed into the maws of the former.

4. The hanging of the ghouls represents a *moralized closure* and a fantasied revenge. The vast frustrations engendered by the catastrophe had no personal cause. The despoiler of the dead was the only accessible scapegoat in a cataclysm brought on by an act of God.

5. Panic-rumors such as these correspond to the final stage of *riot-rumors*. Nothing is too wild to be believed, provided it somehow explains or relieves the current excitement. But, unlike riot-rumors, the tales nourished by panic do not have preceding stages of build-up unless the panic itself developed gradually—a rather unusual situation.

6. There is no evidence here for *rumor-chains*. The catastrophe forged so complete a unity of interest that we can well imagine a survivor telling these stories to a complete stranger. We cannot, however, imagine a citizen of New York or Chicago believing the tales of destruction of his own city. Dwellers in each metropolis had their own secure standards of evidence, making such tales impossible. It is doubtful, too, that the press published any rumors that could be readily checked. Many *unverifiable* stories, however, were published on hearsay evidence alone and were believed widely throughout the country until the quake was no longer a subject of topical interest.

7. One can easily imagine *prestige* accruing to the teller of such horror stories. The whole nation was in a state of agitation and eager for news of any kind. As soon as the outlines of the catastrophe became known, details to fill in the picture were greedily grasped, and a neighbor who supplied latest bits of "news" was welcomed and eagerly listened to. Such a neighbor may oblige by adding lurid inventions.

CASE TWO. The following story circulated during the visit of Madame Chiang Kai-shek to America in 1943. The scene of the incident was usually said to be Baltimore. One day, the story goes, a gentleman entered a jewelry store and asked for a $500 watch.

The jeweler did not carry such expensive stock, but finally managed to find several high-grade timepieces for his customer to choose from. The purchaser selected, in all, $7000 worth of watches and jewelry. When asked by the proprietor how they were to be paid for, the customer replied that he was Madame Chiang's secretary and requested that his purchase be charged to Chinese lend-lease.

Comment: This was typical of the World War II *wedge-driving* rumors, intended to divide the United States from its allies. Such stories gave government officials grave concern. Of the same stamp were the tales that the Russians were using lend-lease butter to grease their guns, and that the British were using their aid funds to purchase nylon stockings and other scarce and luxurious articles, thus depriving our own citizens of the coveted goods.

1. Evidence shows that we can expect such stories to circulate only among a limited *rumor-public*. The Madame Chiang scandal would appeal to people with a pre-existing grudge against China or, more probably, against the Democratic administration in Washington.

2. Like hostility rumors generally, this one is a product of frustration, much of the resulting aggression being *displaced*. Wartime shortages were annoying and high taxes aggravating. If goods in short supply are going abroad and tax revenue is being squandered recklessly by a prodigal administration, why should we not feel annoyed? We are willing to make sacrifices for the war, but it is not the war we are complaining about; it is the scandalous inefficiency of that radical set of long-haired professors and "that man" in Washington. The rumor represents a subtle fusion of antipathies and frustrations, and serves to explain and justify our political animosities.

3. The motivation may also entail *guilt-evasion*. During the wartime boom, many people indulged in luxuries that they could not afford in peacetime and that were hardly compatible with the wartime emphasis upon self-sacrifice and the purchase of war bonds. But our petty extravagances could easily be forgotten and forgiven in the face of the blatant self-indulgence of Madame Chiang, one of the most prominent wartime personages, wantonly wasting *our* national funds in the purchase of fabulous luxuries.

4. There may be an element of *assimilation* to the widely current belief in the waste and corruption of high officials in China. But this factor, if present, is minor, since the victims of the animus are more apparently the American than the Chinese officials.

5. *Concreteness* is used to lend plausibility to the story; precise amounts—$500 and $7000—are mentioned. Part of the rationalizing process is to surround the item with the pseudo-authority of detail.

6. Although the locale of this story was not always given as Baltimore, we know that the *label* first conferred upon an incident tends to remain unchanged, especially if it introduces the story. First items in a series are well retained.

7. Had the story been told without introducing the name of Madame Chiang, its essential function would have been unchanged. But to specify a well-known individual is a common device for personalizing a rumor and for assimilating it to common and conventional subject matter of current interest.

Guide for the Analysis of Rumor

The reader is now invited to make his own analysis of additional cases—selected from the final section, Additional Cases for Analysis, or from his own daily intake of rumor. In undertaking his analyses, he may find the following questions helpful. Each is based on an established principle of rumor; but, needless to say, not all the questions are applicable to all samples of rumor.

1. Is the story a proposition for belief of topical reference?
2. Do teller and listener lack secure standards of evidence for its verification?
3. Are ambiguity and importance both present? Which factor is more prominent?
4. In what way does the rumor reflect an effort after meaning?
5. Does it offer an economical and simplified explanation of a confusing environmental or emotional situation?
6. Does it explain some inner tension?
7. Is the tension primarily emotional or nonemotional?
8. Is the tension anxiety, hostility, wish, guilt, curiosity or some other state of mind?
9. Does the story justify the existence in the teller of an otherwise unacceptable emotion?
10. What makes the story important to the teller?
11. In what sense does the telling of the rumor confer relief?
12. What elements of rationalization are present?
13. Does the rumor contain possibilities of projection?
14. Does it resemble a daydream?
15. May it serve the function of guilt-evasion?
16. Does it reflect displaced aggression?
17. In telling it, is the teller likely to acquire prestige?
18. Might it be told to please a friend or to confer a favor?

19. Might it serve in phatic communication? (That is, does it serve to avoid an awkward silence by giving "someone something to say"?)

20. Can one detect the kernel of truth from which it probably developed?

21. Is it a home-stretch rumor?

22. Might there have been errors in the initial perception?

23. What might have been the course of the creative embedding?

24. Is it likely that it contains elaboration? If so, of what type?

25. Does it probably suffer from a distortion of names, dates, numbers or time?

26. Does its label or locale persist?

27. Is there likely to have been a complete shift of theme?

28. Is there evidence of conventionalization? moralization?

29. What cultural assimilations does it seem to reflect?

30. Does it partake of the character of a legend?

31. Could it conceivably contain a reversal to truth?

32. Does it contain tendency-wit?

33. Do the conditions underlying its circulation illustrate the fecundity of rumor?

34. What may have become leveled out?

35. Have oddities or perseverative wording persisted in the telling?

36. Has there been sharpening through multiplication?

37. Have movement, size or familiar symbols played a part in sharpening?

38. Has there been concretization or personalization?

39. What closure tendencies may be illustrated?

40. Does it deal with current events?

41. Does it contemporize past events?

42. Does it reflect relatively more intellectual or more emotional, assimilative tendencies?

43. Are all details assimilated to the principal theme?

44. May condensation of items have occurred?

45. Is there evidence of good-continuation?

46. In what way is assimilation to expectancy shown?

47. Is there assimilation to linguistic habits?

48. Has there been assimilation to occupational, class, racial or other forms of self-interest?

49. Is there assimilation to prejudice?

50. Is it conceivable that any part rests on verbal misunderstanding?

51. What is the expressive (metaphorical) signification of the rumor?

52. Does it represent a fusion of passions or antipathies?

53. Does it probably travel in a rumor-chain? What is its public? Why?

54. Are people suggestible to this particular tale because their minds are "unstuck" or "overstuck"?

55. Could it be classified as a fear, hostility or wish rumor?

56. Could it be part of a whispering campaign?

57. What relation, if any, does it bear to news? to the press?

58. Is the story labeled rumor or fact? Is it ascribed to an authoritative source? With what effect?

59. Might it perhaps represent a stage in crisis (riot) rumor-spreading?

60. What might be the best way to refute it?

Additional Cases for Analysis

The reader may wish to try his hand at analyzing the following rumors:

CASE THREE. Twenty-four hours before a sizable contingent of navy men were to receive their honorable discharges from the service, a rumor spread among them that the commanding officer had announced they must wait two weeks longer for their discharges, until the ship they were working on had been decommissioned.

CASE FOUR. The Russians, it is said, "nationalize their women."

CASE FIVE. Every few years a story reappears to the effect that a sea serpent has been seen in Loch Ness, Scotland.

CASE SIX. In the early days of World War II, it was rumored that the Philippine Islands (in some versions, the Panama Canal as well) had been attacked by the Japanese a whole week before the Pearl Harbor assault, but that news of this attack had been withheld from the public.

CASE SEVEN. Before taking off on a combat mission, many squadrons were plagued with rumors to the effect that their equipment was in some way defective; that the target was almost inaccessible because of antiaircraft protection; and that the enemy had recently perfected a new and dreadful defense weapon, which would almost certainly be employed against the squadron.

CASE EIGHT. Workers in a New England manufacturing town during the darkest days of the depression in the 1930s believed that the rich were running over the children of the poor in their elegant cars and never caring; also, that the whole depression was some sort of plot by the upper classes to cut the wages of the workers.

REFERENCES

1. R. H. Knapp, "A psychology of rumor," *Publ. Opin. Quart.*, 1944, 8:22-37.

2. H. W. Odum, *Race and rumors of race: challenge to American crisis*, Chapel Hill: University of North Carolina Press, 1943.

3. G. Myrdal, *An American dilemma*, New York: Harper, 1944.

4. H. V. McLean, "Psychodynamic factors in racial relations," *Ann. Amer. Acad. Pol. Soc. Sci.*, 1946, 244:159-66.

CHAPTER 20

Expectancy and war

Psychology tells us that what a child or an adult expects will determine in large part what he learns, thinks and does. Countless experiments have proved this fact in the nursery, classroom and laboratory.

This essay broadens the point. It argues that the scourge of war is also to a large extent a result of expectancies. If we wish to work for peace, we must direct much effort to altering the anticipations of individuals—both the leaders and the led. The task is one for the classroom no less than for mass media, for individual citizens as well as for world assemblies.

Certainly the causes of war are not wholly psychological. But political and economic solutions will not be effective unless they entail a radical change in the expectancies of mankind. It is encouraging to note that recent programs involving exchange of persons, good will tours and summit conferences recognize the validity of this argument.

The essay grew out of a Conference of the UNESCO "Tensions Project" held in Paris in July 1948. It first appeared in the volume *Tensions that cause wars* (1950) under the title "The role of expectancy."

The people of the world—the common people themselves—never make war. They are led into war; they fight wars; and they suffer the consequences—but they do not actually make war. Hence, when we say (as does the Preamble to the UNESCO Charter) that "wars begin in the minds of men," we can mean only that under certain circumstances, leaders can provoke and organize the people of a nation to fight. Left alone, people themselves could not make war.

Having said this, we must hasten to admit that circumstances prevailing today make it tragically easy to fabricate a warlike spirit in the minds of men and to instill in them obedience to war-minded leadership. The crux of the matter is the fact that, while most people deplore war, they none the less *expect* it to continue. *And what people expect determines their behavior.*

Expectations are themselves a complex matter, only partially conscious and only partially rational. To change warlike expectations to peaceful expectations requires, first of all, a careful analysis of the blend of personal and social factors that determines the anticipations of people in the world today.

327

Extreme Views of Aggressive Nationalism

Among the many attempts to explain national aggressiveness we find two that are fatally one-sided. One errs in attributing the aggressiveness wholly to the idiosyncrasies of the individual, the other in attributing it wholly to history and the economic imbalances of world society. We shall see that the concept *expectation of war* is a crystallization of both sets of factors.

Those who locate the sole cause of aggressive nationalism in human nature sometimes say that every person has an instinct of pugnacity. What is more natural than for him to rush to war whenever this biological instinct is provoked? Even if instincts are left out of the explanation, the frustrations of life are said to be so great that anger, hostility and resentment flow in every bosom, only to vent themselves ultimately through war. Personal aggression, we are told, becomes displaced upon an external enemy. The enemy becomes a scapegoat and attracts the wrath aroused by the frustrations we encounter in our occupation or in our unsatisfactory family life.

The fallacy of this purely personal explanation lies in the fact that, however pugnacious or frustrated an individual may be, he lacks the capacity to make organized warfare. He is capable of temper tantrums, chronic nagging, biting sarcasm and personal cruelty; but he alone cannot invade an alien land or drop bombs upon a distant enemy to give vent to his own emotions. Furthermore, whereas national aggressiveness is total—all citizens being involved in offensive and defensive efforts—relatively few citizens feel personally hostile toward the enemy. Studies of soldiers in combat show that hate and aggression are less commonly felt than fear, homesickness and boredom. Few citizens in an aggressive nation actually *feel* aggressive. Thus their warlike activity cannot be due solely to their personal motivations.

An interpretation exclusively in terms of personal life, therefore, will not work. How is it with the historical-economic approach (favored, for example, by Marxist thinkers)? Here too a fatal one-sidedness is evident. No social system has yet succeeded in abolishing war. Aggressive nationalism has flourished under communism as well as under capitalism, in both Christian and non-Christian countries, among illiterate and literate peoples, under authoritarian and democratic political structures. True, some nations, such as Switzerland, have been relatively successful in avoiding war. And some social systems may increase the *probability* of aggression; fascism, for example, by its very nature, engenders a war-minded leadership. But to hold that only one type of social system automatically excludes war, and that all others automatically engender war, is to violate the evidence of history up to the present time.

The Marxist theory of the causes of war overlooks the indispensable role of expectancy. It pivots on the alleged impossibility of achieving basic (and needed) reforms in production and ownership without violence, since the owners of the tools of production (stereotyped as "monopolistic capitalism") will presumably not relinquish their grasp without violence (stereotyped as "class warfare"). "Monopolistic capitalism," the argument runs, "will not destroy itself but must be destroyed." This simple and, I fear, war-engendering formula is itself a reflection of dogmatic expectancy.

Historic inevitability is not involved here. There are, rather, two sets of expectancy—one in the "have-nots," and one in the "haves." Both sets of expectancy have to be built up through psychological stimulation. Poor people, history shows, do not automatically resort to warfare to obtain a fairer share of the world's loot. They must first be led to perceive their interests as their leaders perceive them, and then must be exhorted and pushed into organized revolt.

Similarly history shows that the owners of the tools of production often yield peacefully to the expanding force of nationalization. In many progressive countries, mines, sugar refineries, banks, factories and transportation facilities are leaving private hands without violence. And it is by no means uncommon for peacefully minded owners in certain capitalistic countries to yield gracefully to an effective partnership with labor. On the other hand, the owners' apprehension may be crystallized into a horror of the "commies" and, with the aid of private and public propaganda, into a rigid expectancy that war alone will safeguard the owners' prerogatives.

Class warfare thus reduces largely to the anticipations of the contending parties. So, too, do the "imperialistic wars" decried by Communists—and by decent men everywhere. Wars of expansion, of exploitation or simply of distraction have not been limited to a capitalistic form of social organization. Belligerent sorties have occurred whenever or wherever greedy leaders have succeeded in inducing enough men (usually mercenaries) to carry out their inhuman raids. Highly collectivistic societies have been as guilty of such raiding parties as have the more individualistic societies.

In short, the indispensable condition of war is that people must *expect* war and must prepare for war before, under war-minded leadership, they make war. It is in this sense that "wars begin in the minds of men." Personal aggressiveness does not itself render war inevitable; it is simply a contributing cause when people *expect* to vent their emotions in warfare. Similarly the alleged economic causes of war are effective causes only when people think war is a solution to problems of poverty and economic rivalry. What men expect determines their behavior.

Personal Factors in the Expectancy of War

Expectancy, as I have said, is a complex state of mind. To imply that men anticipate war only in a simple, conscious way, as they anticipate the arrival of a commuter's train on schedule or a change in weather, would be an oversimplification. The deeper the emotions involved, the more unconscious and evasive are the determinants of our expectancies. Let us, therefore, look more closely at the personal conditions involved in hostile expectancies.

Some men have an apparently unbounded capacity for bitter hate, prolonged resentments and envy. Yet, paradoxically, men also have an unlimited capacity for love, friendship and affiliative behavior. No person ever seems able to love or be loved enough to satisfy him. The best psychological thinking, in my opinion, holds that hate and jealousy result from interference with affiliative relationships. Hate springs from interference with love. Aggressive nationalism, therefore, in so far as it entails elements of hate, represents in some devious way an interference with man's basic capacity for affiliative living and loyalty.

Such interference takes a complex course of development. The infant, we know, is at first in a friendly, symbiotic relationship with his mother. Anger is likely to surge up in him whenever this happy situation is interrupted, perhaps in connection with weaning or perhaps when younger brothers or sisters are born. A child who feels thus rejected is likely both to hate and to love the rejecting parent. Since hate and love conflict painfully, the hate may not be recognized. It may be repressed. Outwardly the child lives at peace with his parents, but his bottled up resentment may slip out in unusual ways against many "parent figures"—teachers, policemen, rulers, clergy.

According to this line of thinking, aggression may exist in a personal life and yet be almost unrecognized. The individual is ripe for a channelizing of his hatred upon substitute objects. Freud goes so far as to hold that the common feeling of bitterness and hate toward Jews is due to people's resentment toward God Himself for demanding so much of us. This hatred, repressed through fear of God, gets displaced upon the Jews, who taught us about God and are commonly accused of killing Christ, the son of God. In a deeper sense, the theory continues, we ourselves would like to kill Christ for expecting so much of us. Since we deplore this impulse in ourselves, we blame the Jews, who, legend tells us, have actually carried it out.

It is not necessary to accept Freud's somewhat involved theory of anti-Semitism to recognize that man's hostile impulses are subtle and are capable of much strange channeling. For our purpose, it is enough to note that channeling of hostility in the direction of war or racial and religious prejudice is an authentic possibility. Strange crystallizations take place around the myths available in our folklore. Originally, of course, these myths were created and maintained by like-minded individuals who felt a need to project their personal conflicts outward. In this way, Jews became the mythological cause of people's inner unrest; Communists—or capitalists—became a threat to their very existence. The legend adopted by the individual is available to him in his culture and is often forced on him by his parents, teachers or leaders.

The dark-skinned races, we hear, are ready to pollute our "blood." Symbolisms and displacements of this sort are legion. The conflicts within our bosoms are personified outward. In the myth we find the mirror image of our own disordered lives. When one can no longer tolerate one's own problems, one often seizes upon the institutional interpretation and legend. After a time, organized hostility comes to seem inevitable. In warfare one may act out symbolically the buried and unrecognized conflicts in one's own private life.

Such an analysis as this—appropriate to *some* people—shows how deeply buried the roots of expectancy of war may lie. But men differ exceedingly in the causes of aggression in their lives, in the amount and type of aggression they sustain and in the manner in which it is expressed. Many people are virtually aggressionless; frustrations, deprivations and slights to their pride affect them very little. They have serene and benevolent minds, even when they deal with individuals who are hotbeds of hatred. No doubt genetic factors of temperament that we know little about are involved in aggression. But whether for reasons of inheritance or of training, some men are clearly *extropunitive* and some *intropunitive*. The former will readily blame others when things go wrong; the latter tend to blame themselves and refuse to project their own guilt upon others.

Yet, for all this diversity, it is not difficult to marshal plenty of resentment against a "common enemy." Any society contains a large nucleus of extropunitive aggressors. All that is needed is to persuade these individuals that a particular enemy is responsible for the vague discomfort in their personal lives.

This line of reasoning must not lead us to the mistaken assumption that within every nation there is a fixed reservoir of hostility— hostility that *must* be released somehow, through local conflicts, class prejudices or external warfare. Oddly enough, one does not relieve aggression by expressing it in one channel rather than in another. A country with many internal explosions does *not* have fewer external explosions. Studies show the opposite: nations and tribes that are aggressive within the group are also aggressive outside, while peaceful social units tend to be peaceful in both their internal and their external relations. The Arapesh, though much undernourished, are a placid and peaceful folk at home and abroad. The Dobu are suspicious, vicious and hateful, both among themselves and among strangers. Hence, in speaking of the channeling of aggression, we must avoid the "steam-boiler-with-multiple-valves" fallacy.

The fact is that aggression breeds aggression. One comes to *expect* aggression as a response to problems. Conversely, peaceful relations breed expectancy of peaceful relations. Thus aggression is pretty much of a habit; the more you express it, the more you have of it. It is not enough, therefore, to find a "moral equivalent for war" (that is, a harmless outlet for aggression); it is equally important to change people's false expectancy that *any* outlet for aggression will automatically bring a solution. If wars were simply a relief from tension, they might conceivably have their justification. But experience shows that one war not only engenders another but also brings fierce domestic postwar strain and conflict into the nation itself.

It is true that, while a war is actually in progress, a nation often feels united and friendly within its own borders. This fact, among others, leads some theorists to argue that friendly social relations demand a "common enemy." We never feel so firmly cemented with our friends, they say, as when we are united with them in ridiculing, criticizing or fighting a common opponent. And if a common enemy is needed to guarantee affiliative relations with our allies, is not the vision of one world chimerical? If all nations were friendly, who would be the enemy to cement our internal loyalty?

Three answers come to mind: (1) Whether a common enemy is needed in a more advanced stage of human development is not yet known. (2) If such an enemy is needed, may we not point to the ravages of uncontrolled nature, disease and ignorance—all of which may, if necessary, be personified to satisfy our need for a tangible villain? (3) In the foreseeable future there will certainly be criminals—both domestic and international—as well as dissident outlawed groups against which globally minded citizens may unite in their wrath. The expectancy of peaceful relations with all men will be at best a gradual achievement.

Personal aggressiveness, then, exists in large amounts and in devious forms; it plays many unhappy tricks with our own essential longing for friendship, love and peace. Mental hygiene is profoundly concerned with these ravages of hate, anxiety and envy in the personal life. In complex ways, such individual states of mind intrude themselves into international relations. Sometimes the person with unresolved aggression regards war as a good means of evading a family difficulty and gladly follows a call to the colors. Sometimes he sees in the enemy, with or without some justification, a cause of his own misery. Sometimes he merely wishes to submit to a leader, as many Germans submitted to Hitler, in order to escape from the responsibilities of making the difficult decisions of maturity. "Let the leader be my conscience," says such a person. "If the leader himself is disordered in his inner life—a prey to mythical notions and unresolved hatreds—no matter. I shall follow wherever he calls, for I am too weary with my own conflicts to resist him. Decision is too much of a burden for me. Let the leader interpret the political and economic scene. I will follow."

Social Factors in the Expectancy of War

Left alone, the distress in each personal life would take so many forms and seek so many solutions that a concerted, national, warlike effort would not occur. But the members of a group are, after all, imbued with common values and sentiments. They "know" from their ancestors that their group is much sinned against, that the boundaries of their land are unjustly narrow. They "know" also that theirs is an inherently superior group and therefore most deserving.

One important reason why every national and cultural group feels superior is that, in fact, there existed for this group a golden age—a time when it was superior in culture, prosperity, science or power to all surrounding groups. This golden age may have been a hundred, a thousand or two thousand years ago; but at some time or other it had—as every cultural group has had—a high mark of artistic, material or intellectual distinction. Motivated by our personal pride, we find it easy to identify ourselves with the golden age of our people. What we deserve today we are inclined to estimate by this age of exaltation.

Such ethnocentricism is well-nigh universal among all peoples. Its roots are deep, as deep as our own boundless self-esteem. Expectancy of war grows in part from the latent resentments we hold against other groups who, perhaps centuries ago, violated the rights of our ancestors with whom we now identify ourselves. The fixity of these self-adulating sentiments may be estimated from the ethnocentric tone of much social science. Openly or implicitly, many a social scientist frames his theories and his observations so that his own culture emerges most glamorous and his own nation sinless. Until social science becomes truly transnational, we must heed the criticism that comes from the sociology of knowledge. We cannot expect too much of ordinary citizens, who often follow the myths manufactured by their intellectuals and build their own expectations upon them.

To some youths, war is definitely appealing. It arouses expectations of adventure, novelty and exalted comradeship. It removes the heavy burden of maturity, since in military service one has few important decisions to make. Economic insecurity, family troubles and overbearing or possessive parents are, for the time being, disposed of.

Can peace be made equally exciting? Can it possibly provide expectancies as satisfying as the prospect of war? This particular question has led to an experiment, now rapidly expanding, with what are commonly called "work service camps." In 1920 a small group of internationally minded volunteers, with the permission of local authorities, started to clear and reconstruct the land and buildings around Esnes-Verdun. In April 1921, however, the prefect of the district declared that "recent developments in Franco-German politics" had made it necessary to suppress the work. The first experiment thus ended under duress from aggressive nationalism.

But the efforts continued, particularly in times of local catastrophe. Groups of volunteers have been organized to assist in rebuilding regions affected by flood, fire or avalanche. In the summer of 1948, at least 130 voluntary service camps were flourishing in Europe, principally under the auspices of the *Service Civil Interna-*

tional. In the United States and in Mexico, under the auspices of the American Friends Service Committee, a score more were under way. Nearly all camps are international in composition; all are designed for collaborative work of mutual service without financial profit to the participants. The tasks have a positive social value, and the labor is not regarded by ordinary paid laborers as offering dangerous competition.

Slight though the impact of such work service camps is when viewed on a world scale, their appeal and their success indicate that youth may find constructive peacetime projects both exciting and satisfying. While conscription and military training affect the anticipation of youth in the direction of aggressive nationalism, work service camps affect their anticipations in the direction of internationalism, constructive activity and friendly human relationships. One important purpose of the *Service Civil International* is to persuade governments to accept voluntary service of this order as an alternative to compulsory military training. This goal has obviously not yet been reached, but the issue has been well drawn: *will nations permit youth to have alternative expectations concerning their public duties—expectations entailing international cooperation and constructive service rather than preparation for war?* The prospect seems utopian, but the question illustrates the type of decision that nations will be forced to make if they ever become sufficiently enlightened to consider the psychological importance of expectation on the attitudes of youth.

Like traditions and a sense of adventure, symbols are an important factor in expectancy. Germans think of themselves as belonging to the land of Beethoven and Goethe; Norwegians preserve the relics of the Vikings and in fantasy share in their fabulous exploits. Greeks do not forget Praxiteles and Demosthenes. Flags, martial music and noble ruins are profoundly significant to the citizen whose security and self-esteem are inseparable from the tradition of his people.

Most symbols are of an exclusively parochial order. They mark off my country, or my religion, or my caste, from yours. World symbols are virtually lacking: there are no world parks, gardens and universities; no world currency; no genuine world capital. A few fine words have been spoken—the Atlantic Charter, the United Nations Charter, the Preamble to the UNESCO Charter—but these documents are little known and still fail to rally appreciable loyalty. Yet, just as the diversified egos within a nation cannot be fused into one "we" except with the aid of tradition and symbol, so international loyalty cannot be achieved without the common focus of thought and the common uplift that come from symbols of transnational unity.

Our existing national symbols are not necessarily mischievous. A very considerable amount of national loyalty is compatible with world loyalty. But at times these symbols are deliberately employed for war-making purposes by leaders of government and of public opinion. Patriotic phrases repeated over and over in a warlike context will habituate people to the expectation of war. Nationalistic bureaus of "propaganda and enlightenment" deliberately frame the expectancies of men.

When people's minds have become habituated to accepting a designated enemy as a menace, the next step is to set the final expectation that will lead to war. Leaders usually do this with a formulation of national demands. An ultimatum is sent to the enemy. When it is rejected, people feel that no path other than war remains open.

An ultimatum is a momentous matter. Take the case of two individuals: when they meet to discuss their aims and their needs, they have a fair chance of finding a friendly, common solution; but when one confronts the other with an ultimatum, a fight ensues. If one party yields momentarily under duress, it is only for the purpose of building up his resources for later revenge. So it is with nations in disagreement: demands and prefabricated solutions usually increase tensions, simply because they deny the other fellow a right to participate in matters affecting his own destiny. The price he would pay in loss of pride is too great. He prefers to fight.

Pride of position is the immediate cause of every war. So decisive and final have been the demands made by each national spokesman that to yield ground would be felt humiliating and shameful. Expectancies have become frozen. It is "Fifty-four forty or fight." At this point, war is indeed inevitable.

Before this stage is reached, the art of resolving difficulties through the mutual discussion of desires and needs (in place of demands and ultimata) must be cultivated. The desires and needs of people are seldom incompatible; more often they are parallel and reciprocal, because one nation generally has something to spare that the others require. Since all men need and want freedom from destructive poverty, from irrational fear and from debilitating ignorance, it is plainly through joint action that the pathway to a common goal can best be discovered. The prerequisite of peace lies in developing the habit of discussing *needs* and *desires,* rather than (as now) stating arranged solutions.

Ignorance and Expectancy

One of the most important barriers to international understanding is ignorance of the other fellow's intentions and of his way of life.

Ignorance may be of two kinds: *simple ignorance of the facts,* or *distortion of facts* to accord with one's own motives or with the motives of demagogic leaders who have much to gain from misrepresentation.

Simple ignorance is the easier of these two kinds to repair. Crusades against illiteracy, now under way from Mexico to India and from Nigeria to Siberia are exciting and gratifying in their results. Psychological studies have shown that an appreciable relationship does exist between a high level of general education and freedom from prejudice. The relationship, however, is far from perfect. Even scholars may be intense bigots. Salvation does not lie in schooling alone.

Ignorance due to distortion of facts is harder to remedy. Some distortions are simple and understandable, though often damaging, as when certain white children recoil from colored people because they look "dirty." One's personal history often creates the emotional ground for a distortion, as in the case of the youth who hated "the Irish" because his rather cruel father happened to be of Irish descent. The most mischievous capacity of the human mind is its impulsive tendency to categorize and endow all members of a particular group with one set of alleged attributes. My cruel father is Irish, therefore all Irish are cruel.

A hostile image, once formed, is peculiarly resistant to the onslaught of contrary evidence. An Oxford student is said to have remarked, "I despise all Americans—but I have never met one I didn't like." Thus do tabloid generalizations persist, even when every ounce of firsthand experience contradicts them. We know of no remedy for this mental-emotional tabloidism except the inculcation of habits of discriminating perception and critical thought. Systematic training is possible even in the lower schools.

The emotional economy of a group stereotype is easily seen in the image many Americans hold of the Soviet Union. When the Russians were our allies in World War II, they were readily perceived as courageous, cheerful, progressive and liberty-loving people.

In the postwar period, when circumstances had shifted, the image became one of a cruel, oppressed, atheistic and double-dealing folk. Thus perceived, Russia came to serve as a satisfactory scapegoat—a distant menace capable of explaining many of our frustrations. Communists became the symbolic cause of evil at home. Is my employment jeopardized? Blame the Communists! Am I inconvenienced by inflation? Blame the Communistic labor leaders! Are the colleges advocating dangerous internationalism? Oust the Communist professors! A study has shown that the dislocations in America after World War I were blamed on a diversity of scapegoats: Bolsheviks, hyphenated-Americans, monopolists, the IWW. After World War II the image had sharpened; the ubiquitous villain is simply the "Communist."

Now, in order for a villain to become common property, communication and propaganda are needed. Unless newspapers, politicians and special pleaders of all kinds join in painting the picture, people will not focus their diversity of negative emotions upon one clearly identified menace. Expectancy of a new war within twenty-five years increased in America from 40 per cent of the population in August 1945 to 65 per cent in July 1946. In the same interval, the enemy became clearly identified as Russia. The services of news agencies and public opinion molders were essential to this shift.

But is expectancy never rooted in fact? Are there no natural and inevitable wars, provoked by differences in ideology or by intransigence in one party to a dispute? Are expectancies only a product of designing propagandists or irresponsible leaders and publicists, busily watering the seeds of aggression in the individual life?

The answer, I believe, is as follows: While some serious and basic conflicts of interest may be unavoidable, warlike solutions spring always from warlike expectancies and preparation. The confirmed Marxist who sees class warfare—world-wide revolution preceded by imperialistic wars—as inevitable is merely *seeing* them as inevitable. If enough people on both sides of a dispute expect it to result in a war, then of course war *becomes* inevitable. (I shall have more to say shortly about defensive wars.)

Unfortunately, the images we have of other people are more often condescending or hostile than friendly. Textbooks, legends, traditions, leaders and mass media of communication conspire to keep them so. The reason, I presume, is that hostile images accord best with people's desires to hold firmly to provincial islands of security. That the world itself is our natural island of security is a conception too spacious for our fragmented egos to grasp. But, fortunately, even hostile images are susceptible to change. They change when films, radio, newspapers and textbooks change. They change when people travel observantly and sympathetically. They change when people engage as participants in shared projects of work or recreation. They change when people gain insight into the myth-making process of their own minds as it is manipulated by publicists.

Let me repeat that school knowledge is insufficient. As Sorokin points out, the twentieth century marks the highest educational level in all of human history. At the same time, it is immeasurably the bloodiest century, in terms of civil and international wars, persecution of minorities and criminal violence of all types. One reason is that schools are seldom international in their emphasis. More often, at all hours of the day, they din national glories into the children's minds.

Yet even a new, internationally minded curriculum would not be a magic cure. For intellectual knowledge is not emotional knowledge. Only the sound mind, free from cramping complexes, can turn book learning into international understanding. A scholar may be familiar with all ethical systems and may himself be the author of an altruistic doctrine of ethics; yet in his personal life he may be blatantly egoistic, chauvinistic and war-minded. A man may understand human frailties and the techniques of propaganda, as Goebbels did, and use them to destroy his fellow men.

The Personal Philosophy of Life

It is here that moral and religious leaders have a strong point to make. Only when knowledge is deeply rooted in acceptable values does it become socially effective. Moral inclination is still an essential part of the story of war and peace.

Recent empirical studies have shown an important relationship between one's philosophy of life and one's tendency to hostility. People who are afraid of life, who say that the world is a hazardous place and that men are basically evil and dangerous, are people with much race and religious prejudice. Usually they hate Catholics, Negroes and Jews; they are superpatriotic and find their security only in nationalistic strength and sovereignty. They are generally institution-minded, docile outwardly to parents and traditions. They like fraternities and sororities, and find binding security only in small in-group attachments. They are peculiarly rigid in their approach to practical problems, even to the solution of simple arithmetical tasks. This pattern of rigidity marks the aggressor-personality. It constitutes a belligerent philosophy of life. International and intercultural understanding requires a degree of relaxation and peace with oneself that such personalities lack.

A Jesuit priest, a student of mine, studied the amount of prejudice against Negroes within a Catholic parish. Without being told the purpose of the research, a devoted layman was asked to give the names of members whom he would regard as deeply Christian in their faith and in their lives, and to give names of other members whom he felt were merely "institutional" Catholics, conforming to the rules but not genuinely Christian in respect to their outlook. These two groups were then studied by means of a well-framed questionnaire designed to measure anti-Negro feeling. It turned out that the "institutional" Catholics were vastly more bigoted. To them, apparently, the church was an island of security in a hostile world. Outsiders were objects of distrust. The essential teachings of Christianity had not penetrated into their personalities. They were living their lives rigidly, holding fast to in-group security and hating outsiders. Although this particular study did not deal directly with nationalistic sentiments, it strongly suggests that war-mindedness is closely associated with a philosophy of life that is tense, in-groupish and dependent on small platforms of organized security, not daring to embrace the world as a whole within its view.

We thus have reason to believe that two types of personality formation are especially likely to be swept into the stream of national aggressiveness. One—the most obvious—is the unintegrated, many-minded person, easily controlled through suggestion and through momentary appeals by leaders and publicists. He will see demons where the morning paper puts them. Being unsure of his own values, he will yield to the demagogue and follow the prevailing fashion in blame.

The other type is the individual who has himself developed an authoritarian character structure. To him the world is a jungle. He needs a safety island in his group, his own nation; beyond the in-group he feels helpless. He suspects, rejects and hates the stranger. Such a person quickly perceives menace in a harmless minority group in his own land, or in any foreign power that is pointed out to him as a threat.

We need corresponding studies of the altruistic and world-minded citizen, the man who has no difficulty enlarging his circles of loyalty. Wendell Willkie was no less a good Hoosier or good American for embracing the cause of "One World." On the basis of available evidence, psychologists are inclined to believe that men are less likely to be swayed into irrational fears and national antagonisms if they have spent reasonably secure childhood years in an atmosphere where affection prevailed and where high ideals of altruism were not only taught but practiced. But childhood security is undoubtedly only one of the factors making for strong attitudes of trust and relaxation in dealing with one's fellows. We need to know the other factors involved.

The Role of Parent and Leader in Building Expectancies

The child's philosophy of life grows chiefly from seeds planted by his parents. Studies show that, in general, those who mirror the parents' views in respect to religion, politics and ethics are likely to be bigoted unless the parents' views were exceptionally altruistic. The mature and benevolent outlook on life is not likely to be found among those who cling blindly to parental patterns of security.

Yet, for better or for worse, parental attitudes are always in some degree adopted. Few parents realize that they are imparting attitudes unsuited to life in a world greatly altered since their childhood. To some degree, schools and colleges modify the parental influence, but the content of instruction in schools and colleges is more often parochial than international.

Political leaders and other figures of public importance also play a vital part. If feelings of insecurity prevail, their interpretations of these inward jitters may become decisive factors in our view of the world at large. If I am told by a person to whom I accord prestige that the Jew is threatening my job, or that the Negro endangers my sexual prerogatives, or that a certain foreign country threatens my preferred way of life, I am likely to accept the interpretation and prepare myself perhaps for violent action—or, at least, for a future suspicious separation.

Marxist thinkers and others insist that leaders are mere incidents in the stream of history. Leaders, they say, are not much more than puppets that reflect prevailing tensions and transmit to the individual the dominant ideology. In only a limited sense is this true. Leaders are, of course, subject to their own fears, just as are their followers. They are influenced by current myths, by their predecessors and by the prevailing nationalistic tradition. But aggressive nationalism cannot break out unless war-minded individuals are seated in positions of dominance. The leader is decisive in matters of war and peace, precisely because his followers are themselves ambivalent, or many-minded or charged with hostility. He can play upon the latent hostility or upon the affiliative impulses of his group. It is he who calls the tune.

An important distinction in respect to leadership is between what we may call "person-minded" leaders and "object-minded" leaders. The former are mindful of the human factor, of their responsibility to their constituents and of their constituents' interests. Object-minded leaders love power and pursue a goal forcibly and heedlessly. To them, human beings are mere *things* to be manipulated in the service of a cause. Object-minded leaders often set their eyes on aggressive nationalism and, in the course of their activity, raise people's expectancies to accord with their own desires. People are made to see no other way out but war.

Along with object-minded leaders we may, I think, include a great many incompetent leaders in the international field—men who stumble into war because their position puts demands on them that are too great for their skill in human relations. They quickly reach the point in international dealings where they can engage only in recrimination. Such bunglers drag the people along with them. Their own maladroitness is interpreted by them as villainy on the part of the enemy.

Person-minded leaders hate war because they habitually reckon the human consequences. They are indisposed to utilize propaganda and manipulative techniques, to create false images and over-simplified categories around which to rally their followers. It is harder to be consistently skillful in advancing the interests of persons than of an aggressive cause. But modern experiments in social psychology indicate that it might be possible to train person-minded leaders. Until now we have allowed leadership to rise in haphazard fashion. It was more or less chance whether the leader turned out to be person-minded or object-minded.

Whether the expectations of a population are directed toward war or toward peace, toward arbitration or open break, toward person-centeredness or object-centeredness, depends largely upon the deeds done and the symbols invoked by national leaders. The greatest menace to the world today are leaders in office who regard war as inevitable and thus condition their people for armed conflict. For if men regard war as inevitable, it is inevitable.

Social Structure and Expectancy of War

I have said that war has flourished under all known social systems. The differentiating factor between war and peace, therefore, is not a surface matter of social organization, but deeper human factors

of expectancy and channelizing of attitude. Personality is so un-
stable a unit in nature that it can be swayed to national aggression or
to international amity. War can be avoided as soon as we learn how
to prevent the swaying of expectancies toward warfare. Or am I
overstating the case?

What, for example, about defensive warfare? A peaceful people,
invaded by a warlike neighbor, would normally seize weapons in
self-defense. In this case, is not expectation irrelevant? No; in such
a case, *unilateral* expectation was the cause of war. One side in the
conflict regarded attack as inevitable. If war is to be avoided, *no*
nation can be permitted to have warlike expectations, for one war-
minded land endangers all others and keeps war-mindedness alive
through fear.

What of the "economic causes" of war, so much under discussion
today? I do not for a moment hold such causes to be unimportant.
Prolonged hunger, especially in the face of plenty, will engender an
understandable violence if no other solution is available. Raids and
counter-raids on surrounding tribes are as old as human history.
Often the motives have been hunger; but at times they have also been
desire for revenge and for excitement, escape from boredom and
personal frustration (channelized by the leader). Economic wars are
not the only kinds of war. There are ideological wars, religious wars,
wars of envy and wars of boredom.

And, as I have said, certain political systems make expectancy
of war almost inevitable, while others render this mode of life
relatively unpopular and unlikely. The tradition of a culture may
exalt martial virtues, or it may condemn the outlay of funds and
the exercise of military prowess. Political systems make for war or for
peace, according to the expectancies they create.

The factor of expectancy is decisive. The wants of men, even
acute hunger, do not lead to violence unless people *think* violence
is the way to satisfy them. When those who "have" refuse to yield
to those who "have not" they increase the expectancy of war by
making it seem a reasonable mode of behavior to the "have-nots." To
refuse to negotiate is a way of creating expectancy of violence. The
proud and unbending kings of France brought on the Revolution by
destroying every other alternative in the minds of their subjects.

Organization for war is a peculiarly low-grade form of social
organization, even though in modern times it takes elaborate and
ingenious forms. Young draftees are herded into camps, given routine
tasks to perform, drilled in specialties and discouraged from thinking
as integrated personalities. Essentially, only the young man's capacity

for obedience is played upon, stimulated by patriotic symbols; and the process fulfills some momentary function in relieving personal frustration. The war machine is thus a primitive organization of human resources. As a form of social structure, it segmentalizes the individual; whole personalities are not involved. It is for this reason that the aftermath of war usually brings about demoralization, criminality and shattered personalities.

The way up from this primitive form of social organization is long and hard. We have always had wars because they have been seen as the simplest mode of solving conflicts between groups of people. If wars had not today become so disastrous, we might be tempted to let this easy "solution" of social conflict remain. But we have now no alternative except to change mankind's habit of expecting armed conflict to solve its disagreements.

Summary in Terms of World Organizations

Man's moral ideals, as expressed in the great creeds of the human race, are at a fairly high level. But his capacity to profess one thing and act the opposite seems almost unlimited. At the present time, he appears completely unable to bring his conduct in line with his expressed ideals.

We have seen three principal reasons why this fatal chasm exists:

1. *Men's personalities are seldom well unified.* There are anxieties and repressions, unsatisfied wants and unrequited love, shame, guilt and awe before the unknown. Pressed between two oblivions, man's life is to him mysterious and fearful, yet vaguely beautiful and intensely interesting. Seldom is he able to unite his basic desire for love and understanding of the world about him with an underlying feeling of trust for his fellow men. Relatively few personalities are integrated to such an adequate degree, or so free from fear.

2. *This basic ambivalence in life, and its confusedness, make man a prey to slanderous conceptions of his fellow men.* Security is found only within the in-groups—within the family, the church, the tribe, the nation. All else appears hazardous and unknown. Myths arise exalting the in-group, and legends depicting the menace or inferiority of the out-group. This view of the out-group often entails an expectancy of armed conflict. Images of the "enemy" seldom correspond to reality, because people are ignorant of the facts and because they

tend to oversimplify the motives and characteristics of the out-group in order to justify their inimical sentiments.

3. *Such vaguely hostile expectancies are easily manipulated by war-minded leaders, or by the incompetent who slip willy-nilly into patterns of nationalism.*

For these reasons a state of cynicism results, and men despair of ever achieving their desire for peace. They expect war—and this expectancy itself brings war. Only by changing the expectation, in leaders and followers, in parents and children, shall we eliminate war.

Our perspective on this giant task of attitude change is still limited and the outlook still discouraging. Yet we find hope in the fact that, within the past few years, three significant quasi-global organizations have been formed. The function of each in its own area is to alter the mode of human anticipation from one of war to one of peace. The area of activity of these three organizations corresponds well to the three obstacles I have just enumerated.

World Health Organization. The aim of the World Health Organization, as stated in its constitution, is "the attainment by all peoples of the highest possible level of health." Health is defined as "a state of complete physical, mental and social well-being and not merely the absence of disease or infirmity." Since "mental and social well-being" is included, it is clear that this organization is dedicated to the development of integrated, peaceable personalities, capable of handling personal and interpersonal tensions without resort to violence. Mental hygiene—health on the level of personality—is of primary concern to this organization. With improvement in mental health, the number of relaxed, wholesome, internationally minded citizens will surely increase.

There are, of course, many other agencies whose aim is constructive action on this same level. Wise physicians, parents, teachers, psychiatrists and clergymen, individually and in their professional organizations, work ceaselessly for the same end.

Unesco. This organization is dedicated to erecting the "defenses of peace" in the minds of men. In terms of our analysis, the special function of UNESCO is to correct the distorted images that make for war and thus to diminish expectations of war and rationalizations of war. In its program of international education and cooperation, UNESCO tries to reduce strangeness and strain among the peoples of the world. It facilitates the contributions of schools, international voluntary work camps, artists, publicists and scholars to the process of altering belligerence into friendliness. UNESCO represents only one line of constructive effort in this direction, but its international character makes it particularly significant.

The United Nations. At the level of political and economic relations between nations, the United Nations is dedicated to the task of altering expectancies. It provides a means for seeking peaceful solutions of conflicts, and it brings the leaders of nations together. But public confidence in the efficacy of this activity is still weak. The success of the United Nations will be guaranteed as soon as the people and their leaders really *expect* it to succeed. The great majority of the people of the world have by now heard of the United Nations and know of its efforts. *Confidence* in the United Nations is itself a key to the prevention of war.

These three organizations, and other bodies with analogous functions, are hard at work. Their endeavor in all cases is to build expectancy of peace and to provide machinery for its achievement. That men are hopefully yearning for their success is the first step in acquiring a new expectancy. Yearning may gradually turn into confidence. And when men are fully confident that international organizations can eradicate war, they will, at last, succeed in doing so.

CHAPTER 21

Guidelines for research in international cooperation

This essay argues that prompt and energetic research in the broad field of social science may play a significant role in the prevention of World War III. While it was first published shortly after the close of the last war—in the *Journal of Social Issues* (1947)—its content is no less relevant and urgent today.

The head of a philanthropic foundation, interviewing an applicant for a grant, once asked, "Do you regard your project as 'basic research,' or do you really have something in mind?" This paper shows that the needed social and psychological research can be both scientifically basic and intensely practical.

Confronted with the cheerless spectacle of the modern world, an increasing number of today's prophets are saying that our international troubles are wholly *moral*. Technical progress, they point out, brought in its wake a perilous secularization of life. Among its macabre consequences we reckon technological unemployment, technological warfare and now the black portent of atomic destruction. The present century, in spite of its unexampled inventiveness, has been the bloodiest century on record in terms of international, civil and criminal violence.

Secularization, these prophets insist, led mankind to forget the Commandments of Moses, the ethics of Confucius, the self-discipline of Krishna and the vision of Christian Brotherhood. It were better now, they say, for each man to look to his own salvation. Let religion revive. Let character be restored. Only then may we expect human relations to improve.

Can one doubt that these advocates of moral reformation are right in arguing that the great moral creeds of the world, *if taken in their purity*, would help control the ravages of technology? Were men to backtrack from the present gulf of secularization, were they to start practicing their creeds, peace on earth would be more readily achieved.

The manifest difficulty in accepting this apparently simple counsel lies not in the falseness or inapplicability of our creeds but in their sheer antiquity. Many, perhaps most, inhabitants of the earth would recognize "Love thy neighbor as thyself" as a worthy imperative. But this commandment tells twentieth-century man very little about how he can translate his affectionate purposes into action. How, in an age of giant industries, bureaucracy, instant communication and atomic energy, shall one effectively love one's neighbor?

Suppose a factory owner, a man of good will, wishes to practice the Golden Rule. What does the Rule tell him about fair and just wages? Without research into living costs, the needs and aspirations of his employees and the standards for safety and health, he cannot intelligently be a Christian. The age of shepherds and Sadducees bequeathed him a sound moral orientation but none of the skills or knowledge needed to implement his ideals.

Suppose I am persuaded that I should love my neighbor as myself—or, at least, that I should live at peace with him. My neighbors, I know, are almost three billion in number. What concretely shall I do in my capacity as a world citizen? Shall I press for the Quota Force Control amendment to the United Nations Charter? Shall I work for birth control in India and for a gigantic loan for industrial upbuilding in that country? Shall I approve or disapprove Scheme X for the international control of crime? Only social research, focused upon overlapping problems of nations, will tell the answers.

Sound moral purpose is by no means lacking in the world. It still flows from the great creedal literature of past ages, even while it is being reinterpreted in the light of modern conditions. The present chasm between technology and morals has formed chiefly because physical engineering has outstripped social engineering, because physical science has been allowed to outdistance social science. The worship of technological efficiency for its own sake is an almost universally recognized evil, but its control through moral efficiency awaits knowledge and instrument.

Policy, Research and Operations

Perhaps the most heartening event of our times is the establishment of the Economic and Social Council of the United Nations and its dependent specialized agencies including UNESCO. The last of these, in the Preamble to its Charter, strikes the keynote of a new era: "Since wars begin in the minds of men it is in the minds of men that the defenses of peace must be constructed." The implications are crystal clear: man's moral sense condemns war; let us therefore study scientifically the sources of this evil in men's minds and scientifically remove them.

But here an initial misgiving arises. Can research into the causes of war be translated effectively into action? A certain pessimism has descended upon many of the world's most resourceful social scientists. Aiming to improve morale in wartime, industrial relations in peacetime and amity between races, they have pressed ahead with research and have proffered solutions. For the most part, their findings have been disregarded and their zeal correspondingly dampened. Political expediency, power politics and selfish national purposes have conspired to overlook—to "place on file"—their counsel. Atomic scientists, likewise, were listened to respectfully in their capacity as technological producers; but when they spoke earnestly regarding the moral and economic implications of their discovery, a chorus of special interests tried to drown them out. Today amoral technology is in the saddle; the socially minded engineer is a pedestrian left far behind.

The situation can be remedied in three ways:

First: boldness in taking risks is called for. Everyone knows there are serious inherent limitations in social research. It is likely that social investigation can never attain an exactness equivalent to that of physical technology, whose ravages it aims to control. Unlike physical and chemical research, social studies are infrequently additive, and their powers of generalization are limited. But we cannot know precisely the inherent limitations of social science until it is given an opportunity of adequate scope. The imperfections of social engineering is no excuse for failing either to encourage its growth or to employ its aid wherever practicable.

The United States alone spent two billion dollars on the invention of the atomic bomb. Would it be absurd to spend an equivalent sum, if necessary, on the discovery of means for its control? And, as the Preamble to the UNESCO Charter states, it is undoubtedly in the minds of men that the defenses of peace must be sought. Success cannot be guaranteed; it is entirely possible that social engineering may fail to implement the moral sense of mankind and that mankind may go under. But we shall never know the potential value of social science unless we take the risk.

Second: policy makers (I include the Department of State as well as the highest policy authorities in the United Nations) *can and should open their minds continually to the documented advice of social scientists.* When it is good, they should follow it. Publicity given to relevant research, to the recommendations of social scientists and to the policies finally adopted will reveal the extent to which international practices are determined by selfishness and momentary expediency, and the extent to which they conform to the best social knowledge available.

Third: let social scientists continually strive to attain a standard in research that merits respect. Too often in the past, their findings have been trivial or incompetent. Equally often, they have failed to make even the soundest of their principles intelligible or their applicability clear. Psychologists, sociologists, anthropologists and economists have much to learn about practical orientation of their studies and about effective means for communicating their results to policy makers.[1]

If developments move in the direction of the three suggestions just offered, the integration between policy bodies and social scientists will be greatly improved. Much encouragement comes from the knowledge that, during recent years, some beneficial coordination has been achieved. In numerous instances during World War II, social science gave indispensable aid to the war effort. In spite of resistance and some hostility, social science scored triumphs, notably in the areas of psychological warfare, personnel selection, morale building and effective communication between the government and the public.[2] The scope of this success is sufficiently great to raise our hopes high for the potential results of teamwork between social scientists and administrators in the area of international cooperation.

While the natural scientist or the medical scientist, operating alone in his individual laboratory, may do significant research of importance to the entire world, it is safe to say that almost no social research of international significance can be successfully carried forward in this manner. Even if a whole nation should concentrate its energy upon social investigations, it is unlikely to accomplish much of *world* significance. A single nation's culture-bound outlook is restrictive. True, in the past, social scientists have occasionally traveled abroad in their quest for data, but their reports have seldom been broad-gauged enough and free enough from provincialism to serve as a guide to international policy of any type whatsoever.

At the present time, barriers of language, inadequate facilities (especially in smaller and poorer countries), meagerness of intercommunication and lack of incentive to focus upon common problems conspire to separate and segregate the social scientists of the world. As yet the resources of their knowledge and skill, as well as their eagerness to aid, have not been tapped in the interests of world peace. To obtain the concerted effort of the world's social scientists, even in regard to limited and special topics, we now need international stimulation, facilities and coordination. Thousands of highly skilled physical scientists worked in collaboration on a *national* scale for the production of the destructive atomic bomb. The control of its destructive potential and the realization of its latent benefits will require equally many, and equally able, minds cooperating on an *international* scale.

What Is Known and What Is Needed

International social research need not start at scratch. Already much initial work has been done. A sufficient number of general principles are known, and widely enough agreed upon, to set the guidelines for urgently needed investigations. More important, these principles might *immediately* be applied with immense profit to the conduct of international relations, if the proper officials were so disposed.

As we examine these principles and their usefulness as guides to concrete research and policy, two limitations should be held in mind. *First:* they are offered as illustrations, not as a final system. An adequate survey should have the benefit of wide discussion and concerted approval by a large number of social scientists assembled from many nations.[3] *Second:* the discussion is limited largely to psychological principles, with some borrowing from social anthropology and sociology. The potential contributions of economics, geography, political science and history are unquestionably large; but these disciplines fall outside the range of the present survey.

Trends toward collective security. Perhaps the first principle to which the social scientist would call attention is the unidirectional historical trend toward the formation of a world government. From the cave man to the twentieth century, human beings have formed larger and larger working and living groups. At some time in the dim past, families became clans. Clans turned into tribes and states. Federations followed; empires had their day; commonwealth and regional unions flourished. During the past century, nonpolitical international organizations have sprung up in bewildering numbers, especially among scientific, professional and recreational groups. The League of Nations, followed by Hitler's sinister and abortive New Order, were chapters in the same saga. The United Nations is the latest and best hope mankind has devised. Yet it is not necessarily the final effort; even now it is unclear whether one world is the next step in the series, or whether mankind is doomed first to live through a divided period, a pro- and anti-Russian world.

The social scientist also warns that, though it is bound to come about, the form of the future world government is as yet undetermined. A tyrannical global system is a distinct danger. Precisely for this reason, a maximum effort in study and research is needed to insure that future developments shall be such as to implement the moral sense of mankind. Unless social engineering hastens to the support of democratic ideals, a tyrannical form of world government or an additional period of divisiveness and war may be expected to occur. Almost as bad would be the creation of a benevolent bureaucracy from which individual initiative and participation were excluded. No social structure is solid unless the citizens themselves feel that they themselves have a part to play in shaping their mortal destinies.

Participation in one's own destiny. Various lines of research in recent years have demonstrated the inescapable importance of personal participation in matters affecting one's own welfare. People almost always want to solve their problems for themselves, or at least feel that they play an important part in the process of achieving a solution. International relief organizations have learned that charitable handouts seldom strengthen the recipient or win his gratitude. Apathy, bootlicking or resentment may accompany "benevolence" of any sort, whether it be alms or an imposed political system. On the other hand, personal efforts at upbuilding and rehabilitation are usually undertaken with joy by a person who feels that the product he achieves will be his own and will not suffer destruction or expropriation.

Thus human progress and human happiness seem to depend, not upon what one has in hand, but upon one's freedom to grow and to build. Shortly after World War II, the inhabitants of certain villages in Poland and in Czechoslovakia rebuilt their destroyed communities through cooperative efforts, declaring that they were supremely happy in the process. But in many localities of the world, freedom to build is denied; and the people who are denied such freedom become reactive, bitter, resentful and destructive.[4]

Though the guideline here is clear, and is fortified by much research in group dynamics and industrial relations, we still know far too little about the process of eliciting participation and encouraging cooperative enterprise. We know too little about the techniques of linking the basic motives of self-interest to the best of all means for attaining it—namely, mutual aid. There are also cultural differences to be taken into account, though all peoples seem potentially capable of cooperation. How best to engage this capability, and how best to extend the circle of cooperative endeavor until it reaches an international orbit—these are subjects demanding immediate research.

Economic and social insecurity. Persons who feel that their livelihood or safety is threatened generally make poor citizens—of a town, a nation or the world. They tend to be defensive, restless, suspicious. Since poverty is well-nigh universal and social insecurity widely prevalent, it becomes imperative to determine the types of provisions, guarantees and reassurances that are most needed to allay fear and unrest. What are the standards of security and well-being below which no people can fall without incurring social disaster? Up to now, these standards have been guessed at through intuition and in terms of expediency, but only the results of an objective investigation will serve as a reliable basis for action.

Certain minimum guarantees against starvation and disease may be a legitimate objective for all nations acting in concert at a governmental level. But human interests are best served when people themselves are consulted and permitted to play an active part in providing for their own security. The precise forms of self-help to be encouraged, and the ideal order of priority, are subjects for research, not speculation.

We know that criminality, especially among children, can often be traced directly to feelings of psychological insecurity. National unrest, likewise, is often derived from apprehensiveness. War springs in part from conditions of chronic suspicion and deprivation. All these social ills cry for sustained research into the conditions of, and remedies for, intolerable insecurity. Some available studies suggest that a certain amount of social and economic uncertainty is conducive to personal growth, but that privations which bring morbid anxiety lead to antisocial conduct.

One form of insecurity especially injurious to the cause of peace arises from the frequent inconsistency of national and international policy. An important factor in the downfall of democratic Germany and the rise of Hitler was the German people's dismay at the shifting policies of the Allies. To the Germans, Versailles meant one thing, the Dawes Plan another; reparations indicated one attitude, nonenforcement of reparations another. Punitive treatment was inconsistently mixed with friendship. By such an inconsistent administering of rewards and punishments in a laboratory, a rat can be made neurotic. Under similar circumstances, a child, an adult or a social group grows restless and embittered. It is necessary for each nation to know, at any given moment, precisely where she stands in the international family.

Psychological security on an international scale, therefore, requires a policy of clear commitment, frequently reiterated and carried forward with unvarying consistency. To arouse hopes and let them fall; to start one ill-considered policy and switch it in midstream; to invite cooperation and then reject it—all these are fatal errors. Research seems scarcely needed to prove this point, but the fact should be clearly recorded and prominently advertised in order to influence continually the operations of policy and deliberative bodies.

International conference procedure. At the root of much of the vagueness and inconsistency of international decisions lie the human failings that come to light in the work of committees and assemblies. Men, even trained statesmen, do not know how to deliberate efficiently. Up to now, in social science, only a bare beginning has been made in the study of the processes of discussion, group criticism and decision. We may expect much basic work to be done in the future even without international support. But so essential is it for international groups to learn how to employ the most effective conference procedures that money and time would be well invested in additional investigations.

The parliamentary problems of international bodies are unique, for when individuals come together from contrasting cultural backgrounds, employing different languages and reflecting diverse traditions, the ordinary difficulties of efficient mental coordination are exaggerated. How shall representatives of different nations learn most effectively to deliberate together unless international support and encouragement are given to this vital line of research?

Focusing on children. Social scientists know that within the next generation it is theoretically possible to have a world language, to build universal loyalty to a world state, and to eliminate most racial and national prejudices. They know equally well that the goal cannot be achieved in practice, for it is from their parents that children chiefly learn their social attitudes. The older generation unfortunately inclines to be firmly set in its bitterness and its blindness; and children, with their almost limitless plasticity, will acquire much of this burden. Yet children still constitute the best possible focus for our internationalizing efforts. They can readily identify with symbols of world unity, even while holding inviolate their loyalty to family, neighborhood and nation.

To overlook children is to be stupidly inefficient from the standpoint of social engineering. Twenty-five years is not too long to await results in the perspective of social evolution. Social scientists might reasonably advise that adults be largely disregarded in favor of children. The establishment of health centers, nutritional standards, curricular standards, welfare stations, model schools, a children's village, research in social attitudes, social training and appropriate symbols might well hold the center of the stage. The children of today are the custodians of the United Nations of tomorrow. The problems we cannot solve they will inherit, and their ability to cope with these problems will exceed ours only if their loyalties are stronger and their initial training sounder.

There is a simple psychological reason why international bodies tend to overlook children. Delegates assemble in an atmosphere of cameras, microphones and bald heads. Where are the children? While in an adult world, adults tend to forget them. Would it not be well to arrange the entrance to the General Assembly, the Security Council and the UNESCO headquarters so that it would lead the delegates through a nursery school play yard—just as a reminder?

To focus upon child welfare, education, health and juvenile research would have an extra advantage. What every parent wants (with few exceptions) the wide world over is a better opportunity for his child than he himself had. A United Nations devoted to providing such an opportunity would win the allegiance of adults far faster than through a direct appeal to their adult-centered interests.

One dare not minimize the political obstacles in the way. To take a single example, the task of teaching the children of the world scientific facts about race will turn out to be a vexatious problem. Sovereign rights will seem to be threatened. The senator from Mississippi will scarcely welcome scientific facts about race in Mississippi's public schools, especially if the curriculum is devised in consultation with Russian and Negro scholars. Children are plastic and willing; adults are the bigots. Yet even here, research and patience may discover not only a scientifically sound curriculum for international use, but also, in time, the effective means for introducing this curriculum into backward areas.

The common ground of human nature. To teach children the ways of peace requires, among other things, a factual knowledge of the peoples of the world. What, up to now, have anthropologists given us? And what have the schools been teaching? Broadly speaking, both have accented the *differences* that divide the families of

mankind. There has been little malice in the practice; yet the results have often been harmful. The American child, for example,
learns with horror about headhunters and infanticide; he learns to
laugh at the Dutch, who clop in wooden shoes, and at the quaint
observances of Easter among adherents to the Orthodox faith. The
implication of inferiority is a usual by-product of our present method
of teaching cultural and national differences. Less dramatic, but far
sounder, would be the teaching of the common considerations of
justice and morality that are identical over vast areas of the earth.
Practices that may *seem* to differ dramatically often indicate common
aspirations and common values. The prayer wheels of Tibet and the
silent Quaker meeting have virtually identical functional significance;
so, too, the initiation rites of the Pawnee and the American high
school commencement.

Except for the work of some anthropologists—notably the Cross
Cultural Survey developed under the direction of George P. Murdoch
of Yale University—little effort has been spent in the search for the
common ground of mankind. A vast project of investigation, absolutely basic to the interests of peace and to the success of the United
Nations, is the preparation of an encyclopedia of the uniformities
and similarities of the world's peoples in respect to their aspirations,
beliefs and practices. The successful execution of this project would
call for the cooperation of many kinds of social scientists in many
countries. Such a set of volumes, sure to be epoch making, would
serve as a reference guide for innumerable aspects of world policy
for years to come.

One large aspect of this research will inevitably deal with the
problem of national character. Here lies much virgin territory to be
explored. The common ground for mankind cannot be fully understood or intelligently employed unless the national and ethnic variants
are objectively known for what they are.

The desires and opinions of the common man. It is not only the
enduring uniformities and equivalences in culture that need to be
known, but also the *current* state of world needs and world opinion.
Here, too, internationally sponsored social research is indispensable.

In the modern day it is unnecessary to remain in ignorance of
the aspirations, hopes, wishes or judgment of the common man. Particularly when statesmen find themselves deadlocked through their
incompatible demands for solutions to international problems, it
would be salutary to know what the people of the world think. In

many cases, a knowledge of public opinion would aid in redefining the issues and devising peaceful solutions.

One cannot deny that adults in every nation are frequently as belligerent and uncompromising as their statesmen in matters pertaining to boundaries and sovereignty. But a study of the view of the majority of the common people would probably reveal that more important to them than boundaries are matters of self-respect, pride, food, shelter, marriage, the welfare of their children and the opportunity to identify with some successful group—not necessarily with their own belligerent nation. A focus on matters of prior importance to the citizenry would often bring a redefinition of the issues and disclose unexpected solutions. For the root-desires of two people are seldom incompatible: when they confront each other with their basic *desires,* they can usually satisfy both sets of interests through cooperation. But when they confront each other with rigid *demands,* there is often no solution short of war. (Cf. Chapter 11.)

In brief, the time has come for a continuing international service in public opinion. Polling now exists in more than a dozen countries. Facilities and talent are available; they await international coordination and utilization.

Communication. A reciprocal research service is required in order to achieve effective communication to the public of all lands. How may radio, motion pictures, television, books, news services, periodicals and lecturers be best employed in order that people everywhere may be informed in affairs of international import? Purely local research, such as that done in America, is inadequate. It overlooks entirely the difficulties of polylingualism or varying habits, tastes and practices in other lands. The task of communicating effectively with a world audience requires internationally sponsored research.

A special phase of the communication problem deals with the strategies of propaganda. It is recognized today that propaganda has its uses in the service of good causes, but that it may be a device of doubtful ethical justification. To what extent propaganda techniques may legitimately be employed in the interests of international cooperation is a subject for searching discussion. But such discussion cannot profitably take place unless the essential features, the strategies and the tactics of propaganda are first scientifically analyzed.

Condescension and its perils. A principle upon which social scientists almost unanimously agree is that human relations founded upon an attitude of condescension are perilous. So far as is known, no group of people is content to think of itself as inferior to any other group, nor is any single individual normally willing to regard himself as of less worth or merit than another. In some periods of history, slavery or feudalism seemed to lead a temporarily peaceful existence; but it may be safely asserted that policies based on condescension will sooner or later lead to violence. In the world today the unrest of citizens formerly regarded as second-class is manifest. Dark-skinned people are moving ahead toward independence. The white-skinned third of the world's population cannot prevent the movement; the English-speaking tenth certainly cannot do so. Any attempt to preserve the older imperial and colonial systems is doomed to breed violence and war.

Perhaps the basic principle of the science of human relations is that, to deal effectively with any other mortal, it is necessary to find out how he feels. Xenophobia and condescension give way in the face of psychological knowledge. Mutual understanding grows. Projects of investigation in this area range from the analysis of the genesis and nature of race prejudice to the assembling of a world-wide collection of self-told narratives, graphically illustrated, to serve as material for broadening our appreciation of people who represent other colors, other creeds and other nationalities. Research in the fields of ethnic differences, ethnic similarities and interracial understanding is almost limitless in scope. We must rely upon social engineering derived from this type of research to offset the ravages of hostility and condescension that in the past have poisoned our ethnic attitudes.

Need of symbols. For most people the concept of a single, democratically oriented world is difficult to hold in mind. As a rule, personal loyalty can adhere to an abstraction only when the abstraction is richly symbolized. Christianity rivets attention upon the cross; nations, upon their flags. Greece has its Acropolis, America its Statue of Liberty. The Moslem faces Mecca. International mercy is represented by the Red Cross. On his lapel the serviceman bears insignia of his military history and his status.

The great majority of symbols are now nationalistic. Artists and musicians, architects and designers are to a large extent culturebound; inevitably their productions favor single nations rather than the concert of nations. Does it not follow that an early and urgent task is to stimulate, by commission or competition, the devising of adequate world symbols? It should be done on an international scale; and to carry out this task successfully, research is indispensable.

With modern techniques, world opinion can be consulted. Proposed symbols can be pretested before adoption. Business uses market research to determine the effectiveness of trade marks; why should not the United Nations do the same? Tastes in music can be ascertained; so, too, inclinations respecting a common language. If schools were to teach the vernacular and, in addition, one universal tongue, what should the latter be?

It would be fanciful, of course, to assume that symbols can be arbitrarily or synthetically created. They grow out of a deep feeling and are accepted only on the basis of conviction. But millions of people already have the requisite feeling and conviction; in their search for symbols, they need stimulus and incentive, guidance and research. In time, more and better symbols will inevitably emerge, but they will have a fairer chance of success if deliberate attention is paid to the course of their development. It is in this connection that international parks and universities should be considered. Quite apart from their utilitarian significance, they have profound symbolic meaning as well.

Summary

My plea is for an accelerated development of social engineering based on social research, to the end that we may overtake and control the ravages of a rampant and amoral technology. I am convinced that the basic moral sense of mankind is sufficiently established in direction and motive power to employ with profit the principles and instruments which the nascent science of human relations has already developed—and which it will continue to develop at a rapid rate if adequate support is given.

The principles stated in this paper derive from psychology, sociology and social anthropology. In all probability they would be endorsed by most specialists in these disciplines. But a far more complete list of principles and a fuller account of applications would result if many social scientists were to work in concert upon these problems. Such concerted action should be instigated on an international scale.

Should any "hard-headed" statesman scorn the guidelines here offered as an expression of futile idealism, he himself would stand revealed as the most impractical of men. Scientific facts in the social field, as in any field, can be disregarded only with peril. The Einsteinian equation $e = mc^2$ was once dismissed as pedantry; yet the formula led to the release of atomic energy. The "pedantry" of so-

cial science might even now contribute enormously to the establishment of peace and international cooperation if its applications were
understood and employed by policy makers.

Social science has as yet by no means realized its potential power
as a welder of international relations, nor will it do so until adequate
support is given on both a national and an international scale. Since
the most urgent challenges pertain to world-wide problems, international support is most acutely needed. The cooperation of social
scientists all over the world, though as yet meager, would not
be difficult to achieve.

Some of the research required for international policy is of an
ad hoc and momentary character, often statistical in nature. The
pivotal investigations needed for long-range planning, however, fall
for the most part in the areas this essay has surveyed. The research
here recommended is, in all cases, intimately related to basic principles of social science. These principles, as far as they are now
known—and as rapidly as new ones are formulated inductively with
the aid of research—should be allowed to direct policy.

By way of summation, let me outline the essential areas of research mentioned above. The list is only a hint of the total research
needed, but the topics included are all accessible and important. The
list is intended to serve as a starting point for discussion among interested groups of social scientists and policy makers:

1. Prepare a historical survey of the trend toward larger and larger
   units of collective security.

2. Determine the conditions for democratic mass participation:
   A. The conditions required for a sense of freedom to build
   B. The conditions for linking self-interest to the techniques of
      mutual aid
   C. The conditions for widening the individual's circle of co-
      operative enterprise

3. Determine the effects of economic and psychological insecurity:
   A. Under what circumstances, and to what degree, does inse-
      curity serve as an incentive?
   B. Under what circumstances, and beyond what point, does
      insecurity engender morbid and antisocial reactions?
   C. What is the relation between childhood insecurity and the
      formation of delinquent and hostile attitudes?
   D. What forms of insecurity lead to national unrest and warlike
      sentiments?

E. What international policies, if consistently maintained, would lead to an optimum sense of security?

4. Investigate international conference procedures:
   A. What are the requirements of effective deliberation and group decision in large assemblies? In committees?
   B. How are these requirements modified when participants are from different cultural and linguistic backgrounds?

5. Direct main efforts upon children:
   A. Determine how multiple loyalties can be created without mental conflict
   B. Explore the possibilities of a children's village for shaping favorable international attitudes.
   C. Prepare international standards for health and nutrition
   D. Investigate the conditions for the formation of attitudes
   E. Devise model curricula to eliminate ethnic prejudice and explain the interdependence of nations
   F. Determine on a world-wide scale parental aspirations for children
   G. Devise methods for keeping policy bodies aware of children and their needs
   H. Explore methods for the installation of child training projects in all countries

6. Determine objectively the common ground of mankind:
   A. Prepare an encyclopedia of the uniformities and similarities of cultures
   B. Interpret cultural difference in terms of functional equivalences
   C. Explore in detail the conception of national character

7. Ascertain current opinion:
   A. Establish a continuing operation for revealing the state of men's needs, aspirations and opinions. (Start in countries where machinery is already available)
   B. Center attention upon common needs rather than upon divisive demands
   C. Translate findings into implications for policy

8. Investigate channels of communication:
   A. Study the merits of all media in respect to their value for international cooperation
   B. Experiment with programs and determine their effectiveness

    c. Determine the strategy and tactics of propaganda and devise methods for building immunity

    D. Trace the dissemination of ideas through rumor, through both illicit and authoritative channels

    E. Explore continually the problems of polylingualism and the conditions for a world language

9. Clarify the problem of race:

    A. Solve the problem of identities and differences in racial abilities and temperament

    B. Prepare authoritative ethnographic maps

    c. Examine the psychological effects of policies of condescension

    D. Estimate in advance the probable effects of proposed policies respecting bases and trusteeships

    E. Determine the causes of xenophobia

    F. Determine the conditions for mutual understanding among individuals of diverse backgrounds

10. Develop symbols of international cooperation:

    A. Identify the symbols that appeal to diverse groups

    B. Pre-test plans for world centers, music, parks, universities and other symbols of unity

    c. Determine means for encouraging the development of effective world symbols

REFERENCES

1. Suggestions for bridging the chasm in communication and for improving the relevance of social research are made by A. H. Leighton, *The governing of men*, Princeton: Princeton University Press, 1945, especially pp. 390-97; and in Chapters 12 and 13 of the present volume.

2. Some indication of the variety and nature of the successful wartime applications of social science to administrative policy can be obtained from D. Cartwright, "American social psychology and the war," *J. Consult. Psychol.,* 1946, 10:67-72.

3. The list of principles here offered is not, however, quite as individual and arbitrary as may appear. Several of them are contained in "Human nature and the peace," a statement subscribed to by 2,058 American psychologists, all members of the American Psychological Association. The "Psychologists' statement" is published in full in the *Psycholog. Bull.,* 1945, 42:376-78; also in G. Murphy (ed.), *Human nature and enduring peace* (Yearbook of the Society for the Psychological Study of Social Issues, Boston: Houghton Mifflin, 1945).

4. See Chapter 12 of the present volume.

Bibliography

1921-1960

Gordon W. Allport

BOOKS, MONOGRAPHS AND TESTS

A-S reaction study (with F. H. Allport), Boston: Houghton Mifflin, 1928; rev. ed., Boston: Houghton Mifflin, 1949.

A study of values (with P. E. Vernon), Boston: Houghton Mifflin, 1931; rev. ed. (with G. Lindzey and P. E. Vernon), Boston: Houghton Mifflin, 1951; 3rd ed. (with G. Lindzey and P. E. Vernon), Boston: Houghton Mifflin, 1960.

Studies in expressive movement (with P. E. Vernon), New York: Macmillan, 1933; microfilm ed., Ann Arbor: University Microfilms, 1959.

The psychology of radio (with H. Cantril), New York: Harper, 1935. Reprinted in part as "Speaker versus loudspeaker" (with H. Cantril), in G. E. Swanson, T. M. Newcomb and E. L. Hartley (eds.), *Readings in social psychology* (rev. ed.), New York: Holt, 1952, Part I, A, pp. 96-103.

Trait-names: a psycho-lexical study (with H. S. Odbert), *Psychol. Monogr.*, 1936, 47:1-171 No. 211.

Personality: a psychological interpretation, New York: Holt, 1937. Also published as *Persönlichkeit: Struktur, Entwicklung, und Erfassung der menschlichen Eigenart* (trans. by H. von Bracken), Stuttgart: Klett Verlag, 1949; 2nd ed., Meisenheim/Glan: Verlag Anton Hain, K.G., 1959.

The use of personal documents in psychological science, New York: Social Science Research Council, 1942, Bull. 49.

The psychology of rumor (with L. Postman), New York: Holt, 1947. Also published in Japanese (trans. by T. Minami), Tokyo: Iwanami Gendai Sōsho, 1953; and in Spanish as *Psicologia del Rumor* (trans. by J. Clementi), Buenos Aires: Editorial Psique, 1953.

The individual and his religion, New York: Macmillan, 1950. Also published in Japanese (trans. by T. Haratani), Tokyo: Iwanami Gendai Sōsho, 1953; and in Greek (trans. by S. N. Papadaki), Athens: Christian Union of Christian Workers, 1960.

The nature of personality: selected papers, Cambridge: Addison-Wesley, 1950.

The nature of prejudice, Cambridge: Addison-Wesley, 1954; Boston: Beacon; abridged ed., Garden City: Doubleday Anchor, 1958. Chap. 1 reprinted in W. O. Sutherland and R. L. Montgomery (eds.), *The reader: a study of form and content*, Boston: Little, Brown, 1960.

Becoming: basic considerations for a psychology of personality, New Haven: Yale University Press, 1955. Also published in Danish as *Personlighedens Udformning* (trans. by A. Madsen), Copenhagen: Nyt Nordisk Forlag Arnold Busck, 1956; in Swedish as *Personlighetens Utveckling* (trans. by A. Asker), Stockholm: Alfa Boktryckeri, 1957; in German as *Werden der Persönlichkeit* (trans. by H. von Bracken), Bern: Verlag Hans Huber, 1958; in Japanese (trans. by H. Toyosawa), Tokyo: Risosha Ltd., 1959; and in Korean (trans. by Tong-He Choo), Seoul: Tong-Shin Co., 1960.

Personality and social encounter, Boston: Beacon, 1960.

363

ARTICLES AND REVIEWS

1921

"Personality traits: their classification and measurement" (with F. H. Allport),
J. Abnorm. Soc. Psychol., 1921, 16:6-40.
"Personality and character," *Psychol. Bull.*, 1921, 18:441-55.
Reviews:
W. H. Pyle, *The psychology of learning*, *J. Abnorm. Soc. Psychol.*, 1921-22, 16:414-15.
M. S. Pittman, *The value of school supervision*; W. S. Herzog, *State maintenance for teachers in training*; and A. G. Peaks, *Periodic variations in efficiency*, *J. Abnorm. Soc. Psychol.*, 1921-22, 16:415.

1922

Reviews:
L. Berman, *The glands regulating personality*, *J. Abnorm. Soc. Psychol.*, 1922, 17:220-22.
E. S. Bogardus, *Essentials of social psychology*, *J. Abnorm. Soc. Psychol.*, 1922, 17:104-06.

1923

"Germany's state of mind," *New Republic*, 1923, 34:63-65.
"The Leipzig congress of psychology," *Amer. J. Psychol.*, 1923, 34:612-15.

1924

"The study of the undivided personality," *J. Abnorm. Soc. Psychol.*, 1924, 19:132-41.
"Eidetic imagery," *Brit. J. Psychol.*, 1924, 15:99-120.
"Die theoretischen Hauptströmungen in der amerikanischen Psychologie der Gegenwart," *Zeitschrift f. Pädagog. Psychol.*, 1924, 4:129-37.
"The standpoint of Gestalt psychology," *Psyche*, 1924, 4:354-61.
Reviews:
M. P. Follett, *Creative experience*, *J. Abnorm. Soc. Psychol.*, 1924, 18:426-28.
W. W. Smith, *The measurement of emotion*; and H. Eng, *Experimentelle Untersuchungen über das Gefühlsleben des Kindes im Vergleich mit dem des Erwachsenen*, *J. Abnorm. Soc. Psychol.*, 1924, 18:414-16.

1925

Review:
W. B. Munro, *Personality in politics*, *J. Abnorm. Soc. Psychol.*, 1925, 20:209-11.

1926

Reviews:
K. Dunlap, *Social psychology*, *J. Abnorm. Soc. Psychol.*, 1926, 21:95-100.
O. Selz, *Über die Persönlichkeitstypen und die Methoden ihrer Bestimmung*, *Amer. J. Psychol.*, 1926, 37:618-19.

1927

"Concepts of trait and personality," *Psychol. Bull.*, 1927, 24:284-93.
Reviews:
  A. A. Roback, *A bibliography of character and personality*, *Psychol. Bull.*, 1927, 24:309-10.
  A. A. Roback, *Psychology of character*, *Psychol. Bull.*, 1927, 24:717-23.
  W. S. Taylor (ed.), *Readings in abnormal psychology and mental hygiene*, *J. Abnorm. Soc. Psychol.*, 1927, 21:445-48.

1928

"The eidetic image and the after-image," *Amer. J. Psychol.*, 1928, 40:418-25.
"A test for ascendance-submission," *J. Abnorm. Soc. Psychol.*, 1928, 23:118-36.

1929

"The study of personality by the intuitive method: an experiment in teaching from *The locomotive god*," *J. Abnorm. Soc. Psychol.*, 1929, 24:14-27.
"The composition of political attitudes," *Amer. J. Sociol.*, 1929, 35:220-38.
Reviews:
  E. T. Clark, *The psychology of religious awakening*, *Psychol. Bull.*, 1929, 26:710-11.
  W. McDougall, *The group mind*, *J. Abnorm. Soc. Psychol.*, 1929, 24:123-26.
  H. Meltzer and E. Bailor, *Developed lessons in psychology*, *Dartmouth Alumni Bull.*, 1929.
  T. Munro, *Scientific method in aesthetics*, *Psychol. Bull.*, 1929, 26:711.
  C. Murchison, *Social psychology*, *Psychol. Bull.*, 1929, 26:709-10.
  M. Prince, *Clinical and experimental studies in personality*, *Psychol. Bull.*, 1929, 26:711-12.
  L. T. Troland, *Fundamentals of human motivation*, *J. Abnorm. Soc. Psychol.*, 1929, 23:510-13.

1930

"Some guiding principles in understanding personality," *The Family*, June 1930, pp. 124-28.
"The neurotic personality and traits of self-expression," *J. Soc. Psychol.*, 1930, 1:524-27.
"The field of personality" (with P. E. Vernon), *Psychol. Bull.*, 1930, 27:677-730.
"Change and decay in the visual memory image," *Brit. J. Psychol.*, 1930, 21:133-48.
Reviews:
  J. E. Downey, *Creative imagination*, *Psychol. Bull.*, 1930, 27:408-10.
  K. Young, *Social psychology*, *Psychol. Bull.*, 1930, 27:731-33.

1931

"What is a trait of personality?" *J. Abnorm. Soc. Psychol.*, 1931, 25:368-72.
"A test for personal values" (with P. E. Vernon), *J. Abnorm. Soc. Psychol.*, 1931, 26:231-48.

1932

Reviews:
W. Boven, *La science du caractère*, *Amer. J. Psychol.*, 1932, 44:838-39.
J. C. Flugel, *The psychology of clothes*, *Psychol. Bull.*, 1932, 29:358-59.
D. Katz and F. H. Allport, *Students' attitudes*, *Psychol. Bull.*, 1932, 29:356-58.
F. Künkel, *Vitale Dialektik*, *Psychol. Bull.*, 1932, 29:371-73.
A. A. Roback, *Personality*, *Psychol. Bull.*, 1932, 29:359-60.
J. J. Smith, *Social psychology*, *Psychol. Bull.*, 1932, 29:360.
P. M. Symonds, *Diagnosing personality and conduct*, *J. Soc. Psychol.*, 1932, 3:391-97.

1933

"The study of personality by the experimental method," *Char. & Pers.*, 1933, 1:259-64.
"The determination of personal interests by psychological and graphological methods" (with H. Cantril and H. A. Rand), *Char. & Pers.*, 1933, 2:134-51.
"Recent applications of the *study of values*" (with H. Cantril), *J. Abnorm. Soc. Psychol.*, 1933, 28:259-73.

Reviews:
C. Bühler, *Der menschliche Lebenslauf als psychologisches Problem*, *Sociologus*, 1933, 9:336-38.
N. D. M. Hirsch, *Genius and creative intelligence*, *Psychol. Bull.*, 1933, 30:365-66.
L. Klages, *The science of character* (trans. by W. H. Johnston), *Psychol. Bull.*, 1933, 30:370-71.
M. A. McLaughlin, *The genesis and constancy of ascendance and submission as personality traits*, *Amer. J. Psychol.*, 1933, 45:779-80.

1934

"Judging personality from voice" (with H. Cantril), *J. Soc. Psychol.*, 1934, 5:37-55.

Reviews:
A. Goldenweiser, *History, psychology, and culture*, *Psychol. Bull.*, 1934, 31:363-64.
A. A. Roback, *Self-consciousness and its treatment*, *Psychol. Bull.*, 1934, 31:370.

1935

"Attitudes," in C. C. Murchison (ed.), *A handbook of social psychology*, Worcester: Clark University Press, 1935, Chap. 17.
"The radio as a stimulus situation," *Acta Psychol.*, 1935, 1:1-6.
"The nature of motivation," *Understanding the child*, Jan. 1935, pp. 3-6.

1936

"Are attitudes biological or cultural in origin?" (with R. L. Schanck), *Char. & Pers.*, 1936, 4:195-205.

Review:
G. K. Zipf, *The Psycho-biology of language*, *Psychol. Bull.*, 1936, 33:219-22.

1937

"The functional autonomy of motives," *Amer. J. Psychol.*, 1937, 50:141-56. Also published in C. L. Stacey and M. F. DeMartino (eds.), *Understanding human motivation*, Cleveland: Howard Allen, 1958, pp. 69-81.

"The personalistic psychology of William Stern," *Char. & Pers.*, 1937, 5:231-46. Also published (abridged) in H. Brand (ed.), *The study of personality*, New York: Wiley, 1954, pp. 149-61.

1938

"The Journal of Abnormal and Social Psychology: an editorial," *J. Abnorm. Soc. Psychol.*, 1938, 33:3-13.

"William Stern: 1871-1938," *Amer. J. Psychol.*, 1938, 51:770-74.

"Personality: a problem for science or a problem for art?" *Revista de Psihologie*, 1938, 1:1-15.

Review:

L. B. Murphy, *Social behavior and child personality*, *J. Abnorm. Soc. Psychol.*, 1938, 33:538-43.

1939

"Dewey's individual and social psychology," in P. A. Schilpp (ed.), *The philosophy of John Dewey*, Evanston and Chicago: Northwestern University Press, 1939, Chap. 9.

"Recent applications of the A-S reaction study" (with R. Ruggles), *J. Abnorm. Soc. Psychol.*, 1939, 34:518-28.

"The education of a teacher," *The Harvard Progressive*, 1939, 4:7-9.

1940

"The psychologist's frame of reference," *Psychol. Bull.*, 1940, 37:1-28. Also published as El marco de referencia de los psicologos (trans. by A. Bernal del Riesgo), Havana: University of Havana, 1946.

"Fifty years of change in American psychology" (with J. S. Bruner), *Psychol. Bull.*, 1940, 37:757-76.

"The psychology of newspapers: five tentative laws" (with J. M. Faden), *Publ. Opin. Quart.*, 1940, 4:687-703.

"Motivation in personality: reply to Mr. Bertocci," *Psychol. Rev.*, 1940, 47:533-54. Also published in H. Brand, *The study of personality: a book of readings*, New York: Wiley, 1954, pp. 83-99; and in C. L. Stacey and M. F. DeMartino (eds.), *Understanding human motivation*, Cleveland: Howard Allen, 1958, pp. 105-20.

"Liberalism and the motives of men," *Frontiers of Democracy*, 1940, 6:136-37.

Foreword to H. Werner, *Comparative psychology of mental development* (trans. by E. B. Garside), New York: Harper, 1940; rev. ed., Chicago: Follett Pub. Co., 1948.

1941

"Liabilities and assets in civilian morale," *Ann. Amer. Acad. Pol. Soc. Sci.*, 1941, 216:88-94.

"Psychological service for civilian morale," *J. Consult. Psychol.*, 1941, 5;235-39.

"Personality under social catastrophe: ninety life-histories of the Nazi revolution" (with J. S. Bruner and E. M. Jandorf), *Char. & Pers.*, 1941, 10:1-22. Also published in C. Kluckhohn and H. A. Murray, *Personality in nature, society, and culture,* New York: Knopf, 1948, Chap. 25; and in C. Kluckhohn, H. A. Murray and D. M. Schneider, *Personality in nature, society and culture,* New York: Knopf, 1953, Chap. 27.

"Morale: American style." *Christian Science Monitor* (Weekly Magazine Section), Apr. 26, 1941, pp. 1-2, 13.

Review:

    J. M. MacKaye, *The logic of language. J. Abnorm. Soc. Psychol.,* 1941, 36:296-97.

1942

"The nature of democratic morale," in G. Watson (ed.), *Civilian morale,* Boston: Houghton Mifflin, 1942, Chap. 1.

"Defense seminars for morale study and morale building," *J. Soc. Psychol., SPSSI Bull.,* 1942, 15:399-401.

"Report on the third front: at home," *Christian Science Monitor* (Weekly Magazine Section), Sept. 5, 1942, pp. 6, 14.

"Morale and its measurement," in *Public Policy,* Cambridge: Littauer School of Public Administration, 1942, 3:3-17.

Review:

    F. C. Bartlett, *Political propaganda, Sat. Rev. Lit.,* 1942, 25:18.

1943

"The productive paradoxes of William James," *Psychol. Rev.,* 1943, 50:95-120.

"Test tube for rumors," *Coronet,* 1943, 14:136-40.

"Psychological considerations in making the peace: editorial note," *J. Abnorm. Soc. Psychol.,* 1943, 38:131.

"This clinical supplement: editorial note," *J. Abnorm. Soc. Psychol.,* 38:3-5.

"Do rosy headlines sell newspapers?" (with E. C. Winship), *Publ. Opin. Quart.,* 1943, 7:205-10. Reprinted in D. Katz, D. Cartwright, S. Eldersveld and A. McG. Lee, *Public opinion and propaganda,* New York: Dryden Press, 1954:271-74.

"Social psychology and the civilian war effort" (with H. R. Veltfort), *J. Soc. Psychol., SPSSI Bull.,* 1943, 18:165-233.

"The ego in contemporary psychology," *Psychol. Rev.,* 1943, 50:451-78. Also published in C. L. Stacey and M. F. DeMartino (eds.), *Understanding human motivation,* Cleveland: Howard Allen, 1958, pp. 140-58.

"Morale research and its clearing" (with G. R. Schmeidler), *Psychol. Bull.,* 1943, 40:65-68.

"Restoring morale in occupied territory," *Publ. Opin. Quart.,* 1943, 7:606-17.

Reviews:

    E. P. Aldrich (ed.), *As William James said, J. Abnorm. Soc. Psychol.,* 1943, 38:119-120.

    M. D. Allers, *The psychology of character, Amer. Sociol. Rev.,* 1943, 8:735-36.

    M. A. May, *A social psychology of war and peace, Ann. Amer. Acad. Pol. Soc. Sci.,* 1943, 229:186-87.

A. A. Roback, *William James: his marginalia, personality and contribution,* *New England Quarterly,* 1943, 16:143-44.
C. Schrodes, J. van Gundy and R. W. Husband (eds.), *Psychology through literature, J. Abnorm. Soc. Psychol.,* 1943, 38:203 (No. 2, Clin. Suppl.).
E. C. Tolman, *Drives toward war, J. Abnorm. Soc. Psychol.,* 1943, 38:293-96.

1944

Prefaces to *Educational opportunities in greater Boston,* Cambridge: Prospect Union Educational Exchange, 1944 and annually thereafter.
"The quest of Nellie Wise Allport," privately printed, 1944.
"The roots of religion," *Advent Paper,* No. 1, Boston: Church of the Advent, 1944. Reprinted as "La radici della religione" (trans. by Sac. Prof. G. Zunini), *Orientamenti Pedagogici,* 1958, 4:158-74.
"ABC's of scapegoating" (ed. and author of Foreword), Chicago: Central YWCA College, 1944; rev. ed., *Freedom Pamphlet Series,* New York: Anti-Defamation League of B'nai B'rith, 1948; revised, 1959. Also reprinted as *Treibjagd auf Sündenböcke* (trans. by K. C. Knudsen), Berlin: Im Christian-Verlag, 1953.
"This clinical number: editorial," *J. Abnorm. Soc. Psychol.,* 1944, 39:147-49.
"Social psychology and the civilian war effort" (with G. R. Schmeidler), *J. Soc. Psychol.,* SPSSI Bull., 1944, 20:145-80.
"The bigot in our midst," *Commonweal,* 1944, 25:582-86. Also published in *The Catholic Digest,* 1944, 9:93-96; and in *Common Sense* (Johannesburg, South Africa), 1945, 6:154-56. Rev. ed., New York: Community Relations Service, 1950.

1945

"The psychology of participation," *Psychol. Rev.,* 1945, 52:117-32. Also published in *Occup. Psychol.* (London), 1946, 20:54-62; in S. D. Hoslett (ed.), *Human factors in management,* Parkville, Mo.: Park College Press, 1946; and in D. F. Sullivan (ed.), *Readings in group work,* New York: Association Press, 1952, pp. 239-58, Chap. 19.
"Human nature and the peace," *Psychol. Bull.,* 1945, 42:376-78.
"Is intergroup education possible?" *Harv. Educ. Rev.,* 1945, 15:83-86.
"Catharsis and the reduction of prejudice," *J. Soc. Issues,* 1945, 1:1-8.
"The basic psychology of rumor" (with L. Postman), *Trans N.Y. Acad. Sci.,* Section of Psychology, 1945, 8:61-81. Also published in G. E. Swanson, T. M. Newcomb and E. L. Hartley (eds.), *Readings in Social psychology* (rev. ed.), New York: Holt, 1952, Part II, b, pp. 160-71; in E. E. Maccoby, T. M. Newcomb and E. L. Hartley, *Readings in social psychology* (3rd ed.), New York: Holt, 1958, pp. 54-65; in D. Katz, D. Cartwright, S. Eldersveld and A. McG. Lee, *Public opinion and propaganda,* New York: Dryden Press, 1954, 394-404; and in W. Schramm (ed.), *The process and effects of mass communication,* Urbana, Ill.: University of Illinois Press, 1954, pp. 141-55.

Review:
G. Gallup, *A guide to public opinion, J. Abnorm. Soc. Psychol.,* 1945, 40:113-14.

1946

"Personalistic psychology as science: a reply," *Psychol. Rev.*, 1946, 53:132-35.
"Controlling group prejudice" (ed. and author of Foreword), *Ann. Amer. Acad. Pol. Soc. Sci.*, 1946, vol. 244.
"Psychology and social relations at Harvard University" (with E. G. Boring), *Amer. Psychol.*, 1946, 1:119-22.
"Some roots of prejudice" (with B. M. Kramer), published as a separate and in *J. Psychol.*, 1946, 22:9-39; rev. ed., *Roots of prejudice*, New York: American Jewish Congress, Pamphlet Series *Jewish Affairs*, 1946, 1:13.
"Geneticism *versus* ego-structure in theories of personality," *Brit. J. Educ. Psychol.*, 1946, 16:57-68.
"Effect: a secondary principle of learning," *Psychol. Rev.*, 1946, 53:335-47.
Preface to E. Simmel (ed.), *Anti-Semitism: a social disease*, New York: International Universities Press, 1946.
"The priest and the psychologist," *Bull. of General Theological Seminary*, Sept. 1946.
"An analysis of rumor" (with L. Postman), *Publ. Opin. Quart.*, 1946-47, 10:501-17. Also published in *Science Digest*, 1947, 22:58-61.
Introduction to Swami Akhilananda, *Hindu psychology*, New York: Harper, 1946.

Review:
    A. H. Leighton, *The governing of men*, *J. Abnorm. Soc. Psychol.*, 1946, 41:89-92.

1947

"Guide lines for research in international cooperation," *J. Soc. Issues*, 1947, 3:21-37. Also published in T. H. Pear (ed.), *Psychological factors of peace and war*, London: Hutchinson & Co., 1950, Chap. 7.
Introduction to M. I. Rasey, *Toward maturity, the psychology of child development*," New York: Hinds, Hayden and Eldredge, 1947.
"The genius of Kurt Lewin," *J. Pers.*, 1947, 16:1-10. Also published in *J. Soc. Issues*, 1948, 4:14-21, Suppl. series 1.
"Scientific models and human morals," *Psychol. Rev.*, 1947, 54:182-92. Also published as "Modelos cientificos y moral humana," *Rev. Psicol. Gen. Apl.* (Madrid), 1948, 3:425-47; and "Modelos cientificos y moral humana," *Actas del Primer Congreso Argentino de Psicologia*, 1 (Universidad Nacional de Tucuman, Ministerio de Educacion de la Nacion), 1955.

1948

Foreword to K. Lewin (G. W. Lewin, ed.), *Resolving social conflicts*, New York: Harper, 1948.
"Psychology," in *College reading and religion*, New Haven: Yale University Press, 1948, Chap. 3.
"The religion of the post-war college student" (with J. M. Gillespie and J. Young), published as a separate and in *J. Psychol.*, 1948, 25:3-33. Also published in J. Seidman (ed.), *The adolescent: a book of readings*, New York: Dryden Press, 1953.

Reviews:
    D. Jacobson, *The affairs of dame rumor*, Boston Sunday Post, Oct. 24, 1948.

E. Mayo, *Some notes on the psychology of Pierre Janet, Survey Graphic,* 1948, 37:5, 267.

A. Schweitzer, *The psychiatric study of Jesus, Christian Register,* Apr. 1948.

1949

"Psychology and the fourth R," *New Republic,* Oct. 17, 1949, pp. 23-26.

Editorial note, *J. Abnorm. Soc. Psychol.,* 1949, 44:439-42.

1950

Foreword to M. G. Ross, *Religious beliefs of youth,* New York: Association Press, 1950.

"How shall we evaluate teaching?" in B. B. Cronkhite (ed.), *A handbook for college teachers,* Cambridge: Harvard University Press, 1950, Chap. 3.

"The role of expectancy," in H. Cantril (ed.), *Tensions that cause wars,* Urbana, Ill.: University of Illinois Press, 1950.

"A psychological approach to the study of love and hate," in P. A. Sorokin (ed.), *Explorations in altruistic love and behavior,* Boston: Beacon Press, 1950, Chap. 5.

"Prejudice: a problem in psychological and social causation" (Kurt Lewin Memorial Lecture), *J. Soc. Issues,* 1950, Suppl. Series. Also published in T. Parsons and E. A. Shils (eds.), *Toward a general theory of action,* Cambridge: Harvard University Press, 1951, Part 4, Chap. 1.

Reviews:

S. A. Stouffer *et al., The American soldier* (2 vols.), *J. Abnorm. Soc. Psychol.,* 1950, 45:168-73.

"A five-volume shelf about a sickness of both individuals and society: prejudice" [M. Horkheimer and S. H. Flowerman, eds., *Studies in prejudice* (5 vols.), New York: Harper, 1950], *Sci. Amer.,* 1950, 182:56-58.

1951

"The situation we face: a psychological analysis," in A. W. Loos (ed.), *Religious faith and world culture,* New York: Prentice-Hall, 1951, pp. 35-48. Also published in *New Outlook* (Santa Monica, Calif.), 1955, 8:82-87.

"Basic principles in improving human relations," in K. W. Bigelow (ed.), *Cultural groups and human relations,* New York: Teachers College-Columbia University, 1951, Chap. 2.

Foreword to M. H. Wormser and C. Selltiz, *How to conduct a community self-survey of civil rights,* New York: Association Press, 1951.

Foreword to H. E. Kagan, *Changing the attitude of Christian toward Jew,* New York: Columbia University Press, 1951.

Foreword to E. Powers and H. Witmer, *An experiment in the prevention of delinquency,* New York: Columbia University Press, 1951.

Review:

J. La Farge, S.J., *No postponement, Thought,* 1951, 26:471-472, No. 102.

1952

"An evaluation of AFSC volunteer work service camps in Germany," in H. W. Riecken, *The volunteer work camp: a psychological evaluation,* Cambridge: Addison-Wesley, 1952, Appendix A, pp. 185-220.

"Resolving intergroup tensions, an appraisal of methods," in L. A. Cook (ed.), *Toward better human relations*, Detroit: Wayne University Press, 1952, Chap. 3.

"The individual and his religion," *The Andover Newton Bulletin*, 1952, 44:3-10.

"The resolution of intergroup tensions," an *Intergroup Education Pamphlet*, New York: National Conference of Christians and Jews, 1952.

"The mature personality," *Pastoral Psychol.*, 1952, 2:19-24.

"What is on the student's mind?" proceedings of the Thirtieth Annual Meeting of the *American College Health Association, Bulletin* No. 32, Stanford: Stanford University Press, 1952.

"Why do people join?" interview in *Adult Leadership*, 1952, 1:10-12.

"Reading the nature of prejudice," *Claremont College Reading Conference, Seventeenth Yearbook* (Claremont, Calif.), 1952, pp. 51-64.

1953

"The trend in motivational theory," *Amer. J. Orthopsychiat.*, 1953, 25:107-19. Also published as "Bemerkungen zu dem gegenwärtigen Stand der Theorie der Motivation in den USA" (trans. by H. von Bracken and Leo Canders), *Psychol. Beit.*, 1953, 1:10-28; and in C. E. Moustakas (ed.), *The self: explorations in personal growth*, New York: Harper, 1956; in E. L. and R. E. Hartley, *Outside readings in psychology*, 2nd ed., New York: Crowell, 1957, Chap. 22; and in C. L. Stacey and M. F. De-Martino (eds.), *Understanding human motivation*, Cleveland: Howard Allen, 1958, pp. 54-65.

"The teaching-learning situation," *Publ. Hlth. Rep.*, 1953, 68:875-79.

"The psychological nature of personality," *The Personalist*, 1953, 34:347-57.

Review:

H. G. Trager and M. R. Yarrow, *They learn what they live, The Child*, 1953, 18:30.

1954

"Techniques for reducing group prejudice," in P. A. Sorokin (ed.), *Forms and techniques of altruistic and spiritual growth*, Boston: Beacon, 1954, Chap. 24.

"The historical background of modern social psychology," in G. Lindzey (ed.), *Handbook of social psychology*, Cambridge: Addison-Wesley, 1954, Vol. I., Chap. 1.

Introduction to J. Evans, *Three men*, New York: Knopf, 1954.

"A psychologist views the Supreme Court ruling on segregation," *Nieman Reports*, 1954, 8:12-13.

Comments on: J. L. Moreno, Transference, countertransference and tele: their relation to group research and group psychotherapy. *Group Psychother.*, 1954, 7:307-08.

1955

Youth's outlook on the future (with J. M. Gillespie), New York: Doubleday, Doubleday Papers in Psychology, 1955 (distributed by Random House).

"The limits of social service," in J. E. Russell (ed.), *National policies for education, health and social services* (Columbia University Bicentennial Conference Series), New York: Doubleday, 1955, pp. 194-213.

Bibliography 373

Reviews:
  R. B. Perry, *Realms of value: a critique of human civilization*, *J. Abnorm. Soc. Psychol.*, 1955, 50:154-56.
  S. A. Stouffer, *Communism, conformity, and civil liberties*, *Saturday Rev. Lit.*, 1955, 28:14-15.

1956

"Prejudice in modern perspective," *The Hoernlé memorial lecture 1956*, Durban, South Africa: The South African Institute of Race Relations, 1956.
"The participant citizen," *The sixth annual George Denny lecture*, September 4, 1956, Durban, South Africa: Natal Technical College.
Review:
  M. Freedman, *A minority in Britain: social studies of the Anglo-Jewish community*, *Amer. Anthrop.*, 1956, 58:401-02.

1957

"European and American theories of personality," in H. P. David and H. von Bracken (eds.), *Perspectives in personality theory*, New York: Basic Books, 1957, Chap. 1.
"Cultural influence on the perception of movement: the trapezoidal illusion among Zulus" (with T. F. Pettigrew), *J. Abnorm. Soc. Psychol.*, 1957, 55:104-13.
Review:
  P. A. Bertocci, *Free will, responsibility, and grace*, *Religion in Life*, 1957, 26:612-13.

1958

"What units shall we employ?" in G. Lindzey (ed.), *Assessment of human motives*, New York: Rinehart, 1958, Chap. 9. Reprinted as a paperback, New York: Grove Press, 1960.
Foreword to G. V. Coelho, *Changing images of America: a study of Indian students' perceptions*, Glencoe, Ill.: The Free Press, 1958.
Foreword to E. Mira y Lopez (L. Bellak *et al.*, eds.) *M. K. P. Myokinetic Psychodiagnosis* (trans.), New York: Logos Press, 1958.
"Perception and public health," *Health Education Monographs*, Oakland, Calif.: Society of Health Educators, 1958, No. 2, pp. 2-15.
"Binocular resolution and perception of race in South Africa" (with T. F. Pettigrew and E. O. Barnett), *Brit. J. Psychol.*, 1958, 49:265-78, Part 4.
"Personality: normal and abnormal," *The Sociological Review*, 1958, 6:167-80.
Review:
  P. Lafitte, *The person in psychology: reality or abstraction? Contemp. Psychol.*, 1958, 3:105.

1959

"Normative compatibility in the light of social science," in A. H. Maslow (ed.), *New knowledge in human values*, New York: Harper, 1959, pp. 137-50. Also published in *Relig. Educ.*, 1958, 53:62-68.
Preface to V. E. Frankl, *From death-camp to existentialism*. Boston: Beacon, 1959 (trans.).
"Religion and prejudice," *The Crane Review*, 1959, 2:1-10.

1960

"Uniqueness in students," in W. D. Weatherford, Jr. (ed.), *The goals of higher education*, Cambridge: Harvard University Press, 1960, pp. 57-75.

"The open system in personality theory," *J. Abnorm. Soc. Psychol.*, 1960, 60: No. 5.

"Psychology and religion," in J. Clark (ed.), *The student seeks an answer*, Chap. 2. Ingraham Lectures in Philosophy and Religion, Waterville: Colby College Press, 1960.

Index of Names

375

Index of Subjects

381